MODERN NAPLES
1799–1999

MODERN NAPLES
A DOCUMENTARY HISTORY
1799–1999

BY
JOHN SANTORE

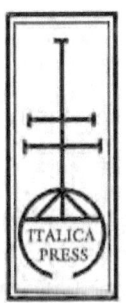

ITALICA PRESS
NEW YORK
2001

COPYRIGHT © 2001 BY JOHN SANTORE

A DOCUMENTARY HISTORY OF NAPLES SERIES

ITALICA PRESS, INC.
595 MAIN STREET
NEW YORK, NY 10044

All rights reserved. No part of this publication may be reproduced, stored in a retrieval system, or transmitted, in any form or by any means, electronic, mechanical, photocopying, recording, or otherwise, without the prior permission of Italica Press.

Library of Congress Cataloging-in-Publication Data

Santore, John, 1941
    Modern Naples : a documentary history, 1799-1999 / by John Santore.
        p. cm. -- (A documentary history of Naples)
    Includes bibliographical references and index.
    ISBN 978-0-934977-53-1 (trade pbk. : alk. paper)
      1. Naples (Italy)–History–19th century–Sources. 2. Naples (Italy)–History–20th century–Sources. 3. Parthenopean Republic–History–Sources. I. Series.

DG848.4.S26 2000
945'.7308–dc21

                                                                                           00-047209

Printed in the U.S.A and E.U.

Cover Art: The Galleria Umberto I. Photo: Eileen Gardiner for Italica Press.
All other artwork from the source credited in List of Illustrations on p. XVIII. The publisher has attempted to provide the proper credits for all images appearing in this book. Please contact us for oversights in this regard.

FOR A COMPLETE LIST OF TITLES IN THIS SERIES
AND IN HISTORICAL STUDIES
VISIT OUR WEB SITE AT:
WWW.ITALICAPRESS.COM

CONTENTS

LIST OF DOCUMENTS	VII
LIST OF ILLUSTRATIONS	XVIII
FOREWORD	XXIV
PREFACE	XXVII
INTRODUCTION. NAPLES: THE TRAGIC CENTURIES	XXXI
NOTES	XLVII

PART I: FOUNDATIONS

1. Naples at the Close of the 18th Century	1

PART II: THE BOURBON CAPITAL, 1799–1860

2. The Revolution of 1799	17
3. Joseph I and Murat, 1806–1815	47
4. Restoration and Reaction, 1815–1848	97
5. The Revolution of 1848	137
6. The Risorgimento, 1848–1861	159

PART III: NAPLES IN ITALY, 1861–1999

7. The Early Years, 1861–1914	187
8. The Era of Catastrophies, 1914–1943	219
9. The Incomplete Recovery, 1943–1999	245
CHRONOLOGY	278
BIBLIOGRAPHY	291
MAPS	300
INDEX	303

■ ■ ■

To my wife,
Frances,
and our son,
John Vincent

DOCUMENTS

CHAPTER 1: FOUNDATIONS

1.	J.W. Goethe on the natural beauty of Naples, February 1787	1
2.	Lady Blessington on the splendor of the Bay, July 17, 1823	2
3.	Lady Blessington on the animation of life in Neapolitan streets, July 19, 1823	2
4.	Hans Christian Andersen's description of the Piazza Florentina, 1841	3
5.	J.W. Goethe on the character and life style of the Neapolitans, March and May, 1787	5
6.	Austrian Emperor Joseph I's description of King Ferdinand IV, 1769	7
7.	Lady Blessington's description of a Neapolitan water-fete, 1824	9
8.	Henri di Stendhal's portrait of the Neapolitan aristocracy, 1817	10
9.	Henry Swinburne on aristocratic extravagance, 1786	11
10.	Lady Morgan on the *lazzaroni*, 1820	13
11.	Lady Blessington on the Neapolitans' love of life and good humor, 1823	15

CHAPTER 2: THE REVOLUTION OF 1799

12.	Queen Maria Carolina, five letters on the Revolution in France and her fears for her sister, Marie Antoinette, December 1792–August 1793	17
13.	Maria Carolina on her determination to struggle against the French to the end, July 1794	19
14.	Gugliemo Pepe's description of the excitement first caused by the French Revolution among Neapolitan youth	20
15.	Maria Carolina on the Neapolitan Jacobins' hatred for the King, 1795	20
16.	Maria Carolina on Napoleon's "greatness," November 1797	21
17.	Ferdinand's appeal to the people of Naples to resist the French, December 8, 1798	22
18.	Wilhelm Tischbein's eye-witness account of the street fighting in Naples in January 1799, n.d.	22

19. A middle-class observer on the "butchery" of the Jacobins, January 1799 — 24
20. General Thiébault on the bravery and ferocity of the Neapolitan defenders, n.d. — 24
21. General Championnet's "Proclamation to the People of Naples," January 23, 1799 — 25
22. Carlo De Nicola's estimation of General Championnet, January 25, 1799 — 26
23. General Championnet's report to the Directory in Paris on the three-day struggle for Naples, January 23, 1799 — 27
24. Instructions of the Provisional Government to the Neapolitan people, February 5, 1799 — 29
25. Vincenzo Cuoco's observations on the Parthenopean Republic and his theory of "passive revolution," 1801 — 31
26. De Nicola on the deteriorating conditions in Naples, February 3, 1799 — 33
27. De Nicola's estimation of the importance of the French dismissal of Championnet, March 1, 1799 — 33
28. De Nicola on the failures of the Provisional Government, April 5, 1799 — 34
29. Cardinal Fabrizio Ruffo's "Proclamation to the Calabrian People," February 7, 1799 — 35
30. General Macdonald's edict ordering the suppression of the counter-revolution, March 1799 — 36
31. Maria Carolina's declaration of support to the people of Calabria, March 1, 1799 — 36
32. The Provisional Government's final call to arms, May 10, 1799 — 37
33. Cardinal Ruffo's recommendation of a policy of clemency towards the rebels, May 8, 1799 — 38
34. Maria Carolina's rejection of negotiations with the revolutionaries, June 14, 1799 — 39
35. Ferdinand IV on the necessity for reprisals, June 17, 1799 — 39
36. Cardinal Ruffo's description of the situation in Naples, June 21, 1799 — 39
37. Ferdinand's insistence on a policy of no compromise with the revolutionaries, June 20, 1799 — 41
38. Maria Carolina on the need to treat Naples like a rebellious city in Ireland, June 25, 1799 — 41
39. Robert Southey's description of the execution of Caracciolo, 1813 — 43

LIST OF DOCUMENTS

40.	The Royal Military Junta in Naples on the need to maintain the execution schedule, August 1799	45
41.	Ferdinand's order to speed up the political trials, August 29, 1799	45

CHAPTER 3: JOSEPH I AND MURAT, 1806–1815

42.	Maria Carolina on the Treaty of Florence between Naples and France, April 1801	48
43.	Baron Alquier's description of Ferdinand's return to the capital, June 1802	48
44.	Baron Alquier on declining influence of the queen, January 1803	49
45.	Maria Carolina's protestations against the French occupation of Apulia, July 13, 1803	50
46.	Napoleon's demand for the removal of the Neapolitan Prime Minister, Lord Acton, July 28, 1803	51
47.	Maria Carolina's expression of rage over Napoleon's imperious manner, June 6, 1804	51
48.	Napoleon's threat to occupy Naples, January 2, 1805	53
49.	Napoleon's "Schonbrunn Declaration" ordering the occupation of the kingdom, December 27, 1805	54
50.	Napoleon's appointment of his brother Joseph as commander-in-chief of French forces in Naples, December 31, 1805	55
51.	Napoleon's letter announcing that the Bourbons had "ceased to reign," January 19, 1806	56
52.	Maria Carolina on the perfidy of Britain's allies, January 6, 1806	57
53.	Maria Carolina's final appeal to Napoleon to spare the kingdom, January 7, 1806	57
54.	Maria Carolina's offer to become a hostage, January 7, 1806	58
55.	Napoleon, two letters to Joseph on military operations, January 27 and 30, 1806	58
56.	De Nicola's description of the French army's entry into Naples, February 14, 1806	59
57.	Joseph's "Declaration to Neapolitan People," February 15, 1806	59
58.	Baron de Damas on the lack of popular resistance to the French, February 1806	60
59.	Napoleon's instructions to Joseph to take the title of "King of Naples," February 27, 1806	61
60.	Napoleon on the need to use "salutary terror" in Naples, March 5, 1806	61

61.	Census report for Naples, 1807	63
62.	Napoleon's criticism of Joseph's domestic policies, March 8, 1806	65
63.	Napoleon on the necessity of establishing French-owned estates in the kingdom, April 11, 1806	65
64.	Maria Carolina on Ferdinand's plans to recapture the city, May 10, 1807	66
65.	Napoleon on the need for reprisals against pro-Bourbon rebels, two letters, 1806	66
66.	Napoleon's warning to Joseph to be on guard against Neapolitan "treachery," May 31, 1806	67
67.	Napoleon, general critique of Joseph's rule and policies, September 25, 1807	67
68.	Napoleon's letter to Joseph informing him that he has been made king of Spain, May 11, 1808	68
69.	Napoleon's appointment of Joachim Murat as King of Naples, May 2, 1808	69
70.	Murat's letter accepting the Crown, May 5, 1808	70
71.	Murat's "Declaration to the Neapolitan People," August 15, 1808	72
72.	Letter demonstrating Murat's initial subservience to Napoleon, August 1808	73
73.	Murat, Declaration of Amnesty, September 21, 1808	73
74.	Napoleon's criticism of Murat's policy towards the émigrés, November 12, 1808	74
75.	Napoleon's demand that the French divorce law be applied to Naples without change, 1808	75
76.	Napoleon, general critique of Murat's domestic policies, December 15, 1808	75
77.	Murat, letter of submission to Napoleon, January 2, 1809	76
78.	Napoleon on Murat's capture of Capri, October 17, 1808	77
79.	Maria Carolina on the Bourbon plan to attack the mainland, March 5, 1809	77
80.	Maria Carolina on the expedition's failure, October 2, 1809	78
81.	Caroline Bonaparte on Napoleon's fear that Murat would invade Sicily, 1809	78
82.	Letter from the Neapolitan ambassador in Paris indicating Napoleon's reluctance to invade Sicily, May 22, 1810	79
83.	Murat's announcement of his decision to postpone the invasion, September 26, 1810	80

LIST OF DOCUMENTS

84.	Napoleon's criticism of Murat's policies towards Sicily, September 1810	80
85.	De Durant on Murat's desire to be independent from Napoleon, August 18, 1810	80
86.	Murat, Decree on Naturalization, June 18, 1811	81
87.	Napoleon's demand for a withdrawal of the decree, July 6, 1811	81
88.	Count Bassano on Napoleon's threat to remove Murat by force, July 7, 1811	82
89.	Murat's offer to abdicate, July 20, 1811	82
90.	Murat's revocation of the Decree on Naturalization, July 20, 1811	83
91.	French census figures for Naples, 1809–1815	84
92.	Murat's letter to Napoleon relinquishing his command of the Grand Army, January 15, 1813	85
93.	Napoleon on Murat's lack of "moral courage," January 1813	85
94.	Napoleon to Murat on his "weakness of character," January 26, 1813	85
95.	Lord William Bentinck on Britain's continuing refusal to recognize Murat as king, 1814	86
96.	Murat, Declaration of Rimini, March 30, 1815	87
97.	Murat's last letter to his wife, Queen Caroline, before his execution, October 1815	88

CHAPTER 4: RESTORATION AND REACTION, 1815–1848

98.	Pietro Colletta, on the state of the kingdom at the time of the Bourbons' return, 1831	97
99.	Prince Klemens von Metternich on the need for a policy of moderation, n.d.	100
100.	Ferdinand IV, Proclamation to the Neapolitan People, May 1, 1815	100
101.	De Nicola on the struggle between the Muratists and the Legitimists, June 28, 1816	102
102.	Henri de Stendhal on the condition of the kingdom in 1817, February–March 1817	102
103.	Society of Guelph Knights, Political Program, c. 1817	105
104.	Metternich, "Political Confession of Faith," 1820	106
105.	General Guglielmo Pepe on the conspiracy to launch a revolution in 1820, 1846	107
106.	Pepe's account of first days of the July (1820) Revolution, 1846	108
107.	Sir William A'Court on the psychological state of the king, August 26, 1820	112

XI

108.	Ferdinand's promise to grant a constitution, July 6, 1820	112
109.	Francis, the duke of Calabria's proclamation establishing a provisional "National Junta," July 9, 1820	113
110.	Keppel Craven's description of the entry of Pepe's troops into Naples, 1820	114
111.	Ferdinand I, Oath of Loyalty to the Constitution, July 13, 1820	115
112.	Metternich's initial reaction to the revolution, two letters, July 1820	116
113.	Pietro Colletta on the increasing difficulties of the revolutionaries, 1831	117
114.	William A'Court on the Neapolitan parliament, October 1820	119
115.	Francesco Ricciardi on the mounting lawlessness in the kingdom, November 6, 1820	119
116.	Pietro Colletta on the king's departure for Laibach, 1831	122
117.	Friedrich von Gentz's description of Ferdinand at the Congress, January 22, 1821	123
118.	Colletta's overview of the situation in the kingdom at the time of the Austrian attack, 1831	124
119.	Marchese de San Saturnino on the corruption in the government during Ferdinand's final years, November 3, 1823	125
120.	Lady Blessington's description of the funeral of Ferdinand I, January 1825	126
121.	Metternich on the continuing corruption and ineffectiveness of the government under Francis I, June 18, 1825	128
122.	Colletta on Francis I's early reign, 1831	128
123.	Monsignor Olivieri's warning that the public viewed the monarchy with "contempt," February 6, 1826	129
124.	Francis' letter of assurance to the Austrians that his government was secure, April 8, 1827	130
125.	Metternich on his determination to keep troops in a state of readiness in northern Italy, February 27, 1827	131
126.	Viennet's speculation on the likelihood of a new revolution in Naples, June 1, 1830	132

CHAPTER 5: THE REVOLUTION OF 1848

127.	Luigi Settembrini's recollections on the high expectations created by Ferdinand II's ascendancy to the throne, 1879	137
128.	William Boulware on Ferdinand's efforts to promote economic development in the kingdom, December 3, 1843	138

129.	William Temple on the Neapolitan government's failures in Sicily, April 14, 1837	140
130.	Boulware on the inevitability of revolution in Italy, March 30, 1844	141
131.	Settembrini, Protest of the People of the Kingdom of the Two Sicilies, 1847	142
132.	William H. Polk on the deepening economic crisis in the kingdom, January 4, 1847	146
133.	Settembrini on the mounting political unrest in Naples in the months prior to the revolution, 1879	146
134.	Settembrini on the outbreak of the revolution in January 1848, 1879	149
135.	Settembrini on the Neapolitan reaction to the revolution in Sicily, 1879	151
136.	Settembrini on the increasing radicalization of the Neapolitan lower classes, 1879	152
137.	Guglielmo Pepe on Ferdinand II's opposition to the war against Austria, 1850	153
138.	Settembrini on the foolishness of the government's decision to participate in the war, 1878	154
139.	Settembrini's description to the street fighting in Naples on May 15, 1848, 1879	155
140.	G.F. Giorgini on the changes in Neapolitan foreign policy after the crushing of the revolutionaries, August 24, 1848	157

CHAPTER 6: THE RISORGIMENTO, 1848–1861

141.	William Ewart Gladstone, two letters to the earl of Aberdeen on the state prosecutions of the Neapolitan government, 1851	159
142.	The New York *Daily Times*, editorial on the repression in Naples, August 13, 1852	161
143.	Count Camillo di Cavour on the need for Neapolitan political reform, October 5, 1856	162
144.	Cavour on the Plombières meeting with Napoleon III, July 24, 1858	164
145.	Ferdinand II on Naples' intention to remain neutral in the event of an Austro-Sardinian war, April 23, 1859	166
146.	Cavour's appeal to the new king, Francis II, to join in the war against Austria, June 25, 1859	166
147.	General Dabormida on Piedmont-Sardinia's demands for a change in Neapolitan domestic and foreign policies, January 11, 1860	168
148.	Giuseppi Massari on Cavour's opposition to the inclusion of Naples in the new Italy, December 29, 1859	169

149. Cavour on his efforts to prevent Garibaldi from attacking Sicily, May 12, 1860 — 170
150. G.C. Abba on the fighting at Calatafimi, May 16, 1860 — 170
151. Cavour on his plans for launching a revolution in Naples, August 1, 1860 — 171
152. Garibaldi's reflections on Cavour's efforts to prevent his conquest of Naples, n.d. — 172
153. Don Liborio Romano's recommendation to Francis II that he abandon the city, August 20, 1860 — 173
154. Francis II on his determination to fight to the end, August 21, 1860 — 173
155. Francis II, Proclamation to the Neapolitan People, September 5, 1860 — 174
156. Liborio Romano's invitation to Garibaldi to enter Naples, September 6, 1860 — 175
157. Alexander Dumas' description of Garibaldi's entry into the city, September 7, 1860 — 175
158. Cesare Cantu on the intimidation of Bourbonists during the plebiscite of October 21, 1860, n.d. — 176
159. Maxime Du Camp's description of Victor Emmanuel's entry into Naples, November 7, 1860 — 177
160. Louise Colet on the somber mood in Naples after Garibaldi's departure, November 1860 — 178

Chapter 7: Naples in Italy, 1861–1914

161. Luigi Farini on the 'hell-pit' of Naples, December 12, 1860 — 187
162. Cavour on the need to impose a centralized system on Naples, December 14, 1860 — 189
163. Constantino Nigra on the further deterioration of the city, March 17, 1861 — 190
164. Massimo d'Azeglio on the failure of Piedmontese policy in the South, August 2, 1861 — 191
165. Legitimist proclamation calling for the re-establishment of Neapolitan autonomy, January 16, 1862 — 193
166. General Galateri on the need to intensify the repression, December, 1860 — 193
167. Nino Bixio on the poverty and backwardness of much of the Italian South, February 18, 1863 — 194
168. Gaetano Negri on the cycle of violence and reprisal in the smaller southern towns, August 1861 — 195
169. P. Cala Ulloa on the repression in Naples, July 1863 — 195

LIST OF DOCUMENTS

170.	Nigra on the Neapolitans' contradictory aspirations, 1860	198
171.	H. Taine on the poverty and overcrowding in Naples in the mid-1860s (1864)	198
172.	Rocco De Zerbi's description of "clientelism" and its operation in Neapolitan elections, n.d.	200
173.	King and Okey on political corruption in the Italian South, 1901	201
174.	King and Okey on the Camorra, 1901	202
175.	Senator Serado on the domination of Neapolitan political institutions by organized crime, 1901	203
176.	The *Edinburgh Review* on the overall deterioration of Naples since unification, July 1883	204
177.	Axel Munthe's description of the cholera epidemic of 1884 (two selections: 1929 and 1889)	205
178.	Agostino Depretis on the need for the nation to commit itself to Neapolitan renewal, 1884	208
179.	Matilde Serao's response to Depretis' call to "gut" Naples, 1884	208
180.	Adolfo Giambarba on the three main objectives of the *Risanamento*, 1885	209
181.	Senator Serado on the fate of those displaced by the rebuilding program, 1901	209
182.	Alberto Marghieri on the failure of the *Risanamento*, 1905	210
183.	Alfonso Cottau on the decline of Naples after 1860, 1896	210
184.	Marco Rocco on the city's "moral and material decadence," 1898	210
185.	Benedetto Croce on the course of Neapolitan history from Unification to 1914	212

CHAPTER 8: THE ERA OF CATASTROPHES, 1914–1943

186.	Arturo Labriola on the collusion between government officials and the Fascists in September 1922	220
187.	Enrico De Nicola's telegram welcoming Mussolini and the Blackshirts to Naples, October 24, 1922	221
188.	Benito Mussolini's speech to the Fascist National Congress in Naples, October 24, 1922	221
189.	Mussolini's declaration to the crowd in Piazza del Plebiscito on the same day, October 24, 1922	223
190.	Carlo Cassola on the Fascists' use of violence in Nocera, February 23, 1923	224
191.	Paolo Scarfoglio, letter declaring *Il Mattino*'s support for Fascism in the wake of the Matteoti crisis, November 28, 1925	225

192. Carlo Levi on the lack of support for Fascism among the peasants in the South, 1946 — 226
193. A Neapolitan industrial worker's recollection of the reception given to Mussolini during a visit to the Royal Shipyard in Castellammare in 1924, 1958 — 227
194. Aurelio Padovani on the need to destroy the "clientele system," November 16, 1922 — 228
195. Ignazio Silone's description of the Fascist Party's organizational structure in Naples, 1927 — 229
196. Mussolini's speech in Piazza del Plebiscito promising new funds for the development of the city, October 15, 1931 — 230
197. Statistical chart comparing the percentage of industrial workers in Naples with the rest of Italy from 1927 to 1939 — 231
198. *Il Mattino*, interview with a Neapolitan fisherman on the impact of League of Nations' sanctions on the city, January 3, 1936 — 232
199. General Narvarrini, Declaration of a State of Emergency in Naples, July 19, 1943 — 232
200. War diary (anonymous) chronicling the frequency and length of bombing attacks on the city, April to August 1943 — 234
201. *Roma*, two articles on the Allied bombing of Naples, August 5 and 6, 1943 — 234
202. German declaration of marshal law in Naples, September 13, 1943 — 236
203. German army order establishing forced labor in Naples, September 22, 1943 — 236
204. Alan Moorehead on Naples at the time of the Allied occupation, October 1943 — 237
205. American embassy in Switzerland on the willingness of the Allies to use the Camorra to implement their policies, January 3, 1943 — 238
206. The *Chicago Daily News* on the cynical relationship between the Allies and the Neapolitan political elite, December 13, 1943 — 238

CHAPTER 9: THE INCOMPLETE RECOVERY, 1943–1999

207. Alan Moorehead on the tragedy of Naples, September 1944 — 245
208. Norman Lewis's description of the devastation in the city at the end of the war, October–November 1943 — 245
209. Lewis on prostitution in Naples (two selections), October 22, 1943 and March 26, 1944 — 249
210. Lewis on the Allied role in reestablishing the Camorra, January and May 1944 — 250

LIST OF DOCUMENTS

211.	The *Whaley-Eaton Newsletter*, note on Churchill's opposition to economic aid for Italy, August 13, 1943	251
212.	Lewis on Neapolitan black-market, May 9, 1944	252
213.	Robert B. Ellis' description of Naples in April 1945, n.d.	252
214.	Two interviews with Neapolitans on the relationship between "clientelism," promotions, and jobs, 1958 and 1963	254
215.	A PCI militant on the discrimination practiced against Communists in job hiring, 1963	254
216.	A Neapolitan worker on the corruption of the state and its indifference to the poor, 1963	255
217.	Statistical table: Voting Pattern in Naples Broken Down by Social Class (1968)	256
218.	Statistical table: Percentage of Votes: City of Naples, 1953–1976	256
219.	Judith Chubb on child labor in Naples, 1982	257
220.	Statistical table: Distribution of Industrial and Commercial Firms by Size, Naples vs. Milan (1971)	258
221.	Luigi Barzini on the destruction of the natural beauty of Naples and Palermo, 1964	259
222.	Antonio Ghirelli on the "Massacre of Naples," 1973	260
223.	Carmine Schiavone's testimony on the power of the Camorra over Neapolitan elections, 1993	261
224.	Alan Cowell's description of the condition of Naples on the eve of the mayoral elections of 1993, November 11, 1993	263
225.	John Tagliabue on the role played by the Camorra in the city's economic structure, March 7, 1994	265
226.	Antonio Bassolino on the Neapolitan cultural revival, March 1994	267
227.	*The New York Times* on the use of Italian troops in Naples to quell Camorra violence, July 14, 1997	267
228.	Frank Viviano on Mayor Antonio Bassolino and the gradual transformation of the city, February 13, 1998	267
229.	Antonio Ghirelli on Naples and its future, 1996	271

■ ■ ■

ILLUSTRATIONS

Cover	Galleria Umberto I. Italica Press.	
1.	Frontispiece: Piergiorgio Branzi. *The vicolo*, c. 1960.	II
2.	Panoramic view of Bay of Naples toward Vesuvio, from the Certosa, 1860/65. Collezione Gafio.	XXVIII-XXIX
3.	Eruption of Vesuvius, April 1872, from Castel Nuovo, with Molo and Lighthouse. Collezione Gafio.	XXX
4.	Queen Maria Carolina, detail of *Portrait of the Royal Family*, by Angelica Kauffmann, c. 1790.	LI
5.	Vincenzo Camuccini, *King Ferdinand IV,* 1818/19. Palazzo Reale.	LII
6.	François Gérard. *Joachim Murat*, c. 1813. Museo di Capodimonte.	46
ARCHITECTURE & URBANISM: 19TH CENTURY		89-91
7.	Angelo Viviani, *Bay of Naples from Castel Sant'Elmo*, c. 1840. Museo di San Martino.	89
8.	School of Posillipo. Ferdinand IV's Return to Naples, 1815. Private Collection.	
9.	Naples and the port from San Martino, 1870/75. Collezione Gafio.	
10.	Porta Capuana from Castel Capuano, c. 1890. Gentile.	90
11.	Waterfront of Santa Lucia, 1885/90. G. Sommer. Gafio.	
12.	Gradinata di Chiaia, 1890/1900. Brunner.	
13.	Port with Molo and Lighthouse, c. 1870. Collezione V. Proto.	
14.	Piazza Poerio (Carità), c. 1890. Gafio.	
15.	Giovanni Antonio Medrano, architect, Teatro San Carlo c. 1840.	91
16.	Villa Pignatelli. Built in 1826 for the Acton family.	
17.	Piazza del Plebiscito (1810) and San Francesco di Paola (1817-32).	
18.	Galleria Principe di Napoli (1883). Cesare de Seta, *Napoli*. Laterza, 1991.	
19.	Galleria Umberto I (1887-90), Cesare de Seta, *Napoli*. Laterza, 1991.	
20.	Covered passage in the Municipio. Gasse (begun 1816).	
DAILY LIFE & MATERIAL CULTURE: 19TH CENTURY		92-95
21.	Traditional female dress, c. 1820.	92
22.	The Feast of Piedigrotta, c. 1840.	

ILLUSTRATIONS

23.	Open-air market, c. 1890. G. Amodio.	92
24.	A street of *fondaci*, c. 1885. G. Sommer. Gafio.	
25.	Salvatore Fergola, *Opening of the Naples-Portici Railroad*, 1840. Museo di San Martino.	93
26.	The *Metropolitana*, Lamont Young project, 1884.	
27.	Via Toledo (Roma), c. 1890. Edizioni K.F.Z.	
28.	Via Foria, c. 1890. Aterocca.	
29.	Homeless family on the beach, c. 1883.	94
30.	*Scugnizzi*, c. 1890.	
31.	Women at a fountain. Santa Lucia, c. 1890. G. Amodio.	
32.	Pasta manufacture, c. 1890. Gafio.	
33.	A water seller, c. 1885.	
34.	A public scribe conducts business on the street, c. 1870. G. Sommer.	
35.	Mealtime at a working-class inn, c. 1890. G. Amodio.	
36.	Gioacchino Toma, *Mass at Home*, 1877. Castel Nuovo, Museo Civico.	95
37.	Playing tennis, 1902. G. Matacena.	
38.	Philippe Benoist (1813–1905), Interior of Teatro San Carlo.	
39.	A bathing club at Posillipo, c. 1900. Gafio.	
40.	Giuseppe De Nittis, *Meal at Posillipo*, c. 1885. Milan: Galleria d'Arte Moderna.	
41.	Francis II, state portrait, 1859.	96

POLITICAL CULTURE & EVENTS: 19TH CENTURY   133–35

42.	Giuseppe Commarano, *Francis I and Royal Family Pay Homage to Ferdinand I*. Caserta, Reggia.	133
43.	Portrait of Cardinal Ruffo. Museo di San Martino.	
44.	A meeting of the Carbonari, c. 1820.	
45.	The Parliament of Naples, 1848.	
46.	*The Barricades on via Sta. Brigida, May 15, 1848*. Castel Nuovo, Museo Civico.	134
47.	Carlo Poerio (1802–1848).	
48.	Luigi Settembrini (1813–1876).	
49.	Gladstone visits political prisoners in 1850.	
50.	E. Matania. *Garibaldi and Bixio at Calatafimi, May 15, 1860*.	135
51.	Casting ballots for the Plebiscite, October 21, 1860.	
52.	Group of brigands, captured near Salerno, 1865.	
53.	A Piedmontese soldier poses with the corpse of the brigand Nicola Napolitano, c. 1865. Editori Riuniti.	
54.	F. Palizzi, *Street Fighting between San Ferdinando and via Toledo, May 15, 1848*. Castel Nuovo, Museo Civico.	136

MODERN NAPLES, 1799–1999

55.	Garibaldi welcomed to Naples on Via Toledo, 1860.	158

LITERATURE: 19TH CENTURY 180–81

56.	Vincenzo Cuoco (1770–1823).	180
57.	Paolo Emilio Imbriani (1840–1886).	
58.	Thomas Lawrence, *Lady Blessington*, 1822. London: Wallace Collection.	
59.	Advertisement for *Il Ventre di Napoli* by Matilde Serao, 1884.	181
60.	Matilde Serao (1856–1927).	
61.	Francesco De Sanctis (1817–1883).	
62.	Ferdinando Russo (1868–1927).	

PAINTING & SCULPTURE 182–85

63.	Neapolitan School, *View of the Port of Naples*, 19th century. Milan: Banca Commerciale Italiana (BCI).	182
64.	Anton Sminck Pitloo, *Castel dell'Ovo from the Seashore*, c. 1825. Torre del Greco: Banca di Credito Popolare.	
65.	Giacinto Gigante, *The Temples at Paestum*, 1854. Solofra Palace.	
66.	Ezechiele Guardascione (1875–1948), *Landscape with Trees and Ruins*. BCI.	
67.	Antonio Mancini (1852–1930), *After the Duel*. Turin: Galleria d'Arte Moderna.	183
68.	Domenico Morelli (1823–1901), *Turkish Bath*. Private collection.	
69.	Gioacchino Toma, *The Shower of Ashes from Vesuvius*, 1880. Florence: Palazzo Pitti.	
70.	Guido Casciaro, *Lago Lucrino*, 1953. BCI.	
71.	Leon Giuseppe Buono, *From My Studio*, 1955. BCI.	
72.	Carlo Brancaccio (1861–1920), *Via Toledo*. BCI.	184
73.	Salvatore De Gregorio, *Landscape on Etna*, 1909. BCI.	
74.	Luca Postiglione, *Impressions*, c. 1920. BCI.	
75.	Giuseppe Carrino, *Celebration*, 1953. BCI.	
76.	Royal Porcelain Factory, *Dancers*, 1800-1806. Museo Filangieri.	185
77.	Vincenzo Gemito (1852–1929), *Fisherman*. Castel Nuovo, Museo Civico.	
78.	Marino Mazzacurati (1907–1969), *Monument to the Martyrs of the Four Days*, Piazza della Repubblica, 1969.	
79.	Piazza del Plebiscito, Annual Installation, 2000.	
80.	Raffaele Giovini, Porcelain plate with costume of Castiglione, 1830-40. Museo Filangieri.	
81.	Vincenzo Buonocore, Majolica vase with floral motifs, 1898. Museo Artistico Industriale.	
82.	O. Goretti, Majolica vase with stylized floral patterns, 1920. Museo Artistico Industriale.	

ILLUSTRATIONS

83.	Poster for 50th Anniversary of the Plebiscito Meridionale, October 1910.	186
PUBLIC HEALTH & RISANAMENTO		214-17
84-85.	Uffici Tecnici del Comune di Napoli. Two of 24 maps showing the density of the central city, 1872–80.	214
86.	Vicolo di Santa Lucia, c. 1890. Gafio.	215
87.	Edoardo Matania. *The Cholera in Naples*, 1884.	
88.	Edoardo Matania. *Umberto I and Agostino Depretis Visit the Cholera Wards*, 1884.	
89.	Plan for the Risanamento, with axes of Corso Umberto I (Rettifilo) and via Nazionale, 1884.	216
90.	Aerial photo of area in 89, showing implementation, c. 1960.	
91.	Elevations along Corso Umberto I after the Risanamento, from Piazza Bovio and Fontana Medina to the train station.	216–17
92.	Plan for the new Corso Umberto I: demolition through the cloister of San Pietro ad Aram.	217
93.	Gennaro D'Amato after Raffaele D'Ambra. Fondaco Calderai a Rua Catalana. Destroyed during the Risanamento.	
94.	Raffaele D'Ambra. Gradelle di San Giuseppe on via Calderai, 1889. Destroyed during the Risanamento.	
95.	*Camorristi* under arrest, c. 1906.	218
POLITICAL CULTURE & EVENTS, 20TH CENTURY		240–43
96.	May 1, 1920. Street fighting disrupts the Socialist May Day Celebration, Piazza Dante.	240
97.	October 24, 1922. The Blackshirt squads take over Naples.	
98.	Benito Mussolini reviews his troops in Naples before the March on Rome, October 1922.	
99.	Edmondo Rossoni, President of the Fascist National Labor Syndicates, addresses the crowds at Piazza del Plebiscito, 1927.	
100.	The "Four Days," September 1943.	241
101.	The Allied Fifth Army enters the city, October 1, 1943.	
102.	Neapolitans greet U.S. soldiers, October 1943.	
103.	Neapolitans sleeping in streets amid bombed-out buildings, 1944. From Aubrey Menen. *Four Days*. New York: Seaview, 1979.	
104.	U.S. sailors and Neapolitan women, 1944.	242
105.	Demonstration against bread shortages, 1947.	
106.	Unemployment after the war: the port area in 1946.	
107-8.	Mayor Achille Lauro at a political rally, 1950s.	243

109.	Women demonstrate for equal pay, 1970s.	243
110.	Crackdown on the Camorra, 1990s.	
111.	Mayor Antonio Bassolino, 1998.	
112.	*Scugnizzi* during the Four Days, 1943.	244

DAILY LIFE & MATERIAL CULTURE: 20TH CENTURY — 272–73

113.	At the Sailing Club of Naples, 1908. Gafio.	272
114.	The prince of Santobono and group at the Agnano racetrack, c. 1903. G. Matacena.	
115.	Industrial workers, Ilva plant, Bagnoli, 1905.	
116.	Work and life in the *bassi*, 1914.	
117.	Child Labor, 1968. Vittorio de Sica.	273
118–19.	Children at play in the *bassi*, 1968. Vittorio de Sica.	
120.	Families separated by emigration. Farewell at the port, 1958.	

ARCHITECTURE & URBANISM: 20TH CENTURY — 274–77

121.	Central Railroad Station, c. 1900.	274
122.	Luigi Cosenza, Palazzo Forquet project for Riviera di Chiaia, 1933.	
123.	Pizzofalcone from the air, 1937.	
124.	Mergellina, c. 1960.	
125.	City and harbor, c. 1965.	
126.	The "urban massacre" on the slopes of the Vomero, c. 1960.	275
127.	Spaccanapoli, c. 1960.	
128.	Uliano Lucas, the Spanish Quarter, c. 1975.	
129.	Bagnoli, Italsider plant, c. 1980.	
130.	The Stazione Marittima, c. 1960. Castel Nuovo in background.	
131.	Enrico Alvino, Casa Armonica Kiosk, Villa Comunale, 1877.	276
132.	Giorgio Botta, Villa Pappone, 1912.	
133.	Gaetano Costa, Stazione di Mergellina, 1924–27. Detail.	
134.	Mostra d'Oltremare, 1937–40.	
135.	Giuseppe Vaccaro, Palazzo delle Poste, 1936.	
136.	Luigi Cosenza, Olivetti Plant at Pozzuoli, 1951. Detail.	277
137.	Angelo Mangiarotti, Prefabricated housing at Caserta, 1962.	
138.	New housings plans for suburbs after earthquake of 1980.	
139.	Plans realized at Maiano, c. 1985.	
140.	Kenzo Tange, Centro Direzionale, begun 1982. View along central axis.	
141.	New Skyline. View across Borgo Marinari from Castel dell'Ovo toward Centro Direzionale, 2000.	

LITERATURE: 20TH CENTURY — 284–85

142.	Benedetto Croce (1866–1952).	284

ILLUSTRATIONS

143.	Salvatore Di Giacomo (1860–1934).	284
144.	Raffaele Viviani (1888–1950).	
145.	Colonnese Bookstore, via S. Pietro a Maiella.	285
146.	Two book covers, from Electa and Alfredo Guida, Naples.	
147.	Luciano De Crescenzo (b. 1928).	
148.	Ann Maria Ortese (b. 1914).	
149.	Fabrizia Ramondino (b. 1936).	

MUSIC   286–87

150.	The Tarantella, 19th century. London: Victoria and Albert Museum.	286
151.	Gioacchino Rossini (1792–1868). Portrait by Gugliemo De Sanctis, 1862.	
152.	Three songsheets. *Funiculi-Funicula* by Luigi Denza (1846–1922); *Torna a Surriento*, words by Giambattista De Curtis (1860–1926), music by Ernesto De Curtis (1875–1937); and *Marechiare*, words by Salvatore Di Giacomo (1860–1934), music by Francesco Paolo Tosti (1846–1916).	
153.	*Io Te Voglio Bene Assaie*, composed before Unification, illustrated by Edoardo Dalbono (1841–1915).	287.
154.	Enrico Caruso (1873–1921).	
155.	Roberto Murolo.	
156-57.	Nuova compagnia di Canto popolare. Album cover & concert photo.	

THEATER & FILM   288–89

158.	Eduardo Scarpetta (1853–1925).	288
159.	Roberto Bracco (1862–1943).	
160.	Eduardo De Filippo (1900–1985).	
161.	Totò (Antonio de Curtis, 1898–1967).	
162–63.	Vittorio De Sica, *The Gold of Naples* (1954) and *Marriage Italian Style* (1964, with Marcello Mastroianni and Sophia Loren).	289
164–65.	Francesco Rosi's *Hands on the City* (1963) and *The Mattei Affair* (1972).	
166.	Lina Wertmüller's *Camorra* (1985).	
167.	Pappi Corsicato's *Libera* (1991).	
168.	Toward Centro Direzionale. Open-air market on via Venezia, 2000.	290

MAPS	300–302
Naples c. 1800.	300
Naples c. 1900.	301
Naples c. 2000.	302

■ ■ ■

XXIII

FOREWORD

Naples, and the kingdom that took its name, has long been a neglected field of history in the United States. There have traditionally been several reasons for this. While the classical heritage of the Bay of Naples, of Pompeii, Herculaneum, Baia, Cumae, Pozzuoli, and Posillipo and their treasures in Naples' museums have long been a central focus of classical studies, both in Italy and in the United States, medieval studies have focused on northern Europe, especially France, Germany, and England; while Renaissance history, even of Italy, has tended to concentrate on the northern and republican centers of the period. This fit well with the liberal and democratic tendencies of the students of Italy in the United States through most of the nineteenth and twentieth centuries. Naples, both the city as capital, and the Regno, as the kingdom was called, were long associated with royalty: with the new Norman dynasty, the imperial dreams of the Hohenstaufen, the dynastic conflicts of Angevins and the house of Aragon, and then with the absolutist monarchies of early-modern Europe: the Spanish and Austrian Hapsburgs and the Spanish and Neapolitan Bourbons.

Coincident with this has been the emphasis of historians to examine the origins and development of medieval and Renaissance culture as expressions of urban and democratic tendencies, of a "civic humanism" that expressed the desires and values of a bourgeois and republican way of life. Thus, again, historians have concentrated on the northern centers of the Middle Ages and Renaissance: Florence, Siena, Venice; and in the High Renaissance, Rome. This tendency has been reinforced by the legacy of Romanticism in the nineteenth and the canons of artistic taste of the twentieth century, which viewed first the Gothic of the North and of northern Italy, and then the flowering of Renaissance style in Tuscany, Lombardy, and the Veneto as the norms of Italian art. Naples, long associated with the glory of the Baroque, shared the disdain of much of the twentieth century for its style and ethic.

More mundane reasons, of course, have contributed to this long neglect of Neapolitan history. Perhaps the most pervasive of these is the tourist image of Italy formed by Americans. With the end of the Grand Tour in the late nineteenth century, Rome, Florence, and Venice became the points of an ironclad triangle of travel, both for the obvious attractions and beauties of these cities and their environs, and for the cultural framework with which Americans have come to view Italy.

This attitude, moreover, belies another American outlook, one that is, unfortunately, still shared by a great many Italians and Europeans themselves: that the modern Mezzogiorno, the "South" of Italy, is a land of poverty and cultural deprivation: a region — and a capital city — beset by corruption, crime, and the stereotype of the *"far niente"* southern Italian. This is an image reinforced in the United States by the daily occurrence of Italian dichotomies: the cultured art, literature, even cuisine, of the North, as opposed to the supposedly poor, peasant culture of Naples and the South.

Such attitudes have long contributed to a certain shyness among Americans to devote much time and effort to the study of things Neapolitan: why contend with so many negative attitudes, such a relatively remote, and perhaps unrewarding, field of research when the bright cities of the North offer much better areas for study? Again, while the Neapolitan kingdom and city have witnessed many events and personalities that have been central to European — and Western — history, they have also suffered the repeated ravages to their historical records: from occasional loses of itinerant archives during the Middle Ages to such popular revolts as those of 1585 and 1647 against Spanish rule (in which tax, court, and other records were destroyed), to the most recent destruction of the State Archives on September 30, 1943 at the hands of the retreating Nazis that forever removed most of the records of the high Middle Ages and Renaissance in Naples. Indeed, Naples never seemed to have recovered from World War II and the impoverishment of the city and its culture that the war left behind.

Recently, however, much of this has begun to change. There has long been a tradition of serious Italian historical and art historical scholarship for Naples and the South. One need only consult the multi-volume *Storia di Napoli*, the *Storia di Campania* or the works of Bologna, Capasso, De Seta, and Gliejeses, among many others, to get some idea of the very well developed field of Italian research there. Indeed, the city and its cultural treasures have once again begun to attract both historians and art historians: the former to the age of the Aragonese monarchy in the Renaissance, the latter to the baroque. Even medieval Naples has begun to attract its students. The reasons are numerous: the broadening of the horizon of historical studies in the United States toward more Mediterranean fields, the search for new areas of fruitful scholarly investigation — now that the chief northern centers of Italian culture have been analyzed with such wonderful results for over a century — and an understanding that Neapolitan politics, culture, and economic life had profound influences on Italy and Europe into the modern world. These trends coincide with renewed development in the Italian Mezzogiorno by the Italian government and private groups that, though slow in materializing, have now restored many of Naples' most important monuments, reinvigorated its urban life and political culture, and given new force to its social and economic potential.

For many of these reasons, in 1995 we conceived the notion of offering a comprehensive documentary history of Naples that would present to English-speaking readers an in-depth survey of the city's history, economy, politics, culture, arts, and spiritual and intellectual life. A five-volume series of carefully selected original texts, translated into English, with brief introductions to their authors' lives and work, is intended to offer a sampling of the rich materials still to be uncovered or further explored. In so doing, we hope to present to the professional researcher the status quo on Neapolitan studies in the United States and offer a base for further study and exploration; and to give the student and general reader a first introduction to the rich and complex history of this famous capital. Our aim was thus to offer a *first*, rather than the last word, on the subject. To accomplish this task we asked many of the most prominent students of Naples and southern Italy in the United States to collaborate on this project. They agreed to participate and responded with equal amounts of enthusiasm and caution: enthusiasm for the enterprise but caution because so much of this territory is either uncharted or still poorly mapped out.

The following volume, *Modern Naples, 1799–1999*, the fifth in the series, is the work of John Santore, professor at Pratt Institute in Brooklyn, New York, and a historian of modern Europe. In contrast with the previously published volume in this series, *Baroque Naples, 1600–1800* by Jeanne Chenault Porter, which appropriately focused on Naples as the flourishing artistic and cultural capital, Professor Santore addresses the last two centuries of Naples' decline as an urban center and a political unit. His text therefore rests on political/diplomatic narrative and social and economic history to reconstruct the city's "tragic centuries." The ensuing story is therefore not triumphalist in any sense. Here the reader will not find the staples of recent Neapolitan myth and memory. The "post-modern" city of song and dance, of film and painting, of poetic and philosophical expression, peopled with world-wise survivors — though discussed — is not the author's intent. Instead a sobering image emerges that offers a faithful interpretation of the historical record and of more recent events and that poses to the reader a challenge both to ponder and to further explore.

— Ronald G. Musto, Series Editor
New York City, January 2001

PREFACE

Few cities have been written about with more passion than modern Naples. Beginning in the Romantic period and continuing into the contemporary era, a long list of famous poets, writers, journalists, and intellectuals have provided vivid descriptions of its people and culture, and depicted its triumphs and tragedies in the most eloquent terms. This book represents an attempt to encapsulate that testimony in the form of a continuous historical narrative. Overall, it contains 229 documents. Many appear for the first time in English and have been selected with both the general reader and the scholar in mind. Among them are travellers' accounts and private letters, newspaper articles and official declarations, ambassadorial reports and governmental legislation, and excerpts from the numerous memoirs, diaries, and statistical surveys of the time.

In presenting these documents, I make no claims to be comprehensive. Indeed, given the abundance of materials available, any such suggestion would be disingenuous at best. Instead, I have tried to select those documents which, in my opinion, are most expressive of the forces that have shaped the last two hundred years of Neapolitan history, and given disproportional weight to those political and economic factors that have had the greatest impact on modern Neapolitan life.

No work of this scope would be possible without the labor of others. In this regard, I would like to acknowledge my debt to a number of scholars in several related fields. Among them, four should be mentioned in particular: Harold Acton (for his two-volume work on the Bourbons); Denis Mack Smith (for his documentary collections on the *Risorgimento*); Frank Snowden (for his study of Naples in the time of the cholera); and P.A. Allum (for his analysis of Neapolitan politics after the Second World War). To each of these authors I express my sincere gratitude.

I would also like to thank Robert Connolly for his help with many of the translations, and Professor Pellegrino D'Acierno of Hofstra University for reading large parts of the text. Finally, I would like to express my appreciation to Pratt Institute for granting me a sabbatical leave so that I could complete my research, and a special Provost's award with additional funds. Any mistakes contained in this volume, of course, are mine.

—John Santore
New York City, September 2000

3. Eruption of Vesuvius, April 1872, from Castel Nuovo, with Molo and Lighthouse.

INTRODUCTION
NAPLES: THE TRAGIC CENTURIES

The history of Naples in the 19th and 20th centuries is woven into the fabric of the books and articles of its most famous citizens. It is a story, by and large, of loss and lamentation. It is a tale of the steady decline of a great city from the towering heights of the 18th century into an abyss of political marginalization and cultural despair. Each of the city's most famous authors — Cuoco, Colletta, Pepe, Settembrini, Serao, Croce — holds a piece of that story. Each bears witness to the relentless character of the city's social and economic deterioration, and to the nostalgic, and often fatal, longing of its foremost citizens for its once brilliant past.

At the start of the 19th century, Naples was still — in terms of size, influence, and culture — among the greatest cities in Europe. In terms of size, its population numbered over 350,000 people, more than twice as large as Rome and greater than Florence, Turin, and Milan combined.[1] In all of Europe, only London and Paris surpassed it in numbers, and future centers, such as Berlin, St. Petersburg, and Vienna, were still far behind. Most of this population lived in a narrow, three-mile arc stretching along the city's famous bay. Within this arc, there existed a vibrant and, often, brilliant artistic and intellectual culture. During the 18th century, Neapolitan philosophers and historians, such as Vico, Giannone, Filangieri, and Genovesi, had contributed enormously to the European Enlightenment, while Neapolitan artists and composers such as Pergolesi, Solimena, Sammartino, and Cimarosa, had made the city a center of European opera, architecture, and art. By the 1780s, the reputation of Naples had grown to such a point that the city became a place of pilgrimage for many European writers and intellectuals. Goethe first visited the city in 1787; and he was followed, in subsequent decades, by a myriad of successors, including Byron, Shelly, Keats, Stendhal, Dickens, and Twain. While there, such visitors were almost uniformly impressed by the beauty of the city's natural setting, the liveliness and spontaneity of its popular culture, the grandeur of the opera performances at the Teatro San Carlo, and the pageantry and splendor that surrounded the royal court. "Naples", as Stendhal put it succinctly in 1817, was "a great capital city... [It] alone, among Italian cities, had the true makings of a [national] capital." Compared to it, the rest [were] nothing more than provincial towns."[2]

The wealth, beauty, and dynamism of Naples in the decades prior to 1800 only served to highlight the severity of its decline in subsequent centuries. During the 19th century, Naples lost its primacy in Italy and was relegated to the periphery of European affairs. The completion of Italian unification in 1861, in particular, had a devastating impact on the city. Within the relatively brief period of a few years, Naples lost its privileged position as the capital of the independent Kingdom of the Two Sicilies and was subjected to a series of fiscal and tariff measures that precipitated a spiraling economic decline. As early as the 1870s, even sympathetic observers began to speak mournfully of the city's loss of prestige and descent into poverty, and to make damaging, and often racially grounded, comparisons between the supposed "lethargy" of its inhabitants and those of the more prosperous North. In 1884, the advent of a cholera epidemic destroyed the last vestiges of the city's image as a thriving metropolis. By 1914, despite repeated, if decidedly half-hearted, attempts by the central government to promote its renewal, Naples had become a city of debilitating slums and grinding poverty, a place where rich and poor mingled uneasily amid a general atmosphere of decay.

The triumph of Fascism in 1922 and the ravages of the Second World War only completed the city's dissolution. Mussolini's populism and authoritarianism, despite their northern genesis, appealed directly to the city's monarchist traditions.[3] Throughout his more than two decades in power, he was able to win substantial support among the Neapolitan population without producing desperately needed economic modernization; and the cumulative effects of his neglect and depredations were compounded by the massive Allied bombing of the city in 1944.

By the end of the war, in fact, Naples had reached its historical nadir. For a brief time, thousands of its inhabitants were forced to flee to the countryside in search of food and shelter, and many thousands more were compelled to sell their bodies and remaining possessions in an effort to survive among the ruins. Efforts by the government in Rome to revive the city during the 1950s and 1960s by financing the creation of a vast industrial zone extending from the city's center to the Vesuvian slopes proved to be only partially successful. While the growth in industry did lead to a significant increase in overall economic production, it permanently marred the city's physical setting and character, and had the unintended effect of polluting much of the city's air and water without effectively transforming the life of the majority of the poor. Throughout the 1970s and much of the 1980s, in fact, Naples continued to have some of the worst slums in Europe. Crime, corruption, and bureaucratic confusion became the hallmarks of Neapolitan life and society, and events such as the return of cholera in 1973 lead some Neapolitan journalists to write gloomily of a "descent into the inferno of the Third World."[4] Only during the 1990s, after many false starts and missed opportunities, would Naples begin to show clear signs of revival. But, by the end of the century, the lingering effects of almost 200 years of deterioration were still everywhere apparent, and its full emergence as a modern metropolis was still far from complete.

2 The reasons for Naples' protracted decline in the 19th and 20th centuries are by no means simple. Most Neapolitan historians, driven as much by local pride as academic reflection, place overwhelming emphasis on the deleterious effects of Italian unification. Specifically, they point to the disastrous impact that the new national government's policies of increased taxation, free trade, and administrative centralization had on the Neapolitan economy, and to the general callousness, corruption, and indifference with which national authorities treated the city's problems after 1861.[5] Other historians, however, while conceding the damaging effect that the Risorgimento had on the city's development, tend to stress more deeply-rooted causes. Building on the work of the late 19th century *meridionalisti*,[6] they emphasize the widespread poverty and backwardness that existed in the South prior to unification, the feudal character of its class structure and interpersonal relations, and the legacy of despotism and obscurantism inherited from the last Bourbon kings. For these historians, the bases for Naples' decline had been already laid in previous centuries. All the Risorgimento did was magnify the disparities between North and South that were already in place.[7]

These two contrasting views of modern Naples — as either the innocent victim of Piedmontese conquest during the Risorgimento or the misshapen product of centuries of economic backwardness, ignorance, and despotism — continue to dominate the historical literature on the city to the present day. They reflect, for the most part, the deep-seated political and geographical divisions in Italian society, and the failure of the Risorgimento to develop a sense of common identity along with its achievement of the national ideal. At the core of the controversy lies the question of why did Naples, whose prospects seemed so promising prior to 1800, fail to develop into a thriving contemporary metropolis? Why did it decline so precipitously in the decades after unification, and why was it unable to mobilize the financial and political resources necessary to guarantee its prosperity as part of a unitary state?

3 A useful starting point for exploring this question is provided by an examination of the pre-19th century Neapolitan economy. During the late 18th century, Naples, and the Italian South in general, was seen by most northern travelers as a place of enormous natural wealth and bounty. Poets, like Goethe, wrote effusively about its warm and nurturing climate and the happiness of its people, while others spoke repeatedly

of the richness of its vegetation and the natural fertility of its soil.[8] In point of fact, however, by the 18th century, the Italian South had long ceased to be the garden of abundance so blithely described by casual observers. Over the previous centuries, population pressures, deforestation, and massive soil erosion had robbed the land of much of its fertility; and blistering summer heat, inadequate rainfall, and poor agricultural techniques had kept yields per acre dismally low. As a result, most of the approximately five million people who inhabited the Kingdom of Naples in 1791 lived in desperate poverty. Of them, about three-quarters were either small farmers, who labored on tiny, and often minuscule, plots, or landless peasants, who toiled endlessly on the estates of the rich. Indeed, throughout the 18th century, the size and concentration of both aristocratic and ecclesiastical landholdings increased dramatically. By 1799, in fact, about 20 percent of all landed income in the Kingdom of Naples was owned by the nobility, and a further 20 to 30 percent more by the Church.[9] Within this group, moreover, there existed a tiny elite of 15 out of 1500 titled families who owned 75 percent of all feudal holdings, with the Pignatelli family alone in possession of 72 fiefs.[10] Since most of these noble landowners were absentees who preferred to live in Naples, they confided the power to run their estates to non-noble stewards. The object of the stewards, in turn, was to maximize income by putting ever greater pressure the area's already-fragile resources, and by constantly heightening the level of exploitation of those who worked the land.

Under such a system, the average peasant was forced to live under conditions that bordered on bondage. As the 18th century wore on, high taxes, increased feudal dues, and the gradual elimination of the common land reduced much of the peasantry to squalor, while natural disasters like a drought or an earthquake sometimes brought calamity to the rural community as a whole. In 1734, a royal report presented to the new King Charles III stated:

> Just a few miles outside of Naples, the men and women you meet are mostly naked...or else clad in the most disgusting rags.... Their basic diet is a few ounces of unleavened bread.... In winter, because there is no regular work...they are forced to eat plants without even oil or salt.... If so much poverty is found in the province of Terra di Lavoro, a region where mother nature is at her most bountiful...what can the situation be like in the other provinces of the kingdom?"[11]

Worse still, during the first half of the 19th century, the poverty of the countryside continued to deepen. From the early 1820s on, in particular, a prolonged slump in agricultural prices produced widespread destitution, and the spread of the cholera epidemic of 1835 from the cities to the villages only added to the despair. By the 1840s, in fact, vagabondage, banditry, and pauperization had all became common — as large landowners tried to take advantage of the situation in order to increase the size of their estates even further, and little or no help came from the Bourbon regime. In 1847, Luigi Settembrini, a Neapolitan liberal who was deeply moved by the plight of the poor, wrote bitterly:

> The foreigners who come to our country seeing the serene beauty of our sky and the fertility of the fields, reading the codes of our laws and hearing the talk of progress, of civilization and religion, might believe that the Italians of the Two Sicilies enjoy an enviable happiness. And yet no state in Europe is in worse condition than ours, not even the Turks.... In the Kingdom of the Two Sicilies, in the country which is said to be the garden of Europe, the people die of hunger, are in a state worse than beasts, and the only law is caprice....[12]

4 In this vast agrarian kingdom of privileged aristocrats and exploited peasants, the city of Naples occupied a unique position. For over five hundred years prior to the 18th century, Naples had been subjected to foreign domination: first, under the French house of Anjou (1266–1442); then, under the kings of Aragon (1442–1504); and, finally, under a long series of royal viceroys appointed from Spain (1504–1707). During these years, the city's main social and cultural characteristics had been gradually established, and its economic relationship with the countryside set in place. As early as 1268, the Anjou King, Charles I, had chosen the city as his royal place of residence. As such, it became the political and administrative center for all of southern Italy and was able to use its privileged position in order to extract surplus wealth from the countryside and to redistribute it among its own narrow political and social elite. Under such conditions, the size and wealth of the city grew rapidly. During the 16th century alone, the population of Naples more than doubled.[13] It became, for a time, the largest city in Europe, and thousands of Spanish nobles were drawn to it in an effort to acquire offices and land. As elsewhere, they brought with them an intense religiosity and an exaggerated sense of honor, and thus provided the city with a decidedly aristocratic tone. Between 1558 and 1597, in fact, the number of marquisates in the Kingdom of Naples tripled.[14] Love of ceremony, religious ritual, and public extravagance became the staples of aristocratic society, and soon were transmitted to the Neapolitan community as a whole. At the same time, the number of benefactions granted to religious institutions grew dramatically, and the Church became the single largest owner of land. By the late 17th century, the number of clerics in the kingdom had grown to over 11,000, and ecclesiastical income was actually greater than that of the state.¹⁵ Thus, by the time that the Bourbons came to power in 1734, the main elements of Neapolitan life and society had already been forged. Indeed, in few other cities in Europe was the power and prestige of the aristocracy and clergy greater, or the domination of the capital over the countryside more complete.

The advent of the Bourbons did nothing to alter these basic relationships. The new Bourbon king, Charles III, had an exalted view of both his own position, and that of his family. During his reign, he spent lavishly in an effort to transform the city into a showplace for his dynasty — constructing new palaces at Capodimonte, Caserta, and Portici, building the great San Carlo opera house and the Biblioteca Nazionale, and sponsoring the first excavations at Herculaneum and Pompeii. By the 1750s, in fact, Naples — even more than in earlier periods — had become the focal point for virtually every important activity in the kingdom: it was the home of the King and the royal bureaucracy; the principle place of residence for the landed nobility and the ecclesiastical hierarchy; the sole place for university studies and the chief artistic and intellectual center; and the kingdom's main commercial port. It was, to use F. Compagna's fortuitous phrase, "like a swollen head on a stunted body,"¹⁶ absorbing energy and resources from the countryside and dissipating them in the capital without giving back anything in return.¹⁷

The parasitic relationship that existed between Naples and its provinces produced more than its share of critics. Starting in the 1750s, a small group of Neapolitan intellectuals, led by the brilliant economist Antonio Genovesi, began to argue that the problems of the peasantry could only be solved if the privileges of the church and aristocracy were diminished, and the balance between town and country was restored. Inspired, in part, by the ideals of the French Enlightenment, they called for a reorganization and rationalization of the administrative and legal machinery, an end to "feudal abuses" by the nobility, and a reinvigoration of agriculture by the introduction of free trade in grain. During the 1770s and 1780s, a number of royal administrators — of whom Bernardo Tanucci, Giuseppi Palmieri, and Domenico Caracciolo were the most prominent — attempted to implement some of these measures. But resistance from the privileged classes soon proved to be insurmountable, and the fears created by the outbreak of the revolution in France in 1789 caused the monarchy to abandon further efforts at reform. In 1792, Palmieri, who as director of the Council of High Finance had proposed to tax feudal estates and give preference to poorer farmers, wrote in obvious disillusion:

> The late Abbé Galiani was right to compare the Council of Finances to a Christmas dinner, in which too much is eaten and everyone ends up with an almighty indigestion. The Council has great projects, it commissions plans and reforms for the public good,

trade, agriculture, arts, crafts, etc. And then it begins all over again without concluding anything; and then things end up worse.[18]

Thus, the Neapolitan Enlightenment, despite the energy and brilliance of its many of its supporters, had only a marginal impact on Neapolitan development. Indeed, right up to the end of the 18th century, the basic political and economic structure of the Neapolitan kingdom remained unaltered, and it would be left to the advancing French armies in 1799 to provide a more formidable challenge to the Old Regime.

5 The French invasion of Italy ushered in one of the most dramatic periods in Neapolitan history. For sixteen years, from 1799 to 1815, Naples was engulfed in war and revolution. Twice, the Neapolitan King, Ferdinand IV, was forced to flee the capital; and, twice, he returned to wreak vengeance on all those who had threatened his regime. After the collapse of the French-inspired "Parthenopean Republic" in 1799, in particular, over one hundred of the city's most prominent citizens, including much of its intellectual and cultural elite, were executed in elaborate public ceremonies. Among those killed were the political writers Mario Pagano and Vincenzo Russo, the jurist Francesco Conforti, the scientist Domenico Cirillo, the noblewoman and journalist Elenora Foncesca de Pimentel, and Admiral Francesco Caracciolo, who was hung from the yard-arm of a ship in the harbor and his body then unceremoniously dropped into the sea.[19] The event proved to be so horrendous that it traumatized over a generation of Neapolitan leaders and intellectuals. Yet the long-term consequences of the failed revolution — and the decade of French domination that followed — were far more ambiguous than they have often been made to seem.

On the one hand, the two French monarchs — Joseph I (1806–1808) and Joachim Murat (1808–1815) — began the process of clearing away centuries of outworn ideas and institutions: feudalism was abolished; legal equality was established; the administrative and fiscal systems were streamlined and rationalized; and the estates of ecclesiastical bodies were confiscated and sold. On the other hand, however, the social structure, both in the city and the countryside, was left untouched in an effort to win the support of men of property; the aristocracy was allowed to consolidate and even increase its estates in the provinces; and the privileged position of the capital in the Kingdom was reinforced. Throughout the period of French domination, Napoleon continued to see Naples primarily as a means for financing his increasingly hard-pressed Army of Italy. As such, he consistently opposed all radical social experimentation, and preferred, instead, to maintain an orderly, hierarchical society based on a cynical toleration for local religious practice, and a narrowly-restricted program of administrative and agricultural reform. Indeed, it has been estimated that 65 percent of all of the property sold by the French after 1806 fell into the hands of about 250 people, almost all of whom were noblemen, high state officials, or members of the wealthy middle class.[20] The devastating impact that Naples' incorporation into the Continental System had on Neapolitan commerce only added to this agrarian bias, and confirms the contradictory effect that the French occupation had on the development of the Neapolitan community as a whole. The ultimate result of the French reforms, in short, was to modernize the administrative and legal machinery of the state without reducing the inequities between rich and poor or town and country. Despite sixteen years of foreign invasion, civil war, and savage reprisal, Naples continued to be a city dominated by a narrow elite of government officials and aristocratic landowners, and its parasitic relationship with the countryside remained complete.

6 The peculiar social and cultural characteristics inherited from the Spanish, the failure of the Neapolitan Enlightenment, and the ambiguous legacy of the Napoleonic reforms set the stage for Naples' decline in the 19th century. By the time of the Bourbon Restoration in 1815, Naples had emerged as a distinctly premodern society, with a narrow, predominantly agriculturally-based ruling elite, a huge economic underclass, and a small and politically-insignificant bourgeoisie. On the surface, the city still sparkled with life as it did in the time of Goethe. But its ostentation and extravagance concealed its basic weakness, since much of its wealth was derived from the countryside and, from at least the 1760s on, the mass of the rural community was growing increasingly poor. In an age of rapidly expanding industrialization, an urban economy based primarily on the expropriation of agricultural surplus could not sustain itself indefinitely with so large a population. In order for Naples to have continued to prosper into the 19th century, therefore, it would have had to transform itself from a regionally-based political capital living off a resident court, church, and aristocracy into a modern industrial and commercial metropolis. It would have had to open up its political system, modernize its economy, and develop its own economically and politically independent bourgeoisie.

Under the conditions of the early 19th century, such a transformation proved to be impossible. First, unlike the more geographically favored cities of Turin and Milan, Naples was located far from the original centers of industrialization in Western Europe. This remoteness retarded the dissemination of technology and capital into the city, and gave overwhelming advantage to the urban centers of the Italian North. Given the importance of transportation costs in early industrial development, it also helped to isolate Naples from lucrative northern markets, and added to the factors — such as a lack of raw materials — that kept the production costs of many Neapolitan industries prohibitively high.

Second, the Neapolitan propertied classes — for all their wealth and political acumen — were both psychologically and socially resistant to economic modernization. Locked in a pre-capitalist mentality, the aristocracy, in particular, preferred to invest its money in land rather than manufacture, and thus deprived Neapolitan industry of the capital that it needed to survive. As for the Neapolitan "middle class" of government bureaucrats, lawyers, merchants, and high state officials, it shared many of the values and aspirations of the aristocracy. With the division and sale of common lands after the abolition of feudalism, many had been able to acquire property in the countryside along with the nobility, and had thus transformed themselves from what had been essentially an administrative class into a landowning bourgeoisie. Like the aristocracy whom they came to emulate, these bourgeois property holders saw land primarily in terms of social prestige rather than productive investment, and shunned the risks associated with investing in manufacture as well.[21] Both groups, in fact, preferred to live amid the pleasures of Naples and dissipate their income on present consumption and hence failed to develop the pattern of saving and investment so crucial to an entrepreneurial bourgeoisie. This failure to create an independent capitalist entrepreneurial class — and, indeed, a large, modern middle class in general — proved to be the single greatest weakness of Neapolitan society. It would place the city at an enormous disadvantage in its competition with the North during the Risorgimento, and, like so many other characteristics inherited from the Bourbon period, would continue to retard the city's modernization after 1861.

Finally, among the factors that inhibited Neapolitan economic and political development, one must not forget the extraordinary size of the city's population. For centuries, Naples had grown in a completely uncontrolled — and largely uncontrollable — fashion. Peasants, fleeing from the hunger and poverty of the countryside, had entered its walls from all over the kingdom, overwhelming local authorities and creating ever-expanding slums. With little or no housing available, many of the new arrivals were forced to live in the streets, in public squares, parks, or doorways. Others, considered more fortunate, found shelter in dilapidated apartments called *fondaci*; or in even more notorious dwellings that Neapolitans referred to as *"bassi"*: small, one-room, windowless, basement lodgings that opened directly onto the street. In 1884, a British journalist described one of these Neapolitan lower-class apartments as follows:

> Imagine the doorway of a cave where on entering you must descend. Not a ray of light penetrates into it except by the one aperture you have passed through; and there, between four black battered walls and upon a layer of filth mixed with putrid straw, two, three, and four families vegetate together. The best side of the cave, namely that through which humidity filtrates the least, is occupied by a rack

and manger to which animals of various kinds are tied; a horse it may be or an ass, a calf, or a pig. On the opposite, a heap of boards and rags represent the beds. In one corner is the fireplace and the household utensils lie about the floor. This atrocious scene is animated by a swarm of half-naked disheveled women; of children entirely naked rolling about in the dirt, and men stretched out on the ground in the sleep of idiocy. Such is the Neapolitan *Fondacho* [sic]. Multiply it by thousands. Remember that a hundred thousand beings at least have no other shelter; that they only live on fruit and vegetables, on snails and onions; without even changing their rags once in a year; without water except such as flows in a dense impure rivulet winding through those lanes.[22]

Living under such conditions, it is small wonder that much of the Neapolitan population existed beyond the reach of modern society. Among the poorest elements of the *lazzaroni*,[23] in particular, ignorance, superstition, and ritual governed the practices of everyday existence; and insularity, fatalism, and petty violence added to the barriers that prevented their integration into the modern world. At the start of the 19th century, it is estimated that from one-third to one-half of the Neapolitan population lived in poverty; and the percentage gradually increased as the century wore on. Like the peasantry from which it had sprung, this huge economic underclass was too poor to constitute a domestic market for Neapolitan manufacturers. Instead, most survived on the meager wages paid to them as craftsmen, laborers, fishermen, or peddlers, and many thousands more remained partially or totally unemployed. It was from this latter group that were drawn Naples' legendary throngs of prostitutes, criminals, and beggars. Crime, in fact, contributed significantly to the cost of doing business in the city, and, by as early as the 1850s, the threat posed to smaller merchants by organized criminal associations like the Camorra already hung over Naples like a pall. Worse still, during their last years in power, the Bourbons used *camorristi* to maintain order in the poorer sections of the city, and thus undermined both respect for the law and their own legitimacy as well.[24]

Overpopulation, in sum—and the myriad problems it created—proved to be a powerful obstacle to Neapolitan economic and political modernization. When added to the other factors already mentioned—the shortage of capital and raw materials; the lack of an entrepreneurial spirit among the propertied classes; the distance of the city from the original centers of industrialization; and the weakness of the domestic market—it is not difficult to understand why Neapolitan industry advanced so slowly in the years between 1815 and 1861. While the progress made in certain areas should not be underestimated, it simply proved to be insufficient to meet the needs of the city's ever-expanding population, and left Naples vulnerable to economic

INTRODUCTION

domination by the more industrially-advanced North after unification had been achieved.[25] As Count Girolamo Giusso, the director of the Banco di Napoli and future mayor of the city, stated:

> Although Naples is the largest city in Italy, its productive capacity bears no direct relation to the number of its inhabitants.... Naples is a center for consumption rather than for production. This is the principle reason for the misery of its populace, and for the slow, almost insensible, increase of that misery over time.... If we want the city to prosper, we must discover and promote ways of putting it to work.[26]

It was this essentially pre-modern city — with its absolutist political traditions, inadequate economic development, and deep social divisions — that would face the challenge of national unification after 1861.

7 The creation of a united Italy destroyed the single greatest asset that Naples possessed — its status as the capital of Italy's largest and still, in many ways, wealthiest, political kingdom.[27] After 1861, Naples lost its privileged position: it lost its role as the principle place of residence of the king, court, and royal bureaucracy, its ability to tax and thus to extract wealth from the countryside, and the economic and political leverage that it gained from its status as the leader of an independent political state. The impact on the city's economy was staggering. Indeed, according to one municipal official, the loss of the royal government alone cost the city 24 million lire a year in public spending.[28] The prestige, power, and patronage that had emanated from the monarchy — and on which so many Neapolitans depended — evaporated. Naples became, both legally and administratively, like any other city in Italy — although its social and economic problems were profoundly different and its historical traditions were unique. Worse still, its lack of a large, politically-independent middle class and huge economic underclass placed serious limitations on its ability to adapt to the new situation. In this sense, Naples had been primed for failure. Its previous history as a privileged capital had prevented it from developing the human and material resources necessary to compete with its northern neighbors, and had thus established the preconditions for its degeneration once unification was complete.

None of this, however, absolves the new national leadership of its responsibility for helping to bring about the city's deterioration. Indeed, Neapolitan historians are right to stress the crucial role played by Piedmontese authorities in contributing to the city's decline. Cavour, in particular, knew very little about Naples; and what he learned from his agents in the city, such as Luigi Farini, filled him with contempt.[29] Deeply suspicious of Garibaldi's popularity among Neapolitans, he was determined to deny the city all autonomy, and thus prevent the possibility of it becoming a focal point for the Mazzinian left.[30] The Piedmontese king, Victor Emmanuel II, and most of his supporters in parliament, shared this opinion, and carried it to its logical conclusion after the prime minister's death.

Between 1861 and 1865, therefore, Naples' centuries-old system of laws, political institutions, and administrative structure was systematically dismantled. The Piedmontese constitution and legal system were extended to the entire country. The high tariff that the Bourbons had used to protect naissant Neapolitan industry was lifted, and a common customs' union was imposed. Taxes, both on property and consumer goods, were increased dramatically, and the Piedmontese state's enormous debt was transferred to the nation as a whole. Most important of all, however, a rigidly centralized administrative system was created, in which a government-appointed prefect was selected for each province and given effective local control. The southern landowning class, in order to preserve its dominant social and economic position in the countryside, accepted these Piedmontese modifications. During the last days of the Risorgimento, it abandoned the Bourbons for Cavour and the Piedmontese liberals, and the Piedmontese army was brought in to maintain the rural status quo.[31]

The compromise, however, proved to be a disaster for Naples. Having lost its traditional sources of income, and being politically and economically marginalized by the new legislation, the city deteriorated rapidly. Almost overnight, cheap northern manufactured goods began to flood Neapolitan markets. Unable to compete, textile and engineering factories closed, trade languished, and the number of artisan workshops dwindled. Many wealthy urban property owners, stunned by the rapidity of events, fled the city for Rome, and took their capital with them.[32] The exorbitant taxes demanded by the central government compounded this problem, and credit and capital, always in short supply in Naples, began to dry up. The decision of the Rothschild Bank to close its Neapolitan branch in 1864 added to the difficulties, and large parts of the economy simply ground to a halt.

The effect on the Neapolitan population was catastrophic. Unemployment, poverty, and destitution — already serious problems in 1861 — reached epic proportions. Hunger, malnutrition, and disease became an integral part of everyday existence; and the city's physical infrastructure fell into massive decay. Between 1878 and 1883, Naples had the highest death rate of any major city in Western Europe — a sign of its poor sanitation, inadequate health care, dilapidated sewage system, and high rate of disease.[33] During a brief period of three months in 1884 alone, a cholera epidemic killed over 7,000 people; and tuberculosis, scurvy, rickets, syphilis, and anemia continued to haunt the city for decades to come.[34] In 1886, the central government, fearful that Naples' health problems might spread to the rest of Italy, announced the start of a vast, twenty-year project designed to rebuild and revitalize large parts of the city. But the funds provided proved to be insufficient to achieve so grand a transformation, and the familiar pattern of poverty, overcrowding, and disease remained undisturbed.[35]

In a report delivered to the city council in 1902, the socialist councilor Leone estimated that among Naples' 500,000 inhabitants, 200,000, or 40 percent, were still unemployed.[36] Among the most destitute, a disproportionate number were women, about three-quarters of whom lacked any occupation whatsoever, twice the percentage of men.[37] Among those who did work, wages — for men as well as women — remained the lowest of any major city in Italy, including Palermo and the rest of the Italian South.[38] In 1896, Alfonso Cottrau, who had been among the city's strongest supporters of unification during the Risorgimento, wrote:

> For the old unrepentant liberal that I am, it is certainly extremely painful to admit that, from 1860 to the present, the progress of my native city has been very slow, and even negative from certain points of view.... The constitution of the Kingdom of Italy has been harmful to Naples...in the sense that among two-thirds of the population the misery is actually worse than it was before.[39]

Two years later, Marco Rocco, an author and keen observer of the city's problems, added ruefully:

> The promises that were made to Naples in 1861 were so extensive that, by this time, she was to have reached the level of the world's great metropolises. In reality, however, after 37 years of long and fruitless waiting, there is no one in our beloved city who does not deplore its present state of moral and material decay.[40]

Thus, by the turn of the century, the feebleness of Rome's response to the city's deterioration had created widespread cynicism and suspicion of the central government among the city's inhabitants; and it was this feeling of alienation that would contribute to the relative indifference with which most Neapolitans reacted to the collapse of the liberal regime after the First World War.

8 The damage done to Naples in the crucial years from 1861 to 1914 sealed the city's fate for much of the 20th century. During the First World War (1914–1919), the gaze of the Italian government shifted away from the city, and the many projects that had been proposed to produce its revitalization simply melted away.[41] With little or no money coming from Rome, and its own internal economic resources still inadequate and shaky, the city declined even further. Between 1915 and 1922 alone, Naples dropped from first to third among Italian cities in population. While its size in absolute terms

XLIII

continued to increase slowly, the rate of growth declined dramatically, falling behind that of Milan, Turin, Genoa, and Rome.[42] Among the causes of the decline, lack of economic opportunity was easily the most important, although crime, disease, corruption, and inadequate housing all added to the city's dwindling appeal.

In 1922, the collapse of the liberal regime and the advent of Fascism brought with it few real changes in the city's basic economic situation. During Mussolini's more than two decades in power, he never developed a coherent plan or strategy for dealing with the city's massive social and economic problems. Instead, he preferred to make up his economic policies as he went along, responding to the city's needs in an ad hoc manner, and reaping whatever political reward he could. Blanketing Naples with propaganda, Fascist authorities eliminated all references to poverty, crime, and corruption from the Neapolitan press and academic publications. Discussion of the so-called "Southern Question" — which had been the focus of intense debate at both the local and national level for decades — was strictly forbidden, and the basic issues that separated North and South were simply declared resolved.[43] As a result, Naples under Fascism never experienced the kind of realistic dialogue or consistent government policy necessary for its economic transformation. While the city did benefit from a number of public works projects and the creation of a small state-sponsored war industry during the late 1930s, the sanctions imposed on Italy by the League of Nations during the Ethiopian War in 1935 more than offset its gains. By 1936, commerce had dried up, tourism had vanished, and a number of smaller industries, like glove making, textiles, and food canning, had been seriously impaired. Indeed, throughout the 1930s, poverty and relative economic backwardness remained the city's two dominant social and economic characteristics; and it was in this essentially weakened condition that it would have to bear the burdens of the Second World War.

World War II brought Naples to the brink of dissolution. For four long years, from 1940 to 1944, the Neapolitan people experienced unprecedented hardship and destruction. During the ten-month period between December 1942 and September 1943, in particular, the city was subjected to savage and, often, indiscriminate bombing. Wave after wave of American and British bombers swept over its center, destroying homes, schools, churches, hospitals, and orphanages, as well as factories, military installations, and docks. On the night of August 4, 1943 alone, over 20,000 people were either killed or wounded in the single most massive air raid of the war. Within a period of less than 24 hours, the city's electrical, gas, and telephone systems were rendered useless, the great 14th-century basilica of Santa Chiara was completely gutted, and virtually all of the ancient buildings between the Piazza Mercato and the waterfront were reduced to ruin. In addition, in late September, the German army, during its hasty retreat from the Campania, made a systematic attempt to

INTRODUCTION

destroy anything left that might be of use to the Allies. Responding to Hitler's order to reduce the city to "ashes," it blew up the remaining port facilities and bridges, destroyed the railway lines, roads, and tunnels, and even set fire to the priceless archives of the former Kingdom of Naples.[44] Thus, by the time that the Allies arrived in early October, Naples had reached the point of disaster. Everywhere there were hungry people and shattered buildings, grief-stricken families living amid mounds of rubble, and hordes of beggars lining the streets. Nothing worked — neither the water system, nor the trams, nor the sewers. Only the black-market seemed to thrive amid its half-starved people, as the city's ability to support itself had all but disappeared.

9 The five decades between the end of the Second World War and the close of the 20th century provide a dreary denouement to Naples' almost 200 years of social and economic deterioration. By the late 1940s, the gap that separated the Italian North from the South, in general, and cities like Naples from Turin and Milan, in particular, had grown so great that only massive intervention by the state could possibly bridge it.[45] In 1950, therefore, the ruling Christian Democratic Party, in an effort to alleviate social tensions in the South, authorized the creation of a special government agency, the *Cassa per il Mezzogiorno*, in order to plan and finance the development of the region. The creation of the *Cassa* aroused great optimism in Naples. During the years between 1957 and 1975, in particular, it spent over 8 billion lire in the South, much of it earmarked specifically for the industrial development of the city.[46] New factories were built, the infrastructure was improved, and thousands of jobs were created. Construction of new housing soared, commercial activity expanded, and vast new industrial zones and residential areas sprang up on the city's periphery.

Nevertheless, despite these gains, the *Cassa* failed to achieve its two main objectives: it neither succeeded in creating an independent, self-sustaining industrial base in the South; nor did it close the gap between Italy's northern and southern regions. With regard to Naples, in particular, the *Cassa's* failure was almost complete. Indeed, in virtually every important social and economic category — per capita income, life expectancy, education, public health, rate of job creation, and level of industrialization — the disparity between Naples and its northern Italian counterparts continued to increase.[47] By 1981, in fact, despite over 30 years of government intervention, Naples still possessed the highest levels of infant mortality and infectious disease in Italy, and its unemployment rate hovered above 25 percent.[48] Poor planning, administrative inefficiency, government corruption, and the blatant use of public funds by the Christian Democrats for political purposes had turned many of the *Cassa's* economic initiatives into a sham.[49] Some of the firms sponsored by the government went bankrupt almost immediately; while others managed to survive only a few years. The collapse of the Bagnoli steel works in 1990 — which had risen to become the third-largest in Italy and were, in many people's minds, the very symbol of southern Italian industrialization — was followed by the mass exodus of businesses throughout the Campania, and the last, lingering hopes of achieving prosperity in Naples through industrial development faded quickly amid an atmosphere of disappointment and despair.

The failure of the *Cassa* to modernize the Neapolitan economy proved to be the last episode in Naples' long history of political and economic degeneration. By the early 1990s, huge, ugly apartment buildings and abandoned factories had replaced many of the city's once-magnificent 18th-century mansions, and an endless stream of automobile fumes and industrial waste polluted much of its water and air. The *Cassa*'s often poorly-conceived industrial schemes, in short, while failing to transform the city's economy, had destroyed much of its physical beauty. It had, as one noted authority on the subject has put it, "inflicted more damage on Naples than the Anglo-American bombings and German demolitions" put together, and made a "foul smelling, pestiferous sewer" out of its once incandescent bay.[50] Worse still, during the peak period of government activity in the 1950s and 1960s, the Camorra had taken advantage of many of the *Cassa*'s initiatives in order to insinuate itself even more deeply into the Neapolitan economy, and had thus managed to bring whole new areas of economic activity under its control. Between 1963 and 1980 alone, the number of criminal cases heard annually in Neapolitan courts rose from 72,000 to 317,000.[51] By the late 1980s, it was estimated that as many as 300,000 people, or 25 percent of the population, actively participated in the "black," or underground, economy, much of it under Camorra control.[52] Indeed, as late as 1992, Italy's main research agency, Cencis, reported that 58 percent of all businesses in the Neapolitan area were forced to pay protection money to *camorristi*, and that many local and national officials openly tolerated such activity in return for votes.[53] Only in 1993, with the advent of new local leadership, did a sustained effort begin to loosen the Camorra's grip on Neapolitan society. Driven by a reformist mayor and fueled by popular indignation, it has made considerable strides towards creating a general Neapolitan political and cultural revival. But, as the 20th century drew to a close, despite many thousands of arrests and hundreds of convictions, the decisive battle against this ancient enemy of Neapolitan prosperity had still to be fought.

■ ■ ■

NOTES

1. Harry Hearder, *Italy in the Age of the Risorgimento* (New York: Longman, 1983), pp. 125-26. Estimates of the Neapolitan population at the beginning of the 19th century vary. The first systemic census, taken by Murat in 1813, placed its number at 326,130. The census, however, had been taken after a decade of war and revolution, and is probably misleading with regard to the size of the city ten years earlier. In 1791, the population of Naples had been officially estimated at over 400,000. For more on Murat's census see: Stefania Martuscelli, ed., *La popolazione del Mezzogiorno nella statistica di Murat*, (Napoli: Guida, 1979).

2. Stendhal, *Rome, Naples, and Florence* (London: George Braziller, Inc., 1959), p. 358.

3. Gabriella Gribaldi, "Images of the South," in David Forgacs and Robert Lumley, eds., *Italian Cultural Studies: An Introduction* (New York: Oxford University Press, 1966), p. 80.

4. Antonio Ghirelli, *Napoli: Gli intellettuali, la metropoli, la questione napolitana* (Milan: Fenice, 1996), p. 90.

5. The origins of this interpretation date from the Risorgimento itself. See, for example, the work of two legitimist historians: Giacinto De Sivo, *Storia delle Due Sicilie dal 1847 al 1861*. 2 vols. (1863 and 1867, reprint, Naples: Arturo Berisio, 1964); and Pietro Cala Ulloa, *Lettres Napolitaines* (Rome: Civiltà Cattolica, 1864). Both provide a negative assessment of the impact of Italian unification on Neapolitan development; and the criticism of Piedmontese policies during the 1860s among historians of various political tendencies has continued ever since. For a more balanced, contemporary account — which still places great emphasis on the negative aspects of unification, see Antonio Ghirelli, *Storia di Napoli* (Turin: Giulio Einaudi, 1973), part V: "L'Unità sbagliata," pp. 257-79.

6. For a discussion of the *meridionalisti* see P.A. Allum, *Politics and Society in Postwar Naples* (London: Cambridge University Press, 1973), pp. 76-79.

7. See, for example, Giuseppe Galasso, *Napoli* (Rome: Laterza, 1987), pp. xi-xxxii, 41-49.

8. J.W. Goethe, *Italian Journey, 1786–1788* (New York: Penguin Books, 1962), pp. 199-207.

9. Stuart Woolf, *A History of Italy, 1700–1860: The Social Constraints of Political Change* (New York: Methuen, 1979), p. 45.

10. Woolf, *History,* p. 46.

11. Cited in Christopher Duggan, *A Concise History of Italy* (Cambridge: Cambridge University Press, 1994), p. 75.

12. Luigi Settembrini, *Opuscoli politici edite e inediti, 1847–1851.* Mario Themelly, ed. (Rome: Ateneo, 1969), p. 3.

13. The exact population of Naples in the 16th century is uncertain, but all historians agree on its phenomenal growth. Guido D'Agostino, in reviewing the evidence, places the figure for 1600 at slightly more than 200,000, over twice that of a century before. See D'Agostino's essay in *Storia di Napoli* (Naples: Società editrice storia di Napoli, 1973), 5:105.

14. Duggan, *History,* p. 69.

15. Woolf, *History,* pp. 47-48.

16. Cited in Allum, *Politics and Society,* p. 23.

17. Galasso, *Napoli,* p. xii.

18. Quoted in Woolf, *History,* p. 143.

19. Giuliano Procacci, *History of the Italian People* (New York: Penguin Books, 1973), pp. 261-62.

20. Procacci, *History,* p. 266.

21. Judith Chubb, *Patronage, Power, and Poverty in Southern Italy: A Tale of Two Cities* (Cambridge: Cambridge University Press, 1982), p. 17.

22. Quoted in Frank M. Snowden, *Naples in the Time of the Cholera, 1884–1911* (Cambridge: Cambridge University Press, 1995), pp. 19-20.

23. On the *lazzaroni,* see below pp. 12-14, 22-25 et passim.

24. Snowden, *Cholera,* p. 40.

25. G. Brancaccio, "Una economia, una società," in Galasso, *Napoli,* pp. 41-49. For a concise summary of Neapolitan industrial development under the Bourbons, see: Ghirelli, *Storia di Napoli,* pp. 212-17.

26. Quoted in Snowden, *Cholera,* p. 32. This statement, which was issued as part of a budget report in 1881, would have been equally valid for Naples at any time between 1815 and 1861.

INTRODUCTION. NOTES

27. Snowden, *Cholera*, p. 36.

28. Ibid.

29. See, for example, Farini's letter to Marco Minghetti, the Piedmontese Minister of the Interior, below, pp. 187-88.

30. For Cavour's attitude towards Neapolitan political autonomy, see his letter to King Victor Emmanuel dated December 14, 1860, quoted below, p. 189.

31. Chubb, *Patronage*, pp. 15-17; Allum, *Politics and Society*, pp. 64-65. As Dr. Domede Pantaleone, Cavour's former agent in Rome and strong supporter of Piedmont in the South, put it to Marco Minghetti, the Piedmontese minister of the Interior, in a letter written on August 14, 1861: "The [southern] landowners feel that without our army they would all be slaughtered by the brigands."

32. Snowden, *Cholera*, p. 37. Snowden's brilliant book is indispensable for anyone seeking to understand the extent of Naples' decline between 1861 and 1914.

33. Snowden, *Cholera*, pp. 13-16.

34. Snowden, *Cholera*, p. 104.

35. On the Neapolitan "Risanamento," see below, pp. 209-11, 214-17.

36. Snowden, *Cholera*, p. 36.

37. Ibid.

38. Ibid., p. 32.

39. Cited in Maryse Jeuland-Meynaud, *La Ville de Naples après l'annexion, 1860-1915* (Aix-en-Provence: Éditions de l'Université de Provence, 1973), p. 49.

40. Ibid.

41. For the prewar proposals to restore and revitalize Naples see Ghirelli, *Napoli*, pp. 56-65.

42. In 1910, Naples was still the largest city in Italy with 723,000 people, followed by Milan with 579,000, and Rome with 542,000. By 1930, Rome was clearly the greatest city in Italy with 1,008,000, compared to Milan's 992,000, and Naples' 839,000. Between 1910 and 1920, Naples' population had actually declined by 1000 people.

43. For a discussion of the "Southern Question" see M.S. Salvadori, *Il Mito del buongoverno: La questione meridionale da Cavour a Gramsci* (Turin: Einaudi, 1960). A useful collection of primary sources can be found in Salvatore Francesco Romano, ed., *Storia della questione meridionale* (Palermo: Pantea, 1945).

XLIX

44. On the German retreat, and the four-day Neapolitan insurrection that helped to precipitate it, see below, pp. 236-38, 241.

45. Chubb, *Patronage*, p. 28.

46. Martin Clark, *Modern Italy, 1871–1995* (New York: Longman, 1996), p. 359.

47. See, for example, Chubb, *Patronage*, pp. 28-55.

48. Chubb, *Patronage*, pp. 39-44, 48-54, 222.

49. See below, pp. 256-61.

50. Ghirelli, *Storia di Napoli*, p. 539.

51. *The San Francisco Chronicle*, February 13, 1998.

52. See below, p. 268.

53. On the Camorra's political activities during the 1980s and early 1990s, see Francesco Barbagallo, *Il potere della Camorra, 1973–1998* (Turin: Giulio Einaudi, 1999), pp. 101-31.

■ ■ ■

4. *Queen Maria Carolina (1752–1814),* detail of Portrait of the Royal Family, *by Angelica Kauffmann, c. 1790.*

5. *King Ferdinand IV (Ferdinand I of the Two Sicilies, 1751–1825)*, Vincenzo Camuccini, 1818/19. Palazzo Reale.

I
Foundations: Naples at the Close of the 18th Century

"In size and number of inhabitants," the English author and diarist John Chetwode Eustace wrote in 1813, Naples "ranks as the third city of Europe, and from her situation and superb show may justly be considered as the Queen of the Mediterranean." This judgment, made at a decidedly difficult moment in Neapolitan history, fairly summarizes the general consensus among European writers and intellectuals on Naples at the start of the 19th century. At the time that it was written, the city's status as one of the premier metropolises of Europe seemed incontestable. The capital of the largest independent political kingdom in Italy, its population in 1791 was estimated at over 400,000 people, and its reputation as an intellectual and artistic center was nearing its height. Writers and scholars came from all over Europe in order to experience its beauty and vitality, and tales of its extraordinary physical setting and the liveliness of its people circulated throughout the Western world. In February 1787, the great German poet, Johann Wolfgang von Goethe — who probably more than any other writer helped to establish the later myth of Naples as a "happy land" full of "carefree people" — wrote during his first visit to the city:

> 1. One may write or paint as much as one likes, but this place, the shore, the gulf, Vesuvius, the citadels, the villas, everything defies description.... One can't blame the Neapolitans for never wanting to leave their city, nor its poets for singing the praises of its situation in lofty hyperboles.... I don't even want to think about Rome. By comparison to Naples' free and open situation, the capital of the world on the Tiber flats is like an old wretchedly placed monastery.
> [J.W. Goethe, *Italian Journey*, 1786-1788. Harmondsworth: Penguin Books, 1962, pp. 186-90.]

Goethe's description of Naples was typical of the almost lyrical way with which most early 19th century Romantics responded to the city's unique architectural design and dramatic topography. In 1823, the peripatetic English aristocrat, Lady

Marguerite Power Farmer Blessington, described her initial reaction to the city's magnificent bay and surrounding islands as follows:

> 2. Naples burst upon us from a steep hill above the Campo Santo, and never did so bright and dazzling [a sight] meet my gaze. Innumerable towers, domes, and steeples, rose above palaces, intermingled with terraces and verdant foliage. The bay, with its placid waters, lay stretched before us, bounded on the left by a chain of mountains, with Vesuvius, sending up its blue incense to the Cloudless sky. Capri, behind which the sun was hiding his rosy beams, stood like a vast and brilliant gem, encircled by the radiance of the expiring luminary, which was reflected in the glassy mirror that bathed its base; and to the right, lay a crescent of blue isles and promontories, which look as if formed to serve as a limit to the waters that lave their bases. The scene was like one of enchantment, and the suddenness with which it burst upon us, added surprise to admiration. We ordered our postilions to pause on the brow of the hill, that we might gaze on the beautiful panorama before us; and as our eyes dwelt on it, we were ready to acknowledge that the Neapolitan phrase of Vedi Napoli e poi mori, had a meaning, for they who die without having seen Naples, have missed one of the most enchanting views in the world. [Margarite Power Farmer Blessington, *Idler in Italy.* Edith Clay, ed. London: Hamish Hamilton, 1979, 2:25-26.]

The splendor of Naples' extraordinary physical setting was not the only aspect of the city that attracted a favorable response from foreign visitors. Equally impressive was the seemingly endless energy of the Neapolitan people, who filled the streets with animation and intensity, and created an atmosphere of fascination and delight. On July 19, 1823, just two days after her arrival in the city, Lady Blessington wrote:

> 3. The gaiety of the streets of Naples at night is unparalleled. Numberless carriages of every description are seen rolling along. The ice-shops are crowded by the *beau monde*, and the humbler portable shops, with their gaudy decorations, which are established in the streets, are surrounded by eager applicants for the *sorbetto* and lemonade, of which the lower classes consume such quantities.... Here all are gay and animated; from the occupants of the coronated carriage down to the *lazzaroni*, who, in the enjoyment of the actual present, are reckless of the future. At one spot was seen one of the portable shops, peculiar to Naples, gaily painted and gilded, illuminated

CHAPTER I. FOUNDATIONS

by paper lanterns in the shape of balloons, tinted with the brightest colours, round which groups were collected devouring macaroni, served hot to them from the furnace from which it was prepared. At another shop, iced watermelons were sold in slices; the bright pink of the interior of the fruit offering a pretty contrast to the vivid green of the exterior. *Frittura*, sending forth its savoury fumes, was preparing in another stall; and *frutti di mare* was offered for sale on tables arranged along the Strada di Santa Lucia. The sounds of guitars were heard mingling with the joyous laugh of the *lazzaroni*; and the dulcet voices of groups in carriages who accosted each other with the animation peculiar to Italians, as their vehicles encountered on the promenade. The sweet-sounding words *signorina, amico, cara*, and *carissimo*, often broke on the ear: and above these scenes of life and gaiety, this motley assemblage of the beautiful and grotesque, was spread a sky of deep azure thickly studded with stars, whose dazzling brightness seemed to shed warmth, as well as light, over the moving picture. The contrast between the solitude and silence of Rome at night, with the hilarity of the crowds that fill the streets of Naples, is striking.... The Neapolitans, like their volcanic country, are never in a state of repose. Their gaiety has in it something reckless and fierce; as if the burning lava of their craters had a magnetic influence over their temperaments. [Blessington, *Idler* 2:27-28.]

The intense and, often, operatic character of Neapolitan street life provided the city with a decidedly anarchistic quality. Overcrowded and desperately short of housing, the city's residents had long been forced to conduct much of their private and business life in public, and the rhythms of their daily existence often unfolded openly in streets and public squares. In 1841, the Danish poet and novelist, Hans Christian Andersen, described the scene beneath his window on the Piazza Florentina as follows:

4. The Piazza... [is] as broad as a common street with us in the North and the length is in proportion to the breath. Opposite to this, and close by a narrow crooked street, extends the facade of a little church, over the open entrance to which the neighbouring dames have hung all their clothes out to dry, from the mysteries which should not be seen to the variegated gowns that should.... Two young priests reading their book of Evangelists, walk up and down the entrance hall. Outside sits an old women selling money.

She is the poor-man's money-changer; the open place is her office; the little table, whose leaf is a box with brass wires across, is her cash chest; and therein lies the small coins which she, for a percentage, sells for larger ones.... Close by her stands a fruit shop, variegated like a picture cut out of an A B C book, with oranges and lemons. The picture above the door, where Madonna quenches the thirst of souls in purgatory, is a very suitable sign. The whole place is paved with broad lava stones; the poor horses cannot keep their footing, and are therefore beaten with screams and shouts. Not less than sixteen shoemakers sit and sew there to the left; the two nearest the door have already lighted their candles; they pull the cap off a poor boy, and throw oranges at him; and he protests loudly. In all the houses the ground floors are without windows, but with broad, open shop doors. Outside one they are boiling a soup of chestnuts and bread, and the man has many customers. Fellows dressed in rags eat out of broken pots. In the highest stories of the houses each window has a balcony, or else it goes the whole story, and has a flourishing garden, in which there are large tubs, with orange and lemon trees.... An Englishman, in his dressing gown, has his rocking chair out there. Now the chair falls backwards, and the Briton strikes the stairs with his proud head. But far above the church and houses rises the rock of St. Elmo, with its fortress; the evening sun is down and the bells ring the Ave Maria. People stream into the church, and the lamps within shine through the windows. The tavern keeper puts lights within his paper lantern; the shoemakers each have a lamp; and the square is completely illuminated. The little old woman shuts up her money shop, and her boy lights her way home with a candle in a paper pottle. There is a song in the church, and there are noises in the streets; they harmonize strangely together. But what is that? There is a procession coming from the narrow street. White figures, each with a large candle in his hand; four men in white frocks, with hoods over their heads, bear on their shoulders a bier with red drapery; a young girl dressed like a bride, with a veil and wreath of white roses around her brow lies in the bier. Everyone takes his hat off for the dead, and the shoemakers kneel.

The procession is now in the church, and the same noise is heard in the streets as before.

CHAPTER I. FOUNDATIONS

> That little square is a faithful picture of this large Naples; yes, a very true one; for the poet sat at his window, and drew every feature of what he saw below. [Hans Christian Andersen, *A Poet's Bazaar.* Boston: Houghton, Mifflin, 1879, pp. 126-29.]

The liveliness of the people, the beauty of the bay, and the benevolence of the climate led many foreign visitors to idealize Naples as a kind of urban paradise — a place of natural abundance in which people lived free from care. Few saw the darker side of the city: the poverty and destitution of an estimated one-third to one-half of its inhabitants; the lack of political freedom; and the squalor and misery of the peasantry in the countryside from whose labor much of the city's wealth was ultimately derived. Instead, writers like Goethe, Blessington, and Andersen — as well as so many others before and after them — concentrated on the pleasures that their positions of wealth and fame afforded them, and the hardships of the ordinary Neapolitan were either minimized or ignored. In March 1787, Goethe, whose sensitivity to human anguish and suffering in his poems and novels would later cause him to be ranked among Europe's greatest authors, wrote:

> 5. Everything one sees and hears gives evidence that this is a happy country which amply satisfies all the basic needs and breeds a people who are happy by nature, people who can wait without concern for tomorrow to bring them what they had today and for that reason lead a happy-go-lucky existence, content with momentary satisfaction and moderate pleasures, and taking pain and sorrow as they come with cheerfull resignation.... [The Neapolitans] display a most ingenious resource, not for getting rich, but for living without care.... [The city] is a paradise, and everyone lives in a state of intoxicated self-forgetfulness, myself included.... It is strange for me to be in a society where everyone does nothing but enjoy himself....

And, again, in May, after returning from a trip to Sicily:

> It is true that one cannot take many steps [in Naples] before coming on some poorly clad, even ragged, individual, but... it is false... to think of these people as miserable; their principle of going without [is] favoured by a climate which [gives] them all the necessities of life. Here a poor man, whom, in our country, we think of as wretched, can satisfy his essential needs and at the same time enjoy the world to the full, and a so-called Neapolitan beggar might well refuse to become a Viceroy of Normandy or decline the honor of being nominated Governor of Siberia by the Empress of all the

Russias.... Here the ragged man is not naked, nor poor he who has no provision for tomorrow.

He may neither have home nor lodging, spend summer nights under the projecting roof of a house, in the doorway of a palazzo, church or public building, and when the weather is bad, find a shelter where, for a triffling sum, he may sleep, but this does not make him a wretched outcast. When one considers the abundance of fish and sea food which the ocean provides,... the abundance and variety of fruits and vegetables at every season of the year, when one remembers that the region around Naples is deservedly called the 'Terra di Lavoro' (which does not mean the land of work but the land of cultivation) and that the whole province has been honored for centuries with the title 'Campagna Felice' — the happy land — then one gets an idea how easy life is in this part of the world. [Goethe, *Italian Journey*, pp. 199-207, 320-21.]

What blinded Goethe and so many other foreign travelers to the social realities of Naples was not only its beauty and the expressiveness of its people, but the spectacle and pageantry that surrounded the royal court. Like many other European capitals in the early 19th century, Naples was primarily a consumer of wealth rather than a producer. Much of this wealth was extracted from the countryside in the form of taxes, and redistributed in the city by virtue of its position as the administrative center of Italy's largest political state. Known as the "Kingdom of Naples" until 1815 (when its name would be changed to the "Kingdom of the Two Sicilies"), the Neapolitan state covered almost 40 percent of the total territory of Italy, and included about 30 percent of its population (or 5 out of 18 million people) in 1791. Ever since 1734, the kingdom had been ruled by a subsidiary branch of the Spanish Bourbons. The king in 1791 was Ferdinand IV, who had succeeded to the throne as a minor in 1759, and had only begun to rule in his own right after the fall of his chief minister, Bernardo Tanucci, in 1776. Mediocre in intelligence and abysmally ignorant, Ferdinand had been born in Naples and was thoroughly Neapolitanized — speaking the dialect fluently and sharing many of the attitudes and values of the population as a whole. In 1768, he had been married by proxy to the able and strong-willed archduchess of Austria, Maria Carolina. The sister of the French queen, Marie Antoinette, for whom she had great affection, the new queen would gradually come to dominate Ferdinand, and would be instrumental in moving him in an anti-French direction after the outbreak of the revolution in 1789. In 1769, the queen's older brother, Joseph I, the Hapsburg emperor of Austria, painted a vivid portrait of Ferdinand while on an official visit to the city:

6. He must be five feet seven inches, and therefore a good inch taller than me, very thin, gaunt and raw boned... his knees bent and his back very supple, since at every step he bends and sways his whole body. The part below his waist is so limp and feeble that it does not seem to belong to the upper part, which is much stronger. He has muscular arms and wrists, and his course brown hands are very dirty since he never wears gloves when he rides or hunts. His head is relatively small, surmounted by a forest of coffee-coloured hair, which he never powders, a nose which begins in his forehead and gradually swells in a straight line as far as his mouth, which is very large with a jutting lower lip, filled with fairly good teeth. The rest of his features, his low brow, pig's eyes, flat cheeks and long neck, are not remarkable.

Although an ugly Prince, he is not absolutely repulsive: his skin is fairly smooth and firm, of yellowish pallor; he is clean except for his hands, and at least does not stink. So far he shows no trace of a beard. But he is very oddly dressed: his hair is smoothed back behind his head and gathered in a net.... and he never wears a hat, sword, or hunting knife indoors, not even when he dines in public, or goes to church, or the theater....

He goes hunting every morning. We asked him if he had had good sport and he drew five domestic pigeons and several other small birds he had shot from his pockets, where he had kept them with tender care. Two or three big pointers followed him. These enjoy the privilege of entering everywhere, lying on all the furniture, which at Portici as at Naples is superb and in excellent taste, and filling all the rooms with their filth. After a few minutes' talk the King went to change his clothes. Several courtiers were in attendance; a chamberlain put on his shoes and stockings and a valet combed his hair, to the accompaniment of much tickling and childishness....

[Once while talking to him] I happened to see the Grand Mistress and other Court ladies waiting in the antechamber and persuaded the King and Queen to let them join us. As they were reluctant I made a joke of it, opened the door and coaxed them in. I wanted to attempt a general conversation, but the King proposed parlour games. I agreed, but as he had to dispatch the Spanish mail I had all the difficulty in the world to make him attend to this and even refused to play until he wrote his letter, whereupon he went off, to return within a quarter of an hour. Then five or six court ladies, my sister, the King and I began to play blindman's bluff and other games.... Throughout these the King distributes blows and smacks the ladies' behinds without distinction.... There is a continuous tussle with the ladies, who are inured to it and throw themselves sprawling upon the floor. This never fails to amuse the King, who bursts into uproarious laughter. As he seldom speaks without shouting and has a piercing voice like a shrill falsetto, one can distinguish it among a thousand....

[At other times while drilling troops indoors] some thirty officers, several aged over forty, have to play this comedy and submit to daily fisticuffs, kicks and even canings from the King who commands them.... The drums and fifes keep up an incessant noise, to which the King's piercing cries are added. He commands, sword in hand, shouting, scolding, laughing, and striking those who miss. They all wear red and blue uniforms like the King. In the middle the sutler is announced. They down arms and everybody rushes to eat, without sitting, without knives or forks, tearing the meat with their fingers, drinking from bottles without glasses, and all in order to have a more martial air. On this occasion I saw the King drink a quantity of unmixed wine without any ill effect....

[One evening he even] begged us to keep him company while he was sitting on the close-stool. I found him on this throne with lowered breeches, surrounded by five or six valets, chamberlains, and others. We made conversation for more than half an hour, and I believe he would be there still if a terrible stench had not convinced us that all was over. He did not fail to describe the details and even show them to us; and without more ado, his breeches down, he ran with the smelly pot in one hand after two of his gentlemen, who took to their heels. I retired quietly to my sister's, without being able to relate how this scene ended, and if they got off with a good fright.... I returned... quite numbed with all the tedious jokes and childishness I had witnessed throughout the day.

Joseph then concludes somewhat despondently:

[Once, during a visit to Pompeii], I spoke to him about the duties of the state, glory, reputation, and liberty; in fact, I tried to find out if there was any hope or probability of shaking off his present degradation, and the subjection and constraint in which he is kept by

Spain. I could detect germs of these sentiments, but so definite an aversion from all innovation, so great an indolence of mind and a distaste for all reflection, that I almost dare assure you that the man has never reflected in his life either about himself or his physical or moral existence, his situation, his interests, or his country. He is quite ignorant of the past and the present and never thought about the future; in fact, he vegetates from day to day, merely engaged in killing time.... [Cited in Harold Acton, *The Bourbons of Naples, 1734-1825.* London: Methuen, 1956, pp. 138-45.]

Despite his intellectual shallowness and frivolity, Ferdinand was enormously popular among the Neapolitan people. A warm and open man, his lack of personal airs and plebeian tastes won him wide support among the city's lower classes, and his liking for special ceremonies and elaborate public spectacles only added to his appeal. In 1824, Lady Blessington described one of these spectacles — a water-fete given in honor of the ex-empress of France, Marie-Louise — as follows:

7. Last night, I witnessed one of the most beautiful scenes imaginable. It was a sort of fete offered to Marie Louise by the King of Naples, and took place on the water. Never was there a more propitious night for such a festival, for not a breeze ruffled the calm bosom of the beautiful bay, which resembled a vast lake, reflecting on its glassy surface the bright sky above which was glittering with innumerable stars. Naples, with its white colonnades, seen amidst the dark foliage of its terraced gardens, rose like an amphitheater from the sea; and the lights streaming from the buildings to the water, seemed like columns of gold. The Castle of St. Elmo crowned the center of the picture, Vesuvius, like a sleeping giant in grim repose, stood on the right, flanked by Mount St. Angelo, and the coast of Sorrento fading into the distance; and on the left, the vine-crowned height of the Vomero, with its palaces and villas, glancing forth from the groves that surrounded them, was crowned by the Mount Camaldoli, with its convent spires pointing to the sky. A rich stream of music announced the coming of the royal pageant; and proceeded from a gilded barge, to which countless lamps were attached, giving it, when seen at a distance, the appearance of topaz, floating on a sea of sapphire. It was filled with musicians, attired in the most glittering liveries; and every stroke of the oars kept time to the music, and sent forth a silvery light from the water which they rippled. This illuminated and gilded barge was followed

by another, adorned by a silken canopy, from which hung curtains of the richest texture, partly drawn back to admit the balmy air. Cleopatra, when she sailed down the Cyndnus, boasted not a more beautiful vessel; and as it glided over the sea, it seemed excited into motion by the music that preceded it, so perfectly did it keep time to the delicious sounds, leaving behind it a silvery track like the memory of happiness. The King himself steered the vessel; his tall and slight figure gently curved, and his snowy locks falling over ruddy cheeks, show that age has bent but not broken him. He looked simple, though he appears like one born to command; a hoary Neptune, steering over his native element; all eyes were fixed on him; but he steadily followed the glittering barge that preceded him. Marie-Louise was the only person in the King's boat; she was richly dressed, and seemed pleased with the pageant. Innumerable vessels, filled with the lords and ladies of the court followed, but intruded not on the privacy of the regal bark, which glided before us like some gay vision of a dream.
[Blessington, *Idler* 2:114-15.]

In theory, the power of the Neapolitan king was absolute: he and his ministers determined all policy, and government officials were responsible solely to him. In reality, however, royal authority was limited by historical tradition, and the ability and inclinations of the individual king. The aristocracy, in particular, possessed a number of irrevocable privileges — including the right to have their own law courts, private military establishments, and freedom from most taxes — which placed them outside the reach of the state. Efforts by royal officials to limit these privileges during the 1770s and 1780s had ended in failure, and, by the close of the century, the nobility's claims to special status as Naples' traditional ruling class had been largely reaffirmed. In 1817, the great French novelist, Stendhal, experienced the pretensions of the Neapolitan aristocracy first-hand while attending an opera at the Teatro San Carlo:

> 8. *San Carlo* is far ahead of *La Scala* in the brilliance of its orchestral performance.... [It] has the status of a patriotic symbol for the good people of Naples [and is an object of] national pride.... King Ferdinand basks in a kind of effulgent glory reflected from the magnificence of the (theater); he can be seen in his Royal Box *sharing* the ecstatic delight of the audience; and, indeed, this word, *sharing* draws the veil of oblivion over a multitude of sins....
>
> This evening, as I went to take my seat, a *gend'arme* came running after me and ordered me to remove my hat. The auditorium is a

CHAPTER I. FOUNDATIONS

good four times the size of the *Grand Opera* in Paris; yet I had failed to notice the presence of God-knows-what insignificant princeling!...
If you explore the galleries, rows of *titles*, redolent of pomp and circumstance, and all writ large upon the doors of private boxes, serve to remind you that you, poor worm, are but a zero, an atom, fit only to be blotted out forever by an *Excellency*....
Among the benches which fill the pit, every seat is numbered, and rows one to eleven are reserved unconditionally for the military — Officers of the Red Guards, of the Blue Guards, of the Guards of the Gateway, etc., etc. — or else are distributed by special favor among the elite of permanent subscribers; in consequence of which, the unhappy foreigner newly-arrived in the city finds himself in the twelfth row.... No such monstrous system prevails in Milan: at La Scala, first come, first served is the rule for every seat. In the fair and fortunate city of Milan, every man may know himself equal of his neighbour; but in Naples, the meanest threadbare Duke without a thousand pounds a year to bolster up his pretensions, may invoke the prestige of the best part of a dozen stars and garters to jab his indolent elbows in my ribs.... Tonight, exasperated by the insolence of the gend'armes, I abandoned the pit and made my way towards my box; and even then, as I climbed the staircase, my temper was scarcely improved by encountering, in descending phalanx, a dozen or fifteen star-spangled Lord-High-Whatnots and Generals, ambling majestically downwards beneath the accumulated weight and grandeur of their mightiness, their braided jackets and their monumental noses. I reflected upon the inscrutable necessity of all this rag-bag of hereditary nobility, stars, privilege, garters and insolence, without which mere courage could never be dreamed of in an army. [Stendhal, *Rome, Naples, and Florence*. New York: George Braziller, 1959, pp. 360-82.]

Many of these aristocrats were absentee landlords who lived in the capital in opulence and luxury. Others, however, having fallen on hard times during the 18th century, possessed little more than their titles, and were the equal of their peers only in the defense of their privileges and their demand for respect. A glimpse into the often ruinous world of aristocratic pride and extravagance was provided by Henry Swinburne in his *Travels in the Two Sicilies* published in 1786:

9. Citizens and lawyers are plain enough in their apparel, but the female part of their family vies with the first court ladies in expensive

dress, and all the vanities of modish fopperies. Luxury has of late advanced with gigantic strides in Naples.... Expense and extravagance are here in the extreme [and] the great families are oppressed with debt... in order to answer the demands of external show.... The nobility, in general, are well served and live comfortably...no ladies or gentlemen finish their toilet till the afternoon, on which account they dine at twelve or one o'clock. The great officers of the state, and ministers, live in a different manner, and keep sumptuous tables, to which strangers and others have frequent invitations.

The establishment of the Neapolitan grandee's household is upon a very expensive plan; the number of servants, carriages, and horses, would suffice for a sovereign prince; and the wardrobe of their wives is formed upon the same magnificent scale.... It is a fixed rule that all ladies, whatever be the circumstance of their husbands, affluent or circumscribed, have a hundred ducats a month allowed to them for pin money... [and that] at the birth of every child the husband makes the wife a present of a hundred ounces [of gold].... [Cited in Desmond Seward, *Naples: A Travelers' Companion*. London: Constable, 1984, pp. 271-72.]

The aristocracy and high state officials constituted the elite of Neapolitan society. Along with the Church, they owned over half the land in the kingdom, and consumed a vastly disproportionate share of national wealth. The Church, in particular, was the single richest institution in the nation, with 21 archbishops, 165 bishops, 50,000 priests, and 60,000 monks and nuns. Beneath these three groups there ranged the vast majority of the Neapolitan people: lawyers and merchants, artisans and fishermen, servants and petty bureaucrats, and the great mass of the peasantry and urban poor. No industrial middle class in the Western sense existed in Naples in the early 19th century. Instead, the population of the city was sharply divided, with the great bulk of its inhabitants occupying the dreary ranks below. It is estimated that there were from 100,000 to 150,000 impoverished people in Naples in 1800. Loosely grouped under the general term *"lazzaroni,"* they included laborers and peddlers, and beggars and con-men — some of whom worked and had permanent residence, and many who lived on the streets and were unemployed. Deeply religious and fiercely loyal to the Bourbons, most lived in unspeakable squalor. Life expectancy in the slums of Naples in the early 19th century was 20 years, and their intense and, often, reckless life style soon became a permanent part of Neapolitan lore. In 1820, the English aristocrat, Lady Morgan, wrote in her book, *Italy*:

CHAPTER I. FOUNDATIONS

10. The large portion of the population of the Kingdom of Naples, called "the people," presents itself more readily to the stranger's observation than the same class in any other civilized nation in the world. Their poverty scarcely leaves them a home to shelter in; and their climate renders a domicile rather a luxury, than a necessity. The roof that screens them from the inclemency of the night, is the only roof they seek or know. The *lazzaroni*, the refuse of the people require not even this: — a bench, or boat, pillows their slumbers, and the sky is their canopy, except in those transient and violent gusts of bad weather to which Naples is subject; when the portico of a palace, or the colonnade of a church, affords them all the temporary shelter they require.

The daylight, which, according to the philosophy of Comus, "alone makes sin," is not shunned by the lower Neapolitans under any presense. In the full glare of its lustre, in the full observance of the public eye, all the duties and all the offices of life are frankly and undisguisedly performed; groups seated at the corner of streets, at the thresholds of the poorer sort of houses, on the shores of the Scoglio or the Mare-chiano, on the Mola or Largo, talking, laughing, menacing, or singing;... wants are supplied or satisfied; trades are carried on; Tasso read aloud; and heads cleaned, or beards shaven — all equally *pro bono publico*....

The weather was occasionally very severe while we were at Naples; it frequently happened, that on returning late from the opera, from *Soirées*, we found the filthy portico of our old palace strewn with *lazzaroni*. Some lay upon the earth, others were flung over a cask, or gathered round a brazier of hot embers, just sufficiently bright to glare upon their marked and grotesque features. Nothing could be more courteous or cordial than their manner: they all jumped up to make way for us, welcomed us home, wished us a good night's rest; and one or two of them, who had got up some English phrases, applied them at random, by way of being particularly polite....

The Mola on Sundays generally presented several circles, each two or three deep; they were composed of the lowest orders and the *lazzaroni*; sometimes seated on benches, sometimes on the ground, according to the price paid to some peripatetic philosopher, or reader, who occupied the center, and who read aloud — Tasso or Mastrillo, stories from 'La Bibbia', or legends of much less edifying character.

The image of one of these *academicians* will not readily escape my memory, as it never failed, during the Sundays of successive weeks, to fix my eye: he was a short square grotesque figure, with a face moulded on the model of the French polichinel — all nose, chin, and bushy eyebrows; he wore an immense wig, a large but torn cocked hat, the jacket, or the fragments of a jacket, of an Italian courier, and a pair of bright yellow buckskin small-clothes, from the cast-off wardrobe of some English groom. He was without shoes or stockings; his spectacles were immense; and he held a filthy tattered Tasso in one hand, and a stick or wand in the other, which he moved with great dignity, and variety of gesture. For every line he recited he gave a commentary of his own, that might fill a page: sometimes pathetic, sometimes humorous, and always with an air so proudly oracular, as to excite the strongest disposition to laughter. Such however was not the effect produced on his auditors: never were countenances more concentrated, or more intensely expressive of the deepest interest — eyebrows were knit, lips distended, cheeks glowed, and heads shook, at the feats and fetes of the 'Goffredo' and the 'Rinaldo', against whom, in vain,

'S'Armo d'Asia e de Libia il popol misto.'

Some half-rose in their emotion — others uttered in deep ejaculation; and the murmur 'Bravo!' circulated with all the restrained emotion of those who feared to interrupt, by their applause, strains that commanded the most enthusiastic admiration!...

The two 'grani' that purchased [a lazzaroni's] daily ration of maccaroni, the two more that went for ice-water and a puppet show, were surely and easily earned; and a little surplus of ingenuity and industry procured a few yards of canvass, which made up their whole wardrobe (a shirt and trousers), allowing even something for the superfluity of their red-worsted sash and cap. These wants supplied, nothing remained but the delicious *far niente* — the lounge in the sun or shade — the laugh raised indiscriminately at friend or foe — a prayer offered at a shrine — or curses given to the scrivano [police magistrate], who mulcts some crime which poverty cannot redeem by a bribe.... [Lady Morgan, *Italy*. London: Henry Colburn, 1821, 3:242-53.]

Lady Morgan was not the only English aristocrat to express her admiration for the conduct and character of the Neapolitan lower classes. Three years later, Lady Blessington wrote with even greater enthusiasm:

CHAPTER I. FOUNDATIONS

11. The more I see of the Neapolitans, the better I like them. I have not detected among the individuals of the lower class that have fallen in my way, a single instance of the rapaciousness so generally, and I am inclined to think unjustly, attributed to them by strangers. Their politeness has nothing in it of servility; and their good humour is neither coarse nor boisterous. The gardeners, and their wives and families, appertaining to the Palazzo Belvedere, seem actuated by the unceasing desire to please us. Fresh flowers are sent in by them, every morning, for the apartments; the finest figs, and grapes, are offered for our acceptance; and smiling faces and courteous enquiries about the health of every individual of the family meet us, whenever we encounter any of them. They sing, and not inharmoniously, while at work in the garden; occasionally in duos and trios, and at other times, one begins a song descriptive of rural occupations, and his companions answer it.... No night passes in which these good people, joined by the *custode* and his family, do not dance the *tarantella* in the court yard, to the music of their own voices, accompanied by the *tamour de basque*. Old and young all join in this national dance, with a gaiety it is quite exhilarating to witness....

The streets of Naples present daily the appearance of a fete. The animation and gay dresses of the lower classes of the people, and the crowds who flock about, convey this impression. Nowhere does the stream of life seem to flow so rapidly as here; not like the dense and turbid flood that rushes along Fleet Street and the Strand in London; but a current that sparkles while hurrying on. The lower classes of Naples observe no medium between the slumber of exhaustion and the fever of excitement; and, to my thinking, expend more vitality in one day than the same class in our colder regions do in three. They are never calm or quiet. Their conversation, no matter on what topic, is carried on with an animation and gesticulation unknown to us. Their friendly salutations might, by a stranger, be mistaken for the commencement of a quarrel, so vehement and loud are their exclamations, and their disagreements are conducted with a fiery wrath which reminds one that they belong to a land in whose volcanic nature they strongly participate. Quickly excited to anger, they are as quickly propitiated; and are not prone to indulge rancorous feelings.

It is fortunate that this sensitive people are not, like ours, disposed to habits of intoxication. Lemonade is sought here with the same avidity that ardent spirits are in England; and this cooling beverage, joined to the universal use of macaroni, is happily calculated to allay the fire of their temperaments....

So far from getting accustomed to the beauty of this place, it creates an increased admiration everyday. The resplendent skies, and the glorious sea that mirrors them, fill me with delight... Idleness, the besetting sin of [Naples], has taken possession of me.... O the *dolce far niente* of Italian life! Who can resist its influence? Not I at least. [Blessington, *Idler* 2:32-59.]

It was this huge and contradictory city — with its well-meaning but indolent king, ambitious queen, unsurpassed natural beauty, and sharp contrasts between rich and poor, and privileged and powerless — that would face the onslaught of the French revolutionary armies in 1799.

■ ■ ■

2
The Bourbon Capital: The Revolution of 1799

The French Revolution began in 1789. From the very beginning, it met with fierce resistance from among the major European Powers. In Naples, in particular, Ferdinand IV was deeply alarmed by the attacks of the revolutionaries on a fellow Bourbon king, Louis XVI, and scandalized by their assault on religion and private property. As early as December 1792, he expressed his "rage" over what he viewed as the bullying and arrogance of French representatives in Naples, and stated his desire "to cut up every Frenchman in the city." This view, moreover, was fully shared by his chief minister, the English aristocrat, Lord Acton, and by the English ambassador, Lord Hamilton — both of whom had gained enormous influence over the government since the fall of Tanucci in 1776. Most of all, however, Ferdinand was supported by the queen, Maria Carolina, whose anxiety over the fate of her sister, Marie Antoinette, had reached the point of obsession, and whose paranoia with regard to France was nearing its peak. On December 4, 1792, she wrote to her life-long friend and confidant, the marchese di Gallo:

> 12.1. My health is bad: my mind is mortally troubled and I do nothing but weep. Six little children to look after and the state in danger.... From one minute to the next we expect the French squadron of fifty-four sails. They assure us that they are coming as brothers and friends.... Finally, the crisis has come: we have stipulated the number of ships we can receive. If the French exceed this number, we have informed them that the surplus will be regarded as hostile. As for us, we have seen what fate has in store for us. I only weep on account of my poor children, for if we suffer a real defeat all is over, and we can consider ourselves irretrievably lost.... [Cited in Acton, *Bourbons*, p. 248.]

And, again, on January 22, 1793, after learning of the execution of Louis XVI:

> 12.2. Knowing your upright mind, I can imagine your emotion on hearing of the appalling crime perpetrated against the unfortunate

King of France in all solemnity, tranquillity, and illegality. We knew it from the Gazette, and...have gone into mourning for four months. He was the head of our family, our kinsman, cousin, and brother-in-law. What an atrocious example! What an execrable nation! I know nothing about the other wretched victims in the Temple. If sorrow does not kill them, other horrors may be expected from this horde of assassins. I hope that the ashes of this good Prince, of this too good Prince who has suffered shame and infamy for four years culminating in execution, will implore a striking and visible vengeance from divine Justice, and that on this account the Powers of Europe will have no more than a single will, since it is a matter in which they are all involved. [Acton, *Bourbons*, p. 254.]

From then on, her preoccupation with her sister became almost continuous. On March 5, she wrote:

12.3. I hear horrible details from that infernal Paris. At every moment, at every noise and cry, every time they enter her room, my unfortunate sister kneels, prays and prepares for death. The inhuman brutes that surround her amuse themselves in this manner: day and night they bellow on purpose to terrorize her and make her fear death a thousand times. Death is what one may wish for the poor soul, and it is what I pray God to send her that she may cease to suffer.... I should like this infamous nation to be cut to pieces, annihilated, dishonored, reduced to nothing for at least fifty years. I hope that divine chastisement will fall visibly on France, destroyed by the glorious arms of Austria.

And, once again, in July:

12.4. They have taken away my unfortunate sister's son and moved him to the apartments of his late father with a certain Simon, a shoe-maker, and his wife. This blow must have been terrible for my unfortunate sister. I could have wished it to end her life. For a long time I have been wishing for a natural death as the best thing that could happen to her. But Providence has decreed otherwise and we shall have to submit. It is certain that she is made to suffer all the sharpest pangs, at such intervals as to drain the full bitterness of each. And just when time and resignation seem to have formed a protective crust, her wounds are torn open again.

And, finally, in August:

CHAPTER 2. THE REVOLUTION OF 1799

12.5. I am increasingly anxious about the fate of my wretched sister and long for it to be over; my imagination always anticipates reality. I do not know what to hope or fear for her and her family. What I wish is that France could be pulverized with all its inhabitants. [Letters cited in Acton, *Bourbons*, pp. 254, 261-62.]

In late October, Maria Carolina learned the sad news that her sister had been guillotined. Returning to her room, she wrote at the bottom a picture of Marie Antoinette that she kept on her desk: *"Je poursuiverai ma vengeance jusqu'au tombeau"* — "I will pursue my revenge to the day of my death" — and she would seek to fulfill that promise for the rest of her life.

■

Given the political conservatism and personal tragedy endured by the royal family, it is small wonder that the kingdom of Naples was among the first of the Italian states to enter the war against the French Republic. In July 1793, Acton and Maria Carolina convinced Ferdinand to sign a treaty of alliance with England, and, one month later, 6,000 Neapolitan troops were dispatched to France to join with the British and Spanish in a futile effort to save Toulon from republican forces. The attempt, however, soon proved to be a disaster. In December, the French took the city by storm, more than 600 Neapolitan troops were either killed, wounded or captured, and, in February, the demoralized contingent was forced to beat a hasty retreat back to Naples. Still, Maria Carolina remained defiant. In July 1794, as French troops were entering Piedmont, she wrote to Gallo:

13. We are determined to hold Gaeta, Capua, Naples, Salerno, Cosenza, Catanzaro, Reggio, Messina, Palermo, Augusta, and, if we are forced to abandon the latter, I will throw my seven children into the sea with my own hands and myself after them. I will neither become the prize of rogues nor a miserable beggar. My mind is made up: I am wretched and I will do my duty to the end. [Quoted in Michel Lacour-Gayet, *Marie-Caroline: Reine de Naples*. Paris: Tallandier, 1990, p. 107.]

Equally alarming to the king and queen was the apparent appeal that the Revolution had among the Neapolitan educated classes. Students, journalists, lawyers, liberal army officers and aristocrats, and intellectuals of all kinds viewed the changes in France with enormous interest, and "Jacobin" ideas were openly discussed in Masonic lodges and at "patriotic" gatherings in all parts of the city. One such student, Guglielmo Pepe, who himself would help to lead a revolution against the Bourbons in 1820, later recalled the excitement generated in Naples by the ideals of the Revolution as follows:

> 14. By 1798, the French Republic had existed for five years and it had awakened in the minds of the youth of Naples the most ardent sympathy for its institutions, and a no less ardent desire to realize the possession of a like form of Government in their own country. The influence of such a feeling was almost universal, but it was more particularly indulged by those who really designed the national welfare, and by the unfortunate beings languishing in state prisons.
>
> The enthusiasm for the French revolution and the knowledge of our own military capacity, of which the conduct of Neapolitan troops, both at Toulon and in Lombardy, had given undoubted evidence, served to inspire...contempt for the weak and ill-advised policy which prevailed throughout the kingdom. I had myself scarcely attained my fifteenth year, but my heart already throbbed with the most enthusiastic feelings of republicanism. [Guglielmo Pepe, *Memoirs*. London: Richard Bentley, 1846, pp. 24-25.]

As early as December 1792, a revolutionary club — "La Società degli amici della Libertà et l'Eguaglianza" — was founded in Naples, and others soon followed throughout the mainland and Sicily. Composed, most often, of some of the most respectable elements in the kingdom, they conducted their meetings in secret and drew up elaborate plans for the modernization of government and society. Confused and frightened, Acton and Maria Carolina responded with wholesale repression: mass arrests were made; the press was censored; and some of the most egregious conspirators were sentenced to long terms in prison or executed. In 1795, the queen wrote to Gallo:

> 15. This infamous revolution has made me cruel. Recently I saved a whole club where many of the nobility spat upon, reviled and finally pierced my portrait with knives, inciting each other to repeat these gestures to the original.... Personally, I scorn the madness of these people, but when it rages against the King — and what a King! — an affectionate father, devoted to them, just and good, such as they do not deserve, I cannot forgive them for it. [Cited in Acton, *Bourbons*, p. 276.]

Meanwhile, the struggle in northern Italy was rapidly reaching its climax. In March 1796, Bonaparte was appointed commander-in-chief of the Army of Italy. Taking the offensive almost immediately, he crushed the Austrians at Lodi and Borghetto,

CHAPTER 2. THE REVOLUTION OF 1799

compelled the Neapolitans to conclude a separate peace and withdraw to Naples, and, in October 1797, triumphantly signed the Treaty of Campo Formio with Vienna, which left virtually all of Italy north of the Papal States under French control. A few weeks later, Maria Carolina wrote of the charismatic French general:

> 16. In spite of all the harm [that Bonaparte] has done us in Italy, I must admit that I hold a high opinion of him, as I love the great in all things and everywhere, even when I find it turned against myself. I wish this rare and extraordinary man to succeed and distinguish himself outside Italy. I foresee that the world will resound with his name, and that history will immortalize him. He will be great in all things, in war, diplomacy, conduct, resolution, talent, genius: he will be the greatest man of our century.... Cultivate in him friendly sentiments for Naples and the desire not to injure us. [Letter to Gallo, published in Acton, *Bourbons*, p. 296.]

The queen's admiration would soon turn to fear and disillusionment. In February 1798, while Napoleon was preparing to launch his adventure in Egypt, the local French commander in Italy, General Berthier, took advantage of popular disturbances in Rome in order to occupy the Holy City. The pope, who had unceremoniously fled to Tuscany, was declared deposed, a Roman Republic was proclaimed, and French troops appeared for the first time on the Neapolitan border.

The event proved to be fatal for Naples. In November, Ferdinand — acting on the advice of Acton and the queen — ordered 50,000 Neapolitan troops under the Austrian General Mack to cross the frontier and clear the French from papal territory. Outnumbered and lacking clear orders from Paris, the French commander in Rome, General Championnet, temporarily withdrew from the city, and, on November 29, Ferdinand and Acton triumphantly entered at the head of the Neapolitan forces.

Their moment of victory, however, was brief. On December 5, Championnet counter-attacked, the Neapolitan army was routed, and Ferdinand and Acton were sent scurrying back to Caserta. As the French advanced, memories of the fate of Louis XVI and Marie Antoinette filled the king and queen with terror. Unwilling to risk capture, on December 21, the entire royal entourage, including children, close friends, and government advisers, boarded the English Admiral Nelson's flagship, the *Vanguard*, and headed for Palermo. Before leaving, however, Ferdinand issued an edict appointing General Francesco Pignatelli as vicar general of the kingdom, and calling on the people of Naples to defend the city against the enemy. The edict — which was backdated to December 8 in order to make it appear as if it had been written in Rome and posted throughout the city — promised support for a war of extermination against the advancing French army:

17. While I am in the capital of the Christian world restoring the Holy Church to its rightful place, the French, with whom I have made every effort to live in peace, are threatening to occupy the Abruzzo. I will return quickly with a mighty army and exterminate them. Meanwhile, let the people arm. Let them succor the Faith, defend their King and Father who is risking his life for them, and who is ever ready to sacrifice himself in order to preserve their religion, possessions, honor and freedom. Remember our ancient valor. Anyone who abandons our flag or fails to rally to our cause will be punished as a rebel, and treated as an enemy of Church and State. [Pietro Colletta, *Storia del reame di Napoli*. Naples: S.A.R.A., 1992, pp. 186-87.]

The appeal produced a resounding response from among the Neapolitan people. Workers, artisans, shopkeepers, priests, and friars — loyal to their king and fearful for their religion — mobilized in a determined effort to defend their city. The ubiquitous *lazzaroni*, in particular, stormed through the streets in near delirium, releasing more than 6,000 criminals from the city's jails, and invading the San Carlo Opera House in search of Frenchmen and "traitors." Weapons were gathered from the city's arsenals; suspected "Jacobins" were rounded up and sometimes massacred; and Pignatelli, who had sought to reach a compromise with the French, was forced to flee to Sicily. Thus, when the French arrived on January 20, they faced the prospect of a bitter confrontation with an armed and impassioned people.

The fighting, in fact, which began the following day with the advance of Championnet's army from Capodimonte, proved to be among the most brutal in Neapolitan history. Within a few days, the city was strewn with burning buildings and rotting corpses, as the struggle proceeded from street to street and house to house with no quarter given. The German painter, Wilhelm Tischbein, who was living in Naples at the time, has left the following account of the fighting in one section of the city:

18. The *lazzaroni*, who [up until January 21] had been dragging cannon through the city every night, shouting, "Look out, look out, the enemy is near!" had fortified themselves in a street off the big square called the Largo delle Pigne. The French, on the other side, just under my windows, had placed a battery, and the explosions now began. Among the high houses, built of stone, these made a reverberation as if the world were about to collapse. One was almost deafened. The door to my house was strongly barred; all the windows were hermetically closed; and there was nothing to do

CHAPTER 2. THE REVOLUTION OF 1799

but wait patiently for death.... I searched for a hole to peep through and it was worth the effort. Not far from my house a joiner had placed a pile of beams from the wrecked mansion of the Duke della Torre, who had been shot with his brother, then cut to pieces and burnt. With those beams the French had made a kitchen fire, and began to roast ribs of pork. A large crowd stood round it. When one finished eating he rose and fired at the *lazzaroni*. Others who had no more cartridges turned and ate, were given fresh ammunition, and began to shoot again. Before the Palazzo degli Studii [across the street], there was a lofty flight of steps on which the bullets beat incessantly like hail. Whosoever stood behind it was safe, because the bullets bounded high up, flying over the houses. Among the French I noticed a fine young grenadier, who was remarkable for his unusual stature. Like the others, he shot assiduously. I thought that the snipers from Solimena's house, facing the door, would take aim at him, because all those who barely put their heads over the steps disappeared. As soon as his bearskin cap and a fraction of his forehead were visible a bullet came: he fell over backwards full length, with his arms outstretched, and never moved a limb.

A large cannon, found at the port, had been placed by the *lazzaroni* under a door in front of my house. After its first discharge, the French began to fire at it, and it soon was abandoned. A youth leapt forward and tried to rescue it, but he was immediately struck dead by a hail of bullets; the others escaped. On this occasion an image of Christ was miserably shattered; only the arms and legs hung from a few splinters. The previous day I had observed that handsome youth, who tried to save the cannon, busily throwing down signs by which the enemy was to distinguish the houses to be burnt. Soon after I heard a Frenchman cry out in agony, and I saw that, struck by a bullet, he had fallen flat on the ground. The weight of knapsack, crammed with stolen goods, had carried him in the same direction....

One of my students was a sculptor. He was passionately pro-French because he believed that they wished to convert the whole of Italy into a Republic.... He [said] that the French had no other desire but to introduce liberty into Italy; they therefore should be supported at all costs. But they did not come as soon as he expected. Hearing that he had consorted with the enemy, the *lazzaroni* wanted to kill him, so that he was forced to go into hiding. He concealed himself in the vast building of the Studii, where he could not be discovered. At last when the French arrived he emerged from his shelter, and rushed with open arms towards his liberators. But these pointed their guns at the chest of their enthusiastic admirer and stole his watch....

[During the fighting, many lazzaroni were captured. As one was being taken off to be shot, he told his French captor:] "What do you want to do to me with your guns? Look here!" [He then twirled his cap in the air to show an image of San Gennaro and the Madonna, which he had stuck to his forehead as a means of protection, like most of his fellows.] The French, however, made short work of him and his amulet: they leveled their guns and his brains bespattered the wall. [Tischbein, *Aus Meinen Leben*, cited in Acton, *Bourbons*, pp. 331-32.]

As the fighting progressed, the hatred of the *lazzaroni* for the French and their Jacobin sympathizers only seemed to intensify. As one middle-class Neapolitan memoirist of the period recorded it:

19. The batteries made a noise which afflicted the human mind. The shops were all shut, and the streets absolutely deserted. Each one, because of the enraged populace, went in fear of death, and because of the French, of a general sack and pillage. The mob...whenever they saw a group of Jacobins, ran thither and made butchery. [Cited in Constance H.D. Gigioli, *Naples in 1799: An Account of the Revolution of 1799 and the Rise and Fall of the Parthenopean Republic*. London: John Murray, 1903, p. 118.]

In reflecting on the ferocity of the conflict, the French General Thiébault later wrote:

20. The Neapolitans taught us to fear them as men. One might say, in fact, that the struggle for Naples only became terrifying after the Neapolitan army had ceased to exist. Although these Neapolitans had been beaten everywhere, and, not counting the losses sustained during the early fighting, had suffered [many tens of thousands of casualties],... we were unable to vanquish them completely within the walls of their city or amid the ashes of their homes. [Thiébault, *Memorie di guerra*, cited in Domenico Capecelatro Gaudioso, *Ferdinando I di Borbone Re Illuminista*, Naples: Adriano Gallina, 1987, p. 86.]

CHAPTER 2. THE REVOLUTION OF 1799

The struggle continued for three days, from January 21 to January 23. Throughout the fighting, the French benefited from the assistance that they received from the Castel Sant'Elmo, which had been seized by Neapolitan republicans prior to their entry into the city, and provided artillery support to the French army during its advance. Resistance was heaviest in the "popular" districts: the Piazza Mercato, Santa Lucia, and the Molo Piccolo, where the *lazzaroni* put up a desperate struggle for two days and nights. By the beginning of the third day, the French had either overrun or penetrated deeply into all three areas. Overall, they had lost over 1,000 men, compared to an estimated 3,000 Neapolitans, with many thousands more either wounded or injured on both sides. On the afternoon of January 23, Championnet—who himself had been stunned by the ferocity of the struggle and wanted to halt the bloodshed—issued a conciliatory "Proclamation to the People of the Kingdom of Naples," in which he promised peace, liberty, and respect for private property and religion to all those who would lay down their arms:

> 21. Neapolitans! You are finally free! Your freedom is the only reward that France wishes to claim from its conquest; it is the only provision of the treaty of peace that the Army solemnly swears to uphold.... May calamity fall on anyone who refuses to sign this honorable agreement in which all of the fruits of victory are for the vanquished and which leaves to the victor only the glory of having increased your happiness.... If there is anyone among you who is ungrateful enough to reject the freedom that we have won for you at the cost of our blood, and if there are men foolish enough to want to bring back a king who no longer has the right to command them, having violated the oath that he made to defend you and fled while committing an ignoble act of perjury, we shall fight them to the death, and they will be exterminated. Do not allow fear to tarnish this unexpected attainment of freedom; the Army will defend you; it stands ready to sacrifice every soldier and to shed its last drop of blood should some tyrant among you try to reestablish the oppression of your families and reopen the grim prisons in which they made you suffer for so long. If the French Army today assumes the title "Army of Naples" it is because of the solemn pledge it has made to raise its arms to defend your independence and preserve the rights it has won for you. Let the people rest assured regarding their freedom of worship, and let the citizen put aside his concern respecting his property rights.... The wave of banditry and assassination of your last king, planned and carried out by his evil henchmen as a means of defense, has had grievous consequences for your city;... but once this evil is eliminated,

it will be easy to rectify its nefarious effects. The Republican authorities will reestablish order and tranquillity based on a benevolent administration, dispelling the fears of the ignorant and calming the furor of fanaticism,... and soon the firmness that appears so readily among the troops of a free People will put an end to the disorder provoked by irrational hatreds, and which the right to retaliate has compelled us to repress. [Championnet, "Proclamazione a tutti gli abitanti del fu Regno," in Tommaso Pedio, *La Republica Napoletana del 1799*. Bari: Levante, 1986, pp. 43-45.]

The contemporary Neapolitan historian and diarist, Carlo De Nicola, wrote of this declaration:

> 22. Championnet later said that, during his nine years of fighting, he had never encountered mass resistance equal to that of the Neapolitans.... He stated that if the Neapolitans were disciplined, they would be the ultimate soldiers.... [Nevertheless, he believed that it was his duty to prevent his forces from sacking the city].... It was Naples' good fortune to have as the commander of the French army a general who shunned unnecessary violence and bloodletting, a humanist and man of good will. If Bonaparte had been the leader of that army, and he had encountered such resistance, Naples would have been destroyed by fire and pillage. [Carlo De Nicola, *Diario Napoletano dal 1798 al 1825*. Naples: Società Napoletana di Storia Patria, 1906, 1:34.]

The leaders of the *lazzaroni* seem to have agreed. Battered by the relentless advance of French forces, pushed into the furthest corners of the city, and devoid of any realistic hope that the king would honor his pledge to come to their assistance with a "mighty army," they accepted Championnet's offer of a cease-fire. The monarchy was ended. A republic was declared, and the Provisional Government made up of Neapolitan "Patriots" lead by Carlo Lauberg was chosen by Championnet to administer the kingdom. A "tree of liberty" was planted in the Castle Sant'Elmo; the French army was formally renamed the "Army of Naples"; and the archbishop of the city was ordered to perform the "miracle of San Gennaro" — in which the dead saint's coagulated blood was made to liquefy in full sight of a credulous population — to show that the changes had the approval of the Church. That evening, while the city was still locked in celebration over its erstwhile transformation, Championnet sent the following dispatch to the Directory in Paris in which he dramatically summarized the three-days' events:

> 23. Citizen Directors:

CHAPTER 2. THE REVOLUTION OF 1799

I am pleased to announce that the French Army has occupied Naples and all of its forts. Three full days of fighting have been necessary in order to subdue the immense population of this city and the remnants of the royal army which supported it. Delirium and fanaticism have armed 60,000 men, and a similar number has harassed my flanks and my rear. The French have had to avenge many outrages; but valor has triumphed over numbers in the end.... By knowing the French Army, I have been able to destroy that of the Neapolitans. General Mack has been forced to retire to Germany; the King has fled to Sicily; the Patriots have gained the upper hand in Naples; the revolution has been made — one monarch less; one republic more; that is the story in brief....

[During the weeks leading up to the attack], I had already learned from newspaper accounts that Naples was in the midst of great agitation.... The *lazzaroni* had disarmed part of the royal army, confiscated its guns and artillery, and were threatening to attack us. In addition, other, disarmed, Neapolitan soldiers had arrived from the front, were warmly greeted by the insurgents, and enlisted in their cause.... Soon after, they attacked our advanced positions at Ponte Rotto and were repulsed....

The next day, I ordered two divisions to advance on Naples and to tighten our hold on the city. I confess that I did not expect any resistance; but attacks on our troops began almost immediately.... Generals Mounier and Duhesme were wounded,... but Generals Broussier and Thiébault continued to pursue the enemy and forced them back into the city.... Many houses were set on fire, the streets were littered with bodies,... and conditions among the inhabitants were horrible.... That night, our soldiers spent the night above Naples on the heights of Capodimonte.

Meanwhile, I learned that the Neapolitan patriots were sincere in their claims to be friends of the French. They had seized the Castle of Sant'Elmo. The brave Moliterno was in command. I took advantage of the night to send two battalions there: they were greeted with cries of "Long Live the Republic!" The canons of the fort thundered. This provided the signal. The army advanced: it attacked with fervor; and the enemy responded in kind. Never was combat more determined: never was a picture more horrifying. The *lazzaroni*, these astonishing men, supported by the debris of an army which had only recently fled before us, were transformed into heroes in Naples. Every street was defended and not one foot of ground was yielded without a fight.... Although shells rained down upon them from the Castel Sant'Elmo and they were faced with repeated bayonet charges, they always retreated in good order, renewing their attacks and advancing with great audacity, and often even regaining ground. Nevertheless, half of the city had been conquered by the end of the first day....

At this point, I hoped that the terrifying possibility of retribution would force the *lazzaroni* to ask for quarter. Instead, they continued to skirmish throughout the night, multiplying their attacks and waiting with courage for the advance of French forces. It was then that I ordered a third attack: the storming of the Castel Nuovo and that of the Carmine, and the burning of the *lazzaroni*'s main district, the Basso Porto. The fighting was renewed with great intensity, and the French were victorious on all fronts: the Castel Nuovo was captured and only the Carmine held out.

The city now faced the threat of a general sacking. [In order to avoid it], I made an offer of peace. I convinced the patriots that it was necessary to avoid such a catastrophe; I persuaded the priests and the people listened to them; one of their leaders was won over. Hope was reborn, peaceful citizens began to appear once again on the streets, calm was reestablished, and the same people who had battled so desperately for a perfidious king, recovering from their delirium, blessed the French and filled the air with cries of "Long Live the Republic!"... The tricolor flag now floats above the city's forts and they are garrisoned by the French army. I have renamed it the "Army of Naples."

History will one day record that this army, lacking adequate provisions and without receiving any reinforcements, invaded the Kingdom of Naples, defeated and destroyed a perfectly organized army of 80,000 Neapolitans, and then confronted an enormous population which was a thousand times more dangerous than the regular army; and that, in the end, in a battle which was as bloody as it was strange, it subdued the people which had been unleashed against it and made them a gift of their liberty. [Championnet, quoted in Pepe, *Memoirs*, pp. 44-49.]

■

CHAPTER 2. THE REVOLUTION OF 1799

The Parthenopean Republic lasted for five fateful months, from January 21 to June 23, 1799. At its head stood the Provisional Government, which had been selected by Championnet from among Patriot leaders on the 23rd, and invested with executive and legislative power. Among its members, were some of the most intelligent and respected citizens in the kingdom. In addition to Lauberg, a chemist and political radical who had been forced to seek refuge in France in 1794, it included Mario Pagano, a legal theorist who had been one of the central figures of the Neapolitan Enlightenment; Melchiorre Delfico, a philosopher and expert on the problems of the Abruzzi; Pasquale Baffi, one of Naples' leading experts on Herculaneum and Pompeii; Domenico Forges Davanzati, a noted archeologist and historian; the prince of Moliterno, who had lead the Patriots in the capture of the Castel Sant'Elmo; Giuseppe Abbamonte, an early convert to Jacobinism who had served as an official in the Cisalpine Republic in 1798; and several prominent Neapolitan lawyers, including Domenico Bisceglia, Prosdocimo Rotondo, and the eloquent and volatile Vincenzo Russo. Intensely idealistic but lacking in practical political experience, the new government made its general objectives clear in a set of "Instructions" that it issued to Neapolitan Patriots on February 5:

> 24. The Neapolitan Republic, created under the auspices of the great French Republic,... under the protection of a victorious and liberating army, [proposes] to reunite promptly all of the parties of the Republic...and to reconcile, to the degree that it is possible, all those with different feelings and points of view.... [Its aim] is to create a benevolent revolution, to make it loved and useful to the People.
>
> Equality and Liberty will form the bases of the new Republic. Equality consists of making the law apply equally to everyone and protecting the weak and innocent against the oppression of the rich and powerful.... It does not recognize the vain and pompous titles that existed under the former tyranny...and decrees that the word "citizen" should be applied to all men.... Liberty consists of the right of each citizen to do anything that is not prohibited by law, and that does not harm another....
>
> [We urge Patriots everywhere to adhere to these principles. We urge them] to plant liberty trees, to wear tricolor cockades...red, yellow, and blue...[and to organize] a municipal government...and National Guard in order to maintain peace and protect the rights of the citizenry....
>
> Representatives of the Provisional Government will be sent to the various departments or provinces of the Republic in order to organize local authority and consolidate the Revolution....

> [All government officials must]...be men of honesty and virtue.... Selfless men, who have dedicated themselves to the glorious pursuit of liberty, will be chosen first to support the rights of the People and to serve the nation as representatives, judges, civil officials, and military leaders.... [All must carry out their duties while showing] unwavering loyalty to the republican regime.... ["Istruzioni generali del Governo Provvisorio della Repubblica Napolitana ai Patrioti," February 5, 1799, cited in Pedio, *La repubblica napoletana*, pp. 34-36.]

Initially, the program of the Provisional Government provoked an enthusiastic response from the Neapolitan middle classes. During the first weeks after the proclamation of the republic, "Jacobin" political clubs and newspapers sprang up throughout the city, and "liberty trees" were planted in front of the royal palace and in all public squares. Political commissioners were sent to the provinces in order to reorganize local government, and a massive propaganda campaign was conducted to weaken the people's monarchist sentiments and imbue them with republican ideals. Streets were renamed, royal statues and aristocratic coats-of-arms were removed, and, in the leading republican newspaper, *Monitore Napoletano*, Eleonora de Fonseca Pimentel devoted herself tirelessly to the elaboration of democratic principles and the promotion of the revolutionary cause.

Nothing, however, seemed capable of bridging the gap between the government and the Neapolitan lower classes. Among the *lazzaroni*, in particular, loyalty to the king and Church remained unshakable; and memories of the bitter struggle with the French and their Neapolitan allies continued to breed resentment despite the altruistic declarations of the new regime. As for the peasants, even Pimentel was forced to admit that they neither valued nor understood the revolutionaries' intellectual abstractions. Most identified the Provisional Government with foreign ideas and military conquest, and many suspected rightly that the middle class secretly looked upon them with fear and disdain.

In his brilliant *Saggio storico sulla rivoluzione napoletana del 1799* (1801), Vincenzo Cuoco, who himself had played a minor role in the Parthenopean Republic, described with extraordinary clarity the chasm that existed between the revolution's leaders and the Neapolitan masses. Noting that the revolution had been imposed on the Neapolitan people by a tiny minority and a foreign army, he emphasized that the majority of the population had neither desired it nor had been prepared historically to understand its possible benefits, and that it was precisely the "passive" character of their participation that doomed the revolution to fail:

CHAPTER 2. THE REVOLUTION OF 1799

25. After the French Army entered Naples, Championnet's first task was to "install" a Provisional Government which, at the same time as it was looking after the immediate needs of the nation, was to prepare a permanent constitution.... But to devise a scheme for a republican constitution is not the same thing as to found a republic. In a form of government in which the public will, or the law, has and ought to have no other support, no other guarantor, no other executive agent than the private will, liberty is only secured by creating free men. Before the edifice of liberty was raised on Neapolitan territory, there were in the old constitutions, in ingrained customs and prejudices, in the present interests of the inhabitants, a thousand obstacles which it was proper to recognize, which it was necessary to remove....

The King had in the Kingdom of Naples itself a good number of supporters, who liked the old government better than the new...[and] the number of those who were decisively on the side of the revolution was very small compared with the population as a whole ....

Our revolution being a passive revolution, the only means of bringing it to a successful conclusion was by winning popular opinion. But the views of the Patriots and those of the people were not the same; they had different ideas, different customs and even different languages. This same admiration for foreigners which had retarded the progress of our civilization in the time of the King now, at the start of our republic, formed the greatest obstacle to the establishment of liberty. The Neapolitan nation could be regarded as divided into two peoples, separated by two centuries and two climatic zones. Since the educated part had been formed on foreign models, its culture was different than that from which the nation as a whole needed and which could be expected to come only from the development of our faculties. Some had become French, others English; and those who had remained Neapolitan and who composed the great majority were still uncultivated. So the culture of the few had not assisted the nation as whole, which in turn almost despised a culture which was useless to it and which it did not understand.

The misfortunes of peoples are often the clearest demonstrations of the most useful truths. One can never help one's country if one does not love it, and one can never love one's country if one does not love the nation. That people can never be free in which the class destined by Nature, on account of the superiority of its intelligence, to govern whether by authority or example, has sold its opinion to a foreign nation. The whole nation has then lost the means of its independence....

It was desirable, amid so many contradictions, to discover a common interest which could summon and re-unite everyone in the revolution. When the nation had once been reunited, all the Powers of the world would have allied against us in vain. If the condition of our nation presented great obstacles, it offered on the other hand great opportunities for the promotion of our revolution.

The population was such that, although it would never have made the revolution by itself, it was docile in receiving it at the hands of others. The decided partisans on both sides were few: the majority of the nation was indifferent....

The immense population of the Capital was more stupefied than active. It was still watching with amazement a change which it had believed almost impossible. In general, it could be said that the people of the Capital were further from revolution than those of the provinces, since they were less oppressed by taxes and more pampered by a Court which feared them. Despotism is generally founded on the dregs of the people, which, having no genuine concern for good or evil, sell themselves to him who satisfies their bellies best. It is rare for a government to fall which is not lamented by the worst elements in society. But it ought to be the business of the new regime to ensure that the best elements do not want it back. But perhaps the overwhelming fear which was conceived of this population caused too much care to be taken of it and too little of the provinces, from which alone there was anything to fear and from which in the event came the counter-revolution. [Vincenzo Cuoco, *Historical Essay on the Neapolitan Revolution of 1799* (1801), pp. 86-93, in Derek Beales, ed. *The Risorgimento and the Unification of Italy*. London: George Allen & Unwin, 1971, pp. 111-15.]

Cuoco's theory of "passive revolution" provided the starting point for all subsequent analyses of the Parthenopean Republic. Since the leaders of the Provisional Government looked to France to provide the model for their revolution, the only way that they could have won the support of the Neapolitan lower classes was to appeal to their material interests by adopting a program of radical social reform. Most of the

CHAPTER 2. THE REVOLUTION OF 1799

Revolution's middle-class leaders, however, rejected such measures. They feared the threat that radical social legislation would pose to private property, and some even argued that the landless peasants were not part of the "people" at all. Thus, while the Provisional Government did outlaw ecclesiastical tithes and aristocratic titles, it failed to issue a general declaration abolishing feudalism or initiating land resettlement among the rural poor. As a result, most of the peasants remained indifferent or openly hostile to the revolution. Like the *lazzaroni* in Naples, they came to resent the French and their "Jacobin" followers for their arrogance and financial exactions, and longed for the relative stability that had existed before the war. On February 3, De Nicola, in reflecting upon the deteriorating political and economic situation, wrote ominously:

> 26. Our condition is worsening daily. The people are in ferment and suffer greatly at the hands of the French, especially since they have attempted to violate our women, something that is deeply resented by the population. It is true that General Championnet has attempted to reign in his troops, but it is impossible to prevent every disorder, and in the meantime we hear more than a hundred Frenchmen have been recently murdered at night.... The French are not numerous enough to control Naples while, at the same time, suppressing the insurrection in the rest of the kingdom.... I have heard it said by people in the streets that the king will return to Naples, and that the French will be forced to leave.... That is what makes me fear a new massacre.... [*Diario Napoletano* 1:45-46.]

The restraining effect that Championnet had on French forces did not last long. In late February, the French civil commissioner in Naples, Guillaume Faypoult, acting on direct orders from Paris, imposed a special war tax on the city, and declared that all royal property — including palaces, art collections, and the antiquities taken from Herculaneum and Pompeii — be turned over to France. When Championnet protested, he was dismissed by the Directory, and replaced by Marechal Macdonald, an officer whose reputation for harshness towards the civil population had been well established in Rome. On March I, De Nicola commented in his diary:

> 27. The news which has arrived today is alarming. It shows that the uproar in the kingdom continues to increase instead of declining, and that the city remains in ferment.... The truth is that no one can be satisfied with the present government. The conduct of the French generals is evil, and it is because of it that they are placed at the head of affairs. So many beautiful promises of happiness and liberty and, meanwhile, we are so unhappy and treated like slaves....

> The French officials disgust everyone with their impertinence...and French soldiers show no respect for the Church or the Sacraments.... The departure of Championnet has only added to the turbulence, since the warm and tolerant manner of that general was able to reduce the hatred of the population. Now it is said that such an attitude will be viewed as a crime...and that the new general Macdonald will be a terrorist. If this proves true, it will only increase our woe....
> [*Diario Napoletano* 1:65-67.]

Meanwhile, as the French attitude towards the Neapolitan people hardened, the Provisional Government was still trying to convince the general population of the benevolence of the revolution. During the spring of 1799, a republican constitution was drawn up. Written largely by Pagano, it ignored much of Neapolitan history and tradition, and was modeled almost exclusively on the French Constitution of 1793. In addition, a republican calendar was introduced, the law of primogeniture abolished, and a pantheon planned to honor the martyrs of the struggle against the king. At the same time, a law abolishing feudalism was discussed but never enacted, priests and monks were ordered to serve in the army, and taxes and prices experienced a steady increase. On April 5, De Nicola wrote wearily:

> 28. It is said that they have drawn up an iniquitous constitution. I shall always say the same thing: the government and the French do not know how to make the people love the revolution and search out ways of constantly increasing the discontent. And the real fact is this: there is no one in the Council who has experience in politics or good judgment; there is a lack of prudence, of conduct, of religion. The result will be as Voltaire said: "The French have always conquered Naples with ease, and lost it with the same ease." Oh! How many would gladly return to their former insignificance. [*Diario Napoletano* 1:99.]

■

The failure of the Neapolitan Jacobins to win the support of the mass of the population set the stage for the Bourbon counter-revolution. The agent of that counter-revolution was the unlikely figure of Cardinal Fabrizio Ruffo, a fifty-five year old Calabrian who had retired to Naples from Rome many years earlier, and had fled to Sicily in December along with the king. Confident and determined, he immediately proposed to return to his native Calabria in order to organize popular resistance to the French. In late January, Ferdinand and Acton accepted his proposal and, on

CHAPTER 2. THE REVOLUTION OF 1799

February 7, he sailed from Messina to the mainland with little money and eight devoted men. Landing at Punta del Pezzo, he immediately proceeded to Palmi, where he issued a ringing declaration calling for an armed crusade to expel the invaders and to restore the monarchy and Church:

> 29. Good and Courageous Calabrians:
> A horde of sectarian conspirators, after having overturned the Altar and Throne in France; after having upset and thrown into confusion all of Italy; after having, with sacrilegious attack, taken prisoner and sent to France the VICAR OF JESUS CHRIST, our Holy Father Pius VI; after having, with treachery and betrayal, scattered our army and invaded and incited to revolution our capital and the provinces, is making every effort to rob us of the most precious gift from heaven, our holy religion, and to the destroy the divine morals of the Bible, depriving us of our possessions and threatening the virtue of our women....
>
> Good and courageous Calabrians! Will you tolerate these outrages? Valiant soldiers of an army betrayed, will you leave unpunished the treachery that...has usurped the throne of our legitimate monarch? No! I can already see that you tremble with righteous indignation and are eager to avenge the offenses made to religion, king, and country.
>
> Gather then under the banner of the Holy Cross and our beloved sovereign. Let us not wait for the enemy to come and contaminate our land. Let us march to confront him, repel him, drive him out of Italy, and cast off the barbarous chains of our holy pontiff. The banner of the Holy Cross will assure us total victory.
>
> And you patriots who have gone astray — mend your ways and give us an unmistakable sign of your change of heart. Our king, in his mercy, will accept with indulgence a sincere demonstration of your conversion. Woe, however, to you who should persist: the lighting of justice will strike you more quickly than you think! [Cardinal Ruffo, "Proclama da Palmi nel Febbraio 1799," *Documenti*, published in Antonio Cimbalo, *La lunga marcia del Cardinale Ruffo alla reconquista del regno di Napoli*. Roma: A. Borzi, 1967, p. 73.]

Ruffo's appeal elicited an overwhelming response from the Calabrian people: priests and monks incensed by the revolutionaries' attacks on the pope and religion; peasants and townsmen hoping for an end to feudalism and greater social justice; and brigands and ruffians seeking loot and plunder — all flocked to his banner and joined in his seemingly relentless march to the north. By early March, the cardinal's self-proclaimed "Christian and Royal Army" already numbered over 20,000. In most towns, panic-stricken republicans fled before his arrival, and murder, torture, and imprisonment awaited those who foolishly chose to stay behind. In mid-March, the French commander in Naples, Macdonald, in an effort to stem the tide, issued an edict threatening draconian punishment to anyone supporting Ruffo's cause:

> 30. Every district or city that joins in the rebellion against the Republic will be burned and leveled to the ground.
>
> Cardinals, archbishops, bishops, abbots, and curates — in sum, all members of the clergy of a region — will be held responsible for rebellions in their area and will be punished by death.
>
> Every rebel will be considered guilty and punished by death; and every accomplice, secular or clerical, will be considered a rebel.
>
> The double ringing of bells is prohibited; should it occur, the clerics of that town will be subject to the death penalty.
>
> Anyone spreading news damaging to the French or to the Parthenopean Republic will be, as a rebel, liable to the death penalty.
>
> The execution of a convicted rebel will also include the loss of his property. [Cited in Colletta, p. 236.]

Posted in every town and village in the kingdom under French control, Macdonald's edict had no effect on the advance of Ruffo's army. In late March, the republican-held towns of Catanzaro and Cotrone were taken by storm. Both were sacked by Ruffo's forces, and their inhabitants were subjected to unspeakable horrors for several grueling days.

The violence, however, only seems to have brightened the mood of the royal family. On March 1, Maria Carolina, exultant over the cardinal's progress, sent him the gift of a hand-sewn flag as a sign of her approval, and issued a declaration encouraging the Calabrians to carry on:

> 31. Good and Valiant Calabrians:
> The bravery and valor that you have shown in defending the holy Catholic religion and your good king and father, decreed by God to sustain you, govern you, and bring you happiness, has stirred such profound feelings of gratitude and satisfaction in our hearts that we have decided to sew and decorate the flag which we have sent you with our own hands. This flag will always remain a luminous token of our sincere affection for you, and of our gratitude for your loyalty and allegiance to your sovereigns; but at the same time, it should serve as a strong incentive to continue to conduct yourselves

with the same valor and zeal, until you have totally defeated and driven out the enemies of our sacrosanct religion and state, so that you and your beloved families and country may tranquilly enjoy the fruits of your toil and your bravery, under protection of your good king and father Ferdinand and all of Us, who will not fail to find occasions to demonstrate to you that We will cherish in our hearts forever the memory of your fidelity and your glorious deeds.

Continue, then, valiant Calabrians, to fight with your accustomed valor under this flag, upon which we have woven with our own hands the Cross, the glorious sign of our redemption. Remember, courageous warriors, that under the protection of such a sign you will be victorious; with it as your guide, hasten bravely into the struggle, knowing full well that your enemies will be defeated totally....

Your grateful and good mother, Maria Carolina. [Cimbalo, p. 75.]

The relentlessness of Ruffo's advance placed the leaders of the Parthenopean Republic in an increasingly difficult position. From the very first days of the revolution, they had been dependent on the French army for their survival, and now their erstwhile protectors were faltering on the battlefield for the very first time. Successful efforts by French troops to put down the uprising in one province were followed invariably by renewed guerrilla attacks in another — as the two sides became locked in a bitter cycle of ambush and reprisal, and the war continued on aimlessly without end.

Under these circumstances, the Directory in Paris began to tire of the whole Neapolitan adventure. Ever since January, it had looked upon Naples primarily as a source of revenue and as a strategic outpost against the British in the Mediterranean — and now, with the republic faltering, its further usefulness seemed to be doubtful on both scores. The creation of the Second Coalition by Austria, Russia, Turkey, and England in March, and the defeats suffered by the French on the Adige and Adda in April, seem to have settled the matter; and, on May 7, Macdonald was ordered to withdraw the majority of his troops from the city in order to help consolidate the French position in the north.

Left alone, the leaders of the Provisional Government decided defiantly to continue on. On May 10, they issued a proclamation aimed at rallying their supporters to further resistance, and assuring them of the ultimate triumph of the revolutionary cause:

32. Brave citizens, we are free. The Republic is already established on the most solid foundation. It is the fruit of that courage, virtue,

and love of fatherland which has ever been engraved in our hearts, and which the former tyrants have only kindled blindly with their actions, to make us, without realizing it, complete the enterprise. If we have courageously driven tyranny from our pleasant land, it behooves us even now to destroy its very seed. Let us unite. The whole nation only presents one single will and an imposing mass of forces. Let us make the remnants of tyranny tremble for the brief span until their destruction. [Quoted in Acton, *Bourbons*, pp. 374-75.]

By this time, however, all realistic hope of victory was gone. On June 11, Ruffo's army captured Nola. One day later, it set out for Naples, and fighting with the republican National Guard began with a ferocious assault on the Maddalena Bridge on June 13. As the defenders began to fall back, the Calabrian cavalry galloped triumphantly into the heart of the city, and thousands of vengeful *lazzaroni* poured into the streets. Anyone suspected of Jacobin sympathies was hunted down and murdered. The bodies of the victims were mutilated and dismembered, heads were placed on pikes, women violated, and houses looted and set on fire. The leaders of the Provisional Government and their families fled frantically to the Nuovo and Ovo castles, which, along with the still French-garrisoned Castel Sant'Elmo, were quickly placed under siege.

The savagery of the Neapolitan lower classes seems to have genuinely alarmed Ruffo. Although his army had perpetrated several massacres during his long march to the capital, he had always hoped that the king would grant a general pardon to the republicans in return for surrender, and thus create the conditions in which a peaceful reconciliation could take place. As early as May 8, he had written plaintively to Acton:

33. I am writing to your majesty with great reluctance, but I feel that the urgency of the situation compels me to express my views.... [I am deeply] concerned with the issue of clemency and pardon.... Most of the [royal] commanders speak only of punishing the rebels. I believe that our course should be totally different. I believe that it would be best to forgive past transgressions.... You have said to me in the past that we do not have sufficient force to combat the Republicans effectively.... Why then should we drive them to desperation?...Those that I have had dealings with have been decent in their behavior, and, knowing that any further misbehavior will not be forgiven, will certainly behave in the future. In such cases, doesn't it make sense to pardon them? [Ruffo to Acton, Matera, May 8, 1799, in Cimbalo, p. 84.]

CHAPTER 2. THE REVOLUTION OF 1799

Nothing, however, seemed capable of softening the hatred that the royal entourage felt for the rebels. On June 14, as Ruffo was just beginning to tighten his ring around the fortresses, Maria Carolina wrote from Palermo:

> 34. I fervently desire to hear that Naples has been taken; I favor entering into negotiations with S. Elmo and its French commander, but no negotiations with our rebel vassals: the king, in his mercy, may pardon them, and may lessen their punishment in his infinite goodness, but he will never capitulate nor negotiate with criminal rebels who are breathing their last and who, even if they wanted, could do no evil, since they are trapped like mice in a trap. I should like, if it is convenient for the good of the state, to pardon them, but not to negotiate with such base, evil creatures: this is my opinion, which I submit like all the others to your wisdom and experience.... [Maria Carolina to Ruffo, Palermo, June 14, 1799, in Cimbalo, pp. 84-85.]

And, on June 17, Ferdinand added:

> 35. I am sure I need not repeat what I wrote to you in my last two letters with regard to treating both the good and the loyal and the infamous rebel Jacobins, especially the ringleaders. Nevertheless, I recommend you fervently not to do anything derogatory to the dignity and decorum which it is so necessary to maintain, both for my honor and yours. As a Christian I pardon everybody, but as he whom God appointed, I must be a strict avenger of offenses committed against Him, and of the injury done to the state and so many poor unfortunates. [Cited in Acton, *Bourbons*, p. 391.]

Still, however, Ruffo persisted. On June 21, after having already quietly begun negotiations with the rebels in the castles on the terms of surrender, he again wrote to Acton:

> 36. I am at the Maddalena bridge; and from all appearances the Ovo and Nuovo castles are about to surrender.... I am so exhausted and worn out that I do not see how I shall be able to bear up if this goes on for another three days. Having to govern, or more precisely to curb, a vast population accustomed to the most resolute anarchy; having to control a score of uneducated and insubordinate leaders of light troops, all intent on pillage, slaughter and violence, is so terrible and complicated a business that it is utterly beyond my strength. By now they have brought me 1,300 Jacobins; not knowing

where to shelter them I have sent them to the granaries near the bridge. They must have massacred or shot at least fifty in my presence without my being able to prevent it, and wounded at least two hundred, whom they even dragged here naked. Seeing me horrified at this spectacle, they console me by saying that the dead men were truly arch-villains, and that the wounded were out-and-out enemies of the human race, well known to the population. I hope it is true, and thus I set my mind at ease a little. By dint of precautions, edicts, patrols and preaching, the violence of the people has considerably abated, thank God. If we obtain the surrender of the two castles, I hope to restore calm here entirely, because I shall employ my troops with this object. It is certain that we are in a cruel plight, having to make war while dreading the enemy's destruction.... The castles have been attacked so vigorously during the night that they are half demolished. The bombs have had the greatest effect against the Castel Nuovo.... The armistice has lasted a few hours, and we are waiting to see if the surrender of the two castles aforementioned will be completed by this evening. The English commander grumbles because the truce involves such a waste of time, and he would like to end it; but the immense danger to the city must not be forgotten, thundered upon incessantly from Sant'Elmo. Meanwhile the populace, and many other outlaws who have come to fight for the King, besides eighty blasted Turks, are robbing and plundering without let or hindrance. Our better soldiers are guarding the houses against pillage, but with little purpose. Often the pretext is Jacobinism: that is what they call it, but in fact it is plunder that often produces Jacobin proprietors. I found the same in small places. To the cry of "Long Live the King!" they dare anything with impunity. It seems to me that this consideration should make us lenient with the rogues in the castles, and compassionate with the many guests locked up with them.

I do not know what the conditions will be, but they will certainly be very clement for a thousand motives which need not be enumerated, and which may be inferred from their antecedents. I do not believe it possible to restore order to the country in a short time without any system, but it would be quite impossible with a new method....
[Cited in Acton, *Bourbons*, pp. 388-89.]

CHAPTER 2. THE REVOLUTION OF 1799

Meanwhile, between June 21 and 23, the final arrangements for the surrender of the castles were concluded. By the terms of the treaty, the republicans were to hand over the forts without any further resistance. In return, Ruffo agreed to guarantee them free passage to France or free existence in Naples, and their persons and property were to be guaranteed.

The agreement produced a bitter reaction in Palermo. On June 20, as rumors of the cardinal's efforts to reach a compromise with the rebels began to circulate in the city, Ferdinand wrote:

> 37. It is bruited abroad that in the surrender of the castles all the rebels shut inside them will be allowed to leave safe and sound, even Caracciolo and Manthone, etc., and proceed to France. This I shall never believe, because God preserve us from them, to spare those savage vipers, and especially Caracciolo, who knows every inlet of our coastline, might inflict the greatest damage on us. [Acton, *Bourbons*, p. 391.]

And, five days later, on June 25, after the actual agreement had been concluded, Maria Carolina added in a letter to the wife of the English ambassador, the influential Lady Hamilton:

> 38. I have received your dear letters from on board, undated, as well as those of Sir William [Hamilton] to the General [Acton].... The General writes the King's wishes, and the King himself writes a note in his own hand for the dear Admiral. Conforming in all things to their will, I can do no less than tell you our own sentiment. From the 17th of this month until the 21st the Cardinal has not written to us. He has written very casually to the General, but not a single line to us. He says little of the negotiations, nothing of military operations and mentions very cursorily those he has appointed, many of whom were guilty, suspect and inadmissible. These are the foundations, according to the King and myself, which we submit to the excellent judgment, heart and mind of our dear Admiral Nelson. The rebels can receive no more help from the French either by land or sea. Consequently they are lost and at the mercy of the King, offended, betrayed, but clement. He offered them a first pardon, and instead of accepting it they defended themselves desperately.... It is therefore impossible for me to deal tenderly with this rebellious rabble.... The garrison of Sant'Elmo must retire, escorted to Marseilles or Toulon, without permission to remove anything. The rebels must lay down their arms and leave at the

King's discretion. Then, to my way of thinking, we must make an example of the leading representatives, and the others will be deported.... Note will be taken of these, and among them will be included the municipality, chiefs of brigades, members of clubs, and the most rabid scribblers. No soldier who has served them will be admitted into our army. Finally there must be an exact, prompt, just severity. The same should apply to the women who have distinguished themselves during the revolution, and that without pity....

The Cardinal must not appoint any official without proposing him beforehand. The sedili, the source of all our evils, the first real assembly of rebels, who ruined the Kingdom and dethroned the King, must be forever abolished, also the privileges and jurisdiction of the barons, to deliver from bondage a faithful people who have restored the King to his throne, from which the treachery, felony, and criminal indifference of the nobles had driven him. This may not be popular, but it is absolutely necessary; without it the King would only govern for six months in peace.... Finally, dear Milady, I recommend Lord Nelson to treat Naples as if it were a rebellious city in Ireland which had behaved in such a manner. We must have no regard for numbers: several thousands of villains less will make France the poorer, and we shall be better off. They deserve to be dropped in Africa or the Crimea. To throw them in France would be a charity. They ought to be branded so that nobody could be deceived by them. Thus I recommend to you, dear Milady, the greatest firmness, force, vigor and rigor. Our reputation and future tranquillity are concerned, and the loyal people desire it. [Acton, *Bourbons*, pp. 396-97.]

Maria Carolina's obvious coolness towards Ruffo and lauding of the British Admiral Nelson was not purely accidental. By this time, Ruffo was seen by the king and queen as a man of equivocation and weakness, and Nelson as a pillar of determination and strength. Ever since he had arrived in Naples in September 1798, in fact, the victor of the battle of Aboukir had been treated by the royal family as a member of the Neapolitan inner circle, and it was largely on his advice — as well as that of Acton and Hamilton — that the king had decided to drive the French from Rome. Now, with his policy in shambles and the royal family in exile, he, like the monarchy itself, was eager to gain retribution on all those who had obstructed his plans. On June 21, therefore, when under the pressure of events communication had broken down between Naples and Palermo, Ferdinand asked Nelson to go to the capital

CHAPTER 2. THE REVOLUTION OF 1799

as his special representative, and to repudiate any concessions towards the rebels that might have been made by Ruffo. Three days later, Nelson arrived in the harbor with a fleet of eighteen warships and instituted a policy of unbridled repression. The treaty with the republicans was repudiated. All republican leaders and suspected sympathizers — a total that eventually numbered over 8,000 people — were arrested and charged with sedition. Public trials were held for all of the leaders and a series of gruesome executions — by firing squad, beheading, or hanging depending on the crime and station of the individual — took place before bloodthirsty crowds. Overall, more than 100 people were executed. Among them were some of the major figures of Neapolitan aristocratic and intellectual life: Admiral Francesco Caracciolo, Mario and Ferdinando Pignatelli di Strongoli, Ettore Carafa, Francesco Conforti, Domenico Cirillo, Giuseppe Riario Sforza, Niccola de Meo, Pasquale Baffi, Mario Pagano, Gennaro Serra, Vincenzo Ruffo, and Eleonora Fonseca de Pimentel. Another 510 people were condemned to life imprisonment or deportation, and over 300 more to shorter terms. The impact on Neapolitan intellectual and cultural development was horrendous. In 1813, the English poet, Robert Southey, who would be named poet laureate two years later, described the trial and execution of Caracciolo in his famous biography of Nelson as follows:

> 39. Caracciolo was brought on board [ship] at nine in the forenoon, and the trial began at ten. It lasted two hours. He averred in his defense that he had acted under compulsion, having been compelled to serve as a common soldier, till he consented to take command of the fleet. This...he failed in proving...for he was brought to trial within an hour after he was legally in arrest; and how, in that time, was he to collect witnesses? He was found guilty, and sentenced to death; and Nelson gave orders that the sentence should be carried into effect that evening, at five o'clock, on the Sicilian frigate *La Minerve*, by hanging him at the fore-yard-arm till sunset, when the body was to be cut down and thrown into the sea. Caracciolo requested that Lieutenant Parkinson, under whose custody he was placed, to intercede with Nelson for a second trial — for this, among other reasons, that Count Thurn, who presided at the court-martial, was a notoriously personal enemy. Nelson made answer that the prisoner had been fairly tried by the officers of his own country, and he could not interfere, forgetting that if he felt himself justified in ordering the trial and execution, no human being could have ever questioned the propriety of his interfering on the side of mercy. Caracciolo then entreated that he might be shot. "I

am an old man, sir", he said; "I leave no family to lament me, and therefore cannot be supposed to be very anxious about prolonging my life, but the disgrace of being hanged is dreadful to me." When this was repeated to Nelson, he only told the lieutenant, with much agitation, to go and attend his duty. As a last hope Caracciolo asked the lieutenant if he thought an application to Lady Hamilton would be beneficial. Parkinson went to see her. She was not to be seen on this occasion — but she was present at the execution. She had the most devoted attachment to the Neapolitan court; and the hatred which she felt against those whom she regarded as its enemies made her at this time forget what was due to the character of her sex, as well as of her country....

[After the execution] the body was carried out to a considerable distance, and sunk in the bay, with three double-headed shot, weighing two hundred and fifty pounds, tied to its legs. Between two and three weeks afterwards, when the king was on board the Foudroyant, a Neapolitan fisherman came to the ship, and solemnly declared that Caracciolo had risen from the bottom of the sea, and was coming as fast as he could to Naples, swimming half out of the water. Such an account was listened to like a tale of idle credulity. The day being fair, Nelson, to please the king, stood out to sea; but the ship had not proceeded far before a body was distinctly seen, upright in the water, and approaching them. It was soon recognized to be, indeed, the corpse of Caracciolo, which had risen and floated, while the great weights attached to the legs kept the body in position like that of a living man. A fact so extraordinary astonished the king, and perhaps excited some feeling of superstitious fear akin to regret. He gave permission for the body to be taken on shore and receive a Christian burial. [Robert Southey, *The Life of Lord Nelson*. London: J.M. Dent, 1906, pp. 151-55.]

The hatred that the *lazzaroni* felt for the revolutionaries often degenerated into blatant sadism. When Eleonora Pimentel was executed on August 20, the entire Piazza del Carmine filled with people. Giuliano Colonna and Gennaro Serra, who went first, were decapitated, and several others were hung, including Pimentel. As she fell, the crowd let out a tremendous roar, several people pulled on the legs of her lifeless body, and the air was filled with sexual barbs. When the Bianchi, a religious order whose vow was to comfort and give spiritual assistance to the condemned, asked for

CHAPTER 2. THE REVOLUTION OF 1799

more time to minister to one of those sentenced to death, the military junta that ran the city sent a note to its leader:

> 40. I have to inform you that the execution must be carried out absolutely at twelve o'clock because afterwards there is to be a drawing of the Lotto, and, therefore, I beg you to send the exhorting fathers to the prison of the Vicaria [early]. "Thus," commented the still-to-be-executed Conforti, "the good populus would not miss the double diversion at the gallows and the Lottery." [Cited in Gigliotti, pp. 345-46.]

On August 29, Ferdinand, who like the rest of royal entourage, was eager to see the whole affair finished, wrote to the now powerless and largely discredited Ruffo:

> 41. The state junta must act with dispatch in all of its operations, and not submit vague and generalized orders. When orders are issued, they must be carried out and verified within 24 hours, the leaders seized, and, without the slightest bit of ceremony, hanged. I hope that the sentence that I am told is to be carried out on Monday has not been delayed; if you show fear, you are done for.... [Things must be done] as simply and as quickly as possible, without making the populace wait for hours or become impatient. [Ferdinand to Ruffo, Palermo, August 29, 1799, in Cimbalo, p. 85.]

Thus ended the Neapolitan Revolution of 1799.

■ ■ ■

6. *Joachim Murat, c. 1813*

3
Joseph I and Murat, 1806–1815

The collapse of the Parthenopean Republic ushered in a tense period in the history of Franco-Neapolitan relations. In September 1799, the Neapolitan army, taking advantage of the vacuum created by the French retreat to the north, reoccupied Rome. One month later, a combined Austro-Russian force of 60,000 men — having destroyed the main body of French troops in the Po Valley — bottled up the last two French armies in the peninsula in Genoa and Ancona, and virtually all of northern and central Italy fell into the Second Coalition's hands. By early December, the French-dominated Cisalpine and Roman Republics — like the Parthenopean Republic before them — had disappeared from the political map of Europe, and the victory of the monarchical powers in Italy seemed complete.

The change in fortune, however, proved to be brief. In December 1799, Napoleon Bonaparte — citing the danger posed to France by the collapse of her satellite states in Italy and Germany — overthrew the Directory in Paris and established himself as de facto head of the republican regime. Taking command of the Army of Italy, he immediately crossed the Alps and descended into Lombardy, crushing the Austrians at Marengo in June 1800 and forcing the Austrian and Russian empires to accept a humiliating peace.

In February 1801, he sent an ultimatum to the Neapolitan government. Incensed by what he viewed as the irrational hatred of the Bourbons, he threatened to attack Naples with 40,000 men unless the Neapolitans (who had foolishly occupied Siena during the fighting) withdrew from the war and evacuated central Italy — adding that only then could the decade-long hostility between the two powers permanently cease. Ferdinand — confused, frightened, and still clinging to the safety of his perch in Palermo — quickly capitulated. On March 29, 1801, therefore, after over a month of negotiation, the two countries announced the conclusion of the Treaty of Florence. Under its terms, the Neapolitans agreed to the evacuation of the Papal States and Tuscany, the payment of a war indemnity of 120,000 ducats and the release of all French political prisoners, and the right of French troops to occupy the port cities of the Abruzzi and Otranto as long as France and England remained at war. Maria

Carolina, who was informed of the terms of the treaty while visiting her daughter in Vienna, commented despondently:

> 42. We have become a Gallo-Spanish province.... The whole treaty is infamous and...the Kingdom of Naples is lost beyond a doubt. Let us save Sicily if possible, and humour allies who will help us to recover Naples at the general peace. Although but a stripped skeleton, at least let my children's patrimony be restored. Our ally can only be England. We must implore her to save and assist us and regard our weaknesses as committed with a pistol at our throat.... I had previously declared what I confirm again, that I should never be able to agree with the French on account of the implacable hatred I bear them, my principles which forbid me to condescend, and the attentions one has to show them now that they are masters in our house. Owing to this inability, I would be more injurious than useful to the King's service. [Cited in Acton, *Bourbons*, p. 448.]

At first, the queen's fears clearly seemed to be exaggerated. On March 25, 1802, Napoleon, seeking to consolidate his position at home and gain international recognition for France's conquests abroad, concluded the Peace of Amiens with Great Britain. Under the terms of the treaty, the British agreed to evacuate Malta in return for a French promise to withdraw from the Kingdom of Naples — a commitment that Bonaparte duly honored the following May. In June, Ferdinand — having spent over two-and-a-half years in exile in Palermo — finally judged the situation on the mainland stable enough to return to the capital. Entering Naples on horseback from Portici on the 27th, a crowd of over 600,000 people lined the streets to give him a tumultuous welcome — as an estimated 200,000 royalist supporters arrived from the countryside to join with the *lazzaroni* in a near hysterical display. One eyewitness to the event, the newly-appointed French ambassador to Naples, Baron Alquier, described the scene as follows:

> 43. Fixed stations had been assigned to the various groups of officials, where appropriate speeches were to be addressed to the King. But this solemn homage was drowned by the tumultuous acclamations of the mob, who cherish a love for Ferdinand IV of which this monarch is well worthy. The pomp of his triumphal march was interrupted to such an extent that the King took more than four hours to traverse a distance that usually takes a little over half an hour, and the lazzaroni would have thrown him from his horse if the transports of their excitement had not been subdued by clubbings.... The diplomatic corps were waiting at the palace, where

CHAPTER 3. JOSEPH I AND MURAT

I was presented by Lord Acton. [As he entered] the King's passage was adorned with temples, porticos and triumphal arches, whose inscriptions recalled the wonders of his reign, and everywhere the titles of invincible and peacemaker were attached to his name....
[Acton, *Bourbons*, pp. 455-56.]

One month later, the queen returned to the capital almost unnoticed from Vienna. Fifty-one years old and exhausted by seventeen children and a decade of turmoil, her once-dominant hold over the king and his ministers was now a thing of the past. In January 1803, Alquier wrote:

44. The Queen is neither good or bad. Born with a great deal of intelligence and natural grace, and, thanks to her education, endowed with more knowledge than women usually possess, she had a fair claim to govern when she came to Naples and found a man on the throne incapable of governing. A relish for pleasure was mingled with a passion to dominate, hence the double intrigues in politics and gallantry; hence also the infinite contradictions which have irritated the most irritable mind that ever was. The Queen's life is a prolonged crisis of vapours, and it is owing to this restless constitution that she has been successively a tender friend or an implacable foe, lenient or vindictive, pious or frivolous, a mistress without restraint and excessively jealous; and that on the same day she is busy intriguing with Vienna, London and Petersburg and prying into the domestic affairs of a Neapolitan burgess....

Her mind, displaced from the feminine sphere and tormented by an ambition to direct policy, has degenerated into a habit of mischief-making which had always been disastrous to the Queen and the kingdom and sometimes, perhaps, to Europe. The Queen hates us assuredly; how can she fail to hate us? Does not the legitimacy of her resentment justify the animosity she bears us? The necessity to intrigue and interfere worries her still, and will never be extinguished. She spends her days in her study and at her desk, and no minister writes so many letters as the Queen of Naples. But the distance from affairs to which Chevalier Acton had driven her has greatly diminished the importance of this activity, and since she cannot correspond with Cabinets she is busy with cafe spying. Another taste which has been conspicuous in her life, that of pleasure, has not abandoned her.... In a private condition she would have produced the same results: she would have been the delight of a few men, but she would have been the torment of her husband and the terror of the neighbourhood. [Acton, *Bourbons*, pp. 468-69.]

The decline in the influence of the queen over governmental policy was accompanied, ironically, by the virtual collapse of Neapolitan relations with France. On May 13, 1803, the British government — which, despite the Peace of Amiens, had never abandoned its primary aim of preserving the balance of power in Europe — ordered British warships to resume the policy of capturing French commercial vessels at sea without prior warning, a policy that it well understood was tantamount to a new declaration of war. Two days later, Napoleon, angered by what he viewed as British perfidy, responded by ordering French troops to occupy Hanover (of which the king of England was the elector), and informed the Neapolitan government that, due to the threat posed by the British to French interests in the Mediterranean, he was sending 15,000 soldiers to reestablish control over the kingdom's southernmost ports. The announcement provoked a bitter reaction from Maria Carolina. On June 13, she wrote to Gallo (who had just been appointed Neapolitan ambassador in Paris):

> 45. I cannot express to you the profound sadness which the wretched and dishonest entry of the French into our country has caused me; and at a moment when we have fulfilled all of the onerous conditions of the peace. By force of arms, they have compelled us, violently and with no other legal right than that of raw power, to accept 15,000 French troops on our territory.... I can see no other reason for this decision than the desire to invade us.... I hope that the English have enough compassion not to seize the ports of Sicily. I say this as the Queen of Naples; but if I were head of the English government, I would have already begun it. Such is the ruinous position that the Corsican Despot has put us in...
>
> The King is furious: he is in such a rage that I fear for his health and sanity, and for the things that, in his anger, he might do in the future. Abdication? Flight to Palermo? Seclusion? Combat? One thought follows the other without resolution. My position is horrible.... We are too old to agree compliantly to serve as a stepping stone for the Little Corsican. [Cited in Lacour-Gayet, p. 232.]

From the very first moment that French troops reentered Neapolitan territory, it was clear that one of Napoleon's primary aims was the removal of Acton. Despite his recognition of the role that Maria Carolina had traditionally played in exacerbating relations between the two countries, he still correctly viewed Acton as the key to Neapolitan policy, and believed that it was essential that the Neapolitan prime

CHAPTER 3. JOSEPH I AND MURAT

minister be dismissed. When, therefore, the queen sent him a letter protesting against the French occupation as a violation of Neapolitan neutrality, he responded coldly:

> 46. I have read your Majesty's letter with great attention, and I beg you will be persuaded that after having done you a great deal of harm, I desire to make myself agreeable.
>
> At the present juncture it is the policy of France to consolidate tranquillity among her neighbors, and to aid a feeble state whose welfare is useful to the prosperity of French commerce.
>
> I desire to reply to your Majesty in the most unreserved manner. In what light must I consider the Kingdom of Naples, geographically and politically speaking, when I see at the head of the administration a foreigner who has centered all his affections and invested all of his wealth in England? And yet the Kingdom of Naples is governed less by the will of its sovereign than by those of its first minister.
>
> I have decided therefore by way of precaution to look upon Naples as a country governed by an English minister. *It is repugnant to my feelings to meddle with the internal affairs of other states;* it is only in order to be sincere towards your Majesty that I have acquainted you with the real reason which justifies all the measures adopted towards Naples....
> [Napoleon to Maria Carolina, July 28, 1803, in D. A. Bingham, ed. *A Selection from the Letters and Dispatches of the First Napoleon*. London: Chapman and Hall, 1884, 2:22. Italics in text.]

Napoleon's reoccupation of Apulia and expression of dissatisfaction with Acton were only the opening salvos in what proved to be a steadily intensifying campaign of intimidation against Naples. After his assumption of the title of Emperor in May 1804, in particular, his willingness to tolerate even a modicum of independence among the smaller states of Europe quickly evaporated, and his determination to reduce Naples to an instrument of French policy rapidly increased. On May 27, Ferdinand, who had earlier stated that he would rather abdicate than part with his prime minister, reluctantly dismissed Acton, and replaced him with Antonio Micheroux, who had proved himself to be far more solicitous of the emperor's interests during his negotiation of the Treaty of Florence with France. One month later, Maria Carolina, who had adopted the habit of filling the air with epithets every time Bonaparte's name was mentioned, wrote indignantly to Gallo:

> 47. It was not worth the trouble to condemn and slaughter the best of kings, dishonor and revile a woman, a daughter of Maria Theresa, a holy princess, to wallow in massacres, shootings, drownings, and

kill six hundred prelates in a church, perpetuating horrors of the most barbarous ages at home and abroad, writing whole libraries on liberty, happiness, etc., and at the end of fourteen years become abject slaves of a little Corsican whom an incredible fortune enabled to exploit all means to succeed, marrying without honor or decency the cast-off strumpet of whom the murderer Barras was surfeited, Turkish or Mohammedan in Egypt, atheist at the start, dragging the Pope after him and leaving him to die in prison, a devout Catholic after that, practicing every deceit, shortening the lives and normal careers of sovereigns who might assert themselves, only allowing dummies to vegetate, then atrociously, without a shadow of justice, assassinating the Duc d'Enghien, plotting himself (and he did not blush to admit it, so blinded is he by his passion) a conspiracy to victimize the rulers he still feared, and on top of all these abominations he is acclaimed Emperor: he and his race of Corsican bastards are to dominate almost half of Europe, yet every thinking person is not revolted. Far from it, their egoism and weakness are such that they study how low they can prostrate themselves before the new idol.... Send me word of the august Emperor's intentions regarding Italy: whether he will deign to accept us as slaves or will leave us in our obscurity.... Tell me what the other Powers are saying. I imagine a *Gloria in Excelsis Demonio* will be the general refrain....

And then she added on Ferdinand:

The King is always at Belvedere. He comes here occasionally for a few minutes. At other times, I go there, which is very trying in the awful heat and dust. We are entirely separated and have to write each other everything.... The Prince attends Councils in his father's absence, and I only attend them on the King's account.... The King dislikes the city and Portici, which bore him, and longs for solitude, as he cannot adapt or subject himself to the supremacy of the French, and be ordered about by them or Bonaparte. He only sighs for Sicily, which he prefers, as he has never been offended or insulted there. In fact he is in a state of fury which depresses me. He is very determined not to receive Alquier's credentials but to let his son represent him...because he declares he would have convulsions or a stroke, which would kill him. In fact, it is beyond

CHAPTER 3. JOSEPH I AND MURAT

belief the rage that is consuming him.... [Maria Carolina to Gallo, June 6, 1804, cited in Acton, *Bourbons*, pp. 490-91.]

Given the unrelenting hostility of the royal family, it is small wonder that Napoleon continued to tighten his grip on the kingdom. In August 1804, he sent 8,000 additional troops to Taranto to reinforce the French garrison in the Mediterranean and demanded that General Damas, a French émigré who had been selected by Ferdinand to reorganize the Neapolitan army, be dismissed. When Ferdinand unexpectedly complied, he refused to be satisfied and insisted that all other foreigners in Neapolitan service should be excluded as well. Nothing, in fact, could alter his belief that the king and queen were secretly plotting against him. On January 2, 1805, after receiving yet another letter from Maria Carolina in which she complained of the bullying of the French ambassador and offered a pledge of Neapolitan friendship and neutrality, he responded acidly:

48. Your letter has been handed to me by the marquis de Gallo. It is difficult to reconcile the sentiments it contains with the hostile projects current at Naples. I have in my hands several letters by Your Majesty which leave no doubt with regard to your secret intentions. No matter what hatred which your Majesty bears France, after the experience you have had of the love of your husband, of your children, of your family, and of your subjects, how comes it that you are not more reserved and do not adopt a line of policy more in conformity with your interests? Cannot your Majesty, who is distinguished among women for your wit, divest yourself of the prejudices of your sex? How can you treat the affairs of your state as love affairs? You have lost your kingdom once already; twice you have been the cause of a war which threatened the total destruction of your paternal house: do you wish then to cause a third war? Already on demand of your ambassador at St. Petersburg 10,000 Russians have been sent to Corfu. What! Is your hatred so implacable, and your love for England so ardent, that you wish, although certain to become the first victim, to set the continent in a blaze, in order to operate a diversion in favour of England? I acknowledge that I should conceive some esteem for such violent passions did the most simple ideas of common sense not make me feel their frivolity and impotence.... Let your Majesty listen to this prophecy: On the occasion of the first war you cause, you and your posterity will cease to reign, and your children, wandering through the different parts of Europe, will demand succor for their parents....

> I have no intention of playing court to your Majesty in this letter; that would be disagreeable to you. However, you may see in it a mark of my esteem. It is only to a person possessed of a force of character far above the ordinary run that I should give myself the trouble of writing so freely.... [Napoleon to Maria Carolina, January 2, 1805, in Bingham, *Letters and Dispatches* 2:114-15.]

From then on, a renewal of hostilities between the two powers seemed inevitable. In July 1805, Austria, Russia, and England — fearful, as always, of French ambitions in Germany and Italy — joined to form the Third Coalition. Maria Carolina, who had remained in contact with the three powers throughout the negotiations, wanted to adhere to the new alliance immediately; but Gallo urged caution, and Ferdinand opted for a more prudent course.

Two months later, Napoleon, faced with the emergency created by the advance of Austro-Russian forces in Central Europe, offered to conclude a formal treaty of neutrality with Naples. Under the terms of the proposal, the French promised to withdraw their troops from Apulia in return for a Neapolitan pledge to exclude British and Russian ships from Neapolitan ports. On October 4, Ferdinand, acting once again on the advice of Gallo, formally signed the agreement; but, at the same time, he secretly informed the Russians that he had no intention of keeping it, since the presence of French troops on Neapolitan territory, he believed, had given him no other choice. On November 19, therefore, after the French had left, he publicly repudiated the agreement, and allowed 20,000 British and Russian soldiers to enter the kingdom unopposed.

The deception would cost the Bourbons dearly. On December 27, 1805, Napoleon — having achieved a spectacular victory over the Austrians and Russians at Austerlitz — issued his famous "Declaration of Schonbrunn." In it, he announced his decision to conquer the Kingdom of Naples and declared that Bourbon dynasty had come to an end:

> 49. Soldiers!
> For ten years I have done everything to save the King of Naples; and he has done everything to ruin himself.
> After the battles of Dego, Mondovi, and Lodi, he could have resisted me but feebly: I trusted him and treated him with generosity.
> After the second coalition was broken at Marengo, the King of Naples, who had been the first to begin that unjust war, abandoned at Luneville by his allies, stood alone and defenseless. He entreated, and I pardoned him a second time.

CHAPTER 3. JOSEPH I AND MURAT

A few months ago you were at the gates of Naples. I had sufficient reason to suspect the treachery which was meditated, and to revenge the outrages which I had received. I was again generous: I acknowledged the neutrality of Naples, and directed you to quit the Kingdom: for the third time the House of Naples was saved and re-established.

Shall we pardon a fourth time? Shall we trust a fourth time a court without faith, or honour, or intelligence? No! No! The Neapolitan dynasty has ceased to reign, its existence is incompatible with the tranquillity of Europe and the honour of my crown.

Soldiers, march; throw into the waves, if they wait for you, the weak battalions of the tyrant of the seas. Show the world how we punish treachery. Let me hear without delay that all Italy is subject to my authority or that of my allies: that the finest of countries is relieved from the most faithless of men: that the sacredness of treaties has been avenged: and that the manes of my brave soldiers, massacred in the ports of Sicily, on their return from Egypt, after having escaped from the desert and from a hundred battles, are at length appeased.

Soldiers, my brother marches at your head. He knows my plans, he possesses my authority and confidence. Give to him yours. [Napoleon, "Declaration of Schonbrunn," in *The Confidential Correspondence of Napoleon Bonaparte with His Brother Joseph*. New York: D. Appleton, 1856, 1:80-81.]

Four days later, he wrote to his brother Joseph in Paris:

50. I am at Munich. I shall remain here a few days to receive the ratification of the treaty, and to give to the army its last orders.

I intend to take possession of the kingdom of Naples. Marshall Massena and General Saint-Cyr are marching on that kingdom with two corps-d'armée. I have named you my Lieutenant commander-in-chief of the army of Naples.

Set off for Rome forty hours after the receipt of this letter, and let your first dispatch inform me that you have entered Naples, driven out the treacherous Court, and subjected that part of Italy to our authority.

You will find at the headquarters of the army the decrees and instructions relating to your mission.

You will wear the uniform of a general of the division. As my lieutenant, you have all the marshals under your orders. Your command does not extend beyond the army and Neapolitan territory. If my presence were not necessary in Paris I would march myself on Naples; but with the generals whom you have, and the instructions which you will receive, you will do all that I could. Do not say whither you are going, except to the Arch-Chancellor; let it be known only by your letters from the army. [December 31, 1805, *Confidential Correspondence* 1:78-79.]

And, again, from Stuttgart on January 19:

51. I wish you to enter the Kingdom of Naples in the first days of February, and I wish to hear from you, in the course of February, that our flag is flying on the walls of that capital. You will make no truce, you will hear no capitulation: my will is that the Bourbons shall have ceased to reign at Naples. I intend to seat on that throne a prince of my own house. In the first place, you, if it suits you; if not another. I repeat, do not divide your forces; let all your army pass the Apennines, and let your three corps march on Naples, so disposed as to be able to join in one day on one field of battle. Leave a general, some depots, some stores, and some artillerymen in Ancona for its defense. Naples, once taken, the distant parts of the kingdom will fall to you for themselves. The enemy in the Abruzzi will be taken in the rear, and you will send a division to Taranto, and another towards the Kingdom of Sicily, to conquer that Kingdom. I intend to leave under your orders the Kingdom of Naples, all this year, and afterwards, until I make some new disposition, 14 regiments of French infantry and 12 regiments of French cavalry, all on a full war establishment. The country must find provisions, clothes, remounts, and all that is necessary for your army, so that it may not cost me a farthing. My troops belonging to the Kingdom of Italy will not remain in the Kingdom of Naples longer than you think necessary, after which they will return home. You will raise a Neapolitan legion, into which you will admit only Neapolitan officers and soldiers, such as choose to adhere to me. [Napoleon to Joseph, January 19, 1806, *Confidential Correspondence* 1:83.]

Faced with Napoleon's determination to overrun the kingdom, the only question remaining was whether the British and Russians would join in its common defense. On November 19, 1805, when the forces of the two powers had entered the country,

CHAPTER 3. JOSEPH I AND MURAT

they had solemnly pledged to defend the nation against outside aggression. Three months later, however, with a French army massing in Central Italy, they quickly reassessed their position, and decided to beat a hasty retreat. On January 6, 1806, Maria Carolina — who, like the king, was stunned by the allies' decision — wrote despairingly to General Damas:

> 52. We live in an abominable age, when honest people are victims.... What times, what horrors! No treaty is sacred; everything is violated. The Russian Emperor is also withdrawing his troops from Holland: this delivers us, bound hand and foot, to the French whom they enticed here; and I see our ruin is certain beyond repair.... It must be admitted that we have been thoroughly duped. [Cited in Acton, *Bourbons*, p. 525.]

Isolated and desperate, the queen decided on one last, dramatic attempt to save the country: she appealed directly to Napoleon. In an extraordinary letter written on January 7, she begged the emperor to forgive her past transgressions, and pledged her eternal friendship if only he would allow the kingdom to survive:

> 53. Victims of the most egotistical and perfidious policy, drawn into the struggle by force of circumstance and then abandoned into the abyss by our so-called friends and allies, the flag with which they have for so long blinded us, *me in particular*, has been torn to shreds forever.
> Your Royal and Imperial Majesty has just provided definitive proof of his military greatness and glory. All that remains left for him to do is to cover himself in new glory by giving to the sovereigns whom he has conquered so easily an example of his generosity, especially in victory, by putting aside all resentment.... It is in ceasing to be an enemy of Your Royal and Imperial Majesty that I appeal to his generosity.... It is as a wife, doubly as a mother of my children and my subjects, who, like me, are victims of the blind faith which I once placed in our egotistical allies and friends. It is by not seeking to hide the truth and admitting the mistakes that I have made, and wishing to make amends for them,... that I do not blush when I ask Your Royal and Imperial Majesty to forget the past, and to establish the basis for a long and sincere relationship which will replace the mutual enmity that has existed between us for far too long.... [Maria Carolina to Napoleon, January 7, 1806, in M.-H. Weil and C.D. Di Somma Circello, eds. *Correspondence Inedité de*

Marie-Caroline, Reine de Naples e de Sicilie, avec le Marquis de Gallo. Paris: Emile-Paul, 1911, 2:656-57. Italics in text.]

And, in an accompanying letter to Gallo, she wrote even more abjectly:

> 54. My letter is frank and sincere.... If I am personally an obstacle to peace, and the emperor asks me to come to Paris as a hostage, I will do so with pleasure and inner peace; if it will only save my country, the patrimony of my children, and serve the welfare of my subjects.
>
> If it is a personal hatred against me, it can be satisfied completely, for I am the most unhappy of human beings and would take my own life if my religion did not forbid it. Sacrifice, if necessary, my personal interests, provided that our country remains in the hands of our son...and we are the only ones sacrificed. [Maria Carolina to Gallo, January 7, 1806, in Lacour-Gayet, p. 302.]

No amount of pleading, however, could convince Napoleon to alter his decision. On January 27, on the very day that he received Maria Carolina's letter, he wrote to his brother Joseph:

> 55.1. ...I reckon on your entering the kingdom of Naples the first week in February. Let nothing affect your plans....
>
> I have this instant received a letter from the Queen of Naples, begging for quarter; I shall not answer it. Do not answer any that you may receive from her. If she sends anyone to you, let her messenger be told that your orders are to occupy Naples. After her breach of treaty, I trust none of her promises. [*Confidential Correspondence* 1:84.]

And, again, on January 30, with even greater determination:

> 55.2. I suppose that by the time you receive this letter you will be master of Naples. I can only repeat to you my former instructions and my intention to conquer the kingdom of Naples and Sicily. As soon as you are master of Naples you will send two corps, one towards Taranto, the other towards Sicily. You will affirm in the strongest manner that the King of Naples will never sit again on that throne, that his removal is necessary to the peace of the Continent, which he has troubled twice. You will insert in your general orders the enclosed proclamation [of December 27]. [*Confidential Correspondence* 1:85.]

Napoleon's unwillingness to accept anything less than the total conquest of the kingdom led to a panicky attempt to flee the capital. On January 10, 1806, the British and

CHAPTER 3. JOSEPH I AND MURAT

Russians unceremoniously disembarked from Naples. Two weeks later on January 23, the king — who had been looking for an excuse to return to Sicily since the spring— once again departed for Palermo. In early February, Gallo, who had been the queen's closest confidant for more than two decades and was one of the country's ablest diplomats, deserted the Bourbons and swore allegiance to Joseph. As for the queen herself, she remained in Naples until February 11 — five days longer than the hereditary prince (the future Francis I), and one day longer than the Neapolitan army itself.

When the French arrived before the city on February 14, therefore, they found it completely undefended. De Nicola, who had refused to leave the capital despite its abandonment by the king and royal advisors, described their entry into the city as follows:

> 56. Today the French army began its entry into Naples by marching down the Via Toledo. At its head was a detachment of cavalry, followed by the infantry, which dragged their artillery and munitions behind them, and had several loaves of bread fixed on their bayonets. Trailing the procession was a herd of cattle. As the army arrived, the city was struck by a tremendous rainstorm; but that did not prevent the troops from advancing; nor did it discourage the large crowd of spectators that jammed the balconies, windows, sidewalks, and streets. Overall, the soldiers passed by quietly, without incident, and in good order. The time of passage was about an hour, and the size of the force numbered roughly 15,000 men. [De Nicola, *Diario Napoletano* 2:205.]

One day later, Joseph arrived amid the sound of marching bands and booming cannons. Proceeding directly to the royal palace, he immediately issued an Italian translation of Napoleon's Declaration of December 27, and then, in an act of inspiration, set off for the Duomo where he placed a diamond necklace on the statue of San Gennaro. At the same time, he issued a second, more moderate declaration of his own:

> 57. People of Naples.
> You have nothing to fear. It is not against you that this war is directed. Your churches, your priests, your laws, your property, and your persons will be respected. The French soldiers are your brothers. [Proclamation cited in *Storia di Napoli*. Napoli: Società Editrice Storia di Napoli, 1967-1978, 9:38.]

This conciliatory approach — backed, as it was, by the might of a 15,000-man army — proved to be totally successful. On February 15, the Council of Regency, which had been left to govern the city after the departure of Francis, capitulated completely. Despite the express orders of the prince not to surrender the fortresses, it turned them over to the French without resistance, and added the surrounding islands of Ischia and Procida as well. As for the *lazzaroni*, it accepted the French occupation with relative indifference. Exhausted by the fighting seven years earlier, it had once again witnessed the desertion of the city by the king in the face of the enemy, and was unwilling to spill its blood in an hopeless struggle for a second time. In commenting upon these events, the Neapolitan General Damas wrote bitterly:

> 58. There is an enormous difference between the present loss of the kingdom and that of 1799: the weak, the discontented, the indifferent, and the timid look upon Joseph Bonaparte as a king, and the people look upon the new government more as a change of dynasty than the creation of a constitutional republic. The weak minded will have a court, and the proud and lazy will be given responsibilities there; the soldiers will be given the false hope that they will no longer have to make war;...the women will have French lovers; the people may pay less in taxes and Acton will not be permitted to return: these are the conditions that will allow the country to grow accustomed to the new regime. [Baron de Damas, *Memoires,* in Lacour- Gayet, p. 308.]

■

The ten years that followed the French reoccupation of Naples in 1806 have gone down in Neapolitan history as *"Il decennio"*: the decade of French domination. There were two French kings of Naples: Joseph I (1806–1808) and Joachim Murat (1808–1815). "Giuseppe Napoleone I," as he was known to the Neapolitans, was Napoleon's elder brother and had been his faithful companion for more than ten years. Talented, educated, and well meaning, he took his new position seriously; but he lacked political experience and had none of his brother's genius for military affairs. His love for Naples was immediate: from his very first days in the city, he was mesmerized by its beauty and exotic culture and aimed to establish himself as a benevolent and popular king. Throughout his reign, in fact, he resisted Napoleon's demands that Naples be treated as a conquered country. Instead, he lavished money on the Neapolitan theater and men of letters and sought to maintain many of the practices of the Bourbon regime. Although he had a reputation as a republican (Napoleon himself had once referred to him as "Prince Egalité"), he basked in the glory of royal

CHAPTER 3. JOSEPH I AND MURAT

splendor — creating his own coat of arms and chivalric order, and even insisting that the ladies of the court assemble each evening to kiss his hand.

Joseph's pretensions to political independence proved to be a continuous source of irritation to Napoleon. Although he had more confidence in Joseph than in any other member of the Bonaparte family, his need to dominate policy in all parts of the empire was overwhelming, and he was determined to demonstrate his control over the kingdom from the start. On February 27, therefore, less than two weeks after Joseph had entered the city, he wrote to him firmly:

> 59. I have ordered 500,000 francs in gold to be sent from Milan to Naples.... I am waiting for your next courier to tell you to take the title of King of Naples. You may in the meanwhile give the name of the ministers to those whom you appoint members of the government. I have already told you that you may have all the Neapolitan officers you like. By this time you can no longer be in want of money. Disarm Naples, and levy contributions of 10 millions upon the town; it will be easily paid. You may safely resort to confiscating all the English merchandise. The loss will fall upon the part of the population that deserves the least consideration. I have sent you some naval officers. I congratulate you upon your reconciliation with San Gennaro. But I suppose that, not withstanding this, you have occupied the forts; that you have taken care to garrison and provision them; that you have disarmed the town, and been rather severe in your government. Many things belonging to the palaces have been removed and concealed. You ought to get them restored. Disarm the populace; send away strangers, the Russians, the English, and even Italians who are not Neapolitans.
>
> Make your army rich, but do not let them rob. [*Confidential Correspondence* 1:92-93.]

And, again, on March 5, after receiving a letter from Joseph complaining of disorders in the city:

> 60. I have your letter of February 22. Let the *lazzaroni* who use the dagger be shot without mercy. It is only by a salutary terror that you will keep an Italian populace in awe. The least that the conquest of Naples must do for you is afford supplies for your army of 40,000 men. Lay a contribution of 30 millions on the whole kingdom. Your conduct wants decision: your soldiers and your generals ought to live in plenty. Of course you will call together the priests, and declare them responsible for any disorder. The *lazzaroni* must have chiefs; let them answer

for the rest. Whatever you do, you will have an insurrection. Disarm. You say nothing about the forts: if necessary, do as I did in Cairo; prepare three or four batteries whose shells can reach every part of Naples. You may not use them, but their mere existence will strike terror. The kingdom of Naples is not exhausted; you can always get money, since there are royal fiefs and taxes which have been granted away. Take care not to confirm these ancient abuses. In a fortnight or three weeks, by a decree of yours or mine, they must be repealed. Every alienation of the royal domains, or of the taxes, though its existence may be immemorial, must be annulled, and a system of taxation, equal and severe, must be established. Naples, even without Sicily, ought to give you 100 millions.... You have no money, but you have a good army and a good country to supply you.... Two regiments of cavalry, two battalions of light infantry, and a company of artillery could put to flight all the mob of Naples. But the first of all things is to have money, and you can get it only in Naples. A contribution of 30 millions will provide for everything, and put you at ease.... Naples is richer than Vienna, and not so exhausted.... Expect no money from me. The 500,000 francs in gold that I sent to you are the last that I shall send to Naples. I care not so much about three or four millions as about the principle. Raise 30 millions, pay your army, treat well your generals and commanders, put your materiel in order. [*Confidential Correspondence* 1:95-96.]

Napoleon's admonition "not to confirm these ancient abuses" set the stage for the great period of Neapolitan reform. Everywhere the French armies went they carried with them the reforms of the Revolution, and it was no different in Naples. Joseph, in fact, was an avid reformer, although his desire for autonomy and popularity often caused him to moderate Napoleon's more radical demands. During his reign, he cleared away much of the debris of the previous centuries and initiated many of the changes later consolidated by Murat.

Foremost among these changes was the abolition of feudalism. On August 2, 1806 (the fifteenth anniversary of the end of feudalism in France), he issued a decree abolishing the feudal rights of the nobility — including the right to maintain separate law courts and military establishments, and the elimination (with government compensation) of feudal dues. In addition, the estates of the émigrés and smaller monasteries were confiscated, new schools and academies were established, and the administrative and financial machinery of the state was modernized along French lines. Finally, the Napoleonic Code and decimal system were introduced into the kingdom, and French experts were brought in to instruct Neapolitan farmers on how best to increase the production of cotton, sugar cane, and grain. At Joseph's insistence, however, the estates of the nobility and the larger monasteries were protected — a decision that, when coupled with the sale of 800 million francs in royal lands and those of the émigrés, actually allowed the aristocracy and middle class to increase their land ownership by 1815.

Joseph's reforms won him a modest popularity among many Neapolitans. By 1808, there were more than 1500 public schools in operation in the kingdom, half of the national debt had been retired, and Naples produced 40 percent of the cotton and sugar kept out of the empire by the Continental System. Nevertheless, despite these achievements, a number of important problems still remained: the persistence of pro-Bourbon sentiment among the Neapolitan lower classes; the threat posed by the British across the straits of Messina; a chronic lack of money; and an insufficient army to defend the kingdom without French military support. Most of all, however, there was the perennial problem of how best to govern the enormous city of Naples. In 1791, a royal estimate had placed the population of the city at slightly more than 400,000. In 1807, Joseph ordered that a census be taken. Compiled by the police, it showed the degree to which the events of 1799 to 1806 had precipitated a demographic decline:

61. Census Report for Naples
Statistical Profile of the City of Naples (1807)

TOTAL POPULATION

	Male	165,612
	Female	175,435
	TOTAL	341,047

BREAKDOWN BY AGE

Under 7 years	Male:	28,262
	Female:	27,359
From 7 to 15	Male:	29,432
	Female:	27,065
From 16 to 25	Male:	25,608
	Female:	38,458
From 26 to 60	Male:	72,058
	Female:	73,525
From 61 to 79	Male &	
	Female	17,352
From 80 to 90	Male	861
	Female	743
Over 90	Male	149
	Female	175
TOTAL		341,047

BREAKDOWN BY STATUS	
Married	119,596
Widowers	16,347
Widows	21,920
Single	85,774
"Zitelli" *	87,267
Priests	3,537
Monks	2,499
Nuns	4,235
Abandoned children	5,827
TOTAL	341,047
BREAKDOWN BY ORIGIN	
Neapolitans	304,100
Provincials	29,282
Foreigners	7,827
TOTAL	341,047

*(Old maids and bachelors)

["Quadro statistico della popolazione di Napoli e dei suoi suborghi di San Giovanni a Teduccio, Fuorigrotta, e Posillipo," in *Storia di Napoli*

Of the 341,047 total, almost 30 percent (101,193) were listed as "professionals" (*"qualifica professionale"*) — of which 6 percent were government officials, and 11 percent were doctors, lawyers, teachers, writers, pharmacists, merchants, and businessmen of various sorts. In addition, about 23 percent were listed as artisans and craftsmen (members of the *"arti meccaniche"*) — stonemasons, carpenters, glass makers, weavers, and blacksmiths — and 46 percent more as practitioners of skilled or semi-skilled trades (*"mestieri"*) — from bakers, fishermen, and gardeners to domestics, coachmen, and porters. Nevertheless, with more than half of the population under the age of 25 and poverty rates still hovering around their traditional levels of 30 to 40 percent, it is small wonder that conditions in the lower-class sections of the city remained unstable. In 1808, the provincial council of Naples noted that, despite Joseph's efforts, times were bad, "subsistence difficult, marriages rare, and the present generation lean and unhealthy." This was also the case in provinces like Calabria, where guerrilla warfare by *"banditti"* continued throughout Joseph's reign.

Napoleon's response to such resistance was to advocate a policy of unrelenting military repression. Drawing from his experience in northern Italy, he argued that enlightened government alone was not sufficient to maintain French authority, and that the *lazzaroni*, in particular, would inevitably engage in future disturbances unless confronted with the constant threat of force.

CHAPTER 3. JOSEPH I AND MURAT

On March 8, 1806, he wrote to Joseph:

> 62. I see by one of your proclamations that you promise to impose no war contribution, and that you forbid your soldiers to require those who lodge them to feed them. It seems to me that your measures are too narrow. It is not by being civil to a people that you obtain a hold on them. This is not the way to get the means to reward your army properly. Raise 30 millions in Naples. Pay well your army; remount well your cavalry and your trains; have shoes and clothes made. This cannot be done without money. As for me, it would be too absurd if the conquest of Naples did not put my army at ease.... It is necessary to establish in Naples a land-tax and stamp-duties as in France. If fiefs are to be given, it must be to Frenchmen who support the crown. I do not hear that you have shot any of the lazzaroni, although I know that they have used their daggers. If you do not begin by making yourself feared, you will suffer for it.... Your proclamations have not enough the style of a master; you will gain nothing by spoiling the Neapolitans.... [*Confidential Correspondence* 1:97-98.]

And, again, one month later, on April 11, in expounding on his view that landed estates be granted to Frenchmen:

> 63. You must not disguise from yourself that you will have real possession of the kingdom of Naples only in so far as you establish there a great number of French. That can only be done by giving to some of them lands, and to others employment, especially in the army, and by entrusting them with the command of towns and of military stations and fortresses.
>
> I see no reason, therefore, why you should be in a hurry to form Neapolitan regiments, or to call for service in your army Neapolitan officers, who you will never really be able to trust. You will have national property to dispose of, that of the clergy, and of the monasteries, and the fiefs of the crown. What you have to do with them need not be begun yet, but ought to be kept in view.... [*Confidential Correspondence* 1:108.]

The continued resistance to the French in Naples and Calabria greatly encouraged the Bourbons. Languishing in Sicily amid increasingly dictatorial British authorities, they longed to reestablish their control over the mainland, and rule independently from the capital once again. Maria Carolina, in particular, viewed the reconquest of

Naples as her sacred duty, and soon convinced the more lethargic king to follow along. On May 10, 1807, she wrote to General Damas:

> 64. Since there is no way to make the English move in spite of our prayers and persuasions, the king has finally decided to do everything to tempt fortune, and four thousand men have been sent to Reggio under the Prince of Hesse's command.... The vexations inflicted on the people [by the French], the spoliations, depredations, and the forced levy to send them to Lombardy has disgusted everybody. There is sporadic fighting everywhere and they appeal to us: consequently we should risk everything to succour our faithful and oppressed subjects.... [Cited in Acton, *Bourbons*, pp. 553-54.]

The expedition, however, proved to be a disaster from the beginning. Landing on the coast on May 22, Hesse's forces were routed by the French at Mileto six days later, and compelled to re-embark for Sicily with a loss of 1,600 men. At the same time, an uprising in Naples that was to have occurred along with the landing was aborted when the plot was discovered by the government and its leaders were arrested by the police. A wave of repression followed. In Naples alone, more than a dozen people were executed. Further executions took place in Apulia and Calabria, and the roundup of royalists and their sympathizers went on for several weeks.

Still, however, Napoleon was not satisfied. In letter to Joseph, he wrote:

> 65.1. I wish the Naples mob would attempt a rising. As long as you have not made an example, you will not be their master. Every conquered country must have its rising. [Quoted in Peter Geyl, *Napoleon: For and Against*. New Haven: Yale University Press, 1964, p.63.]

And, with regard to the repression in the countryside, his demands for reprisals had been increasing for more than a year:

> 65.2. I see with pleasure that you have burned an insurgent village. I suppose that you allowed the soldiers to pillage it. That is the way in which villages which revolt should be treated. It is the right of war, and it is also a duty prescribed by policy.... [Napoleon to Joseph, April 22, 1806, in Bingham, *Letters and Dispatches* 2:227.]

Napoleon's theory of "salutary terror" was never fully accepted by Joseph. Throughout his two years as king, he continued to appoint officials of the former regime to high office and resisted Napoleon's demands that Frenchmen be granted landed estates in order to form a new political elite. Napoleon's response to such recalcitrance was to deluge Joseph with letters filled with angry advice and scornful condescension. In a letter dated May 31, 1806, he wrote:

CHAPTER 3. JOSEPH I AND MURAT

66.1. I have already told you, and I repeat it, that you trust the Neapolitans too much; I tell you this especially as regards your kitchen and the protection of your person, for you run the risk of being poisoned or assassinated. I firmly desire therefore that you should keep your French cooks, and always have a French guard. You have not sufficiently followed my private life to know to what extent, even in France, I have relied on the protection of my most faithful and oldest soldiers.... No one ought to enter your room during the night but your aide-de-camp, who should sleep in the room preceding your bedroom; your door should always be fastened from the inside, and you should never open it to your aide-de-camp until you have recognized his voice, and he himself should not knock at the door until he has shut the door of his own room to make sure that no one is following him.... The character of the Neapolitans has been known for centuries, and you have to deal with a woman who is the personification of crime.... [Bingham, *Letters and Dispatches* 2:234-35.]

When Joseph persisted in his attitude towards Neapolitans, and even boasted to a delegation from the French senate that he was as popular in Naples as Napoleon was in Paris, the emperor responded with obvious irritation:

66.2. ...I have read your speech which contains phrases to which you must permit me to object. You compare the attachment of the French to my person to that of the Neapolitans for you. What kind of love can a people have for you, do you suppose, when you have done nothing to deserve it, and occupy their country by right of conquest, with some 50,000 men?... As for me, I certainly do not need a foreign army to maintain myself in Paris. I see to my sorrow that you are creating illusions for yourself, a dangerous occupation. [Bingham, *Letters and Dispatches* 2:235.]

By late 1807, in fact, Napoleon had come to view the situation in Naples with utter frustration: the Bourbons were still in Sicily; Capri had been seized by British forces; anti-French guerrillas still roamed the countryside in Calabria; and Joseph continued to resist many of his most urgent demands. Naples, in short, had become a bottomless pit into which he poured men and money with little apparent reward. On September 25, therefore, in response to a request from Joseph for additional troops to put down the rebels in Calabria, he wrote bluntly:

67. I have received your letter of the 16th. I cannot imagine how you can want such a number of troops in the kingdom of Naples, which is attacked only by a few wretched banditti. Still less can I

understand...that, with the assistance of the 6,000,000 francs which I send to you, you are not able to pay 25,000 men in a kingdom the population of which amounts to more than 4,000,000. That you have no commerce is not a satisfactory reason. If you can give corn, wine, and bread to an army, the money required for its pay is trifling. It is true that you export no goods, but it is also true that you export no money. Your finances are generally believed to be horribly ill managed. This is very unfortunate. Naples costs me an army, and costs me money besides. The first thing to be done is to allow no arrears in pay of your army. Besides, winter is at hand: what can prevent your merchant vessels from taking your commodities to Genoa and the other French ports?... I have ordered the whole regiment of Isembourg to Naples, and I have also ordered the Viceroy of Italy to send you a reinforcement of from 3,000 to 4,000 men.... This reinforcement will leave Ancona in two detachments, one on October 15th and the other on November 1st. [*Confidential Correspondence* 1:264-65.]

Napoleon's complaints about Joseph's administration of the kingdom continued throughout the rest of his reign. As late as March 1808, he accused Joseph's minister of finance, Roederer, of "ruining the country," and his chief of police, the feared Corsican Saliceti, of "allowing known traitors to live freely in the capital while plotting against the state." Nevertheless, despite his constant criticism, he never seriously contemplated his brother's removal. Driven, in part, by his Corsican atavism, he continued to show strong loyalty towards his family and knew from his agents in Naples that Joseph's reforms and moderate approach towards government had won him considerable support among the Neapolitan aristocracy and middle class.

What ended Joseph's reign, therefore, was not his failure to implement Napoleon's policies, but the need for a new monarch in Spain. Napoleon had first occupied Spain in March 1808 in an effort to integrate the Iberian peninsula into the Continental System. Seeking to consolidate his hold over the country, he forced the incompetent Bourbon king, Charles IV, and his son, Ferdinand, to abdicate and offered the crown to his younger brother, Louis, who promptly turned it down. Left with few alternatives, he then turned to Joseph. On May 11, in a letter written from Bayonne where he still held the Spanish king captive, he informed the Neapolitan monarch:

> 68. My Brother:
> You will find annexed the letter of King Charles to the Prince of Asturias and a copy of my treaty with the King.... King Charles, by this treaty, surrenders to me all his rights to the crown of Spain. The Prince had already renounced the pretended title of King, the

CHAPTER 3. JOSEPH I AND MURAT

abdication of King Charles in his favour having been involuntary. The nation, through the Supreme Council of Castile, asks me for a king; I destine this crown for you. Spain is a very different thing from Naples; it contains 11 million inhabitants, and has more than 150 million in revenue, without counting the Indies and the immense revenue to be derived from them. It is besides a throne which places you at Madrid, at three days' journey from France, which borders the whole of one of its frontiers. At Madrid you are in France; Naples is the end of the world. I wish you, therefore, immediately after the receipt of this letter, to appoint whom you please Regent, and to come to Bayonne, by way of Turin, Mont Cenis, and Lyons.... Before you go, leave instructions with Marshall Jourdan as to the disposition of your troops, and make arrangements as if you were to be absent only to July 1st. Be secret, however; your journey will probably excite only too much suspicion, but you will say that your are going to the North of Italy to confer with me on important matters. [*Confidential Correspondence* 1:320.]

Napoleon's offer of the crown of Spain was not altogether welcome. During his two years as king of Naples, Joseph had developed a deep affection for the city, and he hoped, at first, to be able to maintain his position as ruler of the Neapolitan kingdom as well. Napoleon, however, had other ideas. Of all of the members of his family, only his sister Caroline had not received a substantial position in Europe. With Joseph gone, Naples was now available, and he was determined that she should be its queen. On May 2, therefore, a full nine days *before* he notified Joseph of his intention to transfer him to Spain, he wrote to Caroline's husband, the French commander in Madrid, Joachim Murat:

69. I intend the King of Naples to reign in Madrid. I wish to give you the kingdom of Naples or that of Portugal. Reply at once what you think of this, for it must be done in a day. In the meantime, you will remain lieutenant-general of the kingdom. You will say that you prefer to remain with me; that is impossible. You have a large family, and besides, with a wife like yours, you will be able to absent yourself should war require your presence with me; she is quite capable of being at the head of a Regency.... If you could induce the inhabitants of Madrid to ask for the King of Naples, that would please me, and would appease their amour-propre.... [Bingham, *Letters and Dispatches* 2:387.]

Interestingly enough, Murat too was disappointed by Napoleon's proposal. Having performed brilliantly in seizing control of the Spanish capital, he had hoped (and, indeed, believed that he had been promised) that he would be rewarded with the crown of Spain. Nevertheless, like Joseph, he had neither the will nor the political leverage to defy the emperor, and on May 5, he accepted Napoleon's offer in a self-effacing reply:

> 70. Sire, I am in receipt of your Majesty's letter of May 2, and the tears stream down my eyes as I answer it. Your Majesty would have truly divined the wishes in my heart had you bid me remain at your side. I ask it, nay, I implore it as a favor greater than any I have received at your hands. Familiar as I am with your acts of kindness, accustomed to see you every day, to admire you, to worship you, to depend upon you for everything, how when I am alone and compelled to rely on my own resources shall I ever succeed in acquitting myself of the duties at once so onerous and so sacred? I do not consider myself capable of the task. I beseech you therefore to suffer me to remain with you. Power does not invariably denote happiness. Happiness is only found in affection, and happiness was mine when I was with your Majesty.
>
> And now, Sire, that I have given expression to my grief and to my desires, I must go no further, and I place myself unreservedly at your command. Nevertheless, I will avail myself of the permission which you grant me of choosing between Portugal and Naples, and say at once that my preference goes to the country in which I have already held command and in which I could most usefully serve your Majesty. Yes, I prefer Naples, and I must inform your Majesty that at no price could I accept the crown of Portugal.
>
> If I may be allowed to give expression to yet another wish, it is that I may remain as long as possible with your Majesty. [Murat to Napoleon, May 5, 1808, in Albert Espitalier, *Napoleon and King Murat: A Biography Compiled from Unknown and Unpublished Documents*. London: John Lane, The Bodley Head, 1912, pp. 2-3.]

Several days later an exhausted and somewhat dispirited Murat set out for Naples. At Bayonne, he met with the marquis di Gallo—Maria Carolina's former confidant and Joseph's foreign minister—whom he reconfirmed in office, and then went to Barèges for several weeks of rest. Still brooding over his "loss" of the Spanish kingdom, he would remain in France throughout the summer, and only enter Naples on September 6. On that day, tens of thousands of Neapolitans lined the streets of the

CHAPTER 3. JOSEPH I AND MURAT

city to celebrate his arrival. In the Piazza Mercato, two large statues, one of Napoleon and the other of Caroline, were unveiled to commemorate the occasion as music and dancing filled the square. During the afternoon, Murat attended a *Te Deum* sung by Archbishop Firrao at the church of Spirito Santo, and a spectacular fireworks display lit the skies with color during the night. Early the next day, the new king informed Napoleon that he had taken control of the city. A few hours later, he attended his first meeting of the Council of Ministers, thus marking the official beginning of his reign.

■

Joachim Murat would prove to be one of the most popular and effective rulers in Neapolitan history. The son of a Gascon innkeeper, he had joined the French army prior to the Revolution and had served with great distinction as a cavalry officer in several of Napoleon's campaigns. Handsome, dashing, and courageous, he had been named marshall of France and duke of Berg after the emperor's victory at Austerlitz, and the fact that Napoleon had chosen him as military commander in Spain had deepened his sense of self-importance and pride. In 1800, he had married Napoleon's beautiful and strong-willed sister, Caroline. Although the two would show strong affection for each other at the beginning, political pressures would soon weigh heavily on their marriage, and Caroline's repeated intrigues and infidelities would turn them into implacable enemies for a time.

Despite his many talents and achievements, Murat would never totally free himself from the control of the emperor. From the very first day of his appointment, Napoleon saw him not as an independent king, but as the emperor's representative in Naples, and demanded that the men and resources of the kingdom be employed in his greater design. Everything, in fact, had been worked out prior to his arrival in Naples: a constitution, which seriously restricted his independence as a monarch, had been issued by Joseph prior to his departure; the line of succession, which had traditionally run through the Neapolitan king, was bestowed on the descendants of Caroline; and Murat himself, although not a blood relative, was instructed to adopt the name "Joachim-Napoleon," thus officially carrying the emperor's name. Even his first "Declaration to the Neapolitan People" — which was handed to Gallo on July 21 and promulgated in Naples on August 15 three weeks before Murat's entry into the capital — was drawn up in Paris. Like all declarations of Napoleonic inspiration, it was carefully crafted to highlight the supremacy of the emperor and emphasize the tributary character of the Neapolitan king:

71. People of Naples:
Divine Providence having decreed that his August Majesty, the Emperor Napoleon, bestow on Us the crown of the Two Sicilies, We are highly honored to govern a nation of such noble character, and to restore the former glory that has forever rendered illustrious and memorable its great people. Our deepest thoughts will be concentrated on furthering those developments on which the greatness and prosperity of the country and our crown must depend. Our primary duty, at this moment, is to demonstrate to Europe the gratitude that we feel for the illustrious Napoleon, and to make our people aware of all the benefits that will result from the consolidation of their interests with those of the great French empire. The constitution proclaimed by our august predecessor and upheld by His Majesty, the Emperor, having been solemnly accepted by Us, shall be observed inviolably, and will form the basis of our government. And since our fervent wish is to follow in the footsteps of a sovereign who has brought so much happiness to this populace, We declare that those persons currently holding military, civil, and political positions with the state will continue to hold them, and will continue to hold the rank that has been accorded to them, and continue to exercise the functions that they are currently performing. In a few weeks We hope to be among you with Queen Caroline, our august consort, and the royal prince Achille Napoleon, and be entrusted with your love and loyalty. From that moment, We will begin to acquire the feelings through which We will come to love the country, and to learn the duties through which We can grant it glory and happiness. Meanwhile, We have no doubt that all of the ministers and functionaries of the state will endeavor to carry out the duties that have been assigned to them, so that our people may find the justice and satisfaction that is owed to them, and be assured of our respect and good will. ["Gioacchino Napoleone ai Napoletani," in Giuseppe Talamo, ed. *Napoli da Murat alla Morte di Ferdinando I di Borbone, 1808-1825*. Rome: Elia, 1972, *Testimonianze*, pp. 48-50.]

At first, Murat seems to have accepted the limitations placed on his new position with a certain equanimity. In August, for example, after receiving word from the emperor that he must abandon the name "Joachim Murat" and style himself "Joachim-Napoleon," he responded:

CHAPTER 3. JOSEPH I AND MURAT

72. The crown that your majesty has just given us is no doubt a great gift, but you will permit me to rank still higher the honor you have done me in allowing me to bear your name. I appreciate all the value of this distinguished favor. I know what I am pledged to by the glory of this name. Your Majesty will never have to regret having made me one of your family. [Quoted in A.H. Alleridge, *Marshall Murat: King of Naples*. London: Worley, 1992, p. 199.]

Nevertheless, as the months wore on, the blatant subservience that Napoleon demanded clearly began to rankle. Indeed, everything about Murat's personality — his ambition, talent, and vanity — drove him to seek autonomy, and he soon came to recognize that the surest route to independence lay in a program of popular reform. During his reign, a special commission was set up to adjudicate the literally thousands of conflicting property claims that had arisen out of Joseph's abolition of feudalism. Working day and night, it performed the Herculean task of sorting out precisely what the remaining rights of the barons, communes, and ecclesiastics really were. In addition, the administrative and financial systems were further streamlined and rationalized, roads and bridges built, schools founded, and the size of the army increased to over 80,000 men. Finally, the restrictions that the Continental System placed on fisheries were abolished to the delight of the coastal population, the state of siege was lifted in Calabria, and the property seized from the relatives of émigrés who had fled to Sicily was restored. All of this was done, moreover, with the kind of flamboyance and fanfare that only Murat could muster. Military parades, elaborate religious festivals, and special ceremonies provided the population with endless diversions, and the appearance of the brave and handsome king on horseback in the streets of the capital in his white-plumed hat and white-sashed military uniform only added to his allure. Within a brief time, in fact, Murat had established the basis for a genuinely popular monarchy and began to pursue the freedom of action that was worthy of a truly independent king.

Murat's disputes with Napoleon were virtually endless. One of the earliest grew out of his decision to grant amnesty to deserters from the Neapolitan army. Proclaimed in a decree dated September 21, 1808, it was designed to demonstrate his desire for reconciliation, while expanding the size of Neapolitan armed forces as well:

73. Citizens:
Given that the divisions that once existed in the kingdom, and the agitation and unrest that resulted from them, have led to the desertion of a number of individuals from the Neapolitan army; and in the belief that most of them have recognized their error, and that

> only the fear of being condemned to punishment...has kept them from coming forward, We desire to offer evidence of our clemency and decree as follows:
> Article I: An amnesty is granted to all deserters who, having deserted from the Neapolitan armed forces since February 1806...will present themselves within the period of one month from the publication of this decree before the commander or intendant of each province, or the leader of the corps to which they belonged, and declare their willingness to return under their respective banners to their companies.
> Article II: Any deserter arrested while in a state of desertion and not yet legally tried, will be sent back to his regiment.
> Article III: Deserters who present themselves to the commanders or intendants of the provinces will be assembled in detachments and directed to the corps to which they belonged, if these still exist in the kingdom; and they will be sent to Naples if they belonged to regiments presently outside the kingdom....
> Article IV: Deserters who return, and desert again, or those who do not return within the time limit fixed by this decree, will be considered deserters to the enemy, or as plotters of desertion, and therefore judged and punished as such.... [Gioacchino Napoleone, "L'Amnistia," in Talamo, pp. 57-59.]

One month later, on October 21, Murat decided to extend the amnesty to the émigrés in Sicily and to end the sequestration of their property on the mainland as well. Napoleon's reaction to this decision was characteristically harsh and one-sided. Already alarmed by what he viewed as the reintegration of potentially dangerous, pro-Bourbon elements into the Neapolitan army, he made his feelings known in no uncertain terms on November 12:

> 74. I have seen decrees of yours which make no sense. You are drifting into reaction. Why recall the exiles and restore property to men who have arms in their hands and are conspiring against me? I declare to you that you must take steps to cancel this decree, for I cannot endure that those who are contriving plots against my troops should be received and protected in your States. The decree as to the fisheries is not more prudent. It will be the means for the English to find out all the sooner what is going on. You are making sacrifices to false popularity. It is ridiculous to cancel the sequestration of this property and so provide support for those who are in

CHAPTER 3. JOSEPH I AND MURAT

Sicily. You really must have lost your head! [Napoleon to Murat, November 12, 1808, cited in Atteridge, p. 204.]

In late 1808, Murat made still another attempt to curry favor among the Neapolitans. Recognizing the difficulty of applying French law to Naples without changes, he instructed his minister of justice, Francesco Ricciardi, to exclude the divorce law from the Code Napoleon and then dutifully notified the emperor of his intention to announce the revision by decree. Napoleon's response was to threaten Murat with removal:

> 75. The most important section of the whole code is that which relates to divorce. It is, in fact, the very basis of it. You must not tamper with it in the slightest; it is the law of the country. I would sooner Naples be in the hands of the ex-king in Sicily than permit the Napoleonic Code to be mutilated in such a fashion. [Cited in Espitalier, pp. 21-22.]

Given the adamancy of the emperor's reaction, Murat quickly retreated, but other issues soon prevented a genuine reconciliation from taking place. In early December, he sent a letter to Napoleon complaining about the ruinous financial situation left by Joseph. The treasury, he stated, was empty, all of the ministries were underfunded, and the government was over fifty million francs in debt. As a remedy, he proposed that an entirely new financial regimen be established to rectify the previous government's incompetence and that the interest on the debt be reduced from five to three percent. Napoleon's reaction was volcanic. On December 15, he wrote:

> 76. I have your letter as well as those of your [finance] minister [Agar de Mosbourg]. I have guaranteed the public debt as inscribed in the memorial of the Constitution, and I intend that it shall not be tampered with in any shape or form. I insist that your proclamation be revoked as contrary to the stipulations that I have sworn to maintain. I must also make known to you that I am extremely annoyed at the statements that are perpetually appearing in your decrees reflecting on the king, your predecessor. He had all the difficulties to contend with; you are reaping the fruits of his labours, and you ought to be eternally grateful to him. I am vexed to see that you recognize so imperfectly the extent of your obligation to me, and the grave impropriety of your conduct. As for the individuals at the court of Sicily who are acting in hostility to me, you must confiscate their property, or I shall seize it myself as an indemnity for all that I have disbursed on the Kingdom of

> Naples. That kingdom already costs me several millions. It would have been better to employ the proceeds arising from the sale of these properties for the purposes of paying off the public debt rather than reduce the rate of interest. It is not with stupid and ridiculous phrases that one changes the face of empires. [Espitalier, pp. 22-23.]

Thus, by early 1809, Murat's efforts to establish an independent policy in Naples had reached a virtual dead end. Indeed, almost all of his major proposals — the elimination of the divorce law from the Napoleonic Code, the reduction of government interest, and amnesty for the émigrés — had come under heavy fire from Napoleon, and thus had been summarily withdrawn. On January 2, 1809, in response to the emperor's accusation that he did not appreciate what had been done for him, he wrote plaintively:

> 77. Sire, I am in receipt of your Majesty's letter of December 15. Your heart never dictated expressions which, since you refer to me as the most ungrateful of men, have also rendered me the most unhappy.... I shall never be ungrateful to your Majesty, to whom I owe all, or to King Joseph, to whom I owe nothing. [Espitalier, p. 23.]

Despite the discordant note struck with regard to Joseph, Napoleon accepted Murat's letter as an act of submission. During the summer of 1809, he shifted his attention away from Naples to events in Spain and Austria, and the growing prospect of an open rupture between the two men was delayed for five more years.

■

The disputes between Napoleon and Murat were not limited to domestic policy: they included foreign relations as well. Ever since Murat had entered Naples on September 6, 1808, he had been determined to capture Capri. Occupied by the British in May 1806, the island stood as a standing insult to French forces stationed in the capital, and the new king was convinced that he had to seize it in order to demonstrate the permanence of his regime. On October 3, therefore, a French army led by General Lamarque was ordered to launch an attack on the island. Scaling the rocky cliffs at Anacapri, they besieged the British garrison for two weeks until it ran out of provisions and forced the British commander, Sir Hudson Lowe (Napoleon's future jailer at St. Helena), to surrender his position with scarcely a fight.

Murat was ecstatic. On October 17, he instructed his foreign minister, Gallo, to notify his counterpart in Paris, the French minister of foreign affairs, Champagny, of the Neapolitan triumph. Expecting to be congratulated, Napoleon responded instead with a stinging reply:

78. This is ridiculous. Capri having been taken by my troops I ought to have heard of this event through my Minister of War. You must take care in such matters to do nothing offensive to me and to the French army. [Napoleon to Murat, October 1808, quoted in Alleridge, p. 204.]

Thus, right from the start, Murat had been served notice: although ruler of Naples, he must continue to think of himself primarily as a French officer and avoid using those channels of communication that might create the illusion that he was an independent king.

The recapture of Capri created great alarm among the Bourbons in Sicily. At the court of Ferdinand and Maria Carolina, in particular, it was widely reported that the capture of the island had transformed Murat into a popular hero, and it was decided to strike quickly before he could gather further support. On March 5, 1809, the queen wrote to Damas:

79. From all that I see, read, and presume, the struggle with the Corsican monster will at last begin again. Here we are only waiting to know that the [Austrian] Emperor has started hostilities to march upon Naples. General Stuart, the victor of Maida, will command everything: Hesse has no head, Bourcard is or pretends to be ill, not wishing to leave his dear command in Sicily; you know the rest; thus there is nobody to give the command to and Stuart will lead our troops along with the English. [Cited in Acton, *Bourbons*, p. 567.]

On April 6, the Austrian Archduke Charles proclaimed a war of liberation against the French in Central Europe. Two months later, on June 26, several thousand Sicilian troops under General Nunziante landed in Calabria, while a combined Anglo-Sicilian force under Stuart seized the islands of Ischia and Procida in Naples Bay. For a few days, Ferdinand and Maria Carolina hoped vainly for a direct assault on the city, but a ferocious French counter-attack soon disabused them of so grandiose an idea. On July 5, Napoleon crushed the Austrian army at Wagram. The defeat, which deprived London of its only major ally on the continent, completely demoralized the British. On the 22nd, Stuart decided to abandon the islands and return to Sicily, and his retreat was quickly followed by that of Nunziante from Calabria as well. At the same time, an uprising that was to have taken place in Naples during the Festival of Saints Peter and Paul came to nothing, and the entire expedition vanished without a trace.

The defeat reduced the queen to desolation. Like the king, she had expected the people of Naples to rise in insurrection at the first sign of Bourbon forces, but they had turned out on the Chiaia and cheered Murat and Caroline instead. On October 2—

sick, disillusioned, and increasingly dependent on opium to ease her suffering — she wrote to Damas:

> 80. It is terrible to say and think this, however true: we are in the most deplorable of situations, dominated, degraded, and maltreated by the English, who are the only ones to guarantee us from being invaded by the French. At a distance, it is easy to choose the better of these alternatives, but one must experience what we suffer to understand how painful this bondage is, and how cruelly they make us feel it. [Cited in Acton, *Bourbons*, p. 569.]

The failure of the Bourbons to recapture Naples immediately raised the possibility of a French attack on Sicily. The French had first developed a plan to conquer Sicily in 1794 during their initial descent into Italy. Since then, they had repeatedly reaffirmed their intention of annexing the island, and Napoleon had issued orders to Joseph to seize it after his occupation of Naples in 1806. Starting in the summer of 1808, however, the emperor's opinion slowly began to change. Stung by his defeats in the Iberian peninsula, he began to fear that an invading army would be cut off by the British navy in the Straits of Messina; and he refused to agree to Murat's request for permission to launch an assault on the island with 25,000 men. As Queen Caroline, who knew her brother's views on the subject well, would write:

> 81. [The emperor] knew very well the power of the English and the daring of his brother-in-law, and did not want to run the risk of him becoming a prisoner of the English. He also knew that, if the expedition did not succeed, it was he, Napoleon, who would have to pay the cost. [Quoted in Angela Valente, *Gioacchino Murat e l'Italia meridionale*. Turin: Giulio Einaudi, 1965, p. 160.]

Napoleon's reluctance to sanction an attack on Sicily provided the source of still one more point of dispute with Murat. To the Neapolitan king, the conquest of Sicily seemed absolutely indispensable to the completion of the kingdom, and thus to the consolidation of his political power at home. At a family conference held in Paris in January 1810, therefore, he was among the minority who opposed the marriage of Napoleon to the Austrian archduchess, Maria Louisa, the eldest granddaughter of the exiled Neapolitan queen, Maria Carolina. Fearing that an alliance with the Austrian Hapsburgs would destroy any possibility of an assault on the island, he also believed (correctly as it turned out) that it would provide the Neapolitan queen with a direct line of communication with the emperor, and thus create a long-term threat to his throne.

CHAPTER 3. JOSEPH I AND MURAT

It was, in fact, partially in order to assuage these fears that Napoleon gave Murat permission to begin preparations for an attack in early February. Even then, however, widespread speculation continued as to the emperor's real intentions — especially in light of his demand that all French soldiers remain under the control of French commanders, and his repeated hesitations and delays. On May 22, 1810, the newly-appointed Neapolitan ambassador in Paris, Morile Campochiaro, reported to Gallo:

> 82. According to information that I have received from one of the emperor's ministers, it is not improbable that His Majesty may at any moment put his veto on the Sicilian expedition. Ciphers do not always preserve their secrets, and I therefore refrain from mentioning the name of the minister in question. The object of his communication was to give me to understand that the negotiations with England might result in the abandonment of Sicily. Still, notwithstanding the value I attach to his information as a rule, I cannot bring myself to give credence to such an idea. The emperor is negotiating through Maret [his personal representative] without acquainting Champagny [the French foreign minister] with the real state of affairs. The opinion of the well-informed, or at least of those who wish to appear so, is that the general principle adopted will be that of *uti possidetis*.*[*i.e., that each retain what he currently possesses — ed. Campochiaro's letter cited in Espitalier, p. 76.]

Nevertheless, despite such warnings, Murat continued on undeterred. By the summer of 1810, he had assembled an invading force of 27,000 soldiers, of which less than 5,000 were Neapolitans and a full two-thirds (or 18,500) were French. As bold as Napoleon was cautious, he was determined to bring the matter to a conclusion and, on September 18, he ordered that a crossing take place. On that afternoon, an advance guard of 2,000 Neapolitans and 800 Corsicans landed in Sicily near Messina. Their plan was to draw off the British defenders while the main force — two French divisions under General Grenier — embarked under the cover of darkness from a point near Reggio in the south. As the evening wore on, however, the second crossing never came. Delayed by becalming winds, immobilized by disagreements between Murat and his French general, and surprised by the rapid response of the British navy, the French divisions (either because of secret orders from Napoleon or as an act of prudence) remained in port. By the morning of the following day, the advance guard on the island had to re-embark in order to avoid annihilation, but not before the British had captured almost one-third of its officers and men.

Stunned by the defeat, Murat tried to put the best face on the situation. On September 26, he issued a declaration to his soldiers announcing that, although he had decided to disperse his troops and postpone the invasion, the main objectives of the expedition had been attained:

> 83. Neapolitans!...
> You have solved an important problem. You have proved that the enemy's fleet cannot prevent the passage of the strait and that Sicily will be conquered whenever we decide to make a serious attack....
> [Espitalier, p. 83.]

Napoleon, however, was not so kind. While never keen on the idea of invading Sicily, he had viewed the military build-up in Calabria as useful in that it forced the British to divert troops from the Iberian peninsula, and thus was livid when Murat decided to disperse his army without consulting with Paris first. In a letter to his minister of war, General Clarke, he wrote:

> 84. Inform the King of Naples that I strongly disapprove of his general orders announcing the postponement of the Sicilian expedition. He says that my project has been fulfilled, but he makes a mistake in talking about my plans without authority from me. My purpose was to carry out the invasion of Sicily, and as Sicily is still unconquered it follows that my purpose is not fulfilled. Tell him that I regard his inaccurate statements concerning me as most extraordinary, and that I am surprised that he should have broken up his camp at Reggio without my orders, when I intended to keep the troops there through the winter. Now the British will take their troops to Corfu, to Spain, and add to their forces at Cadiz, while the army that I now have in the Kingdom of Naples will serve no further purpose. [Espitalier, pp. 83-84.]

The failure of the Sicilian expedition seems to have provided a turning point for Murat. Up until then, he had chaffed uneasily under the Emperor's domination. After the debacle in Calabria, however, his mood seems to have become more irritable and embittered, and his desire for his political independence increasingly clear. As the French ambassador in Naples, Baron de Durant, reported to the French foreign office on August 18:

> 85. It is the king's constant anxiety to be in a position to deal with the emperor as an independent power, and to appear in the eyes of Europe as no longer subject to that compelling force to which nevertheless he would not dare refuse obedience. Seeing that all the

advice he receives is given with the object of fostering such aims, the Neapolitans and others who have for a long time past harbored some sort of vision of a United Italy have no difficulty in hurrying him into acts of imprudence. [Espitalier, pp. 160-61.]

In April 1811, a visit to Paris to celebrate the birth of the emperor's new son, the "King of Rome," produced additional quarrels. In a series of heated conversations, Napoleon complained about the quality of Neapolitan troops and the treatment of French officials, the smuggling of British goods into Neapolitan ports and the lack of the respect for the emperor, and the failure of Murat to subordinate Neapolitan policy to that of the empire as a whole. By the spring, rumors began to circulate that Joachim would soon share the fate of the emperor's younger brother Louis, who had been deposed by Napoleon as king of Holland nine months before. The tension grew so great, in fact, that Napoleon even refused to allow the Neapolitan king the right to establish his own embassies in St. Petersburg and Vienna, stating that, in the future, the French foreign office would handle Neapolitan international affairs.

Faced with what seemed to be an imminent confrontation, Murat recklessly decided to rid himself of his Francophile ministers. Believing that the queen and her lover, the French minister of war, marine, *and* police, Jean Daure, were at the center of Napoleon's intrigues in Naples, he promulgated a decree that compelled all Frenchmen in his service to seek Neapolitan citizenship or lose their jobs. Published in the *Monitore* on June 18 but dated four days earlier, the decree gave foreign officials two weeks to make their choice:

> 86. All foreigners holding civil appointments in our realm must, in terms of Clauses 2 and 3 of Article 11 of the Constitution, lodge an application for naturalisation between the date hereof and the first day of August next. Such persons as shall have failed to comply with this regulation shall be regarded as having voluntarily resigned their appointments. [*"Decree on Naturalisation,"* in Espitalier, p. 137.]

The decree created a firestorm in Naples and Paris. In Naples, all of the French members of the cabinet — Agar, the minister of finance; Excelmans, the grand equerry; Lanusse, the grand marshall; and Daure — resigned in protest. In Paris, Napoleon, who was, at the time, preoccupied with the darkening situation in Spain and Russia, responded with angry disbelief. On July 6, he wrote to Clarke, his minister of war:

> 87. Send General Grenier a duplicate of the command that I have given to you for the disbanding of the army of Naples and the formation of a 'corps d'observation' under his orders, and inform him that whatever opposition may be offered by the king of Naples, all

the French are to receive orders from him alone. Say that the king of Naples seems to be yielding himself to the enemies of France, and that I have already pointed out to him the madness of his acts. Tell General Grenier to see to it that a garrison is put into Gaeta and the possession of the place secured, without however allowing his object to become apparent. He must impress upon the French and all who form part of the Guard that they are still French and regarded by me as such, and that by imperial decree French citizens are also citizens of Naples. He must lend his aid to my minister, and second him in extricating the king from his current false position. The king must be told that if his conduct continues to be so far removed from that which duty and gratitude alike impose on him, he will be sternly called to order. General Grenier must speak firmly, and support my minister as someone who is in command of a [French] army corps, and not as a subordinate [of the Neapolitan king]. [Espitalier, pp. 146-47.]

At the same time, he instructed the French ambassador in Naples, Baron de Durant, to increase the pressure within the government and court:

> 88. It is the will of His Majesty that you should express his dissatisfaction to the marquis de Gallo and the other ministers in touch with the King....
>
> His Majesty is displeased in general with the direction given to affairs. Orders are being sent to General Grenier to bring the troops together, whatever the king's views on the subject may be, and to take steps to have them in hand. In all probability His Majesty's commands will be quietly submitted to in Naples, but in the event of there being any grumbling or murmurs of resistance, you could spread the report that twenty thousand men were marching on Naples from Italy. [Bassano to Durant, July 7, 1811, cited in Espitalier, p.147.]

Confronted with such determined opposition, Murat quickly capitulated. Although the decree had transformed him into a hero among those who desired Neapolitan independence, he was unwilling to risk a confrontation with the French army, and, on July 20, he wrote directly to Napoleon asking for forgiveness in the most self-deprecating tone:

> 89. How, Sire, shall men always contrive to make you doubt the loyalty of my sentiments? Must I be forever condemned to act in fear and trembling, when all my thoughts and all my deeds have but one aim, which is never to do anything to hamper your vast

plans, but, on the contrary, to second them with all the energy at my command? Examine my record for twelve years past, scrutinize my conduct from the day I came to Naples: I defy my enemies one and all to cite a single action inconsistent with your policy. Yet calumny speaks, and Your Majesty heaps disgrace upon your brother-in-law, deprives your lieutenant of the command of your troops, holds him up to the French as an enemy of France, while by your decree of July 6 you give the French an advantage for which some of them did not ask and which others are unworthy to receive. Ah Sire, if Your Majesty desires to be rid of me, seek not for pretexts to work your will. More than once I have told you in writing, more often still I have declared it to your face, that if your majesty needs me not, you have but to say the word, and the king of Naples will cease to be a hindrance in your path. Sire, I was stricken with fever immediately after I had replied to the prince of Neuchatel, and I seize the first moment of respite to tell you of my grief, to tell you that you have killed me, that you have lost your best friend, and that my conduct was never such as to compel me to look for treatment so cruel as this. No sooner had the decree arrived than copies were distributed far and wide. They will doubtless fall into the hands of the diplomatic corps. I know not whether Your Majesty will rejoice, but today the king of Naples is a byword among the French employees and ex-contractors, and will soon be a byword to the country. So there is an end to my part in the play; nevertheless, I shall continue until my last breath to be as I have ever been — your most faithful friend. I can write no more, my heart is too heavy. [Cited in Espitalier, pp. 149-50.]

Later that day, he issued a proclamation revoking his previous decree:

> 90. Whereas in accordance with Clause 3 of Article 11 of the Constitution our decree of the 14th June last provided that no foreign subject should hold an appointment within the realm unless he became naturalised, and whereas in accordance with the views expressed by His Majesty the emperor, our august brother and brother-in-law, and with the statements made in his name, it is our wish not to regard French subjects as foreigners, and whereas we eagerly avail ourselves of this opportunity of presenting to His Imperial and Royal Majesty the tokens of our deference and of our desire to perform whatsoever may be pleasing to him and affording a further proof of the

sentiments that we have entertained towards France and its people, we enact as follows:

The provisions of our decree of the 14th June last are not applicable in the case of French subjects. ["Clarification of the Decree on Naturalisation," July 20, 1811, in Espitalier, p. 152.]

■

Murat's capitulation condemned Naples to three more years of foreign domination. After his revocation of the Naturalisation Decree of June 14, he actively pursued a rapprochement with the French party in Naples and was forced into the humiliating position of having to send the queen to Paris to beg for his throne. For a brief time during the winter of 1811, he actually fell ill due the pressures of the situation and was unable to perform his duties as king. Meanwhile, the interests of the kingdom continued to be sacrificed to those of the French imperium, and the city of Naples underwent a steady economic and demographic decline. Indeed, according to statistics produced by the French themselves, the decrease in population, which had begun as far back as the mid-eighteenth century, continued unabated throughout his reign:

91. French census for Naples 1809–1815	
YEAR	POPULATION
1809:	330,236
1810:	330,309
1811:	330,421
1812:	329,187
1813:	326,130
1814:	324,563
1815:	322,662
[*Storia di Napoli* 9:43.]	

Only in May 1812 — after five long months of recrimination and two more of icy silence — did Napoleon relent and allow Murat back into the imperial inner circle; and then it was more due to the demands created by the Russian war than to any fundamental feeling of trust.

Murat joined Napoleon's Grand Armée in Poland in June just two weeks prior to its march on Moscow. He brought with him 25,000 Neapolitan soldiers, and — due to his position as Neapolitan king and grand marshal in the French Army — was

CHAPTER 3. JOSEPH I AND MURAT

appointed head of the cavalry and second in command. Throughout the campaign (which began on June 24), he performed brilliantly, leading a cavalry charge through a hail of bullets at Borodino and entering Moscow at the head of a regiment of hussars on September 14. The burning of the city and Napoleon's disastrous retreat in the dead of winter, however, brought him a change in fortune. On December 5, Napoleon appointed Murat commander-in-chief of the Grand Armée and returned to Paris in order to put down a conspiracy against his government. Left alone amid long columns of starving, ragged troops and thoroughly dispirited, Murat quickly became discouraged and, after turning over his command to Napoleon's stepson, Eugene de Beauharnais, announced that he was returning to Naples on January 15. That same day, he wrote to Napoleon:

> 92. Sire.
> Although I have already written to Your Majesty that I could not retain the command of the Grand Army, nevertheless I would not have taken the step of leaving it, only that the state of illness to which I am reduced during the last five or six days makes it absolutely impossible for me to occupy myself with business. In this state of things I find myself compelled to write the two letters of which I herewith send copies to Your Majesty. I flatter myself that you will do justice to my sentiments towards you to the extent of believing in the sorrow I feel at ceasing for the moment to serve you, but I hope that a stay of some months in the favorable climate of Naples will enable me in the spring to return and resume my old command.

And then he added in a postscript:

> I have a fever and the beginning of a marked attack of jaundice. [Letter cited in Alleridge, p. 244.]

As soon as Napoleon received Murat's letter, he wrote to his sister, Queen Caroline:

> 93. Your husband, the King of Naples, deserted the army on the 16th. He is a brave man on the battlefield, but he is weaker than a woman or a monk when he is not in sight of the enemy. He has no moral courage. I leave it to you to express to him all the displeasure I have felt at his conduct in this matter. [Alleridge, p. 246.]

And, then, in an even angrier tone, he wrote directly to Murat on January 26:

> 94. I don't want to talk to you of the displeasure I feel at your course of conduct since my departure from the army, for that is the result

> of your weakness of character. However, I have thought it right to give my opinion of it frankly to your wife, the Queen of Naples. You are a good soldier on the field of battle, but elsewhere you have neither energy nor character. I presume that you are not one of those who think the lion is dead. If you count on this you make a mistake. Since my departure from Vilna you have done me all the harm you could. The title of king has turned your head. If you want to keep that title you must conduct yourself differently from what you have so far done. The opportunity for reinstating yourself in my good opinion will not be long before it presents itself. [Alleridge, p. 246.]

Napoleon's rancorous condemnation of Murat's abandonment of the Grand Armée only served to increase his determination to free himself from the control of the emperor. In March 1813, after returning to Naples, he secretly initiated negotiations with Vienna. Believing that Napoleon's days were numbered, he offered to switch sides in return for an Austrian guarantee of his throne. In late December, the Austrian prime minister, Prince Klemens von Metternich (who, himself, like Daure, had once been Caroline's lover), accepted his offer, and the two powers concluded the Treaty of Naples in January 1814. Under the terms of the treaty, Murat promised to place 30,000 troops at the disposal of the Allies in return for a formal recognition of his position as king. The British, however, while willing to accept Murat as a co-belligerent, refused to agree to recognize him as a legitimate ruler — even after Caroline sought to demonstrate her good will by expelling all French officials from Naples and banning the import of French goods into Neapolitan ports. As Lord William Bentinck, the British minister plenipotentiary in Sicily, would later state:

> 95. It was lamentable to see such advantages given to a man whose whole life had been a crime, who had been an active accomplice of Bonaparte for years, and who had deserted his benefactor through his own ambition and under the pressure of events. [Quoted in Acton, *Bourbons*, p. 622.]

Given the persistence of British opposition, it is small wonder that Murat continued to remain uneasy about his future. When the Congress of Vienna met in November, therefore, and his representatives were denied admission to the gathering, he decided on one more gamble to save his throne. On March 15, 1815, just two weeks after Napoleon's triumphant march to Paris following his escape from Elba, he declared war on Austria. Hoping to win the support of Italian nationalists and liberals, he lead the Neapolitan army into central Italy, and, on March 30 from Rimini, declared his intention of forming an independent Italian regime:

96. People of Italy!
Providence is at last calling you to be an independent nation. From the Alps to the Straits of Sicily can be heard a single cry: "Italian independence!" By what title do foreigners deny you this primary right of every people? By what right do they lord it over your beautiful country, taking your wealth elsewhere, conscripting your children to fight and die far from the tombs of their ancestors? Was it in vain that nature created the Alps as your defense and gave you that even greater barrier provided by the differences of language, customs and character? No! Away with foreign domination! You were once masters of the world, and have expiated your glory in twenty centuries of slaughter and oppression. But today you can recover that glory by breaking free of your masters.

Every people should keep to the limits assigned to them by nature, and your limits are the sea and the mountains. Do not ask for more than that, but at least drive out the foreigner who violates your territory. Eighty thousand soldiers from Naples led by their King have sworn not to rest until they have liberated Italy. We call on Italians from every province to help this great design. Take up arms again and let your young men learn how to fight. Let every free man who has the courage and intelligence learn to speak for Italy to every true Italian. If national energies can be fully released, that will decide if Italy will be free or else humiliated and enslaved for further centuries. [Joachim Murat, "Declaration of Rimini," March 30, 1815, in Denis Mack Smith, ed. *The Making of Italy, 1796–1870*. London: Macmillan, 1968, pp. 17-18.]

The Rimini declaration helped to establish the legend of Murat as a patriotic king and defender of Italian independence; but it failed to save his throne. On May 3, 1815, the Neapolitan army was defeated by the Austrians at Tolentino. Driven to desperation, he retreated to Pescara, where he issued a liberal constitution and then headed for the safety of France. On May 20, the British and Austrians concluded the Treaty of Casa Lanza restoring the Bourbons to Naples. Forced to flee to Corsica after Napoleon's defeat at Waterloo, Murat made one last daring attempt to reestablish himself as king by landing in Calabria. But his small and ragged band of supporters were met with indifference by the local population, and he was captured and sentenced to death by a military tribunal at Pizzo on October 13. Before being shot, he wrote one last letter to his often estranged, but still beloved, wife Queen Caroline:

97. My Dear Caroline.
My last hour has come. In a few minutes I shall have ceased to live; in a few minutes you will no longer have a husband. Never forget me; my life has not been stained with any injustice. Adieu my Achille, adieu my Letitia, adieu my Lucien, adieu my Louise; show the world that you are worthy of me. I leave you without a kingdom and without resources, in the midst of my many enemies; show yourself superior to misfortune, think of what you are and what you have been, and God will bless you. Do not speak ill of my memory. I declare that my greatest sorrow in the last moments of my life is to die far from my children. [Quoted in Alleridge, p. 292.]

■ ■ ■

ARCHITECTURE & URBANISM: 19TH CENTURY

7. *Angelo Viviani*, Bay of Naples from Castel Sant'Elmo, *c. 1840*.

OFFICIAL PANORAMAS. Natural settings, long vistas of broad boulevards, the city as a human enterprise rests comfortably against the bay and the unlimited sky. But the official view cannot hide the obvious: balance and control are maintained by ever-present military surveillance. Commanding vistas are the instruments of power over the densely packed city below.

8. *School of Posillipo*. Ferdinand IV returns to Naples, *1815*.

9. *Naples and the port from San Martino, 1870/75*.

89

MODERN NAPLES, 1799–1999

PUBLIC SPACES AND SQUARES. The narrow passages, local markets and defensive needs of the medieval city conflict with the new economy, transport needs, and visual sense of the 19th century.

10. Porta Capuana from Castel Capuano, c. 1890.

11. Waterfront of Santa Lucia, 1885/90.

12. Gradinata di Chiaia, 1890/1900.

13. Port with Molo and Lighthouse, c. 1870.

14. Piazza Poerio (Carità), c. 1890.

ARCHITECTURE & URBANISM: 19TH CENTURY

PUBLIC BUILDINGS. Grand neoclassical ceremonial and bureaucratic structures push the streets — and the masses — off to the wings.

The new needs of commerce and government create their own spaces, insular, compact and protected: against sea, sky, and lower classes.

15. *Teatro San Carlo, c. 1840.*

16. *Villa Pignatelli (Acton), 1826.*

17. *Piazza del Plebiscito, 1810; and San Francesco di Paolo, 1817–32.*

18. *Galleria Principe di Napoli, 1883.*

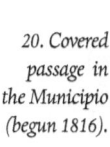

19. *Galleria Umberto I, 1887–90.*

20. *Covered passage in the Municipio (begun 1816).*

21. *Traditional female dress, c. 1820.*

POPULAR LIFE retains its pre-modern behaviors — dress, devotions, economic patterns, and daily life — well into the late 19th century.

22. *The Feast of Piedigrotta, c. 1840.*

23. *Open-air market, c. 1890.*

24. *A street of* fondaci, *c. 1885.*

MODERNITY AND CLASS. New forms of movement, commerce, and housing are available to the upper and middle classes. Two parallel Naples begin to take form that mirror and widen political rifts.

25. *Salvatore Fergola*, Opening of the Naples-Portici Railroad, *1840*.

26. *Lamont Young project for the* Metropolitana, *1884 (left).*
27. *Via Toledo (Roma), c. 1890 (right).*
28. *Via Foria, c. 1890 (bottom).*

29. *Homeless family on the seashore, c. 1883.*

31. *At the fountain, Sta. Lucia, c. 1890.*

30. *Scugnizzi, c. 1890.*

MATERIAL CULTURE for the poor and the working poor — *lazzaroni, scugnizzi,* laborers, servants, peddlers, and small shopkeepers — meant life outdoors: common facilities, daily labor and manufacturing, leisure and hospitality all in the open, with little sense of privacy.

32. *Pasta manufacture, c. 1890.*

33. *A water seller, c. 1885.*

34. *A public scribe conducts business on the street, c. 1870.*

35. *Mealtime at a working-class inn, c. 1890.*

DAILY LIFE & MATERIAL CULTURE: 19TH CENTURY

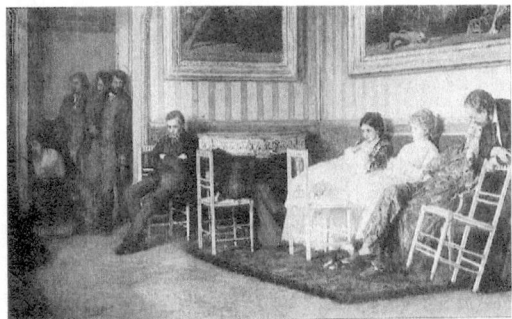

36. *Gioacchino Toma*, Mass at Home, 1877.

MATERIAL CULTURE for the middle classes and rich meant private and ample spaces, both indoors and out. Indoor life protected the extended family, its rituals and sense of privilege; while the outdoors was the realm of leisure: of sport, recreation, display and consumption.

37. *Playing tennis, 1902.*

38. *Teatro San Carlo, late 19th century.*

39. *A bathing club at Posillipo, c. 1900.*

40. *Giuseppe De Nittis*, Meal at Posillipo, c. 1885.

41. *Francis II, State Portrait, 1859.*

4
Restoration and Reaction, 1815–1848

The two decades of French rule in Italy proved to be among the most important in Neapolitan history. For over twenty years — from Ferdinand's fateful decision to enter the First Coalition in 1793 to the fall of Murat in 1815 — the city had been buffeted by war and revolution. Four times — in 1798, 1799, 1806, and 1815 — its leaders had been forced to flee before the onslaught of advancing armies, and its inhabitants had been made to endure a change in regime. Few Neapolitans, therefore, expected a simple return to the pre-revolutionary era. Most recognized the depth of the transformation that had taken place during the preceding decades and were willing to seek accommodation within the framework of a restored Bourbon regime. As the influential Neapolitan general and historian Pietro Colletta — who had served in Murat's army during the war against Austria and whose seminal *Storia di reame di Napoli* provided a justification for many of the changes that had occurred during the revolutionary period — wrote in 1831:

> 98. Although Murat had fallen in 1815, the laws, habits, opinions, and hopes which had been impressed on the minds of the people during the previous ten years did not fall with him.... All of our institutions had been altered, and every part of society and the State had been changed, either for better or for worse. The civil code which had filled a hundred volumes, was now compressed into the Code Napoleon, a monument of political wisdom; and the penal code, which could only be defined with difficulty amidst the various documents and usages among the courts of law, was collected into one body of laws.... Public discussion had succeeded the old secret and iniquitous system of trial; and a wise commercial code had been introduced.
>
> The sources whence the exchequer had formerly been supplied were many and vague...and public finances had been regulated on barbarous principles, and had been confused and unequal in their distribution. But now they were organized into a system and plentiful:

the requirements of revenue regulated taxation,...the public debt had been cleared and audited, a sinking fund had been founded, and a bank of discount projected.... The conduct of the administrators of the provincial and municipal revenues, which had been extremely remiss, was now under regulation. The *Intendente* of the province took the place of the Prefect, an ineffective officer, whose power had been capricious and uncertain; and laws, with almost too many regulations, succeeded the undefined authority exercised by former administrators....

Monasteries had been supressed, the feudal system eradicated, and though the barons had suffered many acts of violence, these had been necessary, because states cannot be renovated as they are maintained....

Religious sentiment had been weakened, and religious belief scoffed at or banished. But no new virtue had arisen to compensate for this loss, nor had it been rendered less injurious by any improvement in morals and manners, since both had degenerated.

Liberal opinions in politics prevailed among the people, and yet while showing little respect for the law, they were too subservient to man; a union of license with servility.

The clergy had degenerated and fallen into disrepute, for the revolution in Naples in 1806 had partaken of the principles and license of French liberty; and the clergy, after the church had been impoverished, sought wealth beyond the pale of the altar, but though not as hypocritical and corrupt as formerly, they were likewise less circumspect in their behavior....

The ancient nobles were poor and decayed, and the new unaccustomed to their position,...and thus more an ornament than a support for the monarchy; [since their] privileges had been abolished, the nobility had become a class of proprietors, and no longer had separate interests from those of the people.

Few of Murat's army remained; the greater number had deserted, including many of the officers and generals. The impatience for promotion in those who remained therefore increased their warlike ardor and desire for glory greater, while discipline was attenuated and morals worse....

Amidst the civil discords the lower orders had become accustomed to dishonest gains, such as the plunder of feudal landowners,...and they were therefore greedy, restless, and only to be governed by force.

CHAPTER 4. RESTORATION AND REACTION

The prestige of the monarchy was at an end from the hour when Joseph and Joachim rose to be new Kings, and were in the eyes of the people greater and more powerful than their former sovereigns. The character of the monarchy had changed, for the old was based on privilege and exclusion, the new on merit and equality. The blind reverence paid by our fathers was converted into a sentiment of fear of the royal power, or approbation of the royal acts; a calculation of interest had succeeded attachment between the sovereign and the people, and this change of sentiment effected a practical change, fruitful in results.

The people who had been afflicted by twenty years of adversity could not forget the cruel persecutions of 1793, the tyranny of 1799, the despotism of the succeeding years, the delusive hopes of modern liberty, the rapine and insolence of foreign armies, and the inefficiencies of their own. They remembered the promises which had been broken, the oaths which had been forsworn, and how often they had been deceived to help other men to wealth and power. They had learnt how both old and new Kings are alike indifferent to the voice of their subjects, and that the first had governed them by the prestige of their race, and the last by force. But now that the prestige had vanished, and the force had been broken, the adherents of either party, Bourbonists or Muratists, were few in number; and the majority of reflecting persons, whether Carbonari or Liberals, though not displeased by the fall of Joachim, felt uneasy and were suspicious of his successor.

The people and their rulers watched one another reciprocally with alternative hope and fear.... The Kings promised to govern better. Some immediately confirmed the recent good laws, and all promised new franchises, while the people rejoiced to hear them express penitence for the past, and the resolution to use moderation in the future. They felt more secure under a mild government in the hands of old rulers taught a lesson by adversity, than in the hands of new sovereigns, the spoiled children of fortune, who used their power with intemperance, and were strong enough to break all restraints. The people therefore hoped to make a new compact by the peace, which should be permanent and equally advantageous to all parties;...and if the promises of legitimacy had been sincere, and not a false demonstration, the people would have adhered to their sovereigns, and Europe would have repose from her labors.

Such was the state of the kingdom at the departure of the French Kings. [Pietro Colletta, *History of the Kingdom of Naples, 1734–1825*. S. Horner, trans. Edinburgh: T. Constable, 1853, 2:244-48.]

Colletta was not the only one who recognized the irreversibility of the changes that had taken place in the Neapolitan kingdom: the Austrians and British were aware of them as well. Metternich, in particular — despite his reputation as an arch-reactionary in most parts of Europe — was outspoken in his desire to prevent the institution of a policy of full-scale repression in Naples. During the negotiations leading up to the restoration of the Bourbons, he and Lord Castlereagh, the British prime minister, had sought to impress upon Ferdinand the advantages to be gained from a policy of moderation and had voiced their concern that an attitude of retribution would lead to a renewal of civil war. As he would later write in his memoirs:

> 99. We proposed as our primary goal to restrict and smother the spirit of partisanship and vengeance among Neapolitans, to guarantee respect for the right of property based upon law, and to prevent the outbreak of a dangerous reaction which would have threatened the tranquillity of the kingdom. [Cited in Rosario Romeo, *Mezzogiorno e Sicilia nel Risorgimento*. Naples: ESI, 1963, p. 53.]

At the same time, however, he was adamantly opposed to the introduction of a liberal constitution such as that instituted in Sicily by Bentinck during the Napoleonic wars. In two separate agreements — the Treaty of Casa Lanza of May 20, 1815 and the Austro-Bourbon Treaty of June 12 — the introduction of a constitution in Naples was strictly forbidden, and the Austrians were given the right to station troops in the kingdom in order to guarantee the safety of the monarchy and to maintain a moderate political course.

At first, Ferdinand was more than willing to accept these conditions. With the uncompromising Maria Carolina dead (September 10, 1814), and a second marriage to the more accommodating princess of Partanna already consummated (November 27), he was eager to resume a normal life in the capital and accepted the necessity of maintaining at least some of the Napoleonic reforms. In a proclamation issued to the Neapolitan people from Palermo on May 1, he declared in a deeply paternalistic tone:

> 100. [People of Naples:]
> The time has come for me to return to my throne.... Your unanimous sentiment recalls me, and the firm and vigorous support of my allies encourages and sustains me.... I come to restore your ancient serenity, and to eliminate all of the evils that have occurred in the past....

CHAPTER 4. RESTORATION AND REACTION

> Neapolitans, return to my arms! I was born among you. I know and appreciate your habits, your character and your customs. My only desire is to give you luminous proof of my fatherly love, and to render the restoration of my government an enterprising period of prosperity and happiness in our common fatherland. One day should be sufficient to extinguish the lamentable series of calamities of many years. The sacred and inviolable pledges of moderation, gentleness, mutual confidence and perfect union should guarantee our tranquillity....
>
> I promise that I will take no action against anyone, without exception, who compromised his allegiance to me during the absence of my government from Naples, or during any period preceding it.
>
> An eternal and impenetrable veil has now fallen over all such past actions and events. I assure you that this will irrevocably remain my policy, and I give you my sacred word that the broadest, most all-inclusive, and complete amnesty will prevail. I promise to preserve for the Neapolitans and Sicilians now serving in the army on land or sea the earnings, ranks, and military honors that they now enjoy. Let God bear witness to the rectitude and resolution of my intentions, and may He bless them with success. ["Proclama di Ferdinand IV," May 1, 1815, in De Nicola, *Diario Napoletano* 3:1-2.]

Ferdinand's renunciation of a policy of repression did not last long. On June 17, he returned to Naples on horseback followed by long columns of British, Austrian, Hungarian, and Sicilian soldiers. As in 1802, noisy crowds lined the streets to witness his reentry into the capital, as canons from the fortresses of St. Elmo and Castle Nuovo sounded a steady drumbeat, and a flotilla of allied ships filled the bay. During the next few months, he and his chief advisor, the cautious and enlightened minister of finance, Luigi de' Medici, carefully acceded to the Austrians' demands for moderation: attacks by ultra-Bourbonists on those who had served in the governments of Joseph I and Murat were strictly forbidden; equality of treatment was extended to Muratists in the army and administration; and legal recognition was given to the changes in lands and titles that had taken place since 1806.

In October, however, Murat's last, desperate attempt to overthrow the dynasty by landing in Calabria brought about a sudden change in the situation. For five full months—from January to June 1816—a veritable wave of terror swept the country. Led by the reactionary and vindictive minister of police, Antonio Capace Minutolo, the prince of Canosa, thousands of Neapolitans in the capital and provinces were arrested and interrogated, hundreds more were harassed and brutalized by royalist extremists armed by the government, and former émigrés were allowed to roam the countryside seeking retribution and revenge. The situation grew so grave that the Austrian and British ambassadors were compelled to intervene in order to force Canosa's resignation; but the conciliatory atmosphere that had characterized the first months of Ferdinand's administration was never fully restored. On June 28, 1816, De Nicola wrote in his diary:

> 101. The prince of Canosa has been dismissed...and there are rumors that he has asked for a passport to go to Spain.... The public is divided by the news: the Muratists are jubilant; the Legitimists humiliated; and the moderates alarmed because they fear that the divisions have now grown so deep that there will never be peace.... The Muratists say that Canosa had organized a revolution against them.... The Bourbonists believe that the Muratists see his fall as the first step [in their return to power].... The gap between them seems unbridgeable.... Only God can save us. [De Nicola, *Diario Napoletano* 3:82-83.]

De Nicola's prayers were answered by de' Medici. Alarmed by the divisions that threatened the country, and aware of the necessity of maintaining the support of Austria, he decided on a policy of political "amalgamation," accepting the best of the revolutionary innovations while, at the same time, opposing the introduction of a constitution and civil rights. The administrative, fiscal, and legal reforms of the French period — so vital to the smooth functioning of the state — were incorporated into the governmental structure, as were many of the Murat's bureaucratic and military personnel. Simultaneously, however, the Carbonari (with its dreams of a liberal regime on the Western model) was outlawed; the constitution granted to Sicily by the British governor Lord Bentinck in 1812 was suspended; and the role of the Church in Neapolitan society was greatly increased. Under the terms of a concordat signed with the papacy in 1818, monasteries and ecclesiastical courts were reestablished, bishops were given the right to censor the press and supervise education, and the pope alone was granted the privilege of consecrating religious officials within the state. By 1819, in fact, despite de' Medici's attempt to establish a relatively enlightened administration, freedom of thought in most parts of the kingdom had all but vanished, and the traditional gap between town and country and rich and poor (which had not been affected by the revolutionary legislation) had sharply increased.

In 1817, Henri de Stendhal, who was visiting Naples for a second time after having spent much of the intervening six years in Paris and Milan, described the situation in the capital and provinces as follows:

> 102. In Italy, the extreme outposts of civilization follow the course of the Tiber. Southward of this river, you may discover all the energy

CHAPTER 4. RESTORATION AND REACTION

and all the happiness of a race of savages. In the Papal State, the only law in force is that of the Catholic faith, which means the *performance of ritual*. Of its quality, you may judge by its effects. Under its authority, all moral philosophy is forbidden, as favouring *a spirit of individual inquiry*.

The Kingdom of Naples, on the other hand, is confined to this one city, which alone among all the towns in Italy has the tone and bustle of a true capital. Its government is an absurd monarchy in the style of Philip II, which yet manages to preserve a few rags and tatters of administrative discipline, a legacy from the French occupation. It is impossible to imagine any form of government of more abysmal insignificance, or with less influence to wield on the population [as a whole]....

On one occasion during a tour of Calabria [I was able to witness] this ineffectuality first hand: I caught illusions to countless robberies committed by a gang of *banditti* known as the company *dell'Indipendenza*.... [Their] practice is to send out warnings to local landowners and *massari*, demanding that on such a day, such a sum be placed at the foot of a tree. Failing compliance with the demand, the house is consigned to flames, and its inhabitants to torture and death....

Some four weeks previous to the occasion on which I was given these details, a certain farmer, enraged by the imperious style of the command which he received to furnish a meal [to the bandits], sent word to the General of the Neapolitan army, and a numerous squadron of cavalry and infantry was brought up to surround the *indipendenti*. The latter, however, were warned...and escaped to the last man....

Three days later, the *banditti* returned and took possession of the farm;...the farmer was put to torture [and] made a full confession.... [The bandits then] picked him up and threw him into an enormous cauldron which was set upon the fire and...as soon as he was fully cooked,...all of the servants on the farm were forced to make a meal of this infernal repast....

[As for] the head of the bandits, he might easily swell the ranks of his company to a thousand.... Indeed, scarcely a day goes by when he does not receive new requests for employment; he, however, makes it a rule to insist upon proper qualifications — i.e., *wounds received in battle, and not testimonials of good conduct*. These are his very own words....

And, then, in an effort to demonstrate the social functions performed by the "bandits" in the absence of government:

> In the spring of this year, the peasants of Apulia were direly oppressed by famine; so the leader of the *banditti* made it his business to distribute among the starving victims a series of regular ration-vouchers, which the more prosperous citizens were obliged to honour. This ration consisted of a pound and a half of bread for a man, one pound for a woman, and two pounds for a woman and child. One woman who had first aroused my curiosity had been receiving six two-pound vouchers a week for the past month. No one, moreover, can ever discover where the *indipendenti* have their headquarters, since all of the spies are on their side. In Roman times, such a brigand would have been a Marcellus....

And, finally, on the repression in Naples itself and the liberal opposition:

> Returning [to Naples] from my Calabrian excursion, I found myself subjected to a certain number of vexations: I learned that the authorities were 'uneasy' about me, while I, for my part, was decidedly uneasy lest I be expelled from the city.... [This would not have occurred] in Bologna; but then Bologna never knew the two years of tyranny and murder that Naples experienced from 1799 to 1801....
>
> Nevertheless, leaving this aside, I have nothing but unqualified admiration for the Neapolitan patriots. Naples may boast the eloquence of Mirabeau and the bravery of Desaix. I am privately convinced, in fact, that this country is destined to achieve its parliamentary constitution before 1840. However, since the gulf which separates a man of merit...from the primeval brutality of the populace is so immeasurably wide, the enlightened classes will of necessity see their schemes flounder more than once upon the rocks, before they succeed in bestowing the gift of liberty on their native land....
>
> [Nevertheless], this realm is still destined to achieve a bicameral government within the next two decades; despotism may crush the nation ten times running, and yet the nation will revolt an eleventh time against the despot. The present regime, with its obsessive resolve to put the clock back, is humiliating to the pride of the aristocracy.

CHAPTER 4. RESTORATION AND REACTION

Even Lord North, one of the most enlightened men in England, agrees with me, albeit with a sigh. [Stendhal, *Rome, Naples, and Florence*, pp. 121-24, 385-86, 428-29. Italics in text.]

■

Given the general poverty and backwardness of Neapolitan society, the lawlessness, lack of political liberty and ineffectuality of the Neapolitan government, and the deep social and political divisions that existed in both the capital and surrounding provinces, it is small wonder that the restored Bourbon monarchy lived in constant fear of revolution. The political compromise that had been engineered by de' Medici had satisfied no one: neither the royalists, who still hungered for full-blown reaction; nor the Muratists, who feared and resented the power of the émigrés; nor the liberals, who wanted the establishment of a constitutional state. Of these, by far the most significant were the liberals, whose ideas had filtered down to a number of loosely-organized secret societies known as the "Carbonari."

The origins of the Carbonari date back to 1806 and the struggle against French domination. Formed by small groups of anti-French activists in Naples and Calabria, they initially combined reactionary pro-Bourbon and pro-religious sentiments with liberal-nationalist ideology in a vague and, often, contradictory set of political ideals. Intensely patriotic, they were determined to expel from Neapolitan soil first Napoleon (the *"grosso lupo"* or "great wolf," as they called him) and then, after 1815, the Austrians. During the early years of the Restoration, the reaction under Canosa had led many of the Carbonari to abandon their support for the Bourbon monarchy. Outlawed by the government and hounded by authorities, they carried on a tireless campaign against "tyranny" and "tyrants," and intensified their efforts to establish a constitutional regime. Between 1817 and 1820, in particular, the Carbonari were able to penetrate virtually every important institution in Neapolitan society. Taking advantage of discontent within the army and administration, they won widespread support among many lower-level army officers and government officials and gained a substantial following among the provincial middle class. In 1817, the "Society of Guelph Knights" — in a typical example of the movement's loosely cast ideology — summarized its general aims as follows:

> 103. The goal of our order is to bring about the independence of Italy, our country. Our aim is to give her a single, constitutional government, or at least to unite the various Italian governments in a confederation. All of these governments, however, shall be based on a constitution, freedom of the press and of worship, the same laws, currency and measures.

> The method of our order is to spread liberal ideas and to communicate them to adherents, friends, and clerics, by firmly convincing them of the unfortunate state of affairs in our mother country. The press, gatherings, and private conversations are opportune means. Cunning and perseverance are needed and, above all, the eradication of all kinds of prejudice. The unprejudiced peasant is more enthusiastic than the rich man, the property owner, and is therefore more useful [to our cause]. [*Carte segrete e atti ufficiali della polizia austriaca in Italia.* Capolago, 1951, 1:116-17, cited in S.J. Woolf, *The Italian Risorgimento.* London: Longman, 1969, p. 41.]

Pitted against such radical ideas were the Great Powers of Central and Eastern Europe, led by the brilliant and enigmatic chancellor of Austria, Prince Klemens von Metternich. The scion of a wealthy German aristocratic family, Metternich had demanded and received a small fortune from Ferdinand in 1815 as payment for his services in restoring the Bourbon monarchy, and continued to draw money from the Neapolitan treasury until the withdrawal of Austrian troops from the kingdom in 1818. An uncompromising enemy of nationalism and liberalism, he had a low opinion of both Ferdinand and the Neapolitan people, but was nevertheless determined to rally the monarchical powers to a defense of the Bourbon regime. In 1820, he wrote to Czar Alexander of Russia:

> 104. There is scarcely any epoch which does not offer a rallying cry to some particular faction. Since 1815, that cry has been "Constitution."... Governments, having lost their balance, are frightened, intimidated, and thrown into confusion by this cry.... We are convinced that society can no longer be saved without strong and vigorous action on the part of these governments.... We are also convinced that this may yet occur, if the leaders of the European states face the truth, if they free themselves from all illusion, and if they join ranks and take a stand on the basis of a set of clear, unambiguous, and frankly announced principles....
>
> The first of these principles must be to maintain the stability of political institutions against the disorganized excitement which has taken place in men's minds....
>
> Let governments, therefore, govern; let them maintain the foundations of their institutions.
>
> Let them announce their determination to their people, and demonstrate it by facts.

CHAPTER 4. RESTORATION AND REACTION

> Let them, in these troubled times,...not confuse the concessions which they make to parties with the good that they do for their people.... Let them be just, but strong; beneficent, but strict.
>
> Let them maintain religious principles in all their purity, and not allow the faith to be attacked and morality interpreted according to the visions of foolish sectarians.
>
> Let them suppress the Secret Societies, that gangrene of modern society.
>
> Let the great monarchs, in short, strengthen their union, and prove to the world that...they alone ensure the political peace of Europe.... [Let them show] that the principles which they profess are paternal and protective, threatening only those who disturb the public order.... Only a strong union between states can protect [us] against the storm [that is approaching].... [Prince Klemens von Metternich, *Memoirs of Prince Metternich, 1815-1829*. Prince Richard Metternich, ed. New York: Howard Fertig, 1970, 3:456-76.]

Metternich's fear that a new wave of revolution was about to engulf Europe was fully shared by de' Medici. In 1816, he had outlawed the Carbonari; but under the unsettled conditions of the first post-Napoleonic decade their numbers had continued to increase. By 1820, they had grown to over 300,000, and the unexpected success of the Spanish revolution in January convinced their leaders that the time had come to strike out against the regime.

At the head of the insurrection was General Guglielmo Pepe, the commander of the Neapolitan army in the district of Avellino. Although not a member of the Carbonari himself, Pepe had enrolled thousands of its followers in the militia as part of his campaign to eradicate banditry in the provinces and had won the confidence of Carbonari leaders by expressing his support for a constitution in 1815. In his *Memoirs*, written more than twenty years later, he described his plan for starting the rebellion as follows:

> 105. It was now the month of May and I came to the resolution of commencing the revolution in the following month.... My plan was extremely simple.... It was my intention to have ordered Major Florio, who commanded fifteen hundred militia in the district of Ariano, to occupy several telegraphic posts upon the route of Apulia and Calabria. He was to write to me officially upon the pretense that the district of San Severo was in a state of open revolt, and then to march with his men in that direction....

> I should then have written to Naples to say that I had marched with the militia of the province of Avellino, a battalion of riflemen, and a squadron of the Bourbon regiment which was stationed at Nola, to put down the insurrection which had broken out in San Severo. While they were holding council in Naples, I should have found myself on the morning of the 25th in Ariano, and two days later in San Severo, with forces more than sufficient to withstand the royal guard and any other body which might have stood by the King. The gensd'arme, both on foot and on horseback, were devoted to me. The constitution would have been openly proclaimed at San Severo on the 27th or the 28th of June. [Pepe, *Memoirs*, 2:206-17.]

Almost immediately, Pepe's plan ran into problems. On the morning of June 24, the day that had been chosen for the start of the revolution, his chief confidant, Colonel Russo, failed to appear at his headquarters in Avellino, and the Carbonari lodge in Salerno, which was to have lit fires on the hills as a signal for the beginning of the insurrection, inexplicably refused to move. Fearing that the conspiracy had been discovered, and that Russo and the others had been arrested, Pepe quickly hurried to Naples, but found the government generally unsuspicious, and the situation strangely undisturbed. It was while still in the capital, on July 2, that he first learned that two junior officers of the Nola regiment, Michele Morelli and Giuseppe Silvati, had started the rebellion by marching to Avellino with about one hundred men. Along the way, they had been joined by a dynamic priest, Luigi Minichini, and numerous local Carbonari, who had been waiting patiently for the signal to strike for more than a week. From then on, Pepe's sole preoccupation became to join his co-conspirators in Avellino. In his *Memoirs*, he provided a dramatic account of his successful attempt to flee the capital, and the warm reception he received upon his return:

> 106. [The revolution having been temporarily postponed], I reached Naples on June 27, having first given directions to the chief of my staff to write me full particulars of everything that might occur in the division.... After arriving in the capital, I visited the different ministers, who began to suspect me, but whose misgivings were somewhat baffled by seeing me far from my headquarters. I had scarcely been two days in Naples, when I received intelligence that General Prince Campana had entered Salerno at the head of his troops to arrest a great number of Carbonari, the most implicated of whom had sought refuge in Avellino.... Although I was in the capital, the fact of my headquarters having become an asylum of

CHAPTER 4. RESTORATION AND REACTION

the fugitive Carbonari of the other provinces caused such suspicion to fall upon me, that I was upon the point of returning immediately to my division...and then proceeding immediately to San Severo.

I had intended quitting Naples on the July 3; but on the morning of the 2nd, Nicholas Staiti, Major of dragoons, came to me saying, that the squadron of the Bourbon regiment composed of a hundred and twenty horse had quitted Nola with the Carbonari banner unfurled, and were directing their course towards my headquarters in Avellino.... Two Carbonari chiefs, the second Lieutenants, Morelli and Silvati...had started out at one o'clock on the morning of July 2 to begin the revolution.... [Their] whole squadron composed of all of the soldiers and non-commissioned officers...had quitted Nola, followed by eleven Carbonari of that city, among whom was a priest named Minichini. The squadron displayed the Carbonari flag, and was increased on its way by some few more Carbonari until it arrived at Mercogliano, a short distance from Avellino....

When intelligence of this movement at Nola reached Naples, the King was on board a man-of-war sailing to meet the Duke of Calabria, his son and heir.... In the absence of his Majesty, the ministers decided that General Nugent [the Austrian general in command of Neapolitan forces] should call into the Council the General Duke of Ascoli, an intimate friend of the King, General Fardella, who had formerly followed the Court to Sicily, and Generals Ambrosio, Carascosa, and Filangieri, so that they might decide the best military measures to be adopted....

It is easy to imagine the agitation that I experienced on learning of the movement of the squadron of Nola.... [My brother] Florestano said that, before long, emissaries of the Government would arrest me.... [But much to his surprise] the Council of Generals concluded that [I] alone could, in such delicate circumstances, quell the rebellion and save the state.... This decision was arrived at in great measure from a resemblance of the events which had taken place in Spain, and from their repugnance to behold their country plunged into the horrors of civil war....

Nugent [himself visited me at my home and], without making any allusion to the Council of Generals, related to me the movement of the rebel squadron, and how it had been reinforced along the way, and asked me whether I hoped to be able to remedy the evil. I replied without hesitation that I was ready to proceed immediately to my headquarters; and that with the militia and the few troops left at my disposal in the province, I would cause every trace of the disorder to disappear.... Nugent then asked me to delay my departure for an hour, so that he might first see the ministers who were in continued deliberation...and might receive the instructions he was to remit to me.... I was afterwards told that [at the meeting]...Medici had said that rather than assume the responsibility of sending General Pepe to oppose the rebels, he would assume that of having him thrown in irons. Had they arrested me, they would have at least acted consistently with their suspicions; but to mistrust me and still to leave me at liberty was indeed an act bordering on idiocy....

It was now impossible to arrive at any decision as to the General to be sent to put down the rebels before the return of the King.... [But] as soon as the King was made aware of what had happened, his first impulse was to remain on board his ship, and it was with great difficulty that he was prevailed upon to come to Naples, on an assurance that he ran no matter of danger. When he did arrive the charge of putting down the rebellion was given to Generals Carascosa and Campana....

[Meanwhile] I employed the days of the 4th and 5th, which seemed to be interminable, seeking the best means of getting to Avellino, and I thought that at the worst I might land in disguise upon the shores of Salerno, and thence reach the mountains.... While I was in this state of uncertainty...General Napoletano came to tell me that a brigade of horse waited for me at the bridge of the Maddalena.... Without saying anything, I got into General Napoletano's carriage, and towards sunset found myself in front of the regiment of dragoons commanded by Lieutenant-Colonel Tapputi, and that of the riflemen under the command of Colonel Celentani.... To arrive sooner, we were obliged to pass through dark narrow roads, called *cupe*, where our horses could only advance one by one. Scarcely had we begun our march, when I was joined by Captain Rappola and his company, and by a regiment of infantry.... The sight of the small body of infantry caused me the greatest pleasure, for without it, the infantry of Carascosa might have fired on my cavalry. We reached Laura at dawn; I caused the

CHAPTER 4. RESTORATION AND REACTION

horses to be fed and rested, and then to recommence our march for Monteforte.... In the villages through which we passed, there were only women, children, and very old men; the rest, militia or Carbonari, were in arms in the mountains between Monteforte and Avellino. The women clapped their hands from the windows, calling out *"Viva la Constituzione."* They addressed me by name, telling me that their husbands, brothers, and sons, were gone to fight for the public cause. This enthusiasm cheered the hearts of the entire brigade....

As I drew near the summit of Monteforte with my troops, I perceived a multitude of armed Carbonari, among them the militia in full uniform.... My column was astonished, for although they had faith in what I said, they had not expected to see so many.... The officers and privates both greeted me with tears...and the soldiers likewise wept with emotion.... In the populous community of Monteforte, the inhabitants were in a delirium of joy. Seeing me among them with two regiments of cavalry, they looked upon the Constitution as already gained. Carascosa and Colletta have both written that the Carbonari and non-Carbonari population were ignorant of the very meaning of the word. [In fact], they knew it only too well; for they shouted: "No more arbitrary taxes; no more wanton arrests!", cries which were loudly repeated, even by the women.

We had scarcely left for Avellino before we encountered a carriage with four deputies from the Carbonari, sent out to meet me.... A few minutes afterwards, Deconcili, Cirillo, the other officers of the corps, and the provincial authorities came to me. [Matteo] Deconcili, a most honorable man, told me that it would give satisfaction to the people were I to ride through the principle streets of the town. I immediately did so, although several Carbonari of respectability entreated me to enter my own house, thinking I was in danger. I perceived that all were excited, and full of enthusiasm at the great event. The population of Avellino, as well as that of the neighbouring communities, received me with many manifestations of joy. After I had ridden through the town, every feeling of doubt or distrust, which had been felt by the worthy citizens disappeared. [Pepe, *Memoirs* 2:218-34.]

Pepe's flight to Avellino proved decisive for the success of the revolution. By the evening of July 6, he had, according to his own testimony, 30,000 men under his command, and the government, viewing its soldiers as unreliable, was hard-pressed to find the means to oppose him. The king, in particular, was desperate to avoid a new confrontation. Terrified and unable to function, he appointed his son, Francis, as vicar-general of the kingdom, and unceremoniously took to his bed. On August 26, the British ambassador in Naples, Sir William A'Court, described his emotional state as follows:

> 107. Last night, His Majesty sent for the French Ambassador requesting to see him immediately. The ambassador went to the palace where he found the King in the most dreadful state of agitation.... He said that he had certain intelligence that a plot was formed to put him to death, as well as the whole of his family.... The mildest proposal was to seize him and shut him up as a hostage. He had been advised by his old and confidential servants to devise a means of escaping.... His Majesty appeared dreadfully ill and agitated.... He only wished, he said, to be removed to a place of safety, where he might spend the rest of his days in peace and tranquility. His conscience reproached him with nothing. He had never had any other wish than the happiness of his people. If he had been mistaken or deceived, it was his misfortune, not his fault.... I do not see the possibility of aiding him in any way. His departure, could we affect it, would be the signal for the massacre of the rest of the royal family.... I am very much embarrassed what line to adopt under the circumstances. [Sir William A'Court, British Ambassador to the Kingdom of Naples, August 26, 1820, quoted in Acton, *Bourbons*, 679-80.]

With the king frozen in fear and the army divided, it was only logical that the government would quickly capitulate to the demands of the revolution. On July 6, 1820, Ferdinand — without even a single battle having been fought — issued a declaration promising a constitution. Drafted in council with the aid of his ministers, it was designed to pacify revolutionary leaders while, at the same time, remaining as vague as possible as to the details of the new constitutional state:

> 108. As the wish to be ruled by a constitutional form of government has been manifested by the nation of the Two Sicilies, We promise, of our own free will, to publish the fundamental laws of this Constitution within a period of eight days. Until the publication of the Constitution, the utmost vigilance of the law will be

CHAPTER 4. RESTORATION AND REACTION

exerted for the maintenance of order. Having thus satisfied the public wish, we hereby order the troops to return to their corps, and all others to resume their usual occupations. [Ferdinand I, "Declaration to the Nation of the Two Sicilies," July 6, 1820, cited in Pepe, *Memoirs* 2:235-36.]

Ferdinand's declaration, however, failed to satisfy Pepe. On July 7, he sent an ultimatum to the Neapolitan government with four specific demands: the convocation of a national assembly; a reorganization of the army; the creation of a provisional "national junta"; and a public commitment by the monarchy to accept the Spanish constitution of 1812. Two days later, on July 9, Francis, acting in the name of his father, issued a second declaration acceding to all of Pepe's demands:

109. We, by virtue of the powers passed on to us by Our august father and sovereign, promise to swear to the constitution drawn up in Spain in 1812, and declare our intention to convoke a national parliament as quickly as possible so that it may draw up a similar constitution for our kingdom....

In order to prepare for the convocation of the parliament, We also *decree* that:

1. A provisional junta of fifteen people be created before which We, and all the princes of our family, will take an oath of loyalty to the Constitution. This oath of loyalty will be repeated before the National Parliament after its legitimate convocation.

2. The Junta will be consulted by us on all government provisions until the installation of the National Parliament: and these will be published by Us according to its wishes.

3. In order to guarantee that the people who compose the national Parliament be the most worthy available, and that they correspond to the votes and desires of the people, We nominate the lieutenant general Don Giuseppe Parisi, the cavalier Don Melchiorre Delfico, the lieutenant general Don Florestano Pepe, the Baron Don Davide Winspeare, and the cavalier Don Giacinto Martucci, and ask them to present us with a list of another twenty persons, out of which We will select ten who, added to those already nominated, will form the Junta.

4. Giuseppe Zurlo, Our minister of internal affairs, will be responsible for carrying out this degree. [Francesco I, "Istituzione della Giunta provvisorio di Governo," Naples, July 9, 1820, cited in Talamo, pp. 242-45. Italics in text.]

That same day, Pepe, having coerced the government into accepting all of his conditions, ordered his forces into Naples. Keppel Craven, an English traveler who happened to be in the capital at the time, described their triumphal march down via Toledo as follows:

> 110. [The revolutionaries]...entered Naples on Sunday, July 9, at about midday, and, proceeding by the Strada Toledo, defiled before the Duke of Calabria, who stood at the window of the royal palace.... The regular troops, headed by General Napoletano, opened the march, and were followed by the mass of the provincial militia, walking rapidly without any order, conducted by General Guglielmo Pepe, and a priest by the name of Minichini, who may be looked upon as the principle mover of all the secret springs which had set the revolution in motion....
>
> The constitution itself, in a palpable shape, made its appearance in the procession, conveyed in a common hackney one-horse chair called a *curriculo*. The spectacle displayed by the bands of provincial militia was singular in the extreme; though they were all formidably armed, their weapons varied as much as their accoutrements: a very small proportion of them were clad in military uniform, the majority being habited according to the different costumes of their respective districts, which at the same time bore a very warlike aspect.
>
> It must be acknowledged that the cartridge belt, the sandalled legs, the broad stiletto, short musket, and grey peaked hats, so peculiarly adapted by painters to the representation of *banditti*, seemed here to realize all the ideas which the inhabitants of the north have formed of such beings; the sunburnt complexions and dark bushy hair and whiskers of the wearer greatly contributed to render this resemblance more striking.
>
> A strange contrast was exhibited by the more opulent classes of these same legions who, though equally well provided with arms of all descriptions, marched among the ranks of their picturesque companions, attired in the full extreme of modern French and English fashions. All bore the Carbonari colours at their breast, while scarves of the same, or different medals and emblems tied to their waistcoat, denoted the rank they severally held in the sect. Banners with inscriptions in honour of this patriotic association were also carried by them. Nearly the whole of these individuals had been absent from their homes nine days, during which they

CHAPTER 4. RESTORATION AND REACTION

had never slept in a bed, or even under a roof, but they all seemed in perfect good humour and spirits and appeared amply repaid for all the hardships they might have endured, by the success which had followed them.

After passing before the palace, they filed off in different divisions, to the respective quarters which had been assigned to them in some of the empty barracks; but more particularly in a long range of buildings on the Portici road, known by the name of the *Granili*. On the first night of their stay in Naples, a considerable proportion of these men slept on trusses of straw, among the oleanders, myrtles, and geraniums of the public walk, or Villa Reale....

[On the evening of July 12] the great theater of San Carlo was illuminated and opened to the provincial troops gratis, who availed themselves of this license to fill it in a degree unparalleled on any former occasion. The sight presented by the seats of the pit, occupied by so motley an assemblage, many of which were armed cap-à-pie, was not one of the least remarkable exhibitions among those witnessed by the public in the short space of twelve days. The Duke of Calabria and his family were present at the representation, and more than divided the applause bestowed on the performers. [Richard Keppel Craven, *A Tour Through the Southern Provinces of the Kingdom of Naples*. London: Rodwel and Martin, 1821, quoted in Seward, pp. 147-49.]

Four days later, on July 13, the king — standing in the royal chapel along with his family, the leaders of the military, and the members of the newly-formed National Junta — faithfully fulfilled his promise to take an oath of loyalty to the Constitution. Fixing his eyes on the crucifix above him, he stated in a grim and solemn voice:

III. I, Ferdinand I, by the grace of God and the Constitution, king of the Kingdom of the Two Sicilies, swear in the name of God and the Holy Scriptures that I will preserve the Roman Catholic religion and will permit no other in the kingdom; and that I will adhere to the political constitution adopted in Spain in 1812 and sanctioned by His Catholic Majesty in March of this year — except for the modifications that the National Assembly of this kingdom, once it is constitutionally convoked, may wish to decree in order to adapt it to the particular circumstances of the Kingdom of Naples. I also swear that in all of my actions I shall have only one goal: the welfare and happiness of my kingdom; and that I shall never cede any part of its territory, nor demand interest or money, or any other thing, that has not been decreed by Parliament; that I shall never take away any man's property, and that I shall respect above all else the political freedom of the nation, and the personal freedom of the individual. If I should violate this oath or any part of it, the people need not obey me, and any transgression that infringes upon their rights shall be declared null and void. In carrying out this oath, let God help me and defend me; and let Him hold me accountable for my deeds. [Ferdinando Borbone, *"Formula del giuramento presento dal re,"* July 13, 1820, in Talamo, 244-45.]

For Pepe and the leaders of the Carbonari, it was a moment of supreme triumph. In just eleven days, from July 2 to July 13, they had toppled the absolutist monarchy and forced the King to agree to the establishment of a constitutional state. The audacity of the secret societies, the weakness of the government, and the divisions within the army had all combined to produce an astonishing victory. Only time would tell whether that victory could be translated into a functioning constitutional regime.

■

The news that Ferdinand had granted a constitution in the Kingdom of the Two Sicilies created enormous alarm among the conservative leaders of Europe. Fearful that the agitation would spread to Berlin and Vienna, Metternich, in particular, was determined to crush the revolution from the beginning and set out almost immediately to organize support for Austrian intervention in both Italy and Spain. On July 15, upon first hearing of events in Naples, he wrote to Count Zichy, the Austrian ambassador to Prussia:

112.1. We have just received news by means of a courier dispatched from Rome that a revolution took place in Naples on July 6, which — although not accompanied by widespread disorders or acts of violence — opens the way to dangers that are impossible to calculate.

[According to the dispatch] the secret societies succeeded by their machinations in inciting a small number of troops in Nola to rebellion, and, at the crucial moment, General Pepe, who was called upon to quell the disorders, choose instead to give a seditious speech to two of the regiments under his control, stating that the nation and the army desired a constitution. In this way, he convinced the two regiments to join the insurgents, who had occupied Avellino on July 3. These acts alone were sufficient to convince the king to agree to grant a constitution and change ministers.... [The country's] military leaders, all of whom held rank in Murat's army, have all, with the sole exception of General Pepe, proclaimed their loyalty to King Ferdinand. But this king, in one of his typically rash and deplorable actions, has nevertheless decided to promise a constitution.

This event calls for the most serious reflection, and compels us, above all, to counsel the emperor to adopt a policy of prudence and firmness.... It is at moments like this that he must take the lead in establishing the principles of unity and trust which unite all [royal] courts.... [Prince von Metternich to Count Zichy, Austrian Ambassador to Prussia, Vienna, July 15, 1820, in Talamo, 257-60.]

And, a few days later, in a more bitter and exasperated tone:

112.2. Two squadrons of cavalry overturn a throne and expose the whole world to incalculable dangers. Things will not go at Naples as they have in Spain. Blood will be shed in torrents. A half barbarous people, utterly ignorant, superstitious beyond limit, as ardent and passionate as Africans, who can neither read nor write and whose final argument is always the dagger, offer promising material for the application of constitutional principles! [Cited in Talamo, p. 212.]

Metternich's determination "to smother the revolution in its cradle" (as he would later put it) was not the only problem confronting the Neapolitan government. Equally disturbing was the outbreak of a revolution in Sicily — which began in Palermo on July 16, and led to a brief but intense civil war. The rebellion — in which the Sicilians formed their own provisional government and demanded a separate constitution — forced the Neapolitans to divert desperately needed men and resources from the Italian mainland and provided a continuous distraction from political reform. In his *Storia di Napoli*, Pietro Colletta — who was an active participant in the struggle — described the reaction of Neapolitan leaders to the Sicilian upheaval as follows:

113. The new form of Government having been established [in Naples], those who had been its chief promoters openly laid claim to its offices and honors.... General Pepe alone, although a Muratist, had adopted the views of the Carbonari...[and] placed himself at the head of the revolution, without possessing any of the qualities necessary for so great a work.... In this, he was urged on by an ardent desire to benefit the people, as well as the hope of gaining fame and power for himself....

The press was made free,... the society of the Carbonari increased,... [and] the Government was obliged to construct a new army, as little remained of the old, owing to the immense number of desertions....

In Sicily, [a second revolution broke out], and the people elected a sovereign Junta, placing Cardinal Gravina at its head.... General Naselli [the Neapolitan commander] had to escape the mob half naked in a boat.... Sicilian envoys [were sent to the mainland] and demanded that the Government of Sicily should be separated from that of Naples, and that the two confederated states be ruled by the same King, with the Spanish constitution in both countries.... The ministers of the Crown, however, gave the Sicilian envoys vague and evasive answers... and neither rejected nor granted the propositions. Naples (as is ever the case among real or supposed liberals) loved to tyrannize over others, and treated the [Sicilian] offers of peace with disdain.... The King, outraged, proposed to inflict a severe and summary chastisement on the rebellious provinces. The ministers, the Junta, and the people, supported him in his resentment, and an expedition of 9000 infantry and 500 cavalry was sent to Sicily at the end of August.... General Florestano Pepe [Guglielmo Pepe's brother] was appointed commander-in-chief...and marched to Palermo by the shortest route with 10,000 men....

[Meanwhile] the people thronged to the electoral colleges to choose a parliament.... Of the 72 deputies elected, 10 were ministers of religion, 8 scientific professors, 11 magistrates, 9 doctors of law, 2 government officials, 3 merchants, 5 military men, 24 landed proprietors, and only 2 nobles.... Of the Sicilian deputies, a third were priests, and the remaining 10 from all classes....

The elections being closed, the deputies arrived in the city on October 1, the day fixed for the opening of the assembly.... General Pepe then resigned the command of the army and received the praises of Ferdinand.... After the convocation of Parliament, the Provisional Junta was dissolved.... When the parliament met, those who belonged to the extreme parts of either side found fault with it: the absolutists called it a meeting of demagogues; the servile, of violent radicals;... just men who took the middle course were abused by both. Liberty was new, and the use of freedom of speech not yet understood; it therefore degenerated into license, and proud men...lost their temper.... The public, also, unaccustomed to the language of the tribune, mistook the audacious or scurrilous language of an individual for that of a parliamentary debate: such was the real or apparent character of this assembly.... [Colletta, *History* 2:351-71.]

Under these conditions, little or nothing constructive was achieved. In October, the British ambassador to Naples, Sir William A'Court, described the assembly's deliberations as follows:

> 114. The proceedings in Parliament are hardly worth relating. The members occupy themselves with anything except what really demands attention. They had a long debate last week, which was pushed to division, whether God was, or was not the Legislator of the Universe. The question was decided in favour of the Deity by a small majority.... The names of the provinces are all to be altered.... The Asiatic pomp of the theater of San Carlo, worthy only of a nation of slaves, has also excited the attention of these sturdy reformers. Colonel Pepe has submitted a motion to Parliament upon the subject which will probably lead to the abolition of this splendid establishment, the delight of the capital and the great attraction of strangers. [Cited in Acton, *Bourbons*, 682-83.]

Amid such chaos, word arrived that Pepe had taken Palermo. The news, according to Colletta, "caused great joy in the city of Naples," but the deterioration of the country continued to increase. On November 6, Francesco Ricciardi, the minister of justice, acting at the urgent request of the deputies, presented the following report on the state of the kingdom to parliament:

> 115. I would like to speak of the state of order in the province of Naples and the capital as subjects of the gravest importance....
>
> The first days of our political rebirth were marked, in the capital and the provinces, by minor disturbances, which did not upset the public order nor compromise the safety of anyone; but the weakness of executive power and the difficulty in rectifying many of the abuses that previously existed has led to a slow reaction against the authority of the government that may produce grave consequences in the future....
>
> The public mood is generally good, even though the cause of the Constitution is not supported by the majority of the people here — as it is, for the most part, in other provinces. Restricted, however, is the number of people who can be called enemies of

the new order; the greater number, in fact, look with indifference on the events that have taken place.... Public education is needed in order to make this majority aware of the benefits of liberal institutions.

[In many parts of the country] the stealing of weapons has become widespread, and many violent acts have been committed.... The many prisoners, who for reasons of individual freedom have been released from the prisons, have increased the numbers of those carrying off arms, and many unfortunate incidents have resulted.... Since there is a shortage of police, it is impossible for the state to take effective action...and the boldness and number of armed robbers has greatly increased.... As a result, the current state of order in the kingdom is far from the point that it should be and much has still to be done....

The morale of the people, in general, is excellent;... but an insidious and deadly poison has attacked the body politic and threatens to subvert the government. The crimes, although minor in most places, go almost totally unpunished. Magistrates and public functionaries are shown little respect; courts of law are without authority; and members of the police force are looked on with contempt.... In a word, the legal framework on which our freedoms rest has been gravely weakened....

The behavior of certain patriotic societies has also become a cause of apprehension with regard to public order. These societies, who gloriously carried out the political reforms and freed us from the yoke of despotism,... did not stop, as they should have, at the moment of our rebirth, and some are continuing to exert a direct influence [on the government] that is inappropriate to the exercise of legislative and executive power.... Out of blind zeal for the public welfare, they create grave obstacles to the improvement of our institutions....

The influence of the patriotic societies in the military, in particular, is fraught with dangers.... The members of the societies, who are not used to recognizing any difference in rank at their meetings, have become habituated to ignoring the restraint prescribed by military discipline and hierarchy.... This is a grievous trend which could lead to the disintegration of the army, which only moral strength and discipline can curb.

CHAPTER 4. RESTORATION AND REACTION

I have taken all the measures that I can to put an end to these irregularities. I have instructed the royal courts and judges to carry out their duties scrupulously. I have insisted on the need for disarmament and the arrest of those causing public disturbances.... I have ordered a rigorous surveillance of suspected thieves, forcing them to show proof of their means of subsistence and have a fixed residence. In Naples, I have restored nightly patrols to insure further the security of citizens against theft and crime....

I must, however, declare to the National Parliament that these measures have not produced the results that I had hoped for, because of the large number of people accused of crimes that have been returned to the streets by the recent legal pardon, and the disgrace into which many functionaries and low-level agents of the administration of public safety have fallen....

As a consequence, I must recommend that you restore the laws to their former force; give greater authority to the executive power; suppress dangerous and illegal enlistments [in the army]; give the police the means to eliminate illegal arms;... and repress the *abuses* that have resulted from the granting of freedom of the press, but not freedom of the press itself....

In this way, public order in the kingdom will not be merely illusionary, foreigners will have reason to admire us,... and we will be able to enjoy the benefits of the constitution that has been so successfully adopted. [Francesco Ricciardi, Minister of Justice, *"Rapporto generale sullo stato della tranquillità del Regno,"* November 6, 1820, in Talamo, pp. 275-87. Italics in text.]

Ricciardi's recommendations on how to strengthen the Neapolitan government came far too late to save the revolution. For at the very time that they were being debated, the European powers were already moving forcefully to bring the constitutional experiment to an end. On November 19, 1820, the representatives of Austria, Russia, and Prussia—meeting in the tiny Moravian town of Troppeau—issued their famous "Troppeau Protocol" in which they granted themselves the right to intervene against any revolution that "threatened other states." One day later, the leaders of the three countries sent three separate, but identically-worded, letters to Ferdinand inviting him to join them in a congress that was to be held at Laibach in January of the following year. The invitations—which were personally signed by the emperor of Austria, the czar of Russia, and the king of Prussia—created an uproar in Naples. The Carbonari, still distrustful of the king, refused at first to allow him to leave the country. The Muratist-dominated ministry, however, more respectful of Austrian power, was willing to agree to a compromise, provided that Ferdinand reaffirmed his loyalty to the Constitution. The matter held fire for ten days until Ferdinand — "with gratitude on his lips and vengeance in his heart," as A.J. Whyte has eloquently put it — accepted the ministry's offer. On January 13 he renewed his oath before Parliament, and three days later he was permitted to leave. Pietro Colletta, who had just returned to Naples from Sicily where he had completed the work of repression begun by Pepe, recalled these dramatic events his *Storia* as follows:

> 116. Meanwhile affairs abroad assumed a more threatening aspect....
> [At home] the finances were impoverished from the great expense of an army and armaments increased to twice their former complement, while the revenue was decreased by the abolition of certain taxes, or by others being lowered, and by want of punctuality in receipts from Sicily, owing to revolutions and financial embarrassments. The hope of recovery was faint, for the threat of an invasion by a foreign army had lowered our credit....
>
> Ferdinand accordingly determined to quit the Kingdom, and wrote privately to the kings assembled at Troppeau, asking their assistance and advice; their answers reached him at the end of November.
>
> The letters from the three sovereigns contained an invitation to meet them at the Congress at Laibach, there to settle the political state at Naples. But by the terms of the Constitution the King could not leave without the permission of Parliament.... The city meanwhile was in a state of great excitement, amidst these various movements by the King....
>
> [As the weeks passed] the city became more and more agitated; for on perceiving hostile preparations in the palace, where the guards were doubled and the guns of the castle were pointed upon the town, numbers hastened to the Parliament to beg for aid and vengeance.... People ran in crowds about the streets, shouting, "The Constitution of Spain or Death!..." The Carbonari aimed at a more formidable movement, dispatching messengers and letters into the provinces in order to excite the revolutionary party of July 6...and sent envoys to Parliament, signifying their desire to preserve the Constitution of Spain inviolate, but to allow the King to depart....
>
> It was observed with surprise that of every possible course, Parliament chose the worst.... It decided to reject the offer of any new constitution, but to permit the King to depart, provided he took a second oath to the Constitution of Spain, and promised to support

CHAPTER 4. RESTORATION AND REACTION

it in the Congress.... By leaving the King free to depart, they lost the opportunity of obtaining the advantage still in their hands.... The pusillanimous King, frightened by popular tumults, believing his guards, servants, and even the crews of the English and French vessels in the harbor his enemies, only thought of flight; he accordingly drew up a new message to the parliament...swearing to maintain the constitution of Spain, and even exceeding the hopes of the people, by declaring that if he could not preserve their rights and those of the crown in the Congress, he would return to Naples in time to defend them by the sword.... After the publication of this final message and the decision of the Parliament, suspicion was lulled, and disturbances ceased.... He then hastened his departure...and embarked on an English vessel on the morning of December 14. [Colletta, *History* 2:371-91.]

Ferdinand arrived in Laibach on January 8, 1821. Initially, he was greeted warmly, but his vacillating personality and unwillingness to work soon caused his welcome to wear thin. On January 22, Friedrich von Gentz, Metternich's personal secretary and advisor, wrote:

117. The King has arrived here without having with him a single man capable of either giving advice or transacting business. He has never himself had the least taste for work; he has now so lost the habit of it that it is difficult to engage him to read a dispatch which consists of more than one page.... Like all weak men, he conceives nothing but extremes; he passes in turn from imprudence to the most fearful reserve, and from terror to temerity. Having subscribed on one evening to the most shameful capitulation, he believes the very next day that he can not only consider this as not having happened, but that he can also dictate the law as an absolute master of those to whom he engaged himself. This is the ally whom heaven has placed in our hands and whose interests we have to reestablish! [Friedrich von Gentz, *Depeches inedités* 2:121-23, quoted in Paul Schroeder, *Metternich's Diplomacy at its Zenith, 1820–1823*. Austin: University of Texas Press, 1962, p. 105.]

In spite of Ferdinand's weaknesses, the conservative powers were determined to restore his authority. On February 9, the monarchs of Austria, Russia, and Prussia sent simultaneous letters to Francis informing him that, because the Neapolitan revolution represented a "danger" to the peace of Europe, they had decided to allow the Austrian army to reenter the kingdom and reestablish order. Two weeks later, on February 23, Ferdinand issued a separate declaration denouncing the Constitution and instructing the people of Naples to greet the invaders as "friends." The declaration proved to be the moment of truth for the Neapolitan government. Already weakened by the Sicilian revolution and deeply divided, it decided to defend the frontier. The difficulties of the government's position were outlined by Colletta who, as minister of war, was responsible for organizing the kingdom's defense:

> 118. It is important to explain what was the condition of the country at this period, when war was inevitable. The hopes of the revolution had failed, or were failing, and the revolutionary party felt that they had been deceived; public confidence was exhausted, the people disabused, the Carbonari demoralized, their followers betrayed, or under the guidance of the crafty agents of those in authority, the King, antagonistic, and volunteering to lead an enemies' army into the Kingdom; the regent, his son, in his father's confidence and subject to him, yet at the head of the Neapolitan Army. The generals disputing among themselves, the officers disobedient, the soldiers insubordinate, the finances impoverished, the fear of invasion great, and the fear of the King's vengeance greater, while mutual suspicions had arisen between the army and the people. In the midst of all these dangers, it was remembered that the revolution was now a fact and irrevocable,... but the acts of public officials, whether ministers, members of Parliament, officers of the army, or Carbonari, all the props of the new government, were men like themselves, disunited and weak. [Colletta, *History* 2:403-4.]

Faced with such difficulties, the struggle went badly from the beginning. On March 7, the Austrian army crushed the Neapolitans at Rieti and headed for Naples. Ferdinand, who was trailing his allies at a distance, issued a declaration threatening draconian punishment to anyone who resisted, and Austrian troops entered the city unopposed on March 23. When they arrived, they found that Pepe and the other revolutionary leaders had already fled the kingdom; and that the Neapolitan parliament had, ten days earlier, "voluntarily" dispensed with the Constitution and passed a resolution submitting to the king. It was an inglorious conclusion to the July Revolution. The divisions among the revolutionary leaders, the civil war in Sicily, the weakness of the middle class in the capital and provinces, and Metternich's determination to crush the Carbonari had all combined to bring the constitutional experiment to an end.

■

CHAPTER 4. RESTORATION AND REACTION

The last four years of Ferdinand's reign provide a dreary tale of governmental corruption and political repression. In April 1821, even before he had reentered Naples, Ferdinand reappointed the reactionary prince of Canosa as minister of police. Canosa — who, like the king himself, had learned little from his long years in exile — immediately launched a policy of retribution. Mass arrests, long prison sentences, and public executions followed. The army and administration were purged of Muratists and Carbonari, and anyone suspected of having been even mildly sympathetic to the revolutionaries was dismissed. Only in July, after three months of brutal reprisals, did General Frimont, the Austrian commander in Naples, intervene to have Canosa removed from office; and, even then, Ferdinand refused to part with him completely, maintaining him as special advisor and counselor of state.

Meanwhile, as the government was busy eliminating its political opposition, the administration was sinking into corruption. On November 3, 1823, the Sardinian ambassador in Naples, the marchese di San Saturnino — who had witnessed the operations of the Neapolitan bureaucracy firsthand in both the capital and the provinces — wrote to the count della Torre, the Sardinian foreign minister in Turin:

> 119. The corruption of the courts throughout the kingdom is, unfortunately, only too easily verified by daily experience. To this is added the corruption of all of the other administrative bodies and almost all of their employees, from those who work alongside the ministers to the lowest subaltern of the intendants. It would take an iron hand to halt this scourge, which has been ingrained over centuries and made chronic by the last revolution. Even the ablest, most foreseeing, most courageous leader would not be able to restore quickly those moral principles upon which the true and intrinsic solidarity of the kingdom depends. [Marchese di San Saturnino to della Torre, Naples, November 3, 1823, in Bianchi, *Storia Documentata* 2:224.]

By 1823, Ferdinand was no longer the man for such Herculean endeavors. Seventy-two years old and absorbed in his personal pleasures, he immersed himself in a daily routine of hunting and evenings with his family, and left his ministers to wield authority in his name. On March 26, 1824, he wrote to Francis I, the emperor of Austria, requesting that Austrian troops be kept in the kingdom in order to prevent "new disorders." Francis, although reluctant, eventually consented, and the costly and unpopular occupation of the country continued for three more years. The last two years of his life, in fact, seem to have been lived like the others, with few regrets and little reflection. On January 25, 1825, he died peacefully in his sleep in the royal palace after a long day of hunting. Having become king at the age of eight in 1759, he had survived two revolutions and two periods of exile, and had still managed to preserve a certain vitality until the age of seventy-five. Lady Blessington, who was in Naples at the time of his death and had visited him only two days earlier, described his funeral as follows:

> 120. The first news I heard on awaking this morning was of the death of the King of Naples. He was found dead in his bed by his attendants, without having suffered any previous illness.... His death seems to have occurred while he slept; for all about him indicated that no struggle had taken place. He is much regretted, for if not a sovereign of superior mental acquirements, he was assuredly a good-natured man....
>
> I myself saw the deceased Sovereign only two days ago, looking healthy and vigorous; and now another sits in his place. His successor, and the Royal Family, have come to the palace of Capo di Monte...and the route is filled by the carriages of the ministers of state, officers of the palace, and courtiers hurrying to worship the new king, and totally oblivious to the departed one.... Innumerable are the virtues, hitherto unsuspected, but now attributed to the [new] king, and the errors discovered in the late. It would seem that in new sovereigns, like brides, their good qualities are lauded, and their defects overlooked. During my long residence in Naples, I have never heard so many anecdotes in favour of Francis as in the last two days....
>
> General Church, who dined here yesterday, proposed to conduct me to see the remains of the late king, lying in state in the palace at Naples; and I availed myself of his offer today. What a changed aspect did the palace present, since I had seen it last, though but a few days before! The staircase, the suite of rooms leading to the chamber of death, were hung with black, and lighted with funeral torches. Mutes and soldiers, with their arms covered with black crape, paced silently along; and all the persons attached to the palace were clothed in deep mourning. In the middle of a large and lofty chamber, lined with black velvet, spotted with silver tears, a high platform, covered with the same material, trimmed with deep silver lace and bullion fringe, was erected. On it a catafalque, surmounted by a royal crown, was placed, composed of gold and silver, and having at the four corners large plumes of feathers. On this catafalque reposed the mortal remains of the deceased king, the head elevated on a pillow, covered with cloth of gold and silver,

CHAPTER 4. RESTORATION AND REACTION

and the face exposed. Officers of the state sat at each corner of the platform; an innumerable quantity of waxen serges of huge dimensions, in silver stands, was distributed around; and large candelabra and sconces of silver, were placed against the walls. Not a sound broke the silence of the place; the floors of the apartments being covered with black carpets, of so thick a substance that no step would be heard. There lay the face I had seen so lately in health; the white locks I had often marked floating over the ruddy cheeks, now pale and marble-like. The hand, thus motionless, a few hours ago swayed a scepter, and at this moment it cannot chase away the insolent fly that has settled on that pallid cheek! Death, at all times a solemn and imposing sight, never appeared to me invested in more solemnity than today, when I saw it surrounded with all the insignia of worldly power and grandeur, over which it waved its triumphal but somber banner. I thought of the evening, only a few months ago, when I beheld him, who now lay so cold and immovable on the splendid catafalque before me, steering his gilded bark over the waters, "the observer of all observers." His nod was then law, and on his cold fiat, life and death depended; yet he is now humbled to dust, the very grandeur of the trophies that surround his earthly remains seeming a mockery when contrasted with the ghastly spectacle which they are meant to dignify.... The silver tears on the hangings were the only ones I witnessed in the chamber of death; and it struck me that they were a happy invention for such occasions. As dead kings are rarely wept for, their disappointed subjects look to their successor for the fulfillment of their frustrated expectations, which the new one, in his turn, is probably equally destined to disappoint. [Blessington, *Idler* 2:127-31.]

Blessington's pessimism with regard to the new regime was certainly borne out by history. For each of the major themes that had dominated the reign of Ferdinand — the persistence of the absolute monarchy; the struggle against liberalism; the continuation of foreign influence at the highest levels of government; and the poverty, crime, and corruption that prevailed in the capital and provinces — continued under his son and successor, Francis I (1825–1830).

Francis was a strange blend of weakness of character and political ambition. Forty-two years old and possessed of none of his father's physical vitality, he had lived in the shadow of power for more than a decade, and immediately set out to make up for lost time by immersing himself in governmental affairs. During his reign, administrative corruption — which had been gathering speed during Ferdinand's last years

— continued without interruption. Bribes, kickbacks, and influence peddling became the standard ways of conducting governmental business, and their insidious effects soon came to be accepted as "normal" by the population as a whole. On June 18, 1825, Metternich, after receiving several alarming reports from his agents in Naples, wrote to Count de Pralormo in Turin:

> 121. The majority of the problem, which seems to be incurable in the Kingdom of the Two Sicilies, is the corruption and venality that reigns among virtually all Neapolitan officials. Public opinion in this kingdom is steadily becoming more cynical and depraved. The king staggers about without principles, the ministers vacillate, the government inspires neither respect nor fear, and the army is penetrated by political sects and thus offers no protection. I am certain that Naples will have a second revolution. But Austria cannot simply stand by and allow so great a calamity to strike Italy a second time; it cannot remain inactive under the pretext that it has no right to meddle in the internal affairs of an independent state.... [Metternich to Pralormo, Vienna, June 18, 1825, in Bianchi, *Storia Documentata* 2:228.]

Accompanying the increase in corruption was an intensification of political repression. Under Francis' competent, but overly-zealous, minister of police, Niccolo Intonti, spies were placed in schools, offices, army barracks, and even churches to report on real or suspected liberals. The activities of the press and the families of émigrés were carefully monitored, and anyone with even a passing acquaintance with a suspected member of the Carbonari was interrogated and harassed. In 1831, Colletta, who like so many other former leaders of the 1820 Revolution had gone into exile, wrote grimly from Florence:

> 122. Francis I surpassed his father in cruelty and cunning while continuing, at the same time, to block any effort to establish a constitution....
>
> During his early years, the harsh and oppressive measures of the late reign continued unabated and the persecution became more systematic and savage. In September 1826, the public functionaries were enjoined "to favor in every way the friends of the throne and altar; to carry on to the death against all who, during the past vicissitudes of the Kingdom, had, by deed or word, rebelled against the absolute government of the King."... The following year, Niccolo Intonti, the Minister of Police, ordered a list of suspected persons to be drawn up in every province; but as the number on the list exceeded 100,000,

CHAPTER 4. RESTORATION AND REACTION

he was compelled to abstain from further proceedings. [Colletta, *History* 2:473-76.]

The continued corruption and heavy-handedness of the royal government tested the loyalty of some of the king's most devoted supporters. Middle-class professionals and intellectuals, in particular, resented the sale of offices to the highest bidder, and the king's unpredictable moods and volcanic temper created a permanent state of tension among many of the members of his staff. On February 6, 1826, Monsignor Olivieri, the duke of Calabria's personal tutor—in one of the most extraordinary letters ever written to a Neapolitan monarch — castigated the entire administration for its venality and corruption. Taking advantage of his special relationship with the monarch, he presented the king with a list of the government's weaknesses in the following terms:

> 123. 1. All honest people, without exception, pity Your Majesty because in a single year you have lost the hearts of your subjects and have become the object of general hatred and public contempt. If anyone tells you to the contrary, he is a false flatterer who deceives in order to betray you.
>
> 2. Your subjects are divided into two classes, conspirators and neutrals. The former are working strenuously in all the provinces to foment a new revolution which is to be decisive...and whose principle aim is to exterminate the royal family and its adherents....
>
> 3. The revolution is to begin in Sicily as soon as Austrian troops quit that island; and from there spread to all the provinces of the kingdom.
>
> 4. The causes of the general discontent are many, but the chief ones are these. First, the despotism of the ministry, which has increased since the death of our father the late King, although Your Majesty may fancy you have curbed it. Second, the paralysis in all affairs. During the thirteen months since Your Majesty's accession nothing has been done, nothing is being done, and everything is put off to a vague, uncertain future. Third, the overweening power, corruption, and venality of the magistrates, secretaries, and all provincial officials, who bring increasing odium on the royal authority. Fourth, Your Majesty's unhappy choice of servants, who are either sectarians, or scoundrels, or fools.
>
> 5. All favours are bestowed on the bad; none on the honest and deserving.

6. The lack of a council of state to examine the conduct of secretaries of state, who are detested by the whole nation.

7. The increase of customs duties and other public burdens, combined with Your Majesty's enormous waste of money on travels, hunting, fishing, luxurious buildings, and every kind of amusement.

8. The dismissal and pensioning off of the best magistrates in Naples and Sicily because they are opposed to the ruinous new systems.

9. Your Majesty's patronage of notorious reprobates and robbers, who not content with robbing Your Majesty, embezzle even the alms of the poor to enrich themselves.

10. The neglect of the army which has become almost entirely hostile to you in consequence; and whoever tells you the contrary deceives you.

11. The chaos and anarchy that are the natural result of what is happening in all of the other administrative branches in the kingdom.

12. Finally, the bad odour surrounding the Queen (pardon this liberty, but I should betray you unless I spoke of it frankly), who is commonly said to be engrossed in coquetry, and the dishonour which this reflects on your daughter Donna Cristina, who will never find a husband, if she loses her reputation.... [Olivieri to Francis I, February 6, 1826, cited in Harold Acton, *The Last of the Bourbons*. London: Methuen, 1961, pp. 19-20.]

Olivieri's criticism, although tolerated, had no effect on government policy. For like so many other Neapolitans, Francis considered the sale of offices and personal gratuities an inherent part of the "system," and opposed any suggestion of administrative reform. Instead, he and his chief minister, the durable and pragmatic Luigi de' Medici, sought to ease the economic burden on the country by asking the Austrians to withdraw. In July 1826, after over a month of difficult negotiations, the reluctant Austrians were compelled to agree to an early departure, and the last Austrian soldier left the kingdom in February of the following year. On April 8, 1827, Francis wrote to the Austrian emperor:

124. I can assure Your Majesty that I do not believe, after having taken every possible precaution, that there is any serious reason to fear for my kingdom, since I have purged not only the army, but also the administration of the kind of pernicious elements that we were forced to keep in 1815, and they have been neutralized completely. My ministers, moreover, having learned from the sad experiences of 1820,

CHAPTER 4. RESTORATION AND REACTION

will certainly be more circumspect and cautious, and will give greater attention to the all important matter of public order.... Given these changes, I have every reason to hope that a recurrence of past disorders is unlikely, and that, even if there is a momentary flare-up in some corner of the kingdom, my army will soon put it out.

As for your concern about possible changes in my system of government,... it is well known that, since I came to the throne, I have been guided by only one set of principles, and that these principles are in perfect accord with those of my August father.... [Francis I, King of the Two Sicilies, to Francis I, Emperor of Austria, Naples, April 8, 1827, in Bianchi, *Storia Documentata* 2:404-6.]

Metternich, however, was not so sure. On February 27, 1827, at the very moment that the Austrians were completing their withdrawal from the kingdom, he wrote to the comte de Bombelles, the Austrian ambassador to Tuscany:

125. Austrian troops have just evacuated the Kingdom of Naples, and, as specified by the terms of the Convention of Milan, they will all be across the Po by the end of March. His Sicilian Majesty, having judged in his wisdom that the reorganization of his army and internal administration has reached the point where he no longer needs the support of the military corps that [we have] placed at his disposal,... requested that they be withdrawn.... Nevertheless, since the future is in the hands of Providence, and the simple laws of caution make it the duty of every government to take whatever steps it deems necessary to combat the evil that threatens us,... His Imperial Majesty has decided to keep these troops for the time being in his Italian provinces, so that they can be redispatched to Naples in the shortest time possible should circumstances demand it.... In taking this precaution, the emperor has no other goal than to provide a warning to the secret societies, and to strengthen the will of governments throughout the peninsula [to resist them].... His Majesty is confident that this decision is in the best interests of all the governments of Italy, and that it will give further proof of his determination to maintain order in this beautiful part of Europe.... [Metternich to Bombelles, Vienna, February 27, 1827, in Bianchi, *Storia Documentata* 2:411-13.]

Metternich's doubts about the future stability of the Neapolitan kingdom proved to be well founded. In June 1828, Carbonari leaders in the district of Salerno, encouraged by the departure of Austrian troops from the country, disarmed the local army garrison in the village of Bosco and began to march from town to town demanding a constitution. Francis, fearful that the rebellion would lead to a repetition of the events of 1820, immediately dispatched 8,000 soldiers to the district with orders to crush the revolution mercilessly before it could spread. The destruction was frightful. The village of Bosco was bombarded by artillery and then razed to the ground by rampaging soldiers. Fleeing rebels were hunted down in the hills around Salerno, and the trials and executions went on for almost a year. Overall, 29 people were condemned to death (including seven in Naples), and 140 more sentenced to long terms in prison. An eighty-year old priest, De Luca, was publicly beheaded, and the episode was held up by the commander of the army, General Del Carretto, as an "example" to anyone who dared threaten the regime.

Meanwhile, as Del Carretto was eliminating the last vestiges of the opposition, the king and queen were heading off to Paris as the honored guests of their equally-threatened Bourbon counterpart, Charles X. Arriving in May 1830 in an atmosphere thick with tension, they were treated to a series of gala receptions at Saint Cloud, the Tuilleries, and the Palais Royal, and a special performance of the Paris opera was given for the Neapolitan king. On June 1, the French diplomat, Guillaume Viennet — who was well aware of the tenuous position of the two monarchs and had noticed the jittery mood that had accompanied the celebrations — wrote in his *Journal*:

> 126. Yesterday I went to the ball given for the King of Naples and his family by the Duke of Orleans. It was the first time I set foot in the rooms of the Palais-Royal.... The Ball was very beautiful. The whole royal family was present and Charles X did not appear to be amused. The sovereigns of Naples are nothing wonderful. The King has the features of a man of eighty and he is not even fifty-four. The dancing was solemn; and solemnity is always sad. There were many deputies in our midst, beset by grim anxieties like everyone else. M. de Salvandy, a wit who enjoys scintillating, has neatly summarized the situation: "We are dancing," he said, "on a volcano." He was quite right. [Cited in Acton, *Last of the Bourbons*, p. 39.]

That same day, Francis and his family began their journey back to Naples; three weeks later, on July 26, riots broke out in the streets of Paris, and Charles X was overthrown.

■ ■ ■

POLITICAL CULTURE & EVENTS: 19TH CENTURY

42. Political Life as Religious Drama. Francis I and the Royal Family worship at the shrine of Ferdinand I.

43. Cardinal Ruffo, the instrument of God and reaction against the Parthenopean Republic: military honors rest comfortably on the cleric's robes.

44. Political heretics: A secret Carbonari meeting, c. 1820.

45. Democracy enshrined: the Parliament of 1848.

MODERN NAPLES, 1799–1999

46. *The barricades on via Sta. Brigida, May 15, 1848.*

47. *Carlo Poerio (1802–1848).*

48. *Luigi Settembrini (1813–1876).*

49. *Gladstone visits political prisoners, 1850.*

50. *Garibaldi and Bixio at Calatafimi, May 15, 1860.*

51. *Casting ballots for the Plebiscite, October 21, 1860.*

52. *Group of brigands captured near Salerno, 1865.*

53. *Piedmontese soldier with the corpse of brigand Nicola Napolitano, c. 1865.*

54. *Street fighting between San Ferdinando and via Toledo, May 15, 1848.*

5
The Revolution of 1848

Francis I's trip to Paris was the last major diplomatic initiative of his reign. Never robust, he arrived in Naples on July 31 depressed and exhausted. Stricken by a variety of illnesses, he died after a convulsion at Castellammare on November 8. Unlike his father, he had never been popular among the Neapolitan people. Even in Naples, where affection for the Bourbons was greater than in the provinces, he had only managed to generate modest enthusiasm, and many were happy to see his regime come to an end.

Francis was succeeded by his son, the young and dynamic Ferdinand II (1830–1858). Twenty years old and brimming with confidence, Ferdinand was determined to change the image of the monarchy and immediately set out to win popular support. Taxes were lowered; a political amnesty was granted; and special efforts were made to stimulate the economy. Political exiles were allowed to return to the country; an attempt was made to establish the kingdom's independence from Austria; and the army was strengthened and reformed. Even the great Neapolitan liberal, Luigi Settembrini — who was later to be imprisoned by Ferdinand as a dangerous revolutionary — was initially convinced of his sincerity. In his *Ricordanze*, written over forty years later, he recalled wistfully:

> 127. When King Ferdinand II ascended to the throne in November of 1830, he began well and to many he seemed to be a good prince.... In one of his manifestos he declared that he "wanted to heal the wounds that for many years [had] afflicted the kingdom," restoring justice, putting the state finances in order, promoting industry and commerce, and assuring in every possible way the welfare of his beloved people. When he later declared an amnesty by which many exiles and prisoners returned to their families, hopes ran high and there was general joy. Wise men...praised him for removing a number of ministers and public servants who had engaged in the worst kind of corruption, and curtailing [personal] expenditures....

Everyone believed him to be courteous because he received everyone in audience: he asked, he answered, he acted promptly, and he remembered the names of everyone, once he met them. He even contented Sicily, which was still yearning for its own king and independence, and sent his own brother, Leopold, to the island as his representative....

I remember with what eagerness we waited for, and read, the newspapers, with what ardor we debated [the issues], and how rosy was the picture that we painted of the future. And not only me, a youth, but also older men of prudence, and even those snail-like plodders at Court, thought that the world had changed. The new political regime [of Louis Philippe] in France, the state of excitement throughout Italy, the innovations that he introduced, the hearty welcome that he gave to liberal men and ideas — everything led one to believe that a great change was about to take place. Not only Neapolitans but other Italians admired him and expected wonders from him, so much so that messengers came from the Marches and the Romagna seeking his aid, and would have proclaimed him king of Italy if he had wanted to send an army to fight the hated Austrians. In short, everyone in the kingdom and without was excited, and believed that, if a revolution should break out, he would be its leader.... [Luigi Settembrini, *Ricordanze della mia vita*. Bari: Guis, Laterza & Figli, 1934, pp. 29-33.]

The favorable impression that Ferdinand made in his early years was not limited to Italians. Non-Italians too were fascinated by his apparent change in direction and openly praised him to their governments at home. On December 3, 1843, the United States chargé d'affaires in Naples, William Boulware, in a report sent to Washington on the Neapolitan economy, wrote to A.P. Upshur at the U.S. Department of State:

128. An observer in this country cannot fail to be impressed by the contrast presented by the advantages conferred by Nature, and the injuries inflicted by the Government. Here is a climate among the mildest, most uniform, and most healthy in the world; a soil in fertility in many parts which even surpasses the valley of the Nile;... a land so picturesque and beautiful that painters from all over the earth have ever been delighted to delineate its scenery and poets have sought successful inspiration [from] its enchantments....

But here is a government which, almost from time immemorial, had made war on the interests of its people, which seems to have

CHAPTER 5. THE REVOLUTION OF 1848

tortured invention to find impediments for the obstruction of commerce, which has burdened agriculture to such a degree that but a mite of products of the soil remains to the producer, [and] which in its stupid efforts to regulate industry and production, has trammeled the exertions of the farmer...[and] extended its harassing interference into the minutiae of [everyday] life....

The present King [however], participating in the spirit of the age, [has] manifested a strong disposition to change the system of his ancestors. He is engaged in the construction of railroads, in facilitating the intercourse between different parts of the Kingdom by means of steamboats, and in various other schemes of internal improvement. He has introduced a most important and useful change, after the example set in Germany, by placing his soldiers to labor on public works.... During his reign commerce has increased with rapidity, and the commercial and naval marine still faster.... [Boulware to Upshur, Naples, December 3, 1843, in Howard R. Marraro, ed. *Diplomatic Relations Between the United States and the Kingdom of the Two Sicilies: Instructions and Dispatches, 1816-1861.* New York: S.F. Vanni, 1951, Dispatch 16, 2:557-61.]

Under Ferdinand, the first iron suspension bridge in Italy, which had been begun by his father four years earlier, was completed over the Garigliano in 1832. In 1839, the first railroad in the peninsula was constructed from Naples to Portici; and the line was extended to Nocera in 1844. Although the country remained overwhelmingly agricultural, progress was palpable. Between 1832 and 1837 alone, the total capacity of the Neapolitan merchant marine increased by over 50 percent, and the number of merchant vessels grew to over 7,000. Buoyed by the general European economic prosperity of the 1830s, public squares in Naples were lit with gas for the first time in 1840, and expensive shops filled with luxury items competed with hawkers for the attention of shoppers on the streets.

None of this, however, had the slightest effect on the Neapolitan form of government. Ferdinand, in fact, was even more committed to political absolutism than his father; and he believed that a strong army and continuous police activity were the only truly effective means of guaranteeing the regime. Even Intonti, whose tactics had terrorized the revolutionaries for more than a decade, was judged to be too liberal for the new government. In 1831, he was replaced by Del Carretto, who kept secret files on his own agents and extended police surveillance to include some of the closest supporters of the king.

In January 1836, the death of the queen, the beautiful and intensely religious Maria Cristina, only added to Ferdinand's deepening mood of alienation and suspicion. Stunned by the suddenness of her death and guilt-ridden over his previous failure of appreciate her, he immersed himself in religious mysticism and withdrew, for a time, almost completely from political affairs. In October, the spread of a cholera epidemic from Central Europe to Italy — which killed almost 14,000 people in the Naples area and over 65,000 in Sicily — completed his drift towards reaction and repression. By the spring of 1837, in fact, the earlier optimism created by his regime had long vanished, and the expectations that the kingdom was entering a new era had clearly passed. On April 14, the British ambassador in Naples, Sir William Temple, wrote:

> 129. The education of the King was unfortunately entirely neglected as to almost all the branches of knowledge which could be useful to him as a Sovereign, and the only principles which the late Monsignor Olivieri, his tutor, appears to have endeavoured to instill in his mind in addition to a blind reverence for the ceremonies and ordinances of the Roman Catholic religion, were a distrust of all persons who might surround him, and a narrow economy which has now almost degenerated into avarice.
>
> These dispositions were probably much strengthened by a consideration of the evils entailed upon this country by the unlimited powers enjoyed by former Ministers, and by the profuse expenditure of the Court and the peculation which pervaded all departments of the State during the reigns of his two predecessors. Unfortunately too, His Majesty has a great distaste for business, and with the exception of military details his Ministers can scarcely induce him to attend to the affairs of state. As there is no minister who has any influence beyond his own immediate department, and each entertains a jealously of his colleagues, consequently there is no directing mind to give influence or unity of action to the march of government, which indeed may be said to stand still.
>
> On the accession of His Majesty to the throne he certainly displayed good sense and energy in recalling many persons who had been banished or who had quitted the country on account of political opinions, a measure which rendered him deservedly popular.... Great expectations were raised of improvements in the administrations of the country, and particularly in Sicily, where on his first visit to that island, he was received with great enthusiasm.... Unfortunately, however, these expectations have not been fulfilled, and on his second visit to Sicily in 1834 his reception was

CHAPTER 5. THE REVOLUTION OF 1848

cold though respectful, and the Sicilians evidently wished to make him sensible to their feelings of disappointment....

It is to be feared therefore that, although the King and his ministers are fully sensible of the evils which exist in Sicily, they do not possess sufficient talent or energy to meet them, and will leave things to take their chance, trusting that as they have gone on so long, they may continue to do so in the same manner, and fearing that their interference would be more likely to lead, as in the case of a corrupt body, to complete dissolution than to a restoration of health and vigour.
[Cited in Acton, *Last of the Bourbons*, pp. 108-10.]

The "feelings of disappointment" indicated by Temple led naturally to a renewal of political agitation. Among the young and educated, in particular, liberalism had continued to grow despite the repression, and unrest in the countryside had never really ceased. During the cholera epidemic of 1836-1837, popular disturbances had occurred in Sicily, the Abruzzi, Apulia, and Calabria, and sporadic disorders reappeared in the provinces throughout the following years. In March 1844, William Boulware, noting the explosive potential of such disorders, wrote to Upshur in Washington:

130. We have recently had an insurrection in this kingdom which, but for the information obtained of the designs of the conspirators, would probably have involved this country, if not all of Italy in civil war. About the middle of this month in the town of Cosenza in Calabria, a considerable body of men rose in the night and paraded in the streets crying *"Viva la Repubblica!"* and *"Giovine Italia!"* They attacked the fortress, but the King's troops, who were stationed [there], succeeded in killing the leader along with various others of the insurgents. This dispirited the party and they retired without gaining their object, though not until they had avenged themselves by the death of the Commander of the troops together with some of the soldiers.

The Government had been previously informed, it is believed, through the kindness of Louis Philippe, by means of discoveries made by the Police at Paris, of what was intended, and were on their guard. But for this fortunate information, it is not improbable that all of Italy would have now been in convulsion....

Italy is volcanic — the smothered fire will explode sooner or later — the first war in Europe will witness a great eruption. Light is diffused, though not rapidly; yet it is diffused. Liberal sentiments are making their way, in spite of all the barriers which can be opposed to

> their progress. Peace, steam, [and] travel are carrying the seeds of
> amelioration everywhere.... [Boulware to Upshur, Naples, March 30,
> 1844, in Marraro, *Diplomatic Relations*, Dispatch 19, 1:567-68.]

The Cosenza rebellion, like the others before it, was met by intensified repression. By the early 1840s, according to Settembrini, 1,500 men were confined in the Vicaria prison in Naples alone. Sleeping in their own stench amid the rats and roaches, political prisoners were mixed with ordinary criminals, and students "who had been late submitting [their] documents" were interned with murderers and thieves. In 1847, Settembrini — driven to desperation by conditions in the kingdom and incensed by the depredations of Ferdinand's minister of the interior, the marchese de Santangelo — published a sweeping condemnation of the regime. Appearing anonymously in Naples under the title *Protest from the People of the Kingdom of the Two Sicilies*, it criticized the king and his administration in the most unrelenting terms:

> 131. Naples saw the birth of economic science and still boasts distinguished economists, yet its administration is in the hands of knaves and fools. The minister of the interior is scandalously corrupt. The minister, together with a few grain merchants, maintains a ruinous hold on the economy, and he personally shares some of the filthy profits of the public-works contractors, choosing those who offer him the highest bribe.... His employees — bootlickers, clowns, and hangers-on — do what he does, and he merely follows the king's bad example.
>
> Our agriculture, which needs government protection and the most assiduous care, comes under a subdepartment run by two or three idiotic clerks. Our land is as fertile as almost anywhere in Italy, but it is deserted, or else is cultivated by a handful of wretched, weary peasants. Immense territories in Sicily, in the Calabrias, in the Abruzzi, in the Principati and even in Apulia are abandoned and malarial. If there is any question of land reclamation, as for instance near the mouth of the Volturno, the minister gives the job to some personal friend who spends and spends but does nothing.... In such a fertile kingdom, which could feed double its present population, there is often a bread shortage and people can be found dead of starvation. Often grain has to be brought in from Odessa, or from Egypt and other so-called "barbarous" states.... All is left to God's providence and to the landowners. When [the king's ministers] see that the people are hungry, they simply forbid the export of grain, remove the flour tax for a couple of

months, and tell the friars to give out generous alms and pray for a good season.

Instead of being protected and helped, landowners are treated as sponges to be squeezed dry. They are oppressed by taxes, by intendants, under-intendants and officials of every kind. Trade is restricted because the provinces lack roads, and the minister and his ultra-rich friends had made road building a sordid monopoly. Growers must sell their produce at a paltry price that barely covers outlay; hence they become poor and reduce their laborers' wages; and the result is that the latter take to robbery and brigandage. The condition of the peasants is appalling. They dig all day for fifteen or twenty grani, just enough to obtain bread and oil and make soup of wild herbs, often without salt. In the winter, hunger forces them to ask the landlord for food; he gives it, but only if they repay him twice as much or even more at harvest time, and only if they let him make love to their wives and daughters. Thus the government leaves the landlord no way of getting rich except usury, while the peasant has to sell his honor for bread. Everyone is offended. The poor rage against the immediate oppressors, failing to see that these too are suffering and that the government is to blame....

When a government is bad, even the best institutions decay into uselessness. We should praise the king (lest it be said that we speak ill of everything) because at least he has partially freed trade; he has signed commercial treaties, and assured that the flag is respected. But when things are decaying within, external polish does not matter; when producers are oppressed, when industries are few and backward, and commerce at home is held up by a thousand obstacles, what is the use of treaties? The balance of trade goes against us, and craftsmen also suffer when agriculture, mother of all, is dying.

Charitable institutions are fine and holy things, but here they are in greedy and pitiless hands.... Poor people [are] ill clad, ill nourished, and shut up in places worse than prisons. For many years now, the director of the Naples poorhouse has been Felice Santangelo, the minister's brother; he filled it with penpushers who battened on the poor orphans like horseflies, and who were in league with the purveyors of clothes and food to steal what they could.... The king, weary of hearing tales of Santangelo's thieving, dealt out justice in his fashion; he removed him from the post of director, but gave him another good job with a large salary, and then set up a commission of eight honest men to run the poorhouse.

The worst place of all, where you see cruelty at its most impious, is the Nunziata, or foundling hospital. Each wet nurse has three or four babies — fleshless, pale, and starving. Out of every hundred, eight-nine die.... To seize bread from the mouths of beggars and these innocent little creatures is a cruelty that could only happen under a government like ours....

The sick and insane have their butchers too. At a recent congress in Naples, a commission of doctors and surgeons was chosen to inspect the hospitals. They made their inspection, were overcome with pity and indignation, and wrote a long, heartfelt report; but nothing was mentioned in the published proceedings, for the report was suppressed by the chairman of the congress, the Minister Santangelo....

The prisons are also in a terrible state. The government grants just over four *grani* a day for each prisoner, on which sum the "contractor" has to provide bread, soup, oil, and earthenware receptacles; he has to whitewash the prison every six months, give good tips, and still make a profit. One single ladleful of fetid beans and a piece of bread are all those wretched men are given to eat.... Here you see not men but beasts, naked as they were when they were born, pale, starving, gnawing at the crusts and remains thrown away by some prisoner who has bought his own food; for a *grano* they submit to any oppression, undergo any shame....

Another affliction in our poverty-stricken country are the beggars who you see all over the kingdom and who pour into Naples from the provinces. The government does nothing to employ this vast number of unemployed. It moves only when some foreign sovereign arrives here;... then all sorts of people are arrested or sent back to the provinces to die of hunger. No country in the world has as many beggars.... [They] multiply daily, and some, with monstrous cunning, even hire a cripple or half-wit and take him out on show through the streets; or they hire babies and teach them to cry, pinching them and hitting them to make them howl and so arouse the pity of the passerby.... Now who is to blame for these tragic crowds of starving people in a country made by nature to be as rich and happy as anywhere in the world? And this king and government call themselves Catholics!

CHAPTER 5. THE REVOLUTION OF 1848

They think they can provide a remedy by public works, the king and Santangelo...are continually congratulating themselves. The king's palace has been restored with money from the city of Naples; another half a million has been spent in a few years to refurbish the San Carlo Theater for the entertainment of the Court, of foreigners, and of high-class tarts; three hundred thousand ducats are going to repair the Posillipo road to provide a more comfortable way for carriage owners. All these works may satisfy the king's childish whim, but they do not benefit the nation.... Two railroads have been built, one from Naples to Nocera with a branch line to Castellammare, and the other from Naples to Capua. This last was made *to link up the two royal palaces* of Naples and Caserta, as is inscribed on the medals struck to perpetuate its memory; and a sleepy branch line extends it as far as Nola where the king can review his troops.

This is all done for Naples. Nothing is done for the provinces, nothing for luckless Sicily.... Railroads are fine and desirable, but only when there are ordinary roads too: otherwise they are, I should say, almost a luxury. Incredible as it may seem, however, when a village wants to build a road at its own expense, the government withholds permission; or else the money is inadequate.... There is only one road in Calabria, and that a bad one; Sicily has two, short and bad; the Abruzzi two; very few cities have connecting roads that link them to these main routes that the French government built [under Napoleon]. In the interior, the only method of transport is on foot, or with difficulty on horseback. Official policy on public works is therefore stupid, and has no serious or useful end; apart from which it is inefficiently carried out. This reflects the character of the king who always acts by whim, who claims he does everything, and in fact does nothing. [Luigi Settembrini, *Protesta del popolo delle due Sicilie*. Naples: 1847, pp. 35-42, cited in Mack Smith, *Making of Italy*, pp. 117-23. Italics in text.]

■

By the time of the appearance of Settembrini's pamphlet, Naples was poised for another revolution. During the winter of 1846-1847, a European-wide economic slump — complete with food shortages, rising prices, and large-scale unemployment — spread to the kingdom. Moving relentlessly from London and Paris to Berlin and

Vienna and then down to Turin, Milan, and Naples, the crisis had a profound effect on the country's already-impoverished population. On January 4, 1847, William H. Polk, who had replaced Boulware as American chargé d'affaires in the capital, wrote ominously:

> 132. The failure of the grain crop in this kingdom this past season is beginning to be felt very severely by the poorer classes of the people, chiefly due to the high prices demanded for food of every description. The Government, influenced by the fear of more extensive want, and with the object of forcing holders to relax in their exorbitant prices, has published an ordinance prohibiting the exportation of every kind of food, with the hope of...forcing a reduction in prices.... Thus far, the ordinance has had no effect....
>
> It cannot be said that actual starving exists,... but scarcity is readily apparent.... Should the approaching season prove to be as dangerous to the agricultural interests of this country as the last, however, there will be no need for royal ordinances to forbid exportations. The miserable cries of the starving thousands will, by quiet or violent means, prevent it; and it will devolve on the United States in such a case to furnish the means of subsistence to millions of people.... [Wm. H. Polk to J. Buchanan, Naples, January 4, 1847, in Marraro, *Diplomatic Relations*, Dispatch 8, 2:630-31.]

Adding to the problems created by the economic crisis in Italy was a change in political leadership in Rome. On June 1, 1846, Pope Gregory XVI died and was replaced by Cardinal Mastai-Ferretti, who took the title Pius IX. Believing that a modernization of the Papal States was inevitable, the new pope immediately set out on a program of political reform: censorship of the press was relaxed; a political amnesty was granted; and a *"Consulta"* of laymen was created to advise the Holy See on domestic and foreign policy.

The reforms set off an explosion throughout Italy. In Genoa, Florence, Pisa, and Lucca, liberal demonstrators descended into the streets and were granted the right of freedom of the press by their frightened governments. In Reggio and Messina, where governmental opposition was stronger, the demonstrations turned into open rebellion and had to be put down by force. Meanwhile, in Naples, agitation for basic civil liberties was growing. In his *Ricordanze*, Settembrini, who participated in this agitation, recalled the mounting unrest in the city as follows:

> 133. The Roman press published every word uttered by the new pope, and it described the hearty welcome accorded to him by the people of the city.... Its reports reached into every corner of Italy.

CHAPTER 5. THE REVOLUTION OF 1848

In Tuscany, it was sufficient to shout "Long Live Pius IX!" in order to obtain freedom of the press, and they began to publish newspapers with fine-sounding names such as *L'Alba*, *La Patria*, and *L'Italia*, proclaiming new ideas and new hopes. In Piedmont, there appeared *Il Contemporaneo*, in which they printed things that the government would have punished them for a year earlier.... Those of us in Naples, when we read those papers and heard the tales of those returning from Rome, felt a stab of pain in our hearts. The Romans urged us on and incited us: "What are you Neapolitans doing? Why can't you follow the example of the Tuscans and the Piedmontese? Ferdinand is harsh: and you have no guts; why don't you have the courage to throw him out?"...

Everywhere, people were talking about the pope...and praised and blessed him. As for us, the police were becoming more ferocious, spying, imprisoning, and torturing; and woe to him who had received letters or newspapers from northern Europe. Some considered meeting in secret in order to take action; but others disparaged them, calling them men with old-fashioned ideas, and said: "This is not a secret society, a small group, but a general consensus, and it is public opinion that will overcome every obstacle, and Ferdinand as well."...

When the news of [the revolts] in Messina and Reggio arrived in Naples, there was great agitation in the city, and the police arrested Carlo Poerio, Mariano d'Ayala, Domenico Mauro, Francesco Trichera, and the barons Stocco, Marsico and Cozzolino, all three Calabrese. But prison no longer frightened anyone, not even those condemned to death, because everyone felt and said that things could not go on that way, and that one day or another things would have to change.... Meanwhile, the king began to waver: he discharged the minister Santangelo, and divided the ministry of the interior into three parts....

To show our general satisfaction with this act, and to push the king to greater things, such as joining the Italian Customs League that was being formed between Rome, Tuscany, and Piedmont, it was decided to mount a public demonstration; and, to hearten the timid, this took place at night. On the evening of November 22, when a large number of people were present in the piazza in front of the royal palace listening to music, some hand-clapping started, and the cry went up: "Long Live Italy, Long Live the Customs League, Long

Live the King!" The shouts continued and grew louder when the music stopped. About three hundred persons ran down the via Toledo inviting everyone to join them, and when they had reached the palace of the nuncio, they intensified their shouts. Then they broke up into smaller groups and dispersed quietly. Few of them were arrested by the police.... A great fact emerged: the police were worried, the king angrily blamed the ministry of Del Carretto, forbade the playing of the music, held a ministerial council, and had a notice prepared in his presence, to be signed by the prefect of police, which was pinned up at all the street corners, saying: "All seditious shouts and cries of 'Long Live the King!' are forbidden, and anyone who starts them will be punished as a disturber of the peace."...

A few days later it was learned that in the Palermo Theater and in the streets outside another demonstration had taken place involving a rather larger number of people, to which it was decided to respond on the evening of December 14.... A large crowd showed up and shouted: "Long Live Palermo and Sicily." Suddenly the police appeared, and a free-for-all followed in which the combatants used clubs, rapiers, rocks, and fists. There were shouts, arrests, blows, and turmoil everywhere, and the via Toledo was quickly emptied by the police....

Meanwhile, in the royal palace the king did nothing but discuss how to increase the repression.... He frequently cursed Pius IX who had disturbed the hornet's nest, and expressed contempt for the weakness of Leopold [of Tuscany] and Charles Albert; mounting his high horse, he would say: "I'll go and be a colonel in Russia or Austria rather than yield and show weakness." And he gave orders that students should be sent away from Naples, because they were full of new ideas, liable to get excited and too quick to act. Immediately many poor young men were chased out at top speed. But everyone's irritation, curses, and complaints were so great that the order was revoked. Could a government last long that knew neither how to be consistently bad nor genuinely good? [Settembrini, *Ricordanze*, pp. 157-58, 163-69.]

The answer was provided by Palermo. On January 12, 1848, the city rose in revolt, expelled its royal garrison, and proclaimed a restoration of the constitution of 1812. During the following weeks, an enraged population drove the 11,000 Neapolitan troops stationed in Sicily to the extreme western part of the island, and, by February 1, only the fortresses at Syracuse and Messina were still in royalist hands.

CHAPTER 5. THE REVOLUTION OF 1848

The victory produced an immediate reaction in Continental Naples. On January 17, in the province of Salerno, members of the secret society in the Cilento district seized control of the region and announced that they were marching on the capital with 10,000 men. Six days later, in Naples itself, Carlo Poerio and several others drew up a petition demanding that the constitution of 1820 be restored throughout the kingdom and backed up their demand on January 27 with a massive demonstration through the streets. Faced with the possibility of an armed uprising in the capital, and already on the defensive in Sicily and Salerno, Ferdinand quickly capitulated: the ministry was dismissed; a liberal government under the duke of Serracapriola was appointed in its place; and a decree was published on January 29 promising a constitution. The announcement produced wild celebrations throughout the city. Luigi Settembrini, who had been forced to leave Naples in January in order to avoid arrest, described the excitement that greeted him after his return to the capital as follows:

> 134. I arrived in Naples on February 7. As the boat entered the harbor and prepared to anchor, I saw several ships with tricolor flags, on one of which was my brother, Peppino, who shouted to me across the water: "Constitution, amnesty. Bozzelli minister of the Interior, Carlo Poerio director of police: everything has changed. Disembark! Disembark!" I embraced him and asked: "How has all this happened?" "There was a great demonstration on January 27, and on the 29th a royal decree was published that promised a constitution and granted full amnesty." "Was so much accomplished just by shouting?" "In Naples there was shouting, but in Palermo there was a terrible revolution that defeated the troops, and a revolution in Cilento." "And Ferdinand...has yielded?" "Yes, and as he signed the constitutional decree do you know what he said? 'Don Pio Nono and Carlo Alberto wanted to trip me up with a stick, so I'll try this girder [*trave*] on them. Now let's try to enjoy ourselves as best we can....'"

When the king heard the alarming news from Sicily, and felt the excitement in Naples growing daily, he asked the advice of those around him. Some advised him to use cannon. Others said he should erect a gallows at the corner of every street. Others, however, stated that force would only further antagonize the people, and that he had to make concessions, especially to the liberals.... All agreed, however, that the cause of the trouble was the abuses of the police; they spoke of the dangerous power of Del Carretto, that he had shown a friendly attitude towards the liberals, that he was reverting to the Carbonarism he had supported in 1820, that the ministry of police should be abolished, and that so much power should never again be given to one man. On the night of January 26, Del Carretto was summoned to the royal palace...and was told that the king had ordered him to leave the kingdom immediately.... [The following day] he left for Livorno,... and his power came to an end....

Meanwhile, the people had been waiting impatiently for a constitution. Bozzelli was drawing it up at the command of the king.... Everyone wanted it as they had imagined,... and many different proposals were drafted and hawked in the streets.... [As for] the Sicilians,... they were only interested in the constitution of 1812; but they wanted it updated by a parliament and not by the king. On February 10, the king accepted [Bozzelli's] constitution, and on the 11th it was published.... It was almost a copy, or rather a translation, of the French Charter of 1830.... The multitude, without examining the document any further, started rejoicing, and, ignoring the heavy rain that was falling, went to the royal palace to show its appreciation to the king.... He appeared on the grand balcony with his family and ministers...and the crowd surged around it and let out a cheer.... The celebration went on into the night...with all of the balconies illuminated and people in coaches and on foot calling to their brothers and embracing soldiers and police.... The lower classes and the young, not knowing what to say, and wanting to shout and perhaps mock, repeated "Vivooo," a meaningless word, because to them the change was meaningless. But words cannot indicate the emotions we felt at hearing many humble people shouting, "Viva Italia! We are Italians!" That word "Italy," which had at first only been uttered by a few and in secret,... sent shivers down my spine and moved me to tears.... [Settembrini, *Ricordanze*, pp. 173-78.]

During the first two months that followed the establishment of a constitution, hopes ran high for a transformation of the kingdom. In February, a general amnesty was granted to all political prisoners. Freedom of the press was established, a national guard was created, and the Italian tricolor flag (which had hitherto been banned in Naples) was adopted as the official flag of the Neapolitan state. Liberal stalwarts, such as Saliceti, d'Ayala and de Tommasi, were appointed to important positions in the provinces, and Carlo Poerio began to draw up a program for educational reform.

Nevertheless, like the revolutionaries of 1820, the leaders of the 1848 revolution were soon confronted with a number of familiar and, seemingly, intractable problems. Among them, by far the most important was the Sicilian desire

CHAPTER 5. THE REVOLUTION OF 1848

for independence. In his *Ricordanze*, Settembrini summarized the development of this problem as follows:

> 135. The greatest concern [of the new ministry] was Sicily, which rejected the Neapolitan constitution of February 10, and stated that it wanted its own constitution of 1812,... desiring to be an entirely separate and independent kingdom, with a viceroy who should be either a royal prince or a Sicilian citizen and should have wide-ranging powers. The Sicilians also stated that the ministers should be nominated by the king but must reside in Palermo, that there should be no more Neapolitan troops in Sicily, and that a mixed commission chosen from the members of both parliaments should be established to deal with common affairs. These conditions seemed extreme not only to the king, but to many Neapolitans and Italians, who believed that Sicily, by separating herself from Naples, would also separate herself from Italy. They wrote that this "Sicilianism" was unworthy, the result of an ancient rancour between Palermo and Naples, the metropolis of the whole kingdom, and that brother nations ought to unite under similar laws and institutions that produce similar customs and sentiments. They also believed that two constitutions would separate the two peoples more than the sea and forever, and that the constitution of February 10...should be accepted as their constitution as well.
>
> In response the Sicilians answered that they were not separating themselves from Italy, and that their desire for independence [from Naples] did no harm to Italy, which ought to unite as a federation and not one kingdom. They stated that they had never lost their constitution since people never lose their rights, and now they had won it back with blood,... and that if Naples was a sister rather than a master, there would be no more hatred and conflict. They knew the Bourbon king and wanted no more of the good that came from him, and they never wanted to see the brother Neapolitans who had bombarded their cities again. The arguments presented by the Sicilians were hotly debated in Naples.... The Minister Scovazzo, who was a Sicilian, submitted his resignation...and the Sicilians opened their own parliament in Palermo on March 25. Ferdinand responded with a protest, and bided his time. [Settembrini, *Ricordanze*, pp. 179-80.]

The Sicilian demand for independence was not the only problem facing the Neapolitan government. In the provinces, thousands of peasants, driven by hunger and incensed by the continuous rise in prices, stopped paying taxes and forcibly began to occupy the land. At the same time, in Naples, where the population had grown by several tens of thousands due to refugees arriving from the countryside, crowds of unemployed denounced the ministry for its "indifference" to their suffering, and radical agitators demanded "the right to work." By early March, the pressure had grown so great that the Serracapriola government had to be reorganized in order to accommodate more radical elements, but the situation continued to deteriorate all the same. In his *Memoirs*, Settembrini, who had become increasingly alarmed by the threat posed to property, wrote:

> 136. The ministry, which had been unable to solve the question of Sicily, did not fall but was reorganized, adding four new and more liberal ministers on March 6, including Saliceti as minister of justice, Poerio as minister of public instruction, and Tofano as minister of police....
>
> The revamped ministry, however, could not prevent the excitement from growing daily. They broke up the great machine of the old government, but with little wisdom. They were able to eliminate the bad, but they failed to find the good to put in their places. The clever and corrupt often remained. The inept substitutes did not know what to do. Everybody chattered, in the streets they complained about everything. They had won a constitution by shouting, so everyone thought he could get a job by shouting. In the clubs there was much talking about every subject under the sun, and those who talked the fastest and aired the most fantastic plans were the most applauded. The press, unrestricted, published scandal, calumny, truth, infamy, and criticized everyone. The masses said: "If there is no work, and we are starving, what liberty is that? Previously the king was one man, and ate for one; now he is a thousand, and they eat for a thousand. We must concern ourselves with our own situation." In the provinces the peasants invaded and divided up the lands of the king, or of the landlords who had seized them earlier and were hated because they had gotten rich through usury and extortion.... And in the city of Naples the mob, not having lands to divide up, contemplated attacking and sacking the houses [of the rich] as had been done in 1799. Into this confusion, like oil on a flame, came the accounts in the journals of the revolution and the republic in France, the movements which had now

CHAPTER 5. THE REVOLUTION OF 1848

started in northern Italy, the constitution granted by Pius IX on March 13 because he couldn't do anything else, the expulsion of the Jesuits from Genoa. Henceforth, people became crazy, the Constitution contented no one anymore, and men said it was necessary to broaden it in order not to go so far as to have a republic.... Every day the tumult grew. Crowds gathered in the streets and shouted down with the ministry, or down with this or that official, as the government trembled in fear.... [Settembrini, *Ricordanze*, pp. 180-83.]

In the middle of this turmoil, on April 3, the Serracapriola ministry fell and was replaced by a new government under the moderate liberal, Carlo Troya. Hoping to win popular support without having to make major social concessions, the Troya government immediately made the fateful decision to join with Piedmont-Sardinia and the newly-formed Italian League in the war against Austria in the north. On April 13, therefore — despite the mounting chaos in the kingdom — 17,000 Neapolitan troops were ordered to leave Naples for Venetia. At the head of the expedition was General Guglielmo Pepe, who had returned to the capital after seventeen years in exile only two weeks before. In his memoirs, Pepe described his plan for the campaign as follows:

137. In my mind, to aid Venice, to be masters of the Adriatic, and to enrich ourselves with the treasures of Trieste...were long-established ideas. I therefore demanded that seven battalions should embark on six magnificent steam frigates, and that with these troops I should disembark in the [Venetian] Lagoon. The king opposed this plan, saying that I would thus place myself in a *cul-de-sac*. I persevered; the minister was on my side, and what I demanded was decided on. Unhappily, in consequence of the agitated life that I was leading, never having a minute's repose, I was attacked with a violent fever, which lasted six days. The king took advantage of this accident to oppose the embarkation of the troops; but being afraid of public opinion, he made the council meet at my house, and wished Florestano to preside.... It would be tedious to detail all of the arguments used against the expedition by sea. Though confined to my bed, I should have been far more successful in inducing them to follow my plan if I had employed intimidation rather than argument; but I was apprehensive that the brigade which was to follow me by land, being *without* me, would never pass the Po.... Thus, it was decided that the troops under my charge should go by

land; and even in this I was thwarted by the Papal government, who demanded that they should proceed by single battalions, and only one squadron a day. They would thus have reached the Po with a delay which would have been ludicrous to the population on the road.

At last the brigade, composed of 17,000 men, started; they were to be followed by 24,000 more, and it was determined that I should embark at Ancona on board the steam corvette Stromboli. Before my departure, I received a letter from the Minister of War, in which he told me, in behalf of His Majesty, that when I reach the Po, I must wait for further orders before crossing it. I placed the letter in my private portfolio, with the firm intention of considering it as not received. It must be evident to everyone that the intention of the King was not to satisfy the noble desire of the nation in sending an army to Lombardy, but...preventing it.... If I had made known the contents of this letter to the public, or even to the Ministry, the King would have inevitably been assassinated. [Quoted in Acton, *Last of the Bourbons*, pp. 227-28.]

For once, Settembrini seemed to agree. In reflecting upon the Troya government's decision to send troops to Lombardy, he wrote:

138. The war against Austria was holy and necessary. But to want Ferdinand II to make war was madness; and to believe that he could be forced to make it was sheer stupidity. He would have resisted in every possible way, and he did, when given the opportunity.... Either we had to remain Neapolitans, and not think of Italy, and be content with the Constitution of February 10 without going any further. Or, if we wanted to fight Austria, we had to broaden the Constitution and chase out Ferdinand, or at least take from him all the power he had over the army and leave him only the name of king....

One day Carlo Poerio said to me: "Between the shouting of the people, the betrayal of the king, and the ministers who don't know what they are doing, what can we do? This morning I handed in my resignation; and I promise you that, as long as I live, I will never hold public office again."... They had insulted him; they had said that he had [conspired] with Ferdinand,... and that he was a traitor. These were the voices of the common people, reckless and stupid.... At the end of March, the whole Ministry, being unable to

CHAPTER 5. THE REVOLUTION OF 1848

ride the tempest, resigned without having done any permanent good: not bad men, from many points of view deserving men, but incapable of governing in these storms.... [Settembrini, *Ricordanze*, pp. 186-88.]

■

The Neapolitan entry into the war against Austria set the stage for the climactic event of the 1848 revolution: the insurrection of May 15. In February, when Bozzelli had drawn up the Neapolitan constitution, he had tried to produce the most conservative document possible. The franchise, in particular, was strictly limited to upper class men of property, and extensive powers were left to the king. In April, therefore, after the elections were held for the deputies to the new parliament, the issue of exactly who should be allowed to vote quickly came to a head. Arriving in Naples with hundreds of their supporters from the countryside, many of the provincial deputies, in particular, immediately demanded an extension of the suffrage. The king, however, encouraged by the activities of the pope who, since April 29, had openly embraced the reaction, adamantly refused to revise the Constitution, and insisted that they take an oath of loyalty to the existing document instead.

Under these conditions — with the country increasingly radicalized by the war and the economic depression and the king resisting further political liberalization — some of the more radical members of Parliament began to advocate a second revolution. On the night of May 14, barricades were built in various parts of the city. By the following morning, over eighty had been constructed, including one less than a hundred yards from the royal palace. At 11 AM, the king, who saw the barricades as an opportunity to reestablish his authority, ordered the royal army to clear the streets. The carnage was frightful. On one side were the royal troops — mostly Swiss mercenaries — supported, in some cases, by small bands of *lazzaroni* yelling "Long Live the King!" On the other, a mixture of radical students, republicans, recent arrivals from the countryside, and isolated members of the National Guard. On most occasions, cannon was used to clear a path through the resistance, and then the fortified positions of the insurgents were taken by storm. Overall, about 500 people were killed (including about 150 Swiss soldiers), and several thousand more wounded. By 11 PM, it was all over, and "order" in the city had been restored. Settembrini, who had tried to discourage the building of barricades, described the immediate aftermath of the struggle as follows:

> 139. It was a night of anguish. There wasn't a light to be seen in the city, not a voice to be heard, a deadly silence reigned. The cries of "Long Live the King!" still rang in my ears, and I thought: "How

many have died? And how many will die tomorrow? The people have gone crazy; they will invade the homes and massacre everyone that they find. And all because of a few foolish people who wanted barricades, not for combat, no, but to frighten a scornful man who had soldiers and cannons and the soul of a Bourbon; and they thought that they could make him flee with a few shouts and threats. They gave him something that he did not possess — an awareness of his strength: before, he feared us; now he scorns us because he has seen us divided and weak. They wanted to imitate the French, to drive Ferdinand out just like [the Parisians] had Louis Philippe.... But you don't drive out an enemy with shouts: you must be prepared; you must mobilize men and arms, establish command posts, and seize the most important places in the city. A hundred well-commanded and well-led men would have won. What did Palermo do! What did Milan do! And what did Naples do!

Barricades! Bloody childishness; a lot of blood spilled for nothing. No, it wasn't Naples, but a few credulous fools who lost everything. And for what? For an oath — whether to change the constitution or not. Oh lawyers, you men of straw, slavery is what you deserve. And what will tomorrow bring?" [Settembrini, *Ricordanze*, pp. 202–3.]

The defeat of the insurrection of May 15 effectively ended the 1848 revolution. The division between Naples and Palermo, the disingenuousness of the king, the split between the middle and lower classes in the capital, the social unrest in the countryside, and the agitation that surrounded the war all combined to bring about its collapse.

In the days following the fighting, Ferdinand moved quickly to reestablish his authority. On May 17, both Parliament and the National Guard were dissolved. One day later, the Neapolitan army was recalled from northern Italy, and the country was placed under martial law. In September, an army of 20,000 men was sent to Sicily. Attacking Messina first, it bombarded the city mercilessly for three full days (an act that earned the king the derisive nickname, *"Bomba"*), and then took it by assault. From there, it moved on relentlessly to recapture the rest of the island — although it would take eight more months before Bourbon authority was completely restored.

Meanwhile, the government had deliberately decided to distance itself from Italy. On August 24, 1848, G.F. Giorgini, the Tuscan minister of foreign affairs, wrote to Giuseppe Griffoli, the Tuscan special envoy in Naples:

CHAPTER 5. THE REVOLUTION OF 1848

140. The distressing events of May 15 in Naples have...changed the attitude of the Neapolitan government towards the Italian question completely.... After May 15, the Neapolitan government recalled not only its plenipotentiaries from Rome, but its troops from the battlefields of Lombardy. Upon hearing of this decision, the Tuscan government made every effort to dissuade that of Naples from taking this step. Advice, reasoning, arguments, exhortations — everything was tried, with unrelenting persistence, but to no avail, and the Neapolitan troops were recalled. This recall of Neapolitan troops has created much distrust, and openly turned the other governments of Italy, particularly that of Piedmont, against the government of Naples.... The Neapolitan government, however,... continues to insist that the recall does not represent a change in policy, but that the measure was only taken in order to maintain internal peace. Nevertheless, despite this explanation, the Neapolitan government has remained effectively isolated from the other Italian governments, and continues to be indifferent, if not openly hostile, to a continuation of the war.... [F.G. Giorgini to Giuseppe Griffoli, August 24, 1848, in Bianchi, *Storia Documentata* 6:400–401.]

This isolation would cost the Bourbons dearly in 1861.

■ ■ ■

55. *Garibaldi welcomed on via Toledo, 1860.*

6
The Risorgimento, 1848–1861

The Revolution of 1848 was followed by a decade of brutal reaction. Traumatized by the May upheaval, Ferdinand reverted to the kind of blind repression practiced by his father, allowing his police to go unfettered, and rejecting any suggestion of political reform. Private homes were broken into without warrants, citizens were arbitrarily arrested and held incognito, charges were falsified for political purposes, and bribery and intimidation were used to elicit evidence in the courts. A police state was created, and whole classes of people lost their rights. Of the 140 deputies who had come to Naples after the elections of April 18, 76 were either arrested or forced into exile. Carlo Poerio and Luigi Settembrini were sentenced to long terms in prison, and a conscious effort was made to eliminate not only political radicals, but moderates as well. The February Constitution, with its guarantee of individual rights, became a dead letter. In the jails, prisoners were kept without light or ventilation, poorly fed and subjected to torture, and left to lie in their own filth for days. Often prisoners were chained together in pairs, and the chains were never removed, even for normal bodily functions — a form of abuse reserved for political offenders alone. While the exact number of political prisoners in the Kingdom of the Two Sicilies can never be known for certain, estimates vary from 10,000 to 20,000. Although conditions were slightly better in Naples than in the provinces, in both places they bordered on the unspeakable and outraged virtually everyone who witnessed them first-hand.

In 1851, the brilliant English politician and statesman, William Ewart Gladstone, had the opportunity to observe the condition of Neapolitan prisons. In two eloquent and passionate letters addressed to the British prime minister, the earl of Aberdeen, he condemned the entire political system in no uncertain terms:

> 141. After a residence of between three and four months at Naples, I have came home with a deep sense of duty incumbent upon me to make some attempt towards mitigating the horrors, I can see no weaker word, amidst which the Government of that country is now carried on....

Without entering at length into the reasons which have led me thus to trouble you, I shall state...that the present practices of the Government of Naples in reference to real or supposed political offenders is an outrage upon religion, upon civilization, upon humanity, and upon decency....

There is a general impression that the organization of the Governments of Southern Italy is defective — that the administration of justice is tainted with corruption—that instances of abuse or cruelty among subordinate public functionaries are not uncommon, and that political offenses are punished with severity, and with no great regard to the forms of justice.

I advert to this vague supposition of a given state of things, for the purpose of stating that, had it been accurate, I should have spared myself this labour.... It is not mere imperfection, not corruption in low quarters, not occasional severity, that I am about to describe; it is incessant, systematic, deliberate violation of the law by the Power appointed to watch over and maintain it. It is such violation of human and written law as this, carried on for the purpose of violating every other law, unwritten and eternal, human and divine; it is the wholesale persecution of virtue when united with intelligence, operating upon such a scale that entire classes may with truth be said to be its object, so that the government is in bitter and cruel, as well as utterly illegal, hostility to whatever in the nation really lives and moves, and forms the mainspring of practical progress and improvement; it is awful profanation of public religion by its notorious alliance, in the governing powers, with the violation of every moral law under the stimulants of fear and vengeance; it is the perfect prostitution of the judicial office, which has made it, under veils only threadbare and transparent, the degraded recipient of the vilest and clumsiest forgeries, got up willfully and deliberately, by the immediate advisors of the Crown, for the purpose of destroying the peace, the freedom, ay, and even if not by capital sentences of life, of men among the most virtuous, upright, intelligent, distinguished, and refined in the whole community; it is the savage and cowardly system of moral, as well as in a lower degree of physical, torture, through which the sentences extracted from the debased courts of justice are carried into effect.

The effect of all this is total violation of all the moral and social ideas. Law, instead of being respected, is odious. Force, and not

CHAPTER 6. THE RISORGIMENTO

affection, is the foundation of Government. There is no association, but violent antagonism, between the idea of freedom and that of order. The governing power, which teaches of itself that it is the image of God upon earth, is clothed, in the view of the overwhelming majority of the thinking public, with all the vices for its attributes. I have seen and heard the strong and too true expression used, "This is the negation of God erected into a system of Government." [William Ewart Gladstone, *Two Letters to the Earl of Aberdeen on the State Prosecutions of the Neapolitan Government*. London: John Murray, 1851, pp. 2-6.]

Gladstone's condemnation of the Neapolitan government blackened the Bourbons' reputation for the rest of the decade. More than fifty pages long, the two letters provided facts, listed names, and cited specific examples of governmental abuse of power at virtually every level. Within a few months, they were translated into Italian and published in pamphlet form in Turin. From then on, the image of Ferdinand as ignorant and savage — the *"Bomba"* who had gratuitously sacrificed the civilian population during the siege of Messina — would appear again and again in the Western press right up until the moment of unification. On April 13, 1852, the New York *Daily Times* wrote in a typically hyperbolic tone:

142. The Neapolitan government pursues the same cold, relentless cruelty as if mankind were not actually aghast at its shocking atrocities. The case seems hopeless indeed, where the criminal is so utterly steeled to shame. The King of Naples, the modern Phalaris, represents, to the reflective mind, murder enthroned and crowned, the incarnated evil, the final result of diabolical malice as practiced upon humanity. Naples is the prey of the foulest and fiercest misrule that ever trampled a nation to dust. All the crimes of the most voluptuous days of Sybaris and Crotona, Pompeii and Herculaneum, pale beside the deep scarlet of more recent times. Phalaris and his tortures are outdone by this Phalaris of the nineteenth century. [Cited in Howard R. Marraro, *American Opinion on the Unification of Italy, 1846-1861*. New York: Columbia University Press, 1932, p. 106.]

The sustained criticism that Ferdinand received in the Western press — despite its often exaggerated and excessively-polemical character — created enormous public pressure among the Western powers for diplomatic intervention. In September 1856, Great Britain and France, yielding to this pressure, took the unprecedented step of issuing a joint declaration to the Neapolitan government demanding the immediate release of political prisoners.

When Ferdinand refused, they ostentatiously broke off diplomatic relations with Naples and seriously contemplated (but eventually rejected) the idea of a naval demonstration in the harbor. On October 5, 1856, the gifted and wily prime minister of Piedmont-Sardinia, Count Camillo Benzo di Cavour — who had secretly encouraged the British and French protest — wrote to Giulio Gropello, the Piedmontese chargé d'affaires in Naples:

> 143. If by chance you are questioned by the Neapolitan government, you must confine yourself to admitting a strong desire to see the King of Naples averting danger by granting wide and wise reforms. You will say that the Sardinian government views the intervention of the foreign Powers in Italian affairs with regret; but that Austria's persistent determination to interfere with all the central Italian states provides England with a plausible motive for interfering in Naples. You will explain that, so long as absolutist governments maintain that an outside Power may aid a sovereign in keeping peoples under an intolerable yoke, it is hardly surprising that liberal governments consider that they, too, can intervene in favor of peoples when oppression goes beyond certain limits.
>
> Regarding the various local parties, you must be very reserved, yet without ever dissimulating the lively interest Sardinia feels for Naples and our ardent desire to see her political situation improve. If you hear of disturbances when foreign fleets call at Naples, you must not encourage them. At the same time you must not condemn them unless there should take place a movement for Italian unity (even in a sense favorable to King Victor Emmanuel). You will tell any supporters of such a project that, at this moment, an uprising for Italian unity would meet with opposition from all the Powers, not excluding England; and that it would therefore have no chance of success.
>
> You must not oppose any project favoring [Lucien] Murat, [Joachim's son] though you yourself must not favor such a movement. Murat is a bad solution, but as it is the only one with any chance of success, we must endure it with good grace. To my mind the success of that claimant will depend on how much support he gets from France. If the French back him, you must help him too. [Cavour to Gropello, October 5, 1856, in Mack Smith, *Making of Italy,* pp. 211-12.]

CHAPTER 6. THE RISORGIMENTO

Nothing, however, was able to convince Ferdinand to modify his policies. As he grew older, he became increasingly stubborn and superstitious, focusing ever more narrowly on the Church and army — two institutions that he simultaneously respected and feared. Even his earlier concern with the country's economic development began to diminish. While the kingdom did participate in the general European economic revival of the 1850s, most Neapolitan industry remained non-competitive and dominated by foreigners, and thus had to be protected by a prohibitive tariff that inhibited trade. Throughout the Bourbon period, in fact, Naples never developed the entrepreneurial class necessary for a rapid transition to industrial capitalism. As late as 1844, only 2 percent of property owners were businessmen or merchants, the vast majority of which chose to invest their money in less risky ventures, such as real estate and land. As for the middle class as a whole, it was overwhelmingly concentrated in the professions, with doctors and lawyers alone comprising an astounding 25 percent.

Thus, Naples — which was still the largest city in Italy in 1860 with 417,000 people — remained a center of consumption rather than production. Although it did possess a naissant industry, it still owed its prosperity to its privileged position as the capital of the Kingdom of the Two Sicilies and its place as southern Italy's largest commercial port. Isolated politically and economically from the more industrially-advanced countries of Western Europe, it would soon be outmaneuvered diplomatically and militarily by Camillo di Cavour.

■

Initially, Cavour had no intention of annexing Neapolitan territory. His aim, on the contrary, was to make Piedmont-Sardinia the dominant power in northern Italy by driving the Austrians from Lombardy and Venetia by force. In order to achieve this aim, he needed the help of Napoleon III of France. Napoleon had his own reasons for wanting to eliminate the Austrians from Italy. As a youth, he had campaigned with the Italian patriots in their ill-fated uprising of 1830, and knew that a victory over France's traditional Austrian rival in Italy would greatly strengthen his prestige at home. In addition, Cavour was willing to offer him the provinces of Nice and Savoy as a reward for his intervention and to acquiesce in his desire to place Lucien Murat on the Neapolitan throne.

On July 23, 1858, therefore, the two men met secretly in the French spa of Plombières to work out the details of a possible agreement. Although no record of the conversations was kept, Cavour left an account of the meeting in a long memorandum that he sent to Victor Emmanuel, the Piedmontese king, the following day:

144. As soon as I was brought to the Emperor's study, he raised the question which was the purpose of my journey. He began by saying that he had decided to support Sardinia with all his power in a war against Austria, provided that the war was undertaken for a non-revolutionary cause, which could be justified in the eyes of the diplomatic circles, and still more, of the public opinion in France and Europe.... I proposed to revive the issues we had used at the Congress of Paris [in 1856] as protests against the illegitimate extension of Austrian power in Italy.... [But] the Emperor did not agree to that proposition.... [Eventually] we agreed that Your Majesty would come to the support of the oppressed population of Massa and Carrara [as a way of providing a legitimate cause]....

This first question being resolved, the Emperor said to me: "Before going any further we must consider two grave difficulties which we shall encounter in Italy: the Pope and the King of Naples.

I must deal with them gingerly: the first, so as not to stir up French Catholics against me; the second so as to keep for us the sympathies of Russia, who makes it a kind of point of honor to protect King Ferdinand." I answered that as for the Pope, it would be easy to maintain him in peaceful possession of Rome by means of the French garrison established there, while letting the provinces of Romagna revolt;... and, as for the King of Naples, there was no need to worry about him unless he took up the cause of Austria; but his subjects should be left free to disencumber themselves of his paternal domination if they seized the chance.

This answer satisfied the Emperor, and we passed on to the main question:... how was Italy to be organized? After a long discussion... we agreed on the following principles.... The valley of the Po, the Romagna, and the Legations would constitute the Kingdom of Upper Italy, under the rule of the House of Savoy.

Rome and its immediate surroundings would be left to the Pope. The rest of the Papal States, together with Tuscany, would form the Kingdom of Central Italy. The borders of the Kingdom of Naples would be left unchanged; and the four Italian states would form a confederation on the pattern of the German Confederation, the presidency of which would be given to the Pope to console him for the loss of the major part of his estates.

This arrangement seemed to me quite acceptable. For Your Majesty, sovereign over the richest and most powerful part of Italy, would be sovereign in fact over the whole peninsula.

The question of what sovereigns would be installed in Florence and in Naples...was left open; nevertheless, the Emperor did not disguise the fact that he could with pleasure see Murat return to the throne of his father; and, for my part, I suggested the Duchess of Parma...might occupy the Pitti Palace. This last idea pleased the Emperor immensely; he appeared anxious not to be accused of persecuting the Duchess of Parma, because she is a princess of the Bourbon family....

The Emperor observed that we should try to isolate Austria, so that we will have no one else to deal with.... [He believes that] to force Austria to renounce Italy would take more than two or three victorious battles.... His estimate is 300,000 men.... France would furnish 200,000, and Sardinia and the other Italian provinces 100,000.... There would be therefore two grand armies, one commanded by Your Majesty and the other by the Emperor personally.... [Cavour to Victor Emmanuel, Baden-Baden, July 24, 1858, cited in Mark Walker, ed. *Plombières: Secret Diplomacy and the Rebirth of Italy.* New York: Oxford University Press, 1968, pp. 27-37.]

The Plombières agreement set off a series of events that would destroy Neapolitan independence forever. Throughout the winter of 1858-1859, Cavour worked assiduously to prepare Piedmont-Sardinia for war and to cast Austria in the role of the aggressor. In January, the Austrian government — as if oblivious to the conspiracy that had been organized against it — played directly into his hands by introducing conscription into Lombardy and Venetia. The move drew heavy criticism in the Piedmontese press and, in March, Cavour, feinting alarm, called up Piedmontese reservists as a precaution against "Austrian aggression." In response, the Austrian government, on April 23, sent an ultimatum to Turin demanding that the Piedmontese disarm, and, when Cavour was slow to respond, recklessly sent the first of 160,000 troops across the border. One day later, France — citing its treaty obligations with Turin — declared war on Austria. During the following weeks, over 200,000 French soldiers crossed into Piedmont, and, by early June, there was major fighting all along the frontier.

From the very first days of the struggle, the Neapolitan government was determined to remain neutral. Ferdinand, in particular — who had become desperately ill during a recent trip to Apulia — had resolved not to become involved in the conflict despite his natural sympathy for Austria. On April 23, 1859, in response to a question from the Russian Prince Gorchakov about the future course of Neapolitan domestic and foreign policy, he told his advisor, Luigi Caraffa:

145. Please thank Prince Gorchakov for his [concern]...and tell him that the kingdom feels no need for a change in [its domestic] policy. As for his question regarding our intentions in the event of a war in northern Italy,... the government of Naples intends to continue to follow the path of neutrality dictated by its principles, its geographical position, and its unswerving desire to maintain peace in southern Italy. ["Appunti di S.M. Ferdinand II di Napoli per il commendatore Carafa," in Bianchi, *Storia Documentata* 8:31.]

One month later, on May 22, he died after several days of bitter suffering at Caserta. A few days earlier, however, he had called in his son, the future Francis II, and had lectured him on what he believed to be the essential elements of Neapolitan domestic and foreign policy. Among them were the maintenance of the Catholic religion, the rejection of constitutionalism, and an unrelenting opposition to an alliance with the Piedmontese.

■

Francis II's ascendancy to the throne ushered in the final period in the 126-year history of Bourbon rule in Naples. Twenty-two years old and lacking political experience, he took power at a critical moment and proved to be utterly unequal to the task. On June 25, 1859, just one day after the decisive French victory over the Austrians at Solferino, Cavour dispatched one of his most able diplomats, Count Salmour, to seek a treaty of alliance with Naples. Hoping that the death of Ferdinand II would lead to a change in policy, he instructed Salmour to emphasize the benefits to be gained from an alliance between Italy's two largest powers — while, at the same, not failing to mention the danger posed by Murat:

146. His Royal Highness has chosen to send Your Lordship on a special mission to the court of Naples, for the purpose of expressing to King Francis II His Majesty's condolences on the death of his illustrious father, and his congratulations on his ascension to the throne....

Your Lordship's appointment, however, must not be considered merely the act of an affectionate relative; it has, also, a highly serious political purpose, which is to unite the two courts in thought and deed....

Today, with the war ongoing, the neutrality that under some circumstances might be considered wise and humane, can be considered, from another point of view, a desertion, or, worse still, a pact with the enemy.... The annals of history, as you know, are replete with examples where this kind of neutrality does not save states, but rather casts them to ruin.

The government of Piedmont-Sardinia does not intend to pass judgment on the internal political system of the previous ruler of the Kingdom of the Two Sicilies. Nevertheless, it is unfortunately well known that there, more than elsewhere, rage burning passions, deep animosities, and long-suppressed hatreds simply waiting to explode.... Your Lordship knows well what these dangers are, and how the desire to change a dynasty can spread among a people; how the presence in Italy of a French army must have enormous appeal in a country where Joachim Murat once ruled and where his death is still mourned.

The new prince has the power to avert these dangers by calling on the love of his people and the gratitude of all of Italy to support his throne. The hatreds would cease and reprehensible desires disappear if, at the beginning of his reign, he would join forces with Piedmont, declare war on Austria, and send part of his army to the Po and Adige to fight for Italy alongside the king of Sardinia and the emperor of France.

Your Lordship must demonstrate to the king, in the interests of his dynasty, the advantages of this alliance, and the benefits it would bring to the entire kingdom.... You must also emphasize the glorious future awaiting the young monarch...and how the affection that is presently shown by the people for Victor Emmanuel and the house of Savoy will be bestowed on Francis II of Naples [as well].... ["Istruzione del conte di Cavour al conte Ruggero Gabaleone di Salmour, inviato in missione straordinaria presso al corte de Napoli," Turin, June 25, 1859, in Bianchi, *Storia Documentata* 8:517-24.]

The Piedmontese offer of alliance immediately put the new monarch to the test. Efforts to seek counsel proved useless: the queen, Maria Sophia of Bavaria, and the queen dowager opted for Austria; the king's uncle, the liberal count of Syracuse, supported Piedmont; and the ministry, led by the aged and pompous Count Filangieri, was divided and inept. The fact that Cavour had also suggested that Francis reactivate the Constitution of 1848 only added to the confusion. In the end, however, Francis followed the advice of his father: he reasserted Neapolitan neutrality and the Constitution was not revived.

From then on, relations between the two countries deteriorated steadily. By January, the whole tone of their diplomatic correspondence had become aggrieved and hostile, and the question increasingly raised in international circles was whether the Bourbon government would be able to survive. On January 11, 1860, the Piedmontese minister General Dabormida instructed the new ambassador to Naples, the marquis di Villamarina, on his duties as follows:

> 147. The current state of affairs in Italy and in Europe has prompted the government of the king to give particular attention to its relations with one of the most important states of the peninsula, the Kingdom of the Two Sicilies....
>
> As a result of the policy of reaction embraced by the government of Naples since 1848, the conduct of the Neapolitan court towards Piedmont has become, if not openly hostile, then certainly cold and almost spiteful in dealing with us.... This cool attitude has convinced us of the futility of further attempts to obtain a close union between Italy's two greatest powers. What we should propose for the present is to dispel the mistrust harbored by the Neapolitan government, and to convince it that, if it finds it impossible to support us,... at least abstain from opposing us, and establish genuinely peaceful and amicable relations....
>
> One thing that we believe to be not only our right but our duty is to draw attention to the deplorable treatment to which our nationals are subjected in the Neapolitan kingdom. In Sicily, in particular, the arrogance and brutality of the police borders on the barbaric.... Your illustrious Lordship must firmly insist that the Neapolitan government put an end to this mistreatment....
>
> In addition, you must also examine the state of our commercial relations with Naples, and take advantage of every opportunity to improve them. The commercial treaty of 1846, which still regulates our dealings with Naples, contains restrictions contrary to the principles of free trade, and does not establish the degree of reciprocity that is normal in such agreements.... Business, which was already meager [before the treaty], has been decreasing daily, and now has been reduced to insignificant proportions....
>
> Some years ago negotiations were begun between the two governments to improve mail service,... but the plans were left in abeyance by the minister of Naples....
>
> We have also expressed our desire for an agreement that would ensure to the literary production of the two countries those rights

CHAPTER 6. THE RISORGIMENTO

of property that today are generally recognized. But the government of the Two Sicilies, suspicious of anything that might favor intellectual development and lead to a free exchange of ideas, abruptly broke off negotiations....

Although it is most unlikely that you will reach an agreement on most of these issues,... you will nevertheless have earned our gratitude if you could clear away some of the mistrust...and thus pave the way for better relations.... ["Istruzioni del generale Dabormida di Villamarina, R. inviato presso la corte di Napoli," Turin, January 11, 1860, in Bianchi, *Storia Documentata* 8:643-50.]

It was under these circumstances that Garibaldi would launch his attack on Sicily and the final drama of Bourbon Naples would begin.

■

The breakdown in relations between Naples and Turin occurred at the worst possible moment for the Bourbon government. By the spring of 1860 — despite the Truce of Villafranca and Austria's continued possession of Venetia — Cavour had achieved virtually all of the aims he had envisioned at Plombières. Under the terms of the Treaty of Turin signed in March, Piedmont had annexed Lombardy, Tuscany, Parma, Modena, and the Romagna, and had doubled in size. The population of the Piedmontese state — or the Kingdom of Upper Italy as it was now called — had increased to over 11 million, and Cavour, worn-out from his struggles, was ready to rest and consolidate his gains. In a conversation with Giuseppi Massari, a Neapolitan exile in Turin, he stated:

148. We must leave Naples out of it. A united Italy will be our children's achievement; I'm satisfied with what we've got, as long as we can reach Ancona. [Giuseppi Massari, *Diario dalle cento voci, 1858-1860.* Emilia Morelli, ed. Bologna: Cappelli, 1959, p. 451. Cited in Mack Smith, *Making of Italy,* p. 300.]

The completion of Italian unity, therefore, was left to Garibaldi. A life-long nationalist and revolutionary, Garibaldi believed that only by adding southern Italy to the newly created Italian kingdom could the *Risorgimento* be complete. Like most supporters of republicanism and democracy, he hated the Bourbons as detestable tyrants and was determined to attack them at their weakest link. On May 6, 1860, therefore, he set out from Quarto with his famous "One Thousand" in an effort to capture Sicily. Cavour — who disliked Garibaldi's political radicalism and feared that his actions would endanger the French alliance — did everything in his power to stop him. On May 12, in response to a protest from the French foreign minister, Edouard Thouvenel, he wrote to his representative in Paris, Constantino Nigra:

> 149. I regret Garibaldi's expedition as much as Thouvenel does, and I am doing, and will continue to do, all that I can to see that it does not lead to new complications. I did not prevent Garibaldi from carrying out his plan because that would have required force.
>
> At the present moment, the government is in too weak a position to withstand the immense unpopularity that we would have incurred if we would have tried to stop him. With the elections imminent...I could not take the vigorous measures necessary to prevent [him from going] to Sicily. But I did try everything in my power to convince Garibaldi not to undertake this mad adventure.... I [even] gave orders for his ships to be stopped at sea.... Please explain this to Minister Thouvenel.... [*Il carteggio Cavour–Nigra dal 1858 a 1861.* Bologna: Zanichelli, 1929, 2:294-95.]

Garibaldi's expedition proved to be a success from the beginning. Confronted by a Neapolitan army of more than 25,000 men, he was able to translate a superiority in the use of guerrilla tactics, the blunders of opposing generals, and the hatred borne by the Sicilians for their mainland oppressors into a sweeping victory in less than two months. In describing the aftermath of the crucial battle of Calatafimi, one of his soldiers, G.C. Abba, wrote in his diary on May 16:

> 150. The dead Neapolitans were a piteous sight. Many of them had been killed by Bayonet. Those who lay at the top of the hill had nearly all been wounded in the head. In the distance, I could see a little hideous monster, who seemed by his clothes to be a local peasant, ferociously stabbing one of the dead Neapolitans. "Kill the brute!" yelled Bixio and spurred against him with raised saber, but the savage creature slid away among the rocks and disappeared; more brute than man. [Cited in Mack Smith, *Making of Italy,* p. 313.]

Meanwhile, as Garibaldi was completing his conquest of the island, Cavour was desperately seeking ways to regain control over the course of events. Convinced more than ever that a Garibaldian victory in the South would strengthen the forces of democracy throughout Italy, he decided on the extraordinary step of launching a pro-Piemontese revolution in Naples before Garibaldi could arrive. On August 1, he wrote to his trusted friend and colleague, Nigra, in Paris:

151. If Garibaldi proceeds to the mainland of southern Italy and captures Naples just as he has already taken Sicily and Palermo, he will become absolute master of the situation. King Victor Emmanuel would lose almost all his prestige in the eyes of Italians, who would look on him as little more than the friend of Garibaldi; and though probably he would remain King, he would merely bask in such reflected glory as this heroic adventurer might decide to allow him.

Garibaldi, if he should reach Naples, would not proclaim a republic, but he would remain a dictator, and would refuse to annex southern Italy to Piedmont. His prestige would then be irresistible, and, as he would dispose of the resources of a kingdom of nine million people, we could hardly cross him. He would be stronger than we were. What then would remain to us? We would be forced to go along with his plans to fight Austria. I am therefore convinced that the king must not receive the crown of Italy from Garibaldi's hands, for his title would then be precarious....

I have no doubts about the grave and dangerous decision I am advocating, but I believe it is essential if we are to save the monarchic principle. Better that a king of Piedmont should perish in a war against Austria than be swamped by the revolution. The dynasty might recover from a defeat in battle, but if dragged through the revolutionary gutter its fate would finally be sealed.

Although I have made up my mind how to act if Garibaldi reaches Naples, it is nevertheless my first duty to the king and Italy to do everything possible to prevent his success there. My only hope of foiling him is if I can overthrow the Bourbon regime before Garibaldi crosses to the mainland — or at least before he has time to reach Naples. If the regime falls, I would then take over the government of Naples in the name of order and humanity, and so snatch out of Garibaldi's hands the supreme direction of the Italian movement. This will need courage, audacity if you like; it will bring outraged protests from other countries, and may even force us sooner or later to fight against Austria. But it will save us from revolution. It will save the national and monarchic character of the Italian movement which is our glory and strength....

A shipload of arms is therefore being sent to Naples for Liborio Romano to use there. Admiral Persano is also going to Naples on the pretext that the Princess of Syracuse has asked for our protection.

> Persano, Romano, and [the Neapolitan general] Nunziante will arrange that a movement takes place among the citizens and in the Bourbon army and navy. If this succeeds, a provisional government will be established under Romano which will immediately invoke Piedmontese protection. Victor Emmanuel will then accept a Protectorate, and troops will be landed to maintain order and stop Garibaldi's further advance. [Quoted in Denis Mack Smith, *Garibaldi*. Englewood Cliffs, NJ: Prentice-Hall, 1966, pp. 44-45.]

In reflecting on Cavour's actions during his southern campaign, Garibaldi would later write:

> 152. Every possible obstacle was raised in our path [by Cavour and the Piedmontese government] between the time we left Genoa and when we arrived at Naples. Some people try to argue that the government could have stopped us and let us go, but I deny that they could have stopped us. Public opinion was irresistibly on our side from the first moment that news spread of the Sicilian rising in April 1860. It is true that the government put no absolute veto in our way; nevertheless they raised every kind of obstacle. I was not allowed to take any of the 15,000 muskets which belonged to our Million Rifle Fund and were kept by us in storage at Milan. This one fact delayed by several days the sailing of our expedition. La Farina [Cavour's agent] then gave us just 1,000 bad firearms and 8000 lire.
>
> However, once we had taken Palermo, the liberation of all Sicily became almost certain, and the Piedmontese government therefore allowed a second expedition of volunteers to join us who proved of great help. But Cavour's new plan was still that we should go no further than Sicily, and with this purpose he sent La Farina and others to campaign in Sicily for immediate annexation to Piedmont. These men did all they possibly could to bring about their petty objective....
>
> Even greater difficulties were placed in my path at Naples. Everyone knows how Cavour sent a host of secret agents there who did what they could with the local conservative committee to bring about their own revolution before I had time to reach Naples. It is common knowledge that, just when I was preparing to fight the battle of the river Volturno, I was forced to leave the army and go back to Sicily in order to calm the agitation there which had been brought about by other agents sent from Turin. [Cited in Mack Smith, *Garibaldi*, pp. 45-46.]

CHAPTER 6. THE RISORGIMENTO

Cavour's efforts to promote a pro-Piedmontese revolution in Naples came to nothing; but Garibaldi's campaign proved irresistible. On August 19, after a 34-hour journey by sea, he landed with 3,360 men at Melito on the southern tip of Calabria. Two days later, after a vicious encounter in which his forces lost over 150 men, he captured the regional capital of Reggio and then began a long, slow march to Naples.

The advance created a near panic in the capital. The Constitution of 1848, which had been resisted by both Francis and his father for over a decade, was reestablished; freedom of the press and individual liberties were granted; and Liborio Romano — a reputed liberal who had secretly maintained contact with *all* sides, Francis, Cavour, and Garibaldi — was appointed minister of the Interior. Even the Camorra — a loosely-knit criminal organization that had grown up in the poorer sections of the city in the 18th century — was recruited to help maintain order in the face of Garibaldi's advance. Nothing, however, could save the dynasty. On August 20, Romano, acting on behalf of the ministry, presented a memorandum to Francis recommending that he leave the kingdom:

> 153. Sire.
> The extraordinary circumstances in which the country finds itself...demand that we speak to you honestly.... We have seen this glorious monarchy of Charles III, which has lasted for 126 years, reduced by force of time and the malevolence of men to a point where it no longer commands the confidence of its people. We believe that it is our duty to advise Your Majesty, therefore, to leave the country and appoint a temporary government in your place.... Everywhere there is mistrust...and discipline in the army and navy have collapsed.... It is no longer possible that public opinion can be changed.... Italy stands before us with the banner of the House of Savoy unfurled.... The only honorable choice is to step aside...in order to spare your people the horrors of [civil] war.... We offer this advice with a clear conscience [since] it is the only advice that we can reasonably give....
> [Memorandum cited in Giacinto De Sivo, *Storia delle Due Sicilie dal 1847 al 1861*. Naples: Arturo Berisio, 1964, 2:165-68.]

Pressured by his own government and threatened by Garibaldi's advancing forces, Francis still, at first, resisted. In mid-August, he wrote bitterly to Napoleon III:

> 154. You advised me to grant a constitution to a people who had not asked for it, and I followed your advice. You made me abandon Sicily without a fight, promising to guarantee my reign, and now I am abandoned completely. But I am resolved not to give up

my throne without a struggle: I will defend my kingdom, and I will appeal to the justice of Europe. [De Sivo, *Storia* 2:164.]

During the following weeks, however, Francis' determination gradually faded. On August 30, 10,000 Neapolitan soldiers — the bulk of the Neapolitan army in the south — surrendered to Garibaldi at Soveria without a fight. The event was followed by a large-scale peasant uprising in Calabria and the rapid advance of Garibaldi's forces to Salerno, only 35 miles from the capital.

On September 5, therefore, Francis — confused, disconsolate, and abandoned by all except a few generals and his family — decided to leave Naples for Gaeta. Before leaving, however, he issued a final proclamation to the Neapolitan people:

155. People of Naples:
Of all of the duties demanded of a monarch, those performed in times of adversity are the most difficult and solemn, and I intend to carry them out in a manner and spirit befitting a descendant of so long a line of kings.... Regretfully, I must now leave Naples. An unjust war, one which was not wanted by the people, has overrun my kingdom, despite the fact that I was at peace with all of the European powers.... My paramount concern now is to protect this illustrious city,... to protect its people from ruin and war, to safeguard its inhabitants and their possessions, the holy temples, the monuments, the public buildings, the art galleries, and everything else that constitutes the patrimony of its civilization and greatness, which, belonging to future generations, must not be sacrificed to the transitory passions of the moment....

War is approaching the walls of the city; and it is with ineffable sadness that I leave.... I commend the devotion of the ministry...and I call upon the honor and civic sense of the mayor of Naples and the commander of the police to spare our beloved city the horrors of internal disturbances....

As a descendant of a dynasty that has ruled over this kingdom for 126 years, after having saved it from the prolonged miseries of the viceregal government, my affections remain here. I am a Neapolitan; and cannot bid farewell to my beloved people, my compatriots, without bitter grief.

Whatever my destiny may be, I will always cherish for them a lasting and affectionate memory. I recommend to them peace and concord and observance of their duties as citizens. Let not an immoderate attachment for my crown become a source of turbulence.

CHAPTER 6. THE RISORGIMENTO

> If the course of the present war should lead me back among you, or if on some future day it may please God to restore me to the throne of my ancestors, rendered more splendid by the free institutions with which I have endowed it, what I most fervently pray for is to find my people united, strong, and happy. ["Proclamazioni de Francesco," September 5, 1860, in De Sivo, *Storia* 2:188-89.]

One day later, Liborio Romano — who had been secretly negotiating with Garibaldi's agents since at least mid-August — issued a declaration inviting the victorious general to enter the city:

> 156. To the invincible General Garibaldi, Dictator of the Two Sicilies.
>
> Naples awaits your arrival with the greatest impatience, so that it may hail the redeemer of Italy, and place in his hands the powers of the state and its own destiny.
>
> Having this in view, I shall make myself responsible for the maintenance of order and of public tranquillity. Your own words which are known to all the people are the surest pledges of success in all such efforts. Awaiting your further command, I remain, with profound respect, Liborio Romano. [*Dispatch*, September 6, 1860, cited in Peter Gunn, *Naples: A Palimpsest*. London: Chapman and Hall, 1961, pp. 205-6.]

On September 7, at 1:30 in the afternoon, Garibaldi arrived by train in the blazing sunshine from Salerno. The French novelist, Alexander Dumas, who had been an active supporter of Garibaldi's campaign since it had first left Quarto, described the near-hysterical reception given to him by the population as follows:

> 157. The whole of Naples followed him from the sea fort to the cathedral and from the cathedral to the palace. An immense shout, which sounded as if from the throats of five hundred thousand inhabitants of Naples, burst forth towards heaven — it was the hymn of vengeance against Francis II, it was the hosanna of gratitude for the liberator. "Evviva Garibaldi!" The general was forced to show himself at the window. The shouts then redoubled; hats and bouquets were then thrown into the air. At every window looking on the palace the women waved handkerchiefs, leaning out at the risk of falling into the streets. The revolution was accomplished, and as I had promised Garibaldi, without shedding a drop of blood. [Cited in Gunn, *Naples*, p. 206.]

No sooner was the celebration over than the Neapolitans were forced to make one of the most fateful decisions in their history. On September 11, Cavour — fearful that Garibaldi would move on to Rome and thus become embroiled with the French forces guarding the city — ordered 33,000 Piedmontese troops into the Papal States in order to block his route north. Moving quickly through the Marches and Umbria, they defeated a papal army that had been sent out against them, and then crossed into the Kingdom of the Two Sicilies where they headed for Naples in full force. Meanwhile, further to the south, Garibaldi, whose army had now grown to over 20,000 men, was in hot pursuit of the last 50,000 Neapolitan troops remaining loyal to Francis — which he defeated at a cost of almost 3,000 dead and wounded in the Battle of the Volturno on October 1.

With virtually all of central and southern Italy now in either Cavour's or Garibaldi's hands, the crucial question became what to do with Naples and Sicily. Most Mazzinians and federalists — sensitive to the differences in history and culture between North and South — believed that local councils should be elected to draw up a new constitution, and thus that annexation should be delayed. Cavour, on the other hand, recommended an immediate plebiscite and incorporation into Piedmont, a tactic that he had already used successfully to extend Turin's control in the North. At first, Garibaldi seemed to side with those who favored a constituent assembly. But Victor Emmanuel — who, unlike Cavour, he considered a friend and trusted — convinced him that a delay would create insuperable obstacles to national unification, and, in the end, he agreed to support a vote on annexation instead.

The plebiscite took place on October 21, 1860. Unlike the earlier ballots in Tuscany and the Romagna, it consisted of only four words: *"Italia Una Vittorio Emmanuele."* The text included no discussion of the future constitution, laws, or administrative system. Voters were simply asked to mark their ballots "Yes" or "No," and then place them in separate boxes. Given the euphoria of the moment, the vagueness of the wording, and the presence of both the Piedmontese and Garibaldian armies on Neapolitan territory, it is small wonder that the vote was overwhelmingly positive. In Sicily, 432,053 people voted "Yes" and only 667 "No." On the Neapolitan mainland, the count was 1,302,064 to 10,302. In Naples itself, where the balloting was held at the university, credentials were rarely verified, and intense pressure was put on the electors to produce a positive vote. Indeed, as one observer, Cesare Cantù, later recalled:

> 158. Here [in Naples] the plebiscite bordered on the ridiculous, since everyone was encouraged to vote on a matter about which the majority knew absolutely nothing, and voters were forced to drop their ballots in urns marked "yes" and "no," thus revealing their choice. In addition, the names given by the voters were almost never authenticated, and even soldiers were permitted to vote. Whistles, catcalls, blows, and even

CHAPTER 6. THE RISORGIMENTO

knifings were inflicted on those who voted "no." One lout shouted: "Long Live Francis II!", and was killed on the spot. [Quoted in Maria Rosa Cutrufelli, *L'Unità d'Italia, guerra contadina, e nascità del sottosviluppo del Sud*. Verona: Bertani, 1974, p. 180.]

Nevertheless, despite such pressures, there can be little doubt that, at the time that the ballot was taken, the vast majority of people in Naples, as well as the inhabitants of the Italian South in general, favored some form of national unification. On October 28, Garibaldi, who had been the virtual dictator of Naples for seven weeks, met with Victor Emmanuel at Teano where he effectively legitimized the vote by acknowledging him as "the first king of Italy." One week later, on November 7, the new king, seeking to take advantage of the general's popularity, invited Garibaldi to sit next to him in an open carriage during his first visit to Naples. The procession, which was so different than Garibaldi's initial entry into the city on September 7, was described by the French writer and Garibaldi supporter, Maxime Du Camp, as follows:

> 159. On November 5 [two days before the visit] all the Garibaldian troops still stationed in Naples received orders to move out to Caserta where the King had agreed to accord them an official review. There they waited all day long on the 6th, but in vain, for Victor Emmanuel...did not deign to appear before our "volunteer bands."... All the volunteers of the southern army were as a result away at Caserta on the 7th when the King was due to make his solemn entry into Naples,... [and] it was the Piedmontese troops and the Neapolitan national guard who lined the road, with the Garibaldians nowhere in sight....
>
> The weather [on that day] was terrible.... It rained in torrents. A fierce west wind blew in continual gusts. In the harbour the swell tossed the ships until their lower yards were awash. Everything was sad and cold.... None of the preparations had, in fact, been completed. Stretched over the wet roads were decorative figures still without heads; and their hands, which were intended to hold flags, were empty. Colored bunting, after being torn by the wind and soaked by the storm, flapped against the bare scaffolding. Triumphal arches were a mere shell and nothing but bare boards. The whole thing was pitiful.
>
> An immense crowd filled the streets all the way from the railway station to the royal palace, but all you could see were umbrellas. From above and from far away they looked like a giant army of mushrooms. At 10 o'clock the guns of the forts thundered out and

> the King rode to the cathedral accompanied by Garibaldi. The latter, as soon as he arrived there, was set upon by the women and embraced far more than he must have liked. Thence Victor Emmanuel travelled by carriage past the shouts and petitions of the crowd to the palace. On his left sat Garibaldi in his grey cloak. In front of the King, wearing a dark suit, was the pro-dictator of Naples, Pallavicino.... The red shirt, in fact, symbolized the revolution which had won Italian independence, and it was this red shirt which should have done the honors to Victor Emmanuel at Naples; nor, I think, could the King have objected to that. Pallavicino was now given the grand cordon of the Order of Santa Annunziata, but Garibaldi...refused it....
>
> Two days later, on November 9, just before dawn, Garibaldi rowed himself in a small dingy to a steamboat placed at his disposal to take him home to Caprera. Of all his army, he took with him only his old faithful friends, Basso and Froscianti. Of the enormous sums which had passed through his hands, he had no more than ten piastres, a mere fifty francs. This was a day of silence for the Garibaldians at Naples. We were all sad, and all knew that something fine had gone out of our lives. That evening, however, an immense procession moved through the town to the cry of "Long live Garibaldi!" [Maxime Du Camp, *Expedition des Deux-Siciles: Souvenirs personnels*. Paris, 1861, pp. 349-51, cited in Mack Smith, *Garibaldi*, pp. 55-57.]

A few weeks later, the French novelist, Louise Colet, who had witnessed the transfer of power, poignantly contrasted Garibaldi and Victor Emmanuel, and their impact on the city, as follows:

> 160. The Neapolitans...love a spectacle...and Garibaldi, with his public speeches just like in a kind of Greek democracy, was their ideal of a sovereign. He was friendly, accessible to everybody, and appreciative of the applause and public demonstrations. At any hour he was ready to show himself on the balcony of a *palazzo*, or he would walk the streets and along the sea-front, listening to the crowd and answering it.... For the ignorant and unfortunate he always had moving words inspired by charity and a fundamental belief in human equality. He conquered this town of Naples not so much by force as by sentiment and real human warmth.
>
> When King Victor Emmanuel subsequently arrived here, he, too, found a genuine welcome and enthusiasm. Even before his arrival

CHAPTER 6. THE RISORGIMENTO

he was already being worshipped as a symbol of Italy. But...the King did not show himself sufficiently to the people when he came to Naples. He excited curiosity but failed to satisfy it. The pomp of kingship and the panoply of war were absent.

It was the same with the soldiers of the northern army, for they produced just the same impression on the people. Duty and discipline came first with them, and they hardly mixed at all with ordinary citizens. And soon these brave soldiers, who came as liberators just like the Garibaldians, were being reproached for their aloofness and for behaving as though they had conquered Naples. Even their uniform was displeasing, as it recalled too much that of the Bourbon army, whereas the varied and picturesque — even theatrical — dress of the volunteers had enchanted everyone.

After Garibaldi's departure, a fair number of his disbanded volunteers were left behind in Naples, uncertain whether they were going to be incorporated into the regular army, or if they would have to return home. They had nothing to do. All day long they could be seen in the streets and cafes, and the citizens always took their part if they quarreled with the Piedmontese soldiers.

Many different types of grievance were now blamed upon the regular government.... But so long as Garibaldi was in Naples, no opposition had dared show itself, for the rapidity of events had left all opponents of the revolution powerless before him. From this fact grew up a popular belief that Garibaldi, in leaving Naples, had taken with him the peace and prosperity of the kingdom. The whole town was afflicted by a profound sadness which no observer could fail to notice. Almost at once the singing and the patriotic shouting were stilled. No longer were there torchlight processions, no more did joyful groups carry flags and cry their vivas. As a poet, I must confess that I shared this general feeling. The Naples of Victor Emmanuel had none of the charm for me possessed by the Naples of Garibaldi. One no longer felt the gaiety, the expansiveness, and the excitement which had affected the whole people after liberation. [Louise Colet, *L'Italie des Italiens*. Paris: E. Dentu, 1863, 3:66-67, quoted in Mack Smith, *Garibaldi*, pp. 130-32.]

■ ■ ■

NEAPOLITAN WRITERS of the 19th century were often very active in the social and political life of their times, combining their literary lives with civic and professional responsibilities.

56. *Vincenzo Cuoco (above, 1770–1823), a politically active historian during the era of Murat, wrote a 3-volume* Historical Essay on the Neapolitan Revolution of 1799, *published in 1801.*

57. *Vittorio Imbriani (above, 1840–1886), was a lecturer at the University of Naples and a Garibaldino. His extraordinary linguistic verve is evident in such works as* Merope.

58. *Marguerite Gardiner, Countess of Blessington (left, 1789-1849), author of* An Idler in Italy, *was just one writer in a long tradition of foreign writers who came to, and wrote about, Naples.*

LITERATURE: 19TH CENTURY

59. Advertisement for Il Ventre di Napoli by Matilde Serao, 1884.

60. Matilde Serao (1856–1927) was the author of more than 40 very popular novels dealing with lower-middle-class Neapolitan life, including The Land of Cockayne and A Girl's Romance. In 1904 she founded the influential Il giorno, which she edited until her death. Initially a supporter of the Risanamento, she later criticized its effects on the city.

61. Francesco De Sanctis (left, 1817-1883), author of the masterpiece, History of Italian Literature, served both as a Bourbon prisoner and as minister of education after the Risorgimento.

62. Ferdinando Russo (1868–1927) wrote both poetry and drama, in Neapolitan dialect, describing life in the Neapolitan bassi, including 'E scugnizze (1897) and Lucilla Catena (1920).

63. *Neapolitan School*, View of the Port of Naples.

64. *Anton Sminck Pitloo*, Castel dell'Ovo from the Seashore, c. 1825.

THE NATURAL BEAUTY of the Bay of Naples, the drama of Vesuvius, and the consequent tourist market for souvenir paintings contributed to the great importance of landscape painting in Naples. Under the influence of Anton Pitloo, the Neapolitan School specialized in exactly composed landscapes that influenced Neapolitan painters throughout the century.

65. *Giacinto Gigante*, The Temples at Paestum, 1854.

66. *Ezechiele Guardascione (1875–1948)*, Landscape with Trees and Ruins.

PAINTING AND SCULPTURE

67. *Antonio Mancini (1852–1930)*, After the Duel.

68. *Domenico Morelli (1823–1901)*, Turkish Bath.

GENRE SCENES were an important component of Neapolitan art, while landscape and cityscape traditions extended into the twentieth century.

69. *Gioacchino Toma*, The Shower of Ashes from Vesuvius, *1880*.

70. *Guido Casciaro*, Lago Lucrino, *1953*.

71. *Leon Giuseppe Buono*, From My Studio, *1955*.

MODERN NAPLES, 1799–1999

72. *Carlo Brancaccio (1861–1920)*, Via Toledo.

73. *Salvatore De Gregorio*, Landscape on Etna, *1909*.

74. *Luca Postiglione*, Impressions, *c. 1920*.

75. *Giuseppe Carrino*, Celebration, *1953*.

PAINTING AND SCULPTURE

PLASTIC ARTS in Naples reflected most of the general European trends from the neoclassical to the Romantic, Beaux Arts, and Art Deco, to the modernist and post-modernist.

76. Royal Porcelain Factory of Naples, Dancers, 1800–1806.

77. Vincenzo Gemito (1852–1929), Fisherman.

78. Marino Mazzacurati (1907–1969), Monument to the Martyrs of the Four Days, 1969.

79. Annual Installation in Piazza del Plebiscito, 2000.

82. O. Goretti, Majolica vase, 1920.

81. Vincenzo Buonocore, Majolica vase, 1898.

80. Raffaele Giovini, Porcelain plate, 1830-40.

83. Poster for the 50th Anniversary of the Plebiscito Meridionale, October 1910.

7
Naples in Italy. The Early Years, 1861–1914

The *Plebiscito Meridionale* (or "southern plebiscite" as it is usually called) changed the status of Naples forever. Almost overnight, the city lost its privileged position as the political capital of Italy's largest kingdom. As such, it lost its place as the home of the royal court and governmental bureaucracy, and the tens of thousands of administrative, judicial, military, and service jobs (from coachmen and gardeners to cooks and housekeepers) that they had produced. In addition — because it no longer possessed its "empire" in Sicily and the mainland — it lost its independent power to tax the provinces, and thus its historic ability to extract wealth from the countryside had been drastically reduced. The prestige, power, and pageantry that had emanated from the monarchy — and from which many Neapolitans drew their identity — had suddenly evaporated, and many Neapolitans felt both materially and psychologically diminished. Naples, in short, had lost its autonomy. It had been set on a path of political and economic marginalization, and the once-powerful feelings of dominance and superiority that its inhabitants had enjoyed for centuries had largely disappeared. The "new Italy" had produced a "new Naples" — although the exact nature of its political identity was still decidedly unclear.

One of the main problems that the Neapolitans had in establishing a new political identity was the attitude of their Piedmontese conquerors. Among the founders of the Italian state, the attitude towards Naples often varied from sympathetic condescension (witness Cavour's remark about "those poor Neapolitans with all their intelligence") to actual contempt. These attitudes, moreover, were often powerfully reinforced by a narrow concern for Piedmontese interests and by a distrust and suspicion of the southern population as a whole. On December 12, 1860, Luigi Farini, who had been chosen by Cavour to be the city's first civilian governor, wrote to Marco Minghetti, the Piemontese minister of the Interior in Turin:

> 161. It is a good thing that the Deputies who have come here from Italian Italy will have seen what a hell-pit Naples is. It will enable them to be fair to us if we fail to turn swine into heroes.

> There is at least this to be said: things cannot get worse. After the fall of Gaeta, I will show our strength and lay down the law. I have had all the heads of the Camorra deported from Naples to the island of Santo Stefano — during the revolution they were in charge of the police and customs. My action is a gross illegality, but there was no means of keeping Naples quiet without getting rid of that lot. Their followers seem to have taken fright, and so far the anti-government press has kept quiet about it.
>
> You know how I used to think it was for Italy's well-being that we should not take Rome soon. Now I have changed my view. By getting to know Naples I have acquired a solid conviction that we must enter Rome in 1861 and complete our national unity, for otherwise this cancer will spread everywhere else. In seven million inhabitants of Naples there are not a hundred who want a united Italy. Nor are there any liberals to speak of.
>
> Nothing matters here except the town of Naples itself. The provinces can hardly maintain man or beast: they are just bossed by the odd baron or landowner. In the capital we have twelve thousand tricksters to contend with, that is to say attorneys, tangle-weavers, law-twisters, casuists and professional liars with the conscience of pimps. They run everything here, whether in public places, in the courts, on the stock exchange, in the cafes, clubs and theaters. What can you possibly build out of stuff like this! And by God they will outnumber us in Parliament unless we in the north stay closely united.
>
> How will the election [for Italy's first parliament] turn out here? Who knows? We have no facts to go on. Will those we rely on turn out to be reliable? I don't think so, at least most of them. *Naturam expelles furca*, etc. They *never* tell you the truth. As a good native of Turin would say, they have a double face. But we are at the dance, and dance we must. Oh if only our *accursed* civilization didn't forbid floggings, cutting people's tongues out, and *noyades*. Then something would happen. We would have a clean slate and create a new people. The land is fertile, and the human animal is prolific here. [Farini to Minghetti, December 12, 1860, quoted in Mack Smith, *Making of Italy*, pp. 330-31. Italics in text.]

Despite his adamancy, Farini, like most Piedmontese leaders, knew almost nothing about Neapolitan law and customs. But he was determined to change them all the

CHAPTER 7. NAPLES IN ITALY, THE EARLY YEARS

same. On December 14, 1860, Cavour — who had never been to Naples and whose understanding of the city and its problems was limited largely to reports that he had received from his representatives — wrote to Victor Emmanuel:

> 162. Far from failing to understand the difficulties with which Your Majesty has to struggle, the inclination here is to exaggerate them, and many think the situation is desperate. I don't agree, for I fully trust Your Majesty's energy and good sense.
>
> It is not an easy matter to say what should be done when one is far from the spot, but I will set down my views frankly. In my opinion the only way to emerge from this business lies in using greater firmness. Once we have captured Gaeta we must make it quite clear that discussion will stop. There must be no compromise with the various parties, whether these be followers of Mazzini or the Bourbons, revolutionaries or autonomists. We must then act in accordance with our views and at once start unifying the various administrative systems.... We need to publish our Piedmontese penal code at Naples, to reform the system of law courts and do a lot else to show that we mean to impose a unified system.
>
> The Neapolitan consultative council will not like this. So much the worse for them! Garibaldi erred in appointing that council and it will be a good thing if it is dissolved. If this causes a public outcry, it will not matter; and if any riots break out, the grenadiers are there to repress unrest with severity. We must convince the country that we intend going ahead despite all obstacles. Nothing will be more fatal than hesitation or doubt. If we show unbending will, people will settle down and adapt themselves to the new regime, because our institutions are in all respects preferable to those from which they were liberated.
>
> Our good Farini will be just the man to follow and carry out this policy — at any rate when he manages to pick up from the nervous crisis brought on by his first experiences of Naples. The goal is clear and is beyond discussion. We must impose national unification on the weakest and most corrupt part of Italy. As for the means, there is little doubt: moral force, and, if that is insufficient, then physical force. [Cavour to Victor Emmanuel, December 14, 1860, cited in Mack Smith, *Making of Italy*, pp. 331-32.]

Cavour's opinion was fully shared by the king. Petty, jealous, and resentful, he never forgave the Neapolitans for the way that they had embraced Garibaldi, and, during his personal encounters in Turin, he often treated his Neapolitan visitors with a coolness that bordered on disdain. Like his prime minister, he too believed in the superiority of Piedmontese institutions and was convinced that military conquest had given him the right to impose them by force.

During the winter of 1860–1861, therefore, a systematic attempt was made to extend the Piedmontese system to the rest of Italy. The Piedmontese constitution — the famous *Statuto* of 1848 — was applied to the entire peninsula. Under it, only 2 percent of the population was granted the ballot, while the percentage who actually voted, in southern cities like Naples in particular, was considerably less. In addition, a rigidly centralized administrative system was imposed on the country, with the state divided into provinces, and each province given a prefect who had an absolute veto over municipal affairs. Although the local town council was elected, the mayor and chief administrative officer, the communal secretary, were also selected from Turin, which gave the central government a virtual stranglehold over Neapolitan affairs. Finally, the Piedmontese legal code and tariff system (with its free trade bias) were imposed on the city without modification. Within a few weeks, shoddy, over-priced goods flooded the market, and Naples' fragile textile and engineering industries (as well as many of its handicraft shops) were wiped out virtually overnight. The anger was palpable. The city's interests, which had always been paramount under the Bourbons, were relegated to secondary importance, as Piedmontese officials and job-seekers flocked to the region, and the "Piedmontization" of the government proceeded apace. On March 17, 1861, Constantino Nigra, the secretary of the Naples administration, described the hostility with which most Neapolitans greeted the changes in a letter to Cavour as follows:

> 163. We are in no way through with the dangers here, especially as there is an infinitude of Bourbon soldiers at a loose end, without work or provisions. We also have brigands who will be occupying the mountains by springtime. We have a hostile clergy; and Garibaldi's followers are discontented, angry, even starving. Five hundred of them who were demobilized with three months' pay are now a prey to that worst of counselors, hunger — they are wandering through the streets of Naples and stealing for their livelihood. We have outbreaks of typhoid raging among the soldiers who have returned from Gaeta, and this causes considerable difficulties. The officers of the former Bourbon navy and army are cross and discontented; and they are looked down on by northern officers. The aristocracy is hostile and in mourning for the Bourbons — Portici has become our Faubourg Saint Germain. The arsenal workers and railway men are restless. The vast number of municipalists,

CHAPTER 7. NAPLES IN ITALY, THE EARLY YEARS

desiring local autonomy, feel their interests to have been badly damaged. The devout have been thrown into confusion by the dissolution of convents and monasteries.

Nothing seems to appease the official employees, the infinite number of lawyers, or the huge mob who used to live on official alms and robbery. The municipal authorities, together with the mayor and corporation, were offended by General Ricotti's letters, and ordinary citizens grumble constantly against the burden of military requisitioning. The Piedmontese officers, the Piedmontese civil servants, and everyone coming from northern Italy, never stop complaining quite openly about the multifarious injustices they find (often quite rightly). Then we have saboteurs; others who just like fishing in troubled waters; a minority who still cling to Murat; and also a handful of Mazzinians. This is the sort of hell you have sent me to.

To add to the difficulties, we are short of carabinieri and men for policing the provinces. The administration is corrupt from top to bottom. The press is appalling. The people may be docile but they are unstable, lazy and ignorant. Food is relatively dear. And dominating the picture we have the gigantic figure of Garibaldi growing bigger and bigger on his rock at Caprera and casting his enormous shadow even at this distance. [Nigra to Cavour, March 17, 1861, in Mack Smith, *Making of Italy*, pp. 366-67.]

Five months later, on August 2, Massimo d'Azeglio, the former prime minister of Piedmont and frequent critic of Cavour, added in a letter to Carlo Matteucci, the Florentine physician and politician:

164. In Naples we drove out the King in order to establish a government based on universal consent. But we need sixty battalions to hold southern Italy down, and even they seem inadequate. What with brigands and nonbrigands, it is notorious that nobody wants us here.

What about universal suffrage you may say! I know nothing about suffrage; but I know that battalions are not necessary to the north of the Tronto River, only in the south. So there must have been some mistake made somewhere. Our principles and our policy must be wrong. We must get the Neapolitans to tell us once and for all whether they want us or not. I realize that we Italians have a right to make war against those who wish to keep the Austrians in Italy;

but we cannot preserve the same hostility towards Italians who, while remaining Italians, reject union with us. I think we have no right to use guns on them, unless you want to put us on the same level of expediency as Bomba when he bombarded Palermo, Messina, etc. I know that this is not the general view, but I have no intention of abandoning my right to use my reason and to say what I think. [d'Azeglio to Matteucci, August 2, 1861, Mack Smith, *Making of Italy*, p. 367.]

Thus, the elation and euphoria that had accompanied Garibaldi's entry into the city in September 1860 had been transformed into bitterness and resentment in less than one year. The disillusionment, moreover, affected *both* sides: among the Neapolitans, there was an increasing feeling that they had been conquered by a "foreign" people; among the Piedmontese, that the Neapolitans were alien and ungovernable, completely devoid of honor and trust. It was out of these two contrasting perceptions that much of the tragedy of Neapolitan history would subsequently emerge.

■

The feelings of powerlessness and alienation that most Neapolitans experienced during the Piedmontese occupation of the city was greatly intensified by the war against "brigandage" in the South. Between 1861 and 1865, the Italian government sent over 100,000 soldiers — almost two-thirds of the Italian army — to maintain order in southern Italy. Driven by poverty, high taxes, and a desire to avoid military conscription, tens of thousands of young men on the mainland and in Sicily took to the hills and launched a bitter struggle against the new Italian state. The conflict — which was conducted with bestial savagery from the beginning — killed more Italians than all of the wars of the *Risorgimento* combined. In Naples, where the strongest military garrison was kept, the police and army were particularly vigilant, with mass arrests, censorship of the press, and the establishment of a military tribunal. The repression, which made a mockery of the Piedmontese claim that unification in the South had been achieved by mutual consent, lead to a revival of pro-Bourbonist sentiment among the poorer classes and raised the whole question of the legitimacy of the new state in the region. As early as August 1861, a major demonstration was held on via Toledo to protest the failure of the first Italian parliament in Turin to adopt legislation to ease the growing economic crisis in the city. During the next two years, further protests and demonstrations followed as democrats, socialists, and legitimists sought to fan the flames of discontent. On the morning of January 16, 1862, the supporters of the exiled king, Francis II, hoping to take advantage of this agitation, posted hundreds of placards throughout the city calling for his return:

CHAPTER 7. NAPLES IN ITALY, THE EARLY YEARS

165. Neapolitans — Sicilians — Noble people of our beloved kingdom!

The voice that calls out to you is not that of a political party or faction but the sorrowful echo of a country that is exhausted and cannot stand anymore....

People of the Two Sicilies — Look out! We are surrounded by dangers and our enemies are watching and mocking us.... We have paid an enormous price in blood and have lost our way....

What can we do to save ourselves? Our goal was to create one great homeland, and instead our country has been torn apart in a series of tragic confrontations by the rogues and scoundrels who have invaded it....

Sons of the Volcano, we who have fire in every drop of our blood, we must avenge ourselves, we must regain our autonomy and remember our legitimate ruler,... we must take a step backwards if we do not wish to be further ravaged by the foreign rabble....

People of Vesuvius and Etna! Patriots! What are you afraid of, why do you hesitate to take action? The need to turn back is imperative; let us go back. But in going back we will once again be free citizens, as we were when we strayed, following the false prophets of false freedoms, only to find ourselves oppressed....

Francis II, the legitimate ruler of the Two Sicilies, and the Constitution. This, simply stated, is our program.... Let us hurry to embrace him and, once we are masters of ourselves, with our parliament and king strengthened, we will make Europe gaze in wonder on the [federated] Italy that the Piedmontese were unwilling to create....

Long Live Francis II! Long Live the Constitution! Long Live the Kingdom of the Two Sicilies! [Cited in Domenico Capecelatro Gaudioso, *Reazione a Napoli dopo l'Unità*. Naples: Delfino, 1976, pp. 79-82.]

Such appeals, however, could produce little response in a city where the opposition was so deeply divided, and the government maintained such overwhelming military force. While Naples did experience a number of violent strikes and protests, *real* resistance was largely confined to the countryside, where a war of often unspeakable horror took place. In December 1860, General Galateri, whose feelings of superiority mirrored those of so many of his Piedmontese colleagues, declared from Teramo:

166. I have come to defend humanity and the rights of private property. Merciful to those who are good, I shall be terrible, unforgiving, inexorable in dealing with brigands. Anyone who gives aid to a

brigand will be shot, regardless of age, sex, or social position. Anyone who has information on the location of brigands, or their movements, and withholds it, will have his house sacked and burned to the ground. [Cited in Domenico Capecelatro Gaudioso, *1860: Crollo di Napoli capitale.* Rome: Ateneo, 1972, pp. 158-59.]

Armed with such uncompromising attitudes, Italian military leaders laid waste to whole regions of the former Kingdom of the Two Sicilies. Villages were bombarded, water supplies cut off, crops burnt, and executions of virtually anyone who seemed sympathetic to the rebels became routine. Still, however, the resistance continued, with the insurgents actually gaining strength in many regions until the spring of 1863. On February 18, Nino Bixio, who had been sent to Naples as part of a parliamentary commission to investigate the conditions that had bred the rebellion, described one of the rebel-held areas in a letter to his wife as follows:

167. Dear Adelaide.

Yesterday afternoon, on the 17th, we returned from our trip with the [parliamentary] subcommittee — we saw the famous woods of Fortore that serve as a hiding place for the brigands, and we visited some villages in the province of Molise.

What places! They are more like pigsties! If I had to live in these parts, I would set myself on fire — and those that I saw are not the only ones. I assure you that in these southern provinces you could keep half the population busy by just having them sweep the streets, or what they call streets here.... Before these places arrive at the level of civilization of our own villages [in the North], long years will have to pass. No streets — no hotels — no hospitals — no schools — no shops — no contact with neighboring villages — in other words, nothing of what one sees today in even the least advanced parts of Europe — poor, wretched, unhappy towns! What kind of government has God permitted them to have! They have no sense of what is right and honest — they are hopeless liars — as timorous as children — and yet there are still Bourbonists here! And millionaires in every village as well! You see vast stretches of land, of great potential — but the man himself has been brutalized — there are terrible hatreds — and in this town adversaries kill each other, but it is not just enough to kill him — he has to be tortured — burned alive over a slow fire, and worse, if possible — and what is truly strange and incredible is their mania to seem courageous. They fill your ears with tales of bravery. Every policeman

CHAPTER 7. NAPLES IN ITALY, THE EARLY YEARS

has miraculously killed countless victims — not the brigands (who by the way are the only truly courageous people here) — but the weak, unarmed, and defenseless — and always fleeing when faced with a few armed men ready to fight. In other words, this is a land that either must be destroyed or at least its population sent to Africa to become civilized! What more can I tell you. [Bixio to his wife, February 18, 1863, in Emilia Morelli, ed. *Epistolario di Nino Bixio*. Rome: Vittoriano, 1942, 2:142-43.]

Living under such extreme conditions, many peasants looked on the "brigands" as heroes in the struggle against the landlords and the state. As such, they developed a natural sympathy for the insurgents and were subjected to repeated reprisals by the Italian high command. In August 1861, Gaetano Negri — a Milanese soldier who would become mayor of his native city twenty-five years later — wrote to his father in a letter from Naples:

168. Dear Father.
The news from the provinces continues to be distressing. Probably even our newspapers have spoken of the horrors of Pontelandolfo. The inhabitants of this village were guilty of the most wicked betrayal and acts of monstrous barbarity; but the punishment inflicted upon them by our army, however merited, was no less barbarous. A battalion of bersaglieri entered the village, killed everyone that they found there, looted all the houses, and then set fire to the entire town, which was completely destroyed. It seems that the instigators of the insurrection were priests, in all the provinces, and especially in the mountain villages. The priests hate us intensely, and take advantage of their position shamelessly in order to incite the inhabitants to brigandage and revolt. If, instead of the brigands, who for the most part are motivated by poverty and superstition, they shot all the curates,... the punishment inflicted would be far more just and the results safer and surer.... [Cited in A. De Jaco, *Il brigantaggio meridionale (Cronaca inedita dell'Unità d'Italia)*. Rome: Riunti, 1969, p. 161.]

Using such tactics, the problem of "brigandage" was gradually brought under control. In July 1863, Pietro Cala Ulloa, the prime minister of Francis II's already-moribund Neapolitan government in exile, wrote ruefully:

169. Piedmontese troops are in occupation of all of southern Italy, but only thanks to a rigorous and pitiless enforcement of martial law. Under the old regime, before 1860, Naples could be placed under

emergency regulations after an insurrection, but just for a matter of three days, and without people being arrested, without suspending freedom of the press. The Piedmontese, on the other hand, have kept Naples under martial law for six months; and Neapolitans are treated by them not as people fighting for their independence, but as slaves who have revolted against their masters. Naturally bloodshed breeds more bloodshed. This always happens in civil strife, and Naples is now the scene of a civil war as well as a war between sovereign states.

Those who will not submit are simply exterminated. Pinelli, Neri, Galateri, Fumel and their kind, have announced a war of extermination in which "pity is a crime." Wherever an insurgent has fallen into Piedmontese hands he has ruthlessly been shot out of hand. Sometimes we have seen human sacrifices of forty or fifty prisoners at once....

The official gazette at Naples announced that a Piedmontese unit had entered Trevigno and killed "forty brigands." The truth is that these were just poor unfortunates who had fled from fear, but who then heard that supporters of the King [Francis II] had recaptured the town, and so were misguided enough to return home with safe-conduct from the mayor. This is known by everyone, but fears make people keep silent. Yet a Piedmontese minister now has the face to tell Europe that, if pacification is proceeding slowly in the ex-Kingdom of Naples, it is because he does not want to override constitutional freedoms!...

Everyone has heard the frightful story of how Pontelandolfo and Casalduni were destroyed. A band of insurgents had fallen on a detachment of Piedmontese and killed some soldiers. In reply, an example was made. Another detachment was rushed up, and soon all of the inhabitants, men, women, the old, the young, were buried in the ruins of their burning homes! General Cialdini, who ordered this extermination, simply gave out that: "Justice has been done at Pontelandolfo and Casalduni." Subsequently, after a massacre at Castellamare in Sicily, the authorities at Palermo inserted these words in the official gazette: "At Castellamare the guilty have been rigorously punished." The magistrate here uses a soldier's language. Not even the conquest of Ireland saw such enthusiastic ferocity, even though Saxons and Celts were quite as different from each other racially as Neapolitans are from Piedmontese....

CHAPTER 7. NAPLES IN ITALY, THE EARLY YEARS

Pardon was promised to every brigand who gave himself up of his own accord. But those who surrendered at Livardi, Caserta, Nola and many other places were at once shot; and their unhappy families, crazed with grief, were seen combing the fields for the remains of their murdered children....

At the end of 1861 several dozen Neapolitans and Spaniards decided to give up the Bourbon cause and flee to the Papal States. When they were surrounded just before reaching the frontier, they surrendered without a fight in the belief that their lives would be saved.... At once they were disarmed and shot.

Compare this with when, in 1844, the Bandiera brothers landed in southern Italy to start an insurrection; they were captured with arms in their hands, and yet were at least given a trial with lawyers to defend them. One of the accused was even found not guilty; and twelve out of the other twenty-one were not executed.... Borjes and his companions, on the other hand, had given up and made no resistance: yet they were ruthlessly shot.... Is this kind of bloody holocaust really necessary to make Italian unity? [P. Cala Ulloa, *Lettres Napolitaines*. Paris, 1864, pp. 87-92, cited in Mack Smith, *Making of Italy*, pp. 369-71.]

Ulloa's question would reverberate in the minds of Neapolitan scholars and intellectuals for generations. At the time it was written, the worst of the fighting on the mainland was already over, although the war in Sicily would continue for several more years. Overall, it was a sad beginning for the new Italy. Administrative centralization and military repression had replaced political absolutism in the southern provinces, and the feelings of trust engendered by Garibaldi had largely disappeared.

■

From the moment that Naples entered into Italy, the role that it was to play in the new Italian state was plagued by ambiguity. In terms of size, it was still the largest city in the peninsula, with 417,000 people in 1860, compared to 78,000 for Turin, 135,000 for Milan, and 163,000 for Rome. Through its port passed more commercial tonnage than any other municipality in the country, and the gold reserves of the Bank of Naples alone were three times greater than those of all of the rest of the banks in Italy combined. Nevertheless, because of the peculiarity of its history, the pre-modern character of its economy and society, and the hostility with which many northern Italians viewed its people, there existed no general agreement as to what its exact relationship with the rest of the country should be. Even the Neapolitans, in fact, were initially undecided about its appropriate place. In 1860, the city's governor, Constantino Nigra, wrote:

> 170. There is a continual clamor: "Simplify, improve, moralize the administration, dismiss Bourbon employees, replace them with the victims of Bourbon tyranny, give the people work and bread, give us roads, schools, industry, and commerce, repress the hostility of the clergy, organize the municipalities, give arms to the National Guard, send us troops and gendarmes." One side cries: "Hurry up with unification, destroy every vestige of autonomy, give the central government entire responsibility for local affairs." The other side replies: "Respect the traditions and institutions already in existence, keep all that is good in local administration, and do not turn away destitute all the servants of the Bourbons." [Cited in Denis Mack Smith, *Italy: A Modern History*. Ann Arbor: University of Michigan Press, 1959, p. 53.]

In the end, however, Naples received neither the economic assistance nor the political autonomy that it craved. Between 1861 and 1876, the leaders of the conservative *destra storica*, or "historical right," which dominated Parliament during the first fifteen years of the country's existence, rigidly adhered to the economic and political program that had been established by Cavour: the government's free-trade policies were continued; the Piedmontese debt was nationalized so as to absorb the financial surplus that had been accumulated by the Bourbons; and Naples' urgent need for improvements in its housing, sanitation, and infrastructure was ignored. In order to balance the budget, the government's finance minister, Quintino Sella, raised taxes while cutting public services. Naples became, along with many of the other cities of the Italian South, one of the most heavily-taxed and least-subsidized metropolises in Europe, and the standard of living of much of its already semi-impoverished population underwent a precipitous decline. By the mid 1860s, there were signs of social and economic deterioration everywhere. In 1864, the noted French historian, Hippolyte Taine, after spending several months in the city, wrote:

> 171. What streets one sees [in Naples]! Steep, narrow, dirty, and bordered at every story with overhanging balconies; a mass of petty shops, open stalls, men and women buying, selling, gossiping, gesticulating, and elbowing each other; most of them dwarfed and ugly.... In the vicinity of the Piazza del Mercato winds a labyrinth of paved tortuous lanes buried in dust and strewn with orange peels, melon rinds, fragments of vegetables, and other nameless refuse; the crowd herd together here, black and crawling, in the palpable

CHAPTER 7. NAPLES IN ITALY, THE EARLY YEARS

shadow, beneath a strip of blue sky. All is bustling, eating, drinking, and bad odors; it reminds me of rats in a rat-trap....
   On the way to the Convent of San Martino, we ascend by the same type of narrow, dirty, densely-populated streets.... We mount up higher and higher, always ascending. One set of steps after another, and no end to them, and always the same rags suspended on surrounding cords; then narrow streets with loaded donkeys feeling their way along slippery declivities, muddy streams trickling between the stones, ragged little scamps of beggars, and full views into interior household arrangements. This mountain is a sort of elephant whereupon crawling, fidgety human insects have taken their abode. You pass a house deprived of its lower story, to which the inmates ascend with a ladder; then another with an open door, through which you see a man with a guitar, surrounded by a lot of women assorting vegetables. Suddenly you emerge from this rag-fair, these rat-holes, this gypsy encampment, and reach the magnificent convent, with all the beauties of nature before you and all its treasuries of art. [H. Taine, *Italy: Rome and Naples*. J. Durand trans. New York: Henry Holt, 1889, pp. 22-33.]

One of main obstacles to the improvement of social conditions in Naples was the extremely restrictive character of the vote. Under the Italian constitution, only men who paid forty lire a year in direct taxes were given the franchise, or about 2 percent of the population. This meant that when the first elections to Italy's parliament were held in January 1861, only 12,700 people in Naples were eligible for the ballot, of which a mere 6,398 (or 1 out of every 65) actually went to the polls. As a result, the government — both at the local and national level — was controlled by a wealthy minority, most of whom were determined to maintain the status quo.

In 1876, the victory of the *sinistra*, or moderate left, in the national elections created widespread hope in the South for a change in the system. Instead, the new prime minister, Agostino Depretis, who had been elected largely with southern support, introduced a strategy in which votes were exchanged for favors, and the electoral process became degraded all the more. Under this strategy — which was known as "transformism" — opposition deputies were induced to "transform" themselves politically by voting for the ministerial majority, and then were paid for their services through state patronage or personal reward. The system — which made party affiliation and political platforms virtually meaningless — had a profound and lasting effect on Naples. There, where the tradition of governmental corruption ran deep, a long list of political "clients" (or *"clientela"*) was drawn up. Using this list, local "notables" (the so-called *"grandi elettori"*) secured votes for parliamentary deputies;

the deputies, in turn, supported specific ministers in Parliament; and the ministers then dispensed protection and patronage to the local notable so that he could maintain his position at home. Political power and personal aggrandizement became an inextricable part of the electoral process, and the vast majority of the population was excluded from political life. Many years later, Rocco De Zerbi, a journalist who himself had been elected and reelected as a deputy from the Avvocata district of Naples for twenty-three years (1870–1893), described how the system worked in an interview with Giustino Fortunato:

> 172. The small elector votes for the promise or threat of the great elector. The great elector is a professional because he receives either a contract or a concession or a similar favor. The City Council is a crowd of people who, being paid with vanity, allow the support which the great electors bring them to be paid out of public funds. It is a group of profiteers who corrupt and are corrupted in the fullest sense of the word. The councilor, in order to have the Council's favors, leaves its hands free; the Council, in order not to antagonize the Mayor on certain matters, closes its eyes to others. The party promises honors, protection and impunity to the most influential and hard-working electors in order to win friends, and these barter electoral agitation as a means of making money, getting jobs…or merely so as not to be imprisoned. The election becomes, therefore, an interest in itself, and the best candidate is not the most intelligent or the one with the greatest integrity, but rather the one from whom you can hope for the greatest advantage and protection in your private interests, whether legal or illegal.

> The intelligentsia wins notoriety by making itself the defender of local interests and the interpreter of discontent and thereby collects little by little a big nucleus of supporters, a ring of political bosses who are strong through control of the streets and who are sustained by regiments of disciplined voters. The credulity of the many makes the strength of the few. The indifference of the majority gives strength to the minority, of whom five thousand voters out of twenty thousand electors is sufficient to win. No longer ambition but appetite, no longer programs but *clientele*, no longer battles over principles but matches of seduction and Camorra; competition succeeds emulation, intrigue replaces merit, base popularity usurps the place of glory. To conserve and consolidate one's own authority is the goal; to form and extend a whole series of networks was the means. A series of corruptions infects

the body of the electorate. [Cited in P.A. Allum, *Politics and Society in Postwar Naples*. Cambridge: Cambridge University Press, 1973, pp. 67-68.]

Under this system, Naples came to be dominated by a long series of political "bosses." Giovanni Nicotera, Alberto Casale, Gennaro Aliberti, Achille Lauro, Antonio Gava: their names were familiar to every Neapolitan, and their power would continue until well after the Second World War. In their late nineteenth-century study of Italian political institutions, the two influential British historians, Bolton King and Thomas Okey, wrote:

> 173. The proportion of the population which has the vote [in Italy] is very small. Before [the reform bill of] 1882, it was only 2 percent; now it is a little over 7 percent, as against 16 percent in Great Britain, 20 in Germany, and 27 in France. The disqualification for illiteracy disfranchises a very large number, especially in the south....
>
> Of those who do go to the poll, a more than normal proportion vote from irrelevant reasons.... The richer and middle classes as a whole have their party ties, and vote in obedience to them. But influence and bribery govern the rest.... The elections at Naples [in particular] are managed by one or two hundred "influential electors," who use the *Camorra* to carry their nominees.... [There] personal influence, governmental pressure, and private bribery reach monstrous proportions.... But everywhere [in the north and the south] the Prefects are used to "prepare" the elections.... All their enormous power is used to return the Government's candidate....
>
> [In addition] newspapers are subsidized from secret funds; school teachers are impressed to assist in canvassing; railway employees are warned, or, if Socialists, are removed to a distant post during the election; Syndics send round circulars recommending the ministerial candidate; policemen are stationed at the polling booth to shut out opposition votes.... Bribery completes the work.... There is, in fact, a hardy and unblushing corruption by Government and private persons, [and] the electoral law which punishes with fine or imprisonment any attempt at direct or indirect bribery is a dead letter....
>
> At all events, Parliament, outside the Extreme Left, represents the wealthier classes only.... "The Italian Parliament," says the *Giornale degli economisti*, "is an assembly of proprietors," with all such an assembly's indifference to social legislation and insistence on the rights of property. "The organization of the Italian State,"

says Signor Franchetti, "is one great *clientele*, and the peasants get no help, because they are not part of the *clientele*."

As a result, Parliament has become divided into two groups, united by personal ties, and each fighting for its own hand....

Since Depretis introduced the system of *trasformismo*, each one has copied his evil model of coalition Governments with weak and inconsistent programs, propped up by the bought support of groups. The result has been that "the Government has never governed Italy, for it has always confined itself to governing Parliament."...

The Executive often allows Southern Deputies and their cliques immunity in their petty local tyrannies and peculations, on the condition that they keep the seats safe and vote for Government. A recent libel action has shown how a Deputy of Naples, by grace of the Government and the Camorra, lived luxuriously by the systematic jobbery of public offices and favors, how the authorities connived, how, though his conduct was notorious, no one dared stand in his way.... Charities are manipulated for party purposes. Communal property is jobbed in the interest of the local magnate, and there is no remedy. Criminal actions for embezzlement of communal funds are suppressed.... For much of this, no doubt, the public is responsible.... The great mass of the educated unemployed are hungry for posts in the Civil Service, and expect the Deputy to procure them. Every small magnate wants to be a commendatore or cavalieri, and even a Socialist has been known to beg a ribbon for a supporter. "Italy," says an ex-Premier, "is governed by decorations." [Bolton King and Thomas Okey, *Italy Today*. 2nd ed. London: James Nisbet, 1904, pp. 14-24.]

And, then, elaborating on the important question of the relationship between the Neapolitan government and the criminal Camorra, they wrote:

> 174. In treating the South...it is necessary to allude to the Camorra.... The Camorra is practically confined to the city of Naples, where it finds a fair field in the deep social degradation of a section of the people. Its picturesqueness lives mainly in the imagination of foreign correspondents; in reality...it is a vicious, malodorous conspiracy of dissolute and criminal poor, who live by blackmailing their fellow-poor and selling their electoral votes to the Government or local deputies. It has a tariff of blackmail on

CHAPTER 7. NAPLES IN ITALY, THE EARLY YEARS

boatmen, porters, prostitutes, gambling-houses; it drives a lucrative trade in unspeakable horrors; it exercises a terrorism at public auctions, and takes care that no one bids against its associates. And such is the fascination which it has on the imagination of its citizens, that its sway is often absolute, and the police are glad to call in its authority when they are powerless.... It is, says Professor [Pasquale] Villari, the natural and necessary form that the social state of Naples takes; the poverty of the city [is]...the environment in which it thrives. And its yet more dangerous feature is that the Government, so far from discouraging it, has often protected it for its own purposes. There is an "upper Camorra" — without the ritual of its lower counterpart, but well understood, — the "kid-glove Camorra" of Deputies and municipal councilors and journalists and professional men, who live on jobs and malversation of public monies. It is their protection that paralyzes the police and allows the Camorra to thrive, while the Government gives tacit support to the system, which keeps the majority of the Neapolitan constituencies for its supporters. The leaders of the Camorra found a quarter of a century ago that "electioneering is the only business that pays at Naples," and they have made themselves adept at it. They are repaid by the certainty that the Government will make no serious effort to disturb their infamous trade in vice and cowardice, that it will wreck every attempt of more honest citizens to purify the air. [King and Okey, *Italy Today*, pp. 117-19.]

In 1901, Senator Serado, after conducting an exhaustive investigation of the inner workings of the city, confirmed King and Okey's judgment completely. In a letter written to Italy's prime minister, Giovanni Giolitti, he stated:

175. Your Excellency has had the salutary courage to tell a sad truth, when you declared that half the communes of Italy are in the hands of the Camorra. I can confirm that nearly all the communes of the Province of Naples and nearly all the charitable institutions are in the hands of groups of delinquents; I add nearly all in order not to exclude the one or two exceptions. [Cited in Allum, *Politics and Society*, p. 67.]

Despite the indifference of the central government and the corruption of local political institutions, Naples did experience some isolated successes in the decades after unification. Between 1876 and 1884, three activist mayors—the duke of San Donato, Girolamo Giusso, and Nicola Amore—worked to improve the city's infrastructure and its overall quality of life. A funicular was constructed on the slopes of Mount

Vesuvius in 1880; the first tramways appeared on the city's streets in the late 1870s; and plans for Italy's first subway, the *Metropolitana*, were drawn up in 1884. Work to improve the Serino aqueduct was begun in 1878; a law making elementary education mandatory was passed in 1877; and some of the most dilapidated *fondaci* in the Mercato and Porto districts were demolished from the late 1870s on.

Nevertheless, with its resources greatly diminished and no real help coming from the central government, the economy continued to stagnate, and the city fell further behind. In 1877, the publication of Jesse White Mario's *La Miseria di Napoli* and Renato Fucini's *Napoli a occhio nudo* revealed the extent of the population's suffering in graphic terms. By the early 1880s, unemployment, crime, and overcrowding — which had already been huge problems under the Bourbons — were clearly among the worst in Europe, while the rate of illiteracy, which was estimated at 72 percent in 1880, was more than twice that of Turin and Milan. Housing, moreover, was totally inadequate, with an estimated 130,000 of the city's 496,499 people in 1884 living in underground dwellings (either *bassi* or *sottoterrani*), and uncounted tens of thousands more living on the streets. In November 1878, an attempt by a Neapolitan anarchist, Giovanni Passanante, to assassinate Umberto I, the new Italian King, during an official visit on via Toledo, although an isolated act, became a symbol of the general alienation and discontent. In July 1883, a correspondent for the *Edinburgh Review*, after a long residence in Naples, summarized the situation in southern Italy as follows:

> 176. The thing that is most striking about the reports coming from the various cities [in the South] is the constant complaint about deterioration; and these complaints are not confined to the mountainous districts, or to the condition of the working classes, but are general, regardless of the place. The one thing that they all point to is the enormous decline that has occurred since unification. [Cited in Gaudioso, *Reazione a Napoli*, pp. 3-4.]

It was under these conditions that the first case of cholera was reported in the city in the summer of 1884.

■

Disease and demographic catastrophe were not new to Naples. In 1656, the plague had killed almost half of the city's estimated population of 450,000 people, and the disease had returned, along with a devastating famine, in 1764. During the first half of the 19th century, cholera had struck Naples at least once in every generation, but never with the virulence seen in 1884. Starting in June and reaching its peak in September, the disease killed 7,143 people, with 17,420 more being taken ill. Panic and hysteria soon gripped the city, as medical facilities proved totally inadequate and

CHAPTER 7. NAPLES IN ITALY, THE EARLY YEARS

virtually anyone with sufficient means took flight. In the majority of cases, high fever, wrenching pain, and a convulsive vomiting of blood were the most common symptoms; in others, the victim simply fell over dead without any sign of being ill. As in the previous outbreaks in 1836 and 1854, the disease spread most rapidly in the poorer sections of the city, where extreme overcrowding and the lack of clean water and sanitation put the population at increased risk.

For most Neapolitans, it was a tragedy of incalculable proportions. In his memoirs, the brilliant Swedish physician, Alex Munthe — who went to Naples in 1884 to help combat the epidemic and whose contemporaneous *Letters from a Mourning City* caused a sensation throughout Europe — recalled the terror which he felt upon first arriving in the city as follows:

> 177.1. [When I first arrived in Naples] I was horribly afraid of the cholera and death from the start.... As I stepped out of the train...I passed long convoys of carts and omnibuses filled with corpses on the way to the cholera cemetery [and] I spent the whole first night among the dying in the wretched *fondaci* of the slums. Had there been a train back to Rome, to Calabria, to the Abruzzi, to anywhere,... there would have been no *Letters from a Mourning City*. As it was, there was no train until noon the next day...[and I therefore] had to return to Santa Lucia trembling with fear. In the afternoon my [earlier] offer to serve on the staff of the cholera hospital of Santa Maddalenna was accepted.... Two days later, I vanished from the hospital having discovered that the right place for me was not among the dying in the hospital, but among the dying in the slums.
>
> How much easier it would have been for them and for me, I thought, if only their agony was not so long, so terrible! There they were lying for hours, for days in the *stadium algidum*, cold as corpses, with wide-open eyes and wide-open mouths, to all appearances dead, and yet still alive. Did they feel anything, did they understand anything? So much the better for the few who could still swallow the tea-spoonful of laudanum that one of the volunteers of the *Croce Bianca* rushed in to pour into their mouths. It might at least finish them off before the soldiers and the half-drunk *beccamorti* came at night to throw them all in a heap in the immense pit on the *Camposanto dei Colerosi*. How many were thrown there still alive!
>
> As the epidemic [grew]...they began to fall in the streets as if struck by lighting, to be picked up by the police and driven to the cholera hospital to die a few hours later. Often when I returned

in the evening...I threw myself on the bed as I was, without even washing myself. What good was washing in this filthy water, what good was disinfecting myself when everybody and everything around me was infected, the food I ate, the water I drank, the bed I slept in, the very air I breathed! Often I was too frightened to go to bed, too frightened to be alone. I had to rush out into the street again, to spend the remainder of the night in one of the churches.... All the hundreds of churches and chapels of Naples were open the whole night, ablaze with votive candles and thronged with people. All their hundreds of Madonnas and saints were hard at work night and day to visit the dying in their respective quarters. Woe to them if they ventured to appear in the quarter of one of their rivals. Even the venerable *Madonna della Colera* who had saved the city in the terrible epidemic of 1834 [sic], had been hissed days before at *Bianchi Nuovi*.

But it was not only of the cholera that I was afraid. I was also terrified...of the rats. They seemed as much at home in the fondaci, bassi, and sottoterrani of the slums as the wretched human beings who lived there.... When the sanitary commission started on its vain attempt to disinfect the sewers...my fear grew into terror. Millions of rats who had been living unmolested since the time of the Romans invaded the lower part of the city. Intoxicated by the sulfur fumes and carbonic acid, they rushed about the slums like mad dogs. They did not look like any rats I had ever seen before, they were quite bald with extraordinary long red tails, fierce blood-shot eyes and pointed black teeth as long as the teeth of a ferret.... The whole Basso Porto quarter was in terror. Over one hundred severely bitten men, women, and children were taken to the hospital.... Several small children were literally eaten up. I shall never forget the night in the fondaco in Vicolo della Duchessa. The room, the cave is a better word, was almost dark, only lit up by a little oil-lamp before the Madonna. The father had been dead for two days but the body was still lying there under a heap of rags, the family having succeeded in hiding him from the police in search of the dead to be taken to the cemetery, a common practice in the slums. I was sitting on the floor by the side of the daughter, beating off the rats with my stick. She was already quite cold, but she was still conscious. I could hear the whole time the rats crunching at the body of the father. At last it made me so nervous that I had to put

CHAPTER 7. NAPLES IN ITALY, THE EARLY YEARS

him upright in the corner like a grandfather clock. Soon the rats began again eating ravenously at his feet and legs. I could not stand it any longer. Faint with fear I rushed away. [Axel Munthe, *The Story of San Michele*. New York: E.P. Dutton, 1957, pp. 157-62.]

And, with equal horror, in *Letters from a Mourning City*:

> 177.2. The doctor must not be too particular with regard to the peoples' feelings about his profession, nor must he be too sensitive to their want of confidence in his skill; the *lazzaroni* are as skeptical with regard to the infallibility of his medicines as maybe the doctor is in his heart. But they go further, for they believe that all sorts of horrible things lie at the bottom of his bottles — various unknown poisons, the evil eye, serpent's tongues, a few hairs of the devil himself, and other ingredients which, as far as I know, are excluded from pharmacopoeia.... The acquaintance with doctors and officials is so new to these inhabitants of the poor quarters.... In ordinary times, no policeman ever puts in an appearance in these slums...and the inhabitants of the Mercato, Pendino, Porto, and Vicaria quarters enter the world and leave it without a doctor's help....
>
> [One day] I went to the cholera cemetery where I remained for an hour and, during that time, eighty-five bodies were brought there (the official report announced fifty-seven). The corpses were laid out in a row before they were buried. As they are being lowered into the grave their names are written down in the register. It made a singularly uncanny impression to see the many blank spaces in the book, nothing to distinguish them — death without names, no home during their lifetime, and a big cholera pit after death!
>
> The poor [in fact] are everywhere in this city. You usually find them rolled up in rags on the street, on the steps of churches, under boats at Mergellina, and on the benches in squares and gardens.... [And] the children! What an amazing multitude of children! They are supposed to be a token of God Almighty's special blessing, and if it is so, to what a terrible extent have these poor, starving people been blessed!... Half of them are fatherless and motherless and all of them are down with *la febbre*. A boy nearby greets us with a dull expression in his eye, and the hoarse giggle of the idiot on his lips, he has got tabes, and had been a cripple for two years.... His father is a convict, and his mother and two sisters died

[of the cholera] last week.... The woman standing there, with a baby at her breast, had taken him into her own house since his mother died, although she has six children of her own and nothing to keep body and soul together.... Poverty, awful, unspeakable poverty, was then the misery that follows in your steps not enough for these poor people? [Alex Munthe, *Letters from a Mourning City.* 2nd ed. London: John Murray, 1899, pp. 30-96.]

The suffering of the Neapolitan people created an enormous wave of sympathy throughout Italy. In many newspapers and journals, the epidemic was held up as the symbol of the failure of national unification to solve the problems of the southern provinces, and of the overwhelming need to arrest the deterioration in Italy's largest commercial port. Even the central government — which had callously ignored the plight of Naples for more than two decades — recognized the threat that the city posed to the rest of the nation. In a speech before the Chamber of Deputies, the prime minister, Agostino Depretis, expressed the fears of many northern Italians when he stated:

> 178. Under the conditions that prevailed [prior to unification], the disease could be largely localized — confined to the city and vanquished there. That is no longer possible. The largest urban center in the nation is linked to the other leading cities by bonds of family, friendship, commerce, speculation, and industry. Standing open on every side by land and sea, and emerging as the hub of a major railroad network, Naples cannot be isolated from the rest of Italy, no matter how grave the danger. [Cited in Frank M. Snowden, *Naples in the Time of the Cholera, 1884-1991.* New York: Cambridge University Press, 1995, p. 191.]

On September 9, at the height of the epidemic, Depretis and the king visited Naples. Moving through the poorest sections of the city along with the mayor, Nicola Amore, they were visibly shaken by the extent of the suffering and vowed to undertake a program of urban reform. Naples, as Depretis put it succinctly, must be "gutted." The remark, which was repeated *ad nauseam* in the Italian press, provoked a cynical reaction from those who knew the city best. In a series of articles published under the title *Il Ventre di Napoli* (*The Bowels of Naples*), the impassioned Neapolitan novelist, Matilde Serao, who understood the inner workings of Naples as well as anyone, wrote:

> 179. This government, which knows everything: from how much meat is eaten each day and how much wine is drunk...to how many

CHAPTER 7. NAPLES IN ITALY, THE EARLY YEARS

> women disgrace themselves and how much money is made in the lottery,... this government does not know the bowels of Naples....
> In order to eliminate the material and moral corruption of the city, in order to restore the health and honesty of the poor, in order to teach them how to live — for, as we have seen, they already know how to die — in order to say to them that they are our brothers, it is not enough to gut Naples, it must be rebuilt almost completely. [Matilde Serao, *Il Ventre di Napoli*. Milan: Treves, 1884, pp. 2-11.]

Driven by such exhortations, and fearful that the epidemic would spread to the rest of Italy, Depretis announced a massive program of urban reform. The program — which became known as the *"Risanamento"* — envisioned a vast transformation that would rid the city of the disease once and for all. In 1885, the municipal engineer who drafted the project, Adolfo Giambarba, listed its three main objectives as follows:

> 180. [1] A demolition of the fondaci and the worst labyrinths. [2] The opening of longitudinal streets in order to rip out the most unhealthy zone, which will be rebuilt with regular and hygienic buildings that allow the free circulation of light and air. And, [3] Elevation of the streets above the present level of ground water. [Cited in Snowden, *Cholera*, p. 186.]

Between 1887 and 1898, the Italian government spent 100 million lire in an effort to rebuild the city. Large parts of the Porto, Mercato, Pendino, and Vicaria districts were demolished; new buildings, broad boulevards, and huge public squares were constructed; and Naples' antiquated seventeenth-century sewer system was entirely replaced. Overall, more than 56,000 people were displaced by the construction, most of them residents of the Lower City and desperately poor. In 1901, the Serado commission described the fate of these residents as follows:

> 181. With regard to the inhabitants of the quarters that were demolished, some crowded, beyond all means of containing them, into the [official] low-cost housing; others, such as the residents of Santa Lucia, were forced to leave the center of their own city and to settle in distant Fuorigrotta; and the others, finally, occupied the unhealthy bassi of the new constructions or squeezed into those of the Old City that were not included in the demolition. [Snowden, *Cholera*, p. 214.]

Thus, one of the main objectives of the *Risanamento* — the reduction of population density in the Lower City — was never achieved. In some areas, in fact, such as the Vicaria, it actually increased. As a result, whole sections of the city remained

209

overcrowded and unsanitary, with foul-smelling air and dilapidated houses, and thousands of homeless still on the streets. Many years later, Alberto Marghieri, who as an alderman during the 1880s and 1890s had been in charge of public works during the implementation of the project, would write:

> 182. From the point of view of housing and hygiene, a very substantial part of the city remains in dreadful condition, despite the work of demolition and reconstruction. Dark, narrow streets, teeming with fondaci and filthy bassi still play host to many thousands of impoverished people. These teeming slums provide the material for macabre reports that all too accurately describe the many foci of infection.... Nicola Amore's marble stature still contemplates...urban caves, rat-holes, alleyways, tenements, and rookeries that the pickax never destroyed. Today, more than twenty years on, they still cause visitors to tremble in horror. Here Neapolitans live out their hard lives, or are struck down by consumption, typhoid, gastro-enteritis, and the comma bacillus. [Cited in Snowden, *Cholera*, p. 220.]

The failure created a deep sense of gloom among many inhabitants. In 1896, the influential Neapolitan journalist and historian Alfonso Cottrau wrote:

> 183. For an old unrepentant liberal like me, it is certainly extremely painful to admit that, from 1860 to the present, progress in my native city has been very slow and even negative from certain points of view.... The constitution of the Kingdom of Italy has been harmful to Naples...in the sense that, among two-thirds of the population, misery is actually worse now than it was before. [Alfonso Cottrau, *La crisi della città di Napoli* (1896), p. 331, cited in Maryse Jeuland-Meynand, *La Ville de Naples après l'annexation, 1860–1915*. Aix-en-Provence: Éditions de l'Université de Provence, 1973, p. 49.]

And, two years later, in the introduction to his book on conditions in the city, Marco Rocco would add:

> 184. The promises that were made to Naples were so extensive that, by this time, she was to have reached the level of the world's greatest metropolises, whereas, after thirty-seven years of long and fruitless waiting, there is no one in our city who does not deplore its present state of moral and material decadence. [Marco Rocco, *Le condizioni del commune di Napoli* (1898), pp. 3-4, cited in Jeuland-Meynand, p. 49.]

CHAPTER 7. NAPLES IN ITALY, THE EARLY YEARS

Thus, despite all of the expense and hardship, Naples failed to rid itself of the cholera. Poor planning, lack of alternative housing for displaced residents, and widespread speculation and corruption at the local level had combined to render its transformation incomplete. As late as 1910, in fact, 126,000 of Naples' 713,000 inhabitants still lived in *bassi*, with families of up to eight-to-ten people going about their daily activities in a single, windowless room. Under these conditions, the cholera returned again in 1910-1911. This time — although the government made every effort to suppress the figures — the number killed was between four and five thousand people, with children under five in the poorest sections being particularly hard hit. It was an unnecessary sacrifice in an age in which medical science had freed most Western cities from the terrors of the disease.

■

One of the most remarkable features of Neapolitan economic and political decline in the second half of the 19th century was the continued creativity of its culture. Indeed, during the years between 1860 and 1914, Neapolitan artists, writers, musicians, and intellectuals produced a body of work that made the city famous throughout Italy and then propelled it onto the international stage. Among them were Salvatore Di Giacomo, Ferdinando Russo, and Ernesto Murolo (poetry), Vincenzo Gemito (sculpture), Matilde Serao (literature), Eduardo Scarpetta and Raffaele Viviani (theater), Giuseppe De Nittis (painting), Giuseppe Turco, Edoardo Di Capua, Francesco Paolo Tosti, Mario Costa, and Giambattista and Ernesto De Curtis (music), Edoardo Scarfoglio (journalism), Francesco De Santis and Benedetto Croce (philosophy), Arturo Labriola (Marxist theory), and Pasquale Villari and Giustino Fortunato (meridionalist studies). By 1914, Neapolitan songs, plays, and ideas were known all over Europe. Neapolitan popular music, in particular, had a huge dissemination internationally during the first half of the 20th century, and the iconography of the city — Vesuvius with its funicular and the Bay of Naples with its sweeping panorama — came to represent Italy in eyes of many people as far away as Argentina and the United States.

None of this, however, could change the social realities of the city. By 1914, most Neapolitans still lived in unbelievable filth and poverty, with death rates in almost every category among the highest in Europe and thousands of sick and elderly lying upon the streets. Special laws for Naples passed by Parliament in 1904, 1908, and 1911 had little impact on the situation, and by the time of the outbreak of the First World War many Neapolitans looked on their city with a combination of horror and shame. In 1925, the great Neapolitan philosopher, Benedetto Croce, in reflecting upon the first fifty-four years of Naples' history as part of a unified Italy, wrote:

185. With the end of the Kingdom of Naples and the annexation of the South to the rest of Italy [in 1860], the history of the Kingdom as a political entity came to an end.... [Since then] there have been many complaints and accusations against the South: without it Italy would have had a more homogeneous distribution of wealth and culture, the percentage of illiteracy would not have been so high, governments would not have won so many bought votes, the monarchy would have given away to a republic, excessive centralization could have been avoided, to the gain or preservation of regional autonomy, general policy would have been more liberal and democratic, and there might even have been an opening toward an ultra-democratic and socialistic social structure. To which, by way of defense or counteroffensive, it has been pointed out that without the South, northern and central Italy would have been restricted to a narrow and trivial existence; the South provided a marketplace for northern manufactures, thereby losing its own local industries; the intellectual drive of the south raised the level of Italian scholarship and science; Italy was lucky to have, in the South, a counterweight or ballast such as to hold it back from certain follies; and this ballast was no dead weight but rather an element of common sense; the idea of a monarchy and a strong central government was not simply a demonstration of traditional subservience but, in the form espoused by the greatest Southerners, grew out of realistic perception and serious historical and political considerations. All these pros and cons are, as such, inconclusive, because every union obviously has its advantages and disadvantages...and each of these observations possesses a grain of truth....

Evidence of many of these problems [in fact] came in the first days of unification. After the Bourbons had been driven out and a new liberal constitution had been put into effect, the government of the new Italy was faced not by the vision of a liberated and happy land but by brigandage in the provinces, crime in the ancient capital, and general lawlessness, confusion, and abjection. Even the returning exiles were aghast, as if a veil had dropped from their eyes. "The dirt and rot are sickening," said a letter from [Silvio] Spaventa [the city's first minister of police]. "One doesnot see how this country can ever return to a reasonable condition; it is as if the hinges of morality had been wrenched loose."... [Yet] of all the ministers that followed [Cavour], only Peruzzi believed that the

CHAPTER 7. NAPLES IN ITALY, THE EARLY YEARS

problem [of the South] should be faced unequivocally. His successors chose the easier path of abstract legislation. Practically speaking, they abandoned the southern provinces to their fate, dealing out small favors to their representatives and indulging them in their vote-getting manipulations.

[Even] the former exiles who belonged to the early cabinets and their conservative southern colleagues...lost interest in the South and treated it with scorn as well as neglect.... Buried in their books, then jailed or driven into exile, they knew little of the country's real conditions...and were reluctant to plunge back into the miseries and vagaries of their native region. We may guess at the accumulated bitterness of these men...by the words of General Filangieri, the son of the author of *La scienza della legislazione*, who wrote to his own son: "Believe me, for anyone with a sense of honor and red blood in his veins it is a great calamity to be born a Neapolitan." In the judgments passed by these newly Italianized Neapolitan moderates there is an echo of the witticism of King Ferdinand II when he supposedly answered a foreign ambassador who pinned the adjective "African" upon certain of the Kingdom's police procedures: "Well, Africa begins here." I remember hearing similar barbed remarks on the part of Spaventa, who, for love of country, had been a conspirator in 1848 and spent ten years in prison. Now, feeling that he had done his duty, he held himself disgustedly aloof, to the point of preferring to represent a northern district in the Chamber of Deputies. He came back only reluctantly to Naples, which he called "that place," and mocked those who favored the establishment of republics and federations because (he said to me): "In that case you Neapolitans would have for a president the Duke of San Donato." Ill-humored and oversimplified exaggerations and injustices, no doubt,... but they "go down in history," and in a way that does not add to the region's reputation or prestige. [Benedetto Croce, *History of the Kingdom of Naples*. H. Stuart Hughes, ed. Chicago: University of Chicago Press, 1970, pp. 238-43.]

■ ■ ■

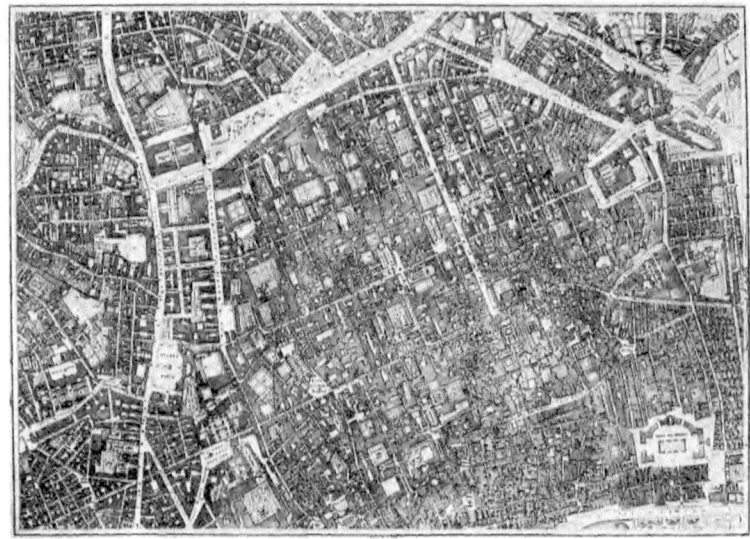

THE SETTING FOR DISASTER. Two of the 24 maps developed for the Ufficio Tecnico show the city from Piazza Cavour (above center) to the harbor (below) and graphically illustrate the high density, overpopulation, and pre-modern street system of the urban core, essentially untouched from its ancient and medieval roots.

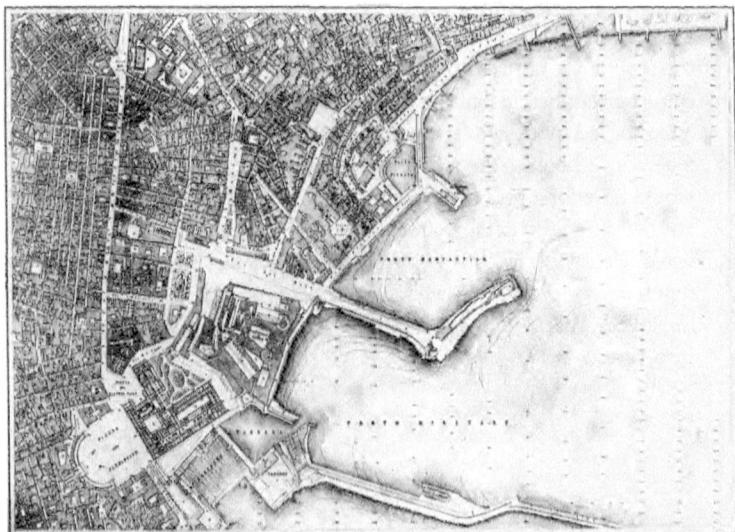

84-85. *Ufficio Tecnico del Comune di Napoli. Maps showing the density of the central city, 1872–80.*

PUBLIC HEALTH & RISANAMENTO

A STREET IN SANTA LUCIA, in an area untouched by the Risanamento, shows the conditions of most of the old urban core: cramped quarters, much of daily life lived outdoors amid narrow streets and dark, damp alleys. Such conditions proved the ideal breeding ground for the outbreak of communicable disease, including the great cholera epidemic of 1884.

86. *Vicolo di Santa Lucia, c. 1890.*

87. *Edoardo Matania.* The Cholera in Naples, *1884.*

88. *Edoardo Matania.* Umberto I and Agostino Depretis Visit the Cholera Wards, *1884.*

MODERN NAPLES, 1799–1999

89–90. *Plan for the Risanamento, with axes of Corso Umberto I (Rettifilo) and via Nazionale, 1884 (above); and aerial photo of same area, showing implementation, c. 1960 (left).*

91. *Below, pp. 216–17. Elevations along Corso Umberto I (Rettifilo) after the Risanamento, from Piazza Bovio and Fontana Medina (left) to the train station (right).*

PUBLIC HEALTH & RISANAMENTO

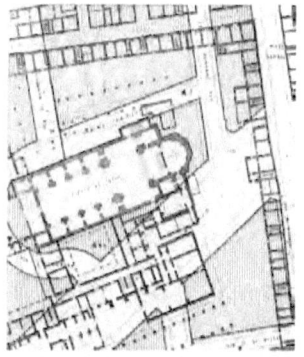

92. *Plan for the new Corso Umberto I: demolition through the cloister of San Pietro ad Aram.*

94. *Gradelle di San Giuseppe on via Calderai, 1889. Destroyed during the Risanamento.*

93. *Fondaco Calderai a Rua Catalana. Destroyed during the Risanamento.*

A NEW CITY CARVED FROM THE OLD. The Risanamento's response to overcrowding and disease was to level entire sections of the old city and replace them with new streets and piazzas, most famously along the Rettifilo, exchanging the pedestrian and the neighborhood for the free flow of traffic and commercial development.

95. Camorristi *under arrest, c. 1906.*

8
The Era of Catastrophes, 1914–1943

If the first period of Naples' integration into Italy was difficult, the second period (1914–1943) proved to be a disaster. In August 1914, when the First World War broke out, most Neapolitans, like the majority of Italians everywhere, were opposed to Italy's entry into the struggle. Alienated from the state and perplexed by the issues involved in what appeared to be a distant conflict, they were relieved when the Salandra government decided to renounce its treaty commitments with Germany and Austria-Hungary and declared its neutrality at the start of the war.

During the next eight months, however, the attitude of many Neapolitans slowly began to change. Spurred on by a small group of politically active university students and subjected to increasingly intense interventionist propaganda, many younger Neapolitans, in particular, began to see the war as a great national adventure. Although only a vocal minority, they were able to whip up popular support for the Salandra government at the time of its decision to enter the struggle and maintained a continuous patriotic drumbeat throughout the rest of the war.

Between May 1915 and November 1918, therefore, tens of thousands of Neapolitans sacrificed themselves on the battlefields of northern Italy for what was (for most at least) only a vaguely-perceived *"Italia irridenta."* Neapolitan women went into the factories in great numbers for the first time in order to manufacture arms and munitions; songwriters wrote patriotic lyrics in order to encourage resistance to the Germans; and Neapolitan industry hummed along at a level which would have been unthinkable prior to the war. Even the appearance of an Austrian dirigible in March 1918, which dropped bombs in the center of the city and killed sixteen people, failed to dampen the determination to continue the struggle. By 1919, many Neapolitans felt themselves to be part of Italy for the first time in their history, and they looked to the future with greater expectations than ever before.

In the end, however, all such hopes proved to be an illusion. For the war had not solved, but exacerbated the city's problems, shifting the government's attention away from the "southern question" and ending all further efforts at social reform. Between 1919 and 1921 alone, prices in Italy more than doubled and national unemployment grew to over 500,000. In Naples, as elsewhere, tensions between factory owners and workers exploded into strikes and disorders — as Fascists fought Socialists in city's streets and factories and the situation quickly spun out of control. By late 1920, armed groups of men roamed the Campania striking out against their political opponents, and the entire country seemed on the verge of civil war.

The first Fascist squads in Naples were formed on April 14, 1919, less than one month after Mussolini had founded the *Fasci di combattimento* in Milan. Led by the dynamic and determined local "party boss" (or *"raz"*), Aurelio Padovani, they consisted largely of ex-soldiers, anti-Bolshevik university students, and low-level government officials, many of whom had been unable to readjust to civilian society after the war. Although they never possessed the numbers of their counterparts in northern and central Italy, they made up for their lack of size with their fanaticism and violence and were able to count on many local property owners and administrative officials for support. In 1929, the Neapolitan Socialist leader, Arturo Labriola, described one of the early efforts of the Fascists to intimidate him as follows:

> 186. At that time (September 1922) the Fascists of Giugliano, a small town near Naples belonging to the constituency which I represented in Parliament, had forbidden me to enter the town. Notices to this effect were posted on the walls throughout the constituency. Though the Fascists were not in power the authorities paid no attention. To me the notice was sent by telegram as follows: "Labriola Naples. Command to Fascists of Giugliano. Cudgels up against Labriola. Signed Giuseppi Cante Secretary." The examining magistrate opened an inquiry and questioned me. I showed him the telegram but the magistrate closed the inquiry declaring that the author of the threat was unknown — though Signor Cante is perfectly well-known and still alive. [Cited in Allum, *Politics and Society,* p. 73, note 1.]

On May 1, 1920, armed Fascist squads broke up a workers' rally in the Piazza Dante. In April 1921, they launched a series of attacks on striking workers in the nearby town of Capua, and the assaults grew more daring as the months wore on. Far from discouraging potential supporters, the violence seemed to attract them. At the start of 1921, in the province of Naples, the Fascist party numbered about 3,000 members. By the end of the year, its membership had tripled to 9,000 as its ranks were swelled by an ever-growing number of middle-class youth. In the parliamentary elections of March 1921, the party surprised virtually everyone by polling over 5,000 votes in the city of Naples — only

CHAPTER 8. THE ERA OF CATASTROPHES, 1914–1943

slightly less than the Catholic Popular Party, and a clear indication of its mounting appeal.

By early 1922, except for the Socialists and a few isolated individuals, virtually no one in the Neapolitan political establishment was willing to take the risk of authorizing state intervention to suppress Fascist violence. Whether due to personal fear, hatred for socialism, or nationalism, all were willing to collaborate with the *squadristi* to some degree. In mid-October, Mussolini, sensing that the time and place were right, decided to hold a national party congress in Naples as part of his final push to power. The meeting — which was attended by the entire Fascist "general staff" — took place on October 24. On that day, 40,000 Blackshirts descended on the city from all over Italy. As they arrived, Enrico De Nicola — who had represented Naples in Parliament for thirteen years and, at the time, was president of the Chamber of Deputies — sent a telegram to Mussolini welcoming him to the city. The greeting, although tersely worded, proved to be a harbinger of the mass capitulation that was to come:

> 187. I want personally to extend to you and all of your colleagues arriving in Naples my cordial and affectionate greetings. De Nicola. [Cited in Giacomo De Antonellis, *Napoli sotto il regime*. Milan: Donati, 1972, p. 104.]

That day, the Fascists owned Naples. For more than two hours beginning at 9 AM, a vast army of *squadristi* paraded past Mussolini — arms raised and banners flying — shouting "To Rome! To Rome!" One hour later, the *Duce* withdrew to the filled-to-capacity Teatro San Carlo, where he threw down the gauntlet to the government:

> 188. Fascists! Citizens!
> Today we have come to Naples from every part of Italy…[and] we have been greeted with enormous enthusiasm.… The whole country is watching our meeting because there is no movement in postwar Europe or the world that is more interesting, original, or epoch-making than Italian Fascism.…
> Do you remember the time in Parliament when my friend Lupi and I proposed the question that concerns not only Fascism, but all of Italy: legality or illegality? Parliamentary or revolutionary conquests? How is Fascism to become the state? For we want to become the state. On October 3, I answered this question [in a speech in Milan].… And yet, the government still asks: what do the Fascists want? To this, I have responded: we want a dissolution of the Chamber, electoral reform, elections on short notice. We want the state to abandon its grotesque neutrality, which has

made it stagger between the national and international forces.... We have demanded five ministerial portfolios, and a government committee for emigration. We have asked specifically for the ministry of foreign affairs, the ministry of war, the ministry of the navy, and the ministries of labor and public works....

The government's answer [to these demands] has been ridiculous. They said that we should accept a nominal position in the Cabinet, or be satisfied with some subordinate post. Ministries without portfolios, undersecretaryships were discussed, all of which is contemptible. We have no intention of getting into the government by the back door, of selling our wonderful birthright for a ministerial mess of pottage. This problem, as a problem of history, has been misunderstood; now it has to be faced as a problem of force....

In the discussion of our intentions, the question of the monarchy is often raised.... There can be no doubt that the unitary regime of Italian life rests solidly on the Savoy monarchy. There can likewise be no doubt that the Italian monarchy, by virtue of its origins and history, cannot oppose the tendencies of the new national force.... Would the monarchy be in the right if today it opposed Fascism, given the fact that the latter, far from intending to attack the monarchy, seeks only to liberate it from all the superstructures that obscure the historical position of this institution?...

Parliament,... and all the trappings of democracy that surround it, have nothing to do with the monarchy as an institution. But I do wish to add that we have no intention of depriving the country of its parliamentary "toy." I say "toy" because that is the way that much of the Italian nation sees it....

As for the...army, it should know that...we defended it at a time when the ministers were advising its officers to go about in civilian dress in order to avoid clashes!

We have created our own myth. A myth is a belief, a passion.... Our myth is the greatness of the nation. To this myth, to this greatness, which we desire to translate into a comprehensive reality, we subordinate everything....

[As part of this reality], I can see the future greatness of Naples, the true metropolis of the Mediterranean.... I can see it joining together with Bari and Palermo in a powerful triangle of strength, energy, and ability; and I can see Fascism harnessing and coordinating

CHAPTER 8. THE ERA OF CATASTROPHES, 1914–1943

> that energy...and gathering it under its banner.... Fascists of Italy, raise your flags and salute Naples, queen of the Mediterranean! [*Opera omnia di Benito Mussolini*, Eduardo Susmel and Duilio Susmel, eds. Florence: La Fenice, 1951-1962, 18:453-59.]

After the speech, a huge, excited crowd gathered outside the theater in the *Piazza del Plebiscito*. Once again, the cry, "To Rome! To Rome!" rose up, and Mussolini, obviously stirred by its enthusiasm, responded ominously:

> 189. Leaders! Legionnaires! Blackshirts of Naples and all Italy! Today, without striking a single blow, we have conquered the burning, vibrating soul of Naples, the burning soul of the South of Italy. The demonstration is now complete and cannot be turned into a battle. But I say to you with all the seriousness that the moment demands, that it is only a matter of days, perhaps even hours, before the government is either handed over to us, or we will seize it for ourselves by marching on Rome! [Mussolini, *Opera*, 18:459-60.]

After the Naples conference, Mussolini moved quickly to implement his plan for coercing the government into giving the Fascist Party a share of power. On the morning of October 27, small groups of *squadristi* — operating with the active or passive support of local prefects and garrison commanders — seized control of key points in towns and cities all over northern and central Italy. Simultaneously, three columns of Blackshirts (totaling about 17,000 men) gathered up their arms and headed for Rome. The government — led by the weak and irresolute Luigi Facta — immediately asked for a declaration of martial law. But the king, Victor Emmanuel II, misinformed about the strength of the Fascist mobilization and thoroughly intimidated, refused to sign the decree. With this, resistance to Mussolini within the ministry completely collapsed. On October 29, Facta resigned and Mussolini was appointed Italian prime minister. Two weeks later, on November 16, the Italian parliament (led by the Liberal and Popular parties) gave him an overwhelming vote of confidence, and he unexpectedly became the master of Rome.

The refusal of Italy's national leadership to defend the country's liberal institutions destroyed any hope of organized resistance in the South. On December 15, 1922, the Fascist squads were formally sworn in as part of a newly-created "national militia." Operating, for the first time under the imprimatur of the state, they immediately launched a new series of attacks on their political opponents, and a large part of the southern population was "converted" almost overnight. On February 23, 1923, the Neapolitan anti-Fascist, Carlo Cassola, who observed this process first-hand in the nearby town of Nocera, wrote:

190. Up to February 5 [1923], Nocera counted about 100 Fascists and the section was in crisis because of the resignation of the executive.... Today [two weeks later] the town has, perhaps, only about 50 of its responsible citizens who say that they are not Fascists (and I am not sure of that). It is the fault of Fascist *violence* and the *venality* of our ruling class.... On the eve of the elections, the prefecture and Fascists believed that the Socialists might present a list and do very well.... This led to the use of violence. *Lorries* of Fascists drove through the town with rifles and revolvers firing, the Socialist club was destroyed and the Democratic Union club occupied.... Two armed *camorristi*... in black shirts...were the executants of this base act of justice.... The incidents terrorized the town and the terror grew when the leaders of the so-called Socialist Party were arrested.

A crowd of people of all political persuasions made requests for Fascist membership where only a few had previously. Nobody had the courage to protest.... An excuse for my fellow citizens is this: the authorities protect the Fascist excesses. One must add that the citizens whose duty it is to protest against the violence and abuses, have not lifted a finger: Guerritore and Lunzara [two former deputies] deluded themselves, in their stupidity, right up to the last moment, that they would be able to enter the [electoral] list with their supporters...because it was officially Fascist. [Cited in Allum, *Politics and Society,* pp. 72-73.]

A similar "pacification" took place in Naples. There virtually the entire political governing class, led by De Nicola, accepted Mussolini's offer to join in the Fascist-dominated "national list" in the crucial 1924 elections. Overall, in the South as a whole, eighty ex-ministers and deputies joined the coalition, including Vittorio Orlando and Antonio Salandra, both former prime ministers. In the balloting—which took place in an atmosphere of violence and intimidation—over seventy percent of the votes cast in the Neapolitan and Terra di Lavoro constituencies went to the Liberal-Fascist coalition, compared to sixty-five percent in the country as a whole.

Even the murder of the Socialist leader, Giacomo Matteotti, in April 1924 — which shocked the nation and shook the Fascist regime to its very foundations — failed to stiffen the backs of the Neapolitan political "opposition." Although, for a time, a number of prominent Neapolitans — including Giovanni Amendola, Croce, Serao, Fortunato, and Paolo Scarfoglio, the editor of the city's preeminent liberal newspaper, *Il Mattino* — attempted to mobilize public opinion around the issue, their efforts quickly collapsed when Mussolini regained his equilibrium and the Blackshirts renewed their attacks. On November 28, 1925, Scarfoglio — the son of the newspaper's

CHAPTER 8. THE ERA OF CATASTROPHES, 1914–1943

venerable founder, Eduardo Scarfoglio — wrote to Mussolini in the hope of avoiding suppression:

> 191. Your Excellency.
> In defense of the four hundred families that we have the pleasure of employing...I submit to your chivalry and admirable sense of justice the following facts. *Il Mattino* has supported Fascism for four years, from 1920 to 1924. When You assumed power, You had never seen me. In March of 1924, when the separation between liberalism and Fascism became apparent, we decided that we could not renounce thirty-four years of tradition at *Il Mattino*.... Our campaign of opposition did not in any way coincide with the Matteotti crime, but preceded it considerably; it was decidedly anti-Ventinian, it emphasized normalization, and avoided the trap of the moral question. It was, to use one of Your Excellency's own phrases, an act of useless gallantry. It was an obligatory homage to a tradition that did not deserve to be abandoned by us, simply because everyone else was abandoning it. And, at the same time, *Il Mattino* was enthusiastic in its praise of all the works that had been accomplished by the Fascist government. The solution to the problem of the South, which we owe to Your Excellency, was in fact the occasion for a modification of our position, which from that point on was one of unconditional support.... I want our moral position to be clear, and our Fascism, nurtured when Fascism was not yet powerful, not marred by malicious distortions.... There are those who want to misrepresent our position. They want to depict us as unyielding and self-serving.... An attempt to abolish *Il Mattino* is an attempt to suppress a newspaper that was founded by Edoardo Scarfoglio...among whose merits was to oppose Nitti and Amendola, anti-Fiumianism, popularism, Turatism and Misiano.
>
> Your Excellency: You will acknowledge that in suppressing *Il Mattino*, a certain part of Fascism is also being suppressed.... During the campaign waged against us in April 1924, You had the generosity to intervene with a letter that reestablished the reputation of my brother Carlo. Gestures of this nature are proof of a moral superiority which, to my eyes, represents the surest sign to your integrity. In a similar way, I hope that this letter will eliminate the necessity for any further demonstration of my support. [Cited in De Antonellis, *Napoli*, pp. 90-92.]

Thus, Fascism came to power in Naples with the aid of the liberal opposition. Despite Mussolini's claims to have brought about a political revolution, the traditional Neapolitan ruling class was not eliminated, but simply absorbed. In 1929, De Nicola was rewarded for his services by being appointed to the Italian Senate, and thousands of local government officials — the *"clientele"* of the previous generation of liberal administrations — were allowed to remain in their positions undisturbed.

■

The support that Mussolini received from southern Italy's traditional ruling class was not matched by that of the peasants and workers. Among the peasants, in particular, the combination of poverty and physical isolation had created a barrier to all forms of political indoctrination and made them resistant to most aspects of the modern world. During the late 19th and early 20th centuries, hundreds of thousands had emigrated to the Americas. Moving through Naples, they had transformed the city into the country's main port of departure, with as many as 200,000 leaving in a single year. In 1946, Carlo Levi, who had spent one year under house arrest in the small provincial town of Gagliano in Basilicata for his opposition to Fascism during the 1930s, wrote:

> 192. The peasants...were not Fascists, just as they would never have been Conservatives or Socialists, or anything else.... There were hailstorms, landslides, droughts, malaria...and the State. These are inescapable evils; such as have always been and always will be.... [To them] Rome means very little; it is the capital of the gentry, the center of a foreign and hostile world.... [There is] Naples...[but] their other world is America.... New York, rather than Rome or Naples, would be the real capital of the peasants of Lucania, if these men without a country could have a capital at all. [Carlo Levi, *Christ Stopped at Eboli*. London: Cassell, 1948, p. 76.]

A similar, but somewhat different, problem existed among the industrial workers. Like the peasants, they too were alienated from the state and harbored a deep distrust for political authority. But unlike the rural laboring class, they had a highly-developed sense of class solidarity and long-standing socialist tradition, both of which had been strengthened by the disorders that had followed the First World War. The fact that the *squadristi* had often intervened against them in their struggles with employers only added to their hostility and gave credibility to the claims of their leaders that Fascism was part of a "general capitalist reaction" that had to be combated at all costs. In an interview given many years later, one Neapolitan

CHAPTER 8. THE ERA OF CATASTROPHES, 1914–1943

laborer recalled Mussolini's first encounter with the workers at a shipyard in Castellammare as follows:

193. In 1923, the Fascist government, abusing its emergency powers, imposed the Reform on all the government shipyards: the workers of the naval shipyards of Castellammare lost their security of employment (for which an annual contract was substituted), their right to a state pension and, what was worse, their wages were cut by half, real hunger wages, all of this as a result of the reform: it was a serious defeat. Many workers emigrated out of sheer desperation. A patrimony of technical skill and experience passed on from father to son for more than a century was thrown away....

On June 22, 1924, the most infamous political crime that history records was perpetrated: the assassination of Matteotti. With the assassination of the Secretary General of the P.S.I. [the Italian Social Party], it seemed that Fascism had overstepped the mark and thus its end was near. Hope was reborn in our hearts, the fighting spirit burned stronger than ever in the working class of Castellammare as in all of Italy. Demonstrations, general strikes, protests, and marches took place everywhere.... But quickly we had to reconsider: it was not the end, but the beginning of a long, bloody, and painful struggle that would last for decades....

In the month of September 1924, it was announced that Mussolini would visit the shipyards. The Manager and all of the members of the Board, all leaders of the local Fascist Party, alarmed, worked themselves into a great to-do in order to persuade the workers to give the *Duce* a grandiose welcome. But imagine the Board's disappointment and stupor, impossible to describe, when the *Duce* passed between the two closed ranks of workers lining his passage to receive his much hoped-for grandiose welcome, and he was met by a funeral silence and looks of hate and contempt from all the onlookers. It was at this moment that he turned to the members of the hierarchy and looked at them with a terrible expression on his face and said: "I am not pleased with you! You assured me that all the workers had been won over and instead what do I see!..."

So he was furtively taken to the spa, a few yards away behind the shipyards and put, almost hidden, into a car and sped to the town hall. In the afternoon speaking from the balcony, looking down on the curious and hostile workers in the square below, he said: "I am aware of your discontent and will take the necessary measures." ["L. D.M." in 1958, cited in Allum, *Politics and Society,* pp. 114-15.]

The failure of the Fascists to win the support of the peasantry and industrial working class, and their willingness to seek accommodation with the old Neapolitan political elite, met with sharp criticism from Padovani. Like many of the original *raz,* he believed that the party had a "moral" duty to purge the country of its former rulers and create a new, genuinely-revolutionary, Fascist state. In an interview granted to the newspaper *Mezzogiorno* on November 16, 1922, he stated:

> 194. Recent events have shown that the public has a strong preference for Fascism, and new members, therefore, will be allowed to join the party. All new members, however, must be carefully screened. Anyone who was a member of another party or who has held public office...will be denied entry.... The Fascist movement in the South must change its current policies: it must eliminate anyone from the movement who can never be a true Fascist because of their past....
>
> The salvation of the South, above all, depends upon the elimination of the old clientele system. Southern Fascism must be in the forefront...of the fight against these politicians. Only uncompromising firmness will succeed in rendering Fascism in the South effective, repudiating those who are unworthy, and rejecting the tactic followed by the Nationalists in Naples...where they accept anyone who asks to be admitted. We did not wish to play the usual game of false friends and self-serving parties; we rejected communal office holders, large and small, who were anxious to save themselves and asked for our support. The Nationalist Party has not behaved in this way, and if it continues in its present policies...we would be obliged, reluctantly, to wage war against it, even though it is our ally. [Cited in De Antonellis, *Napoli,* pp. 105-7.]

On May 17, 1923, Padovani went to Rome where he voiced his opposition to further compromise directly to Mussolini. The *Duce,* however, believing that a tactical alliance with local notables was necessary in order to keep the party in power, strenuously disagreed. One month later, Padovani resigned from the Fascist Party. From then on, he worked steadily to create an independent movement in the Campania, until the collapse of a balcony under mysterious circumstances ended his life in 1926.

Padovani was replaced as the leader of the Neapolitan Fascist Federation by Achille Starace. Under Starace, the party continued its policy of buying off the most important Neapolitan notables, appointing them to high positions in the government and administration, and ignoring the corruption that had continued more or less

CHAPTER 8. THE ERA OF CATASTROPHES, 1914–1943

unabated since the Bourbon regime. Under these conditions, the party grew rapidly. By May 1927, its membership had risen to 44,000; but it seems to have lacked the efficiency and organizational coherence of many of its fraternal federations in the North. In 1927, the writer, Ignazio Silone, drafted the following report on the Neapolitan Fascists for the Italian Communist Party:

> 195. It is the largest federation of the PNF but one of the weakest. The Neapolitan sections only exist in theory. Internal life (thanksgiving fêtes, dances, banquets, and tombola) is limited to district clubs which are grouped in 8 zones; each zone is controlled by an inspector appointed by a secretary (who in turn is appointed by a National Chairman, who is appointed by the Duce who is chosen by God...and this system is defined as "a new form of popular sovereignty" by the Hon. Bottai).
>
> The Inspectors form the Executive of the Neapolitan section. Since the time of Padovani no section assemblies have been held. "It is forbidden to speak of politics" in the district clubs as it is in the cafes. As a result of the internal crisis of Neapolitan Fascism, it has never provoked the formation of well-defined factions. Neapolitan Fascism reflects the internal crisis of the Neapolitan bourgeoisie, disintegrated, fragmented, and without a strong ruling group. Neapolitan Fascism is incapable of organizing itself around a homogeneous group of leaders from the city bourgeoisie but only around the state apparatus: the intervention of the National Executive to resolve personal quarrels has become less frequent since the federation has been placed under the control of the prefect. This is a point of fundamental importance for the study of southern Fascism: the understanding of the particular importance of relations between the fasci and state apparatus. [Cited in Allum, *Politics and Society,* pp. 74-75.]

The undercurrent of discontent and disorganization that existed within the Neapolitan Fascist Party during the 1920s caused Mussolini to attempt to increase its popularity by promoting an extensive program of economic development. Although he had spent much of his early life in the North, he knew that the city had a unique history and culture and recognized many of its special problems: high population density, poor sanitation, inadequate schools, lagging industry, decaying infrastructure, and dilapidated housing. Even before he had come to power, he had made several speeches reminding the Neapolitan people of their past glories and promising them a brighter future under Fascism.

During the early 1930s, therefore, as the Great Depression made its first inroads into the city's already-fragile economy, he returned to Naples to renew his pledge of economic modernization. Speaking on October 15, 1931, before a large crowd in the Piazza del Plebiscito, he told an excited audience:

> 196. Blackshirts! People of Naples!
>
> Once more Destiny affords me the good fortune to hear your heart beating in unison with mine! The first time, nine years ago, when I called together the generation of Vittorio Veneto in this same square, I brought up the problem, which involved not the life of one man, an insignificant event, but the fate of a movement and the future of a people.
>
> I said then: "Either they will hand over power or we will take it!" After four days, the promise was kept.
>
> Two years later, I returned...to see with my own eyes the magnitude of the problems that confronted you...[and] I ordered that the necessary steps be taken to assure that they be resolved....
>
> Today...I can see that my orders have been carried out.... During the past nine years, we have accomplished so much, and the scale of our work has been so great, that it can only silence those who still indulge in useless protestations....
>
> But we would have accomplished so much more if, at the end of 1929, when our ship was already in sight of port, the world-wide tempest had not broken out, forcing us to slow the pace of our labor....
>
> The world-wide crisis, which is no longer merely economic, but is also spiritual and moral, must not hold us back: the greater the obstacles, the stronger must be our will.
>
> Naples has already been transformed: Italians and foreigners alike confirm this. But it is not enough: Naples must live! And it must define its plan of action for the future.
>
> Among our goals, five stand out: first, agriculture, for which we must find outlets for the products of your fertile soil; then, industry, which must be promoted by special laws; third, navigation, whereby your port, completed and modernized, will once again flourish; forth, craftsmanship, which will show the world the skill and genius of your artisans; and finally, tourism, because you alone can offer the world enchanting panoramas and cities that have been brought to light that have no equal on earth.
>
> If your ruling classes will march resolutely along these lines, Naples will achieve its prosperity and the general overall wealth of the nation will be increased.

CHAPTER 8. THE ERA OF CATASTROPHES, 1914–1943

Blackshirts! In 1935, when many other works have been completed, and the hospital and sanitarium and the maritime station and the monumental post office and other areas of your city have been renewed...you will hear me again on this balcony and you will find that nothing in me has changed: neither my spirit, nor my voice, nor my will, and that all of my promises have, once again, been faithfully kept! [*Scritti e Discorsi di Benito Mussolini*. Duilio Susmel, ed. Milan: Ulrico Hoepli, 1934, 7:315-19.]

Mussolini's performance rarely equaled his rhetoric, but during his two decades in power a number of important improvements in the city were made. Between 1924 and 1940, the city's port facilities and railway network were expanded, the Carità district replaced the old San Giuseppe quarter, and a new airport and subway system (the *Metropolitana*) were built. The Teatro San Carlo, Villa Floridiana, and Museo Nazionale were renovated, a funicular was erected on the Vomero, and a huge curvilinear post office was constructed in the European modern style. Finally, an enormous exhibition hall, the Mostra delle Terre d'Otremare, was built to act as a showcase for Mussolini's "Mediterranean Empire," and a number of new streets, including the beautiful via Petrarca, were carved into the Posillipo hills.

None of this, however, proved sufficient to revitalize the Neapolitan economy. For Mussolini's plan for economic development showed a far greater concern for prestige and propaganda than economic health. As a result, colossal sums of money were allocated for grandiose buildings and historical restorations, while only a small portion of the total expenditure went for housing, sewers, and schools. By 1940, over 25,000 *bassi* were still in existence in the heart of the city, and the problems of disease and hunger in the poorer sections remained as great as ever. Worse still, the sanctions imposed on Italy by the League of Nations during the Ethiopian War (1935–1936) had a disproportionately deleterious effect on the Neapolitan economy, and Neapolitan industry (as illustrated by table 197) fell further behind:

197. Number of Workers Employed in Industry in Italy's Major Cites
1927–1939

City:	1927	1939	Change	% Change:
Milan	237,836	342,247	104,441	43.9
Turin	142,569	189,189	46,620	32.7
Genoa	78,798	114,489	35,691	45.3
Naples	75,785	90,119	14,334	18.9

[Cited in Paolo Varvaro, *Una città fascista: Potere e società a Napoli*. Palermo: Sellerio, 1990, p. 176.]

By 1940, in fact, Naples had long lost its place as Italy's largest city, dropping to third behind Rome and Milan. The Depression, the Ethiopian War, and the government's misplaced priorities had resulted in a decade of relative economic stagnation and, by some measures (such as the percentage of the population actively participating in the work force and real wages), actual decline. On January 3, 1936, a Neapolitan fisherman, Gennaro Trapenese, in response to the question of whether League sanctions (which included meat, flour, eggs, butter, sugar, rice, olive oil, coffee, and many other items of popular consumption) had affected his family, answered:

> 198. We live as we always have. Meat has never been a regular part of our diet. It is a luxury that we allow ourselves at Easter and Christmas. Bread, vegetables, and fish, that is our life. [*Il Mattino*, January 3, 1936, quoted in De Antonellis, *Napoli*, p. 201.]

It was a sad commentary on the degree to which Fascist "modernization" had failed to improve the standard of living of the average Neapolitan's life.

■

The modest gains achieved by Mussolini in Naples during the years between 1924 and 1940 were wiped out almost completely during the Second World War. Between 1940 and 1943, Naples was bombed 105 times. During the bombing, over 22,000 people were killed, and countless tens-of-thousands more injured or wounded. In addition, the city lost 90 percent of its telephone network, 65 percent of its metallurgical industry, and virtually all of its electricity and gas. Over 230,000 "*vani*" or "living quarters" were either destroyed or rendered uninhabitable, and its expanded port facilities and railway systems (on which Mussolini prided himself) were left completely in ruins. It was, in relative terms, the worst damage suffered by any city in Italy, and Naples would not recover for many decades to come.

The most intensive bombing of Naples came after the Allied invasion of Sicily in July 1943. From then on, an attack on the mainland seemed inevitable, and British and American bombers came virtually every day. On July 19, 1943, the Commander of the 19th Italian Army Corps in Naples, General Enea Navarrini, issued the following declaration to the people of the city:

> 199. Ordinance 1: State of Alarm.
>
> 1. In the event of an imminent enemy attack, all or part of the Campania will be placed under a "state of alarm."
>
> 2. The state of alarm will be announced by military authorities by means of town criers, posted notices, and bulletins in newspapers.

CHAPTER 8. THE ERA OF CATASTROPHES, 1914–1943

3. During the state of alarm the following regulations will take effect for the civilian population:

No circulating outside of inhabited areas, on foot, or by any means of transportation whatsoever.

No circulating within inhabited areas during the hours of blackout (curfew)....

4. Persons authorized to circulate (such as doctors, priests, employees of the gas and water companies and other vital services) must have a valid document with their photograph confirming their identity.

5. During the state of alarm all telephone and telegraph service will be suspended for private citizens.

State of Emergency.

1. In the event of an actual enemy attack, all of the Campania or part of it will be declared to be in a state of emergency.

2. The state of emergency will be announced by military authorities by means of alarm bells ringing six times for one minute each, and then confirmed by means of town criers.

3. During the state of emergency...the following regulations will apply:

a. The population must remain in their homes or in the air raid shelters during the day and at night.

b. Doors and windows must remain closed.

c. Schools and public gathering places (taverns, bars, cafes, clubs, cinemas, theaters, etc.) will remain closed.

d. Trolley, bus, taxi, and hackney carriage service will be suspended.

4. Functionaries and persons employed in indispensable public services (hospitals, pharmacies, gas and electric light offices, water systems, etc.), however, must remain at their posts.

5. All other authorizations (with the exception of priests and doctors) will be suspended.

Warning.

The military and police will take immediate action against anyone who does not comply with these directives. Delinquents who try to take advantage of either the state of alarm or the state of emergency in order to commit robberies or other misdeeds will be summarily shot. [Cited in Aldo Stefanile, *I cento bombardamenti di Napoli: I giorni delle Am-lire*. Milan: Alberto Marotta, 1968, pp. 117-19.]

During the following two months, the bombing was unrelenting. The population —tired, sick, and short of food, medicine, and clothing—was often forced to take shelter in make-shift bomb shelters in subways, cellars, and caves. In a "War Diary" kept from April to September 1943, one anonymous Neapolitan recorded:

> 200. April 2: Duration: 1 hour 25 minutes, from 6:45 to 8:10 PM 2 aircraft downed by a fighter plane.
> April 3: Duration: 20 minutes, from 3:55 to 4:15 PM
> April 4: Duration: 1 hour 15 minutes, from 3:00 to 4:15 PM
> April 4: Duration: 50 minutes, from 7:40 to 8:30 PM In these last two incursions 2 aircraft were shot down by anti-aircraft fire.
> April 10: Duration: 1 hour 30 minutes, from 6:30 to 8:00 PM 3 aircraft shot down by a fighter plane. 1 by anti-aircraft fire.
> April 11: Duration: 1 hour 15 minutes, from 6:45 to 8:00 PM 6 aircraft shot down by fighter planes. 2 by anti-aircraft fire.

[And so on until August]

> August 4: Duration: 30 minutes, from 3:00 to 3:30 AM
> August 4: Duration: 20 minutes, from 11:00 to 11:20 AM
> August 4: Duration: ? ? , from 1:20 PM to ? ? The sirens did not sound the all-clear alarm. 4 aircraft shot down.
> August 4: Duration: ? ? , from 6:30 to ? ? The all-clear sirens no longer sound.
> August 4: Duration: ? ? , from 9:35 PM to ? ? We left [the shelter] at 1:00 AM.
>
> [Sergio Lambiase and G. Battista, *Napoli, 1940–1945*. Milan: Longanesi, 1978, pp. 82-83.]

For Naples, in fact, August 4, 1943, was the single most devastating day of bombing of the war. On that day, American and British aircraft came right through the heart of the city and over 3,000 people were killed. Churches, hospitals, schools, homes, museums, and even orphanages were either severely damaged or completely gutted. In two articles written on August 5 and 6, a correspondent for the Neapolitan newspaper *Roma* described the scene as follows:

> 201.1. Ferocious, savage, merciless, the ninety-sixth enemy incursion has wreaked havoc on our martyred city.
> This time the Anglo-American airmen deliberately set out to launch a full-scale terrorist raid, raining bombs on every part of

CHAPTER 8. THE ERA OF CATASTROPHES, 1914–1943

the city, sparing nothing: neither hospitals, monuments of art, historic villas, nor humble workers' homes.

Bombs of every size rained down everywhere, branding with infamy the military tactics employed by the Anglo-Americans....

Along the Via Foria, from the Piazza Cavour to the Piazza Carlo III, the incredible violence of the attack is shown...by the solid line of buildings that have been damaged on both sides of the street.... The Piazza Carlo III, near Via Tanucci, has been devastated...and the splendid structure built for the poor of Naples by the first Bourbon king has been seriously damaged. Also struck in the same area were the Via Sant'Antonio Abbate and several buildings opposite the Albergo dei Poveri [the Shelter for the Poor]....

In Via Mario Pagano, more destruction, more workers' houses directly hit. The Mercato area and even the old section of the Vomero were targeted and devastated as well....

[And, again, one day later:]

201.2. The more one ventures out into the streets and stops to look around and let it sink in, the more the full extent of the devastation of Naples...becomes apparent.

The hail of bombs has made it cry out, tearing to pieces its vital arteries, shattering its homes and churches, and destroying its majestic buildings. A macabre scene of buildings ripped open, exposing to the sun an immense pile of bricks and beams, walls and ceilings, floors and furniture,... the remains of the people who had nurtured them and whose lives have been violently snuffed out....

The many bombs that fell on the Gallery [Galleria Umberto I] have cracked its sturdy iron vault in several places. It is as though a cyclone of glass had been hurled down against the transept, posts shattered, boards unrooted, and metal shutters split, twisted, and dislodged.... A vast layer of shards of mirrors, plate glass, crystal and window panes from all of the shop windows and its many gathering places — bars, cafes, theaters — covers the marble floor. [Quoted in Lambiase and Battista, *Napoli*, pp. 48-49.]

The bombing of August 4, 1943, set the stage for the final act in Naples' wartime destruction. Between August 18 and September 2, the Allies made 4,500 sorties against the Italian mainland. Altogether 6,500 tons of bombs were dropped on Naples and the surrounding provinces, and towns, such as Benevento and Foggia, were left in ruins. On September 9, the Allied High Command, believing that the enemy had been sufficiently weakened, launched the first of its assaults on the beaches at Salerno. Three days later, on September 13, the Germans occupied Naples. As they entered, the German commander, Colonel Scholl, alarmed by the hostility with which his soldiers were greeted, issued a declaration placing the city under marshal law:

> 202. Attention! German forces have assumed control of the city of Naples. All civil and military authorities are subject to its orders. Every citizen who behaves in a calm and disciplined manner will be protected. Anyone who acts openly or clandestinely against the German Armed Forces will be crushed by force. For every German soldier killed or wounded revenge will be taken a hundred fold. [Cited in De Antonellis, *Napoli*, p. 244.]

The German occupation of Naples proved to be brutal from the beginning. Like his fellow Nazi officers in occupied Eastern Europe, Scholl saw the local population solely from the point of view of the needs of the German army and was determined to use it to serve the German war effort at all costs. On September 22, therefore, as part of his efforts to strengthen the city's defenses, he issued a decree establishing compulsory labor for the general population. Ignoring the weariness and latent hostility of the mass of the people, the decree — which would have mobilized almost 200,000 workers — read as follows:

> 203. All men living in the city of Naples and the towns of Pozzuoli and Resina who belong to the classes of 1910 through 1925 are called for mandatory national labor service. Those who do not present themselves voluntarily will be compelled to do so by force. Anyone impeding them will be dealt with under the laws of war. [De Antonellis, *Napoli*, p. 249.]

The decree provided the final outrage for a battered and exhausted population. On September 27th, the city rose in rebellion. For four full days — the famous *"Quattro giornate di Napoli"* — fighting raged from the Vomero to Vesuvius. Moving, most often, without outside leadership or coordination, small groups of lightly-armed men — workers, students, laborers, professionals — ambushed German patrols in the streets and set fire to German tanks on the Toledo. At first, the Germans fought doggedly to maintain their position but, with the Allies approaching and the numbers against them, they decided, on September 30th, to withdraw from the city. Before leaving, however, they made a systematic effort to destroy everything that could be of possible use to the enemy. In the port, every remaining tug, barge, and ship was sunk in order to block access to the harbor. Cranes and cargo equipment were destroyed, pipe lines and power cables torn up, and hundreds of mines strewn about the bay. In the city, the remaining electricity plants and transportation facilities

CHAPTER 8. THE ERA OF CATASTROPHES, 1914–1943

were blown up, the water supply was polluted, and the city's priceless historical archives were deliberately burned. Finally, hundreds of time bombs — with fuses set for up to 42 days' delay — were hidden in the post office, police stations, army barracks, hotels, open-air markets, and other public places. Then they left; amid a weary but still defiant population.

One day later, on October 1, the British and Americans, having fought their way up the coast from the bloody beaches of Salerno, arrived to the accompaniment of an almost unbelievable disorder. Alan Moorehead, an English writer who moved along with the King's Dragoon Guards as they approached the city, described the scene in unforgettable terms as follows:

> 204. As we drove over the Sorrento peninsula and caught sight of the city for the first time it seemed that nothing had changed. The black cone of Vesuvius smoking gracefully on the right. The isle of Capri serenely floating beyond the mouth of the bay. The crenellated city spilled along the shore, and that same mesmerizing blueness in the water. Sunshine and orange groves. Brilliant creepers on tumbling walls. The enervating atmosphere of a long lazy summer's afternoon.
>
> Driving through Castellammare and Pompeii the crowd thickened steadily along the road. On the outskirts of Naples itself it was one tumultuous mob of screaming, hysterical people, and this continued all the way into the center of the city. They had been cruelly bombed. There had been spasmodic street fighting for a week. And now they stood on the pavement and leaned out of their balcony windows screaming at the Allied soldiers and the passing trucks. They screamed in relief and in pure hysteria. In tens of thousands the dirty ragged children kept crying for biscuits and sweets. When we stopped the jeep we were immediately surrounded and overwhelmed. Thrusting hands plucked at our clothing. *Pane. Biscotti. Sigarette.* In every direction there was a wall of emaciated, hungry, dirty faces.
>
> I had had the notion that the people would be hostile, or resentful, or perhaps reserved. I had expected that they would indicate in some way the feelings they had had as enemies in the past three years.
>
> But there was no question of war or enmity here. Hunger governed all. There were some who in their need fawned and groveled. They thrust their dribbling children forward to whine and plead. When a soldier threw out a handful of sweets there was a

mad rush to the pavement, and women and men and children beat each other as they scrambled on the cobblestones....

What we were witnessing in fact was the moral collapse of a people. They had no pride any more, or any dignity. The animal struggle for existence governed everything. Food. That was the only thing that mattered. Food for the children. Food for yourself. Food at the cost of any debasement and depravity. And after food a little warmth and shelter. [Alan Moorehead, *Eclipse*. London: Hamish Hamilton, 1967, pp. 60-61.]

■

Amid this chaos, the Allies made no effort, at first at least, to feed or purge the city. On the contrary, their sole concern was to find individuals who might work well with military authorities, and thus allow them to concentrate on the prosecution of the war. On January 3, 1943, the United States embassy in Switzerland, in response to a query by the U.S. State Department as to who such individuals might be, responded succinctly:

> 205. The following influential Italians are said to be pro-Ally and willing to work for the United Nations:
> Comm. Agnelli...Torino.
> Giovanni Rodrigueze, Porto Lonjone, Isola Elba — Mayor.
> Comm. Berlingieri, Rossano Calabro, large property owner and very influential.
> Conte de Lusio, Messina, large property owner and very influential.
> Elso Battistini, Anversa, head of the Cammora.
> Carmelo Albo, at present in jail, head of the Mafia.
> [Quoted in David W. Ellwood, *Italy, 1943-1945*. New York: Holmes & Meier, 1985, pp. 58-59.]

In this atmosphere of expediency, a de facto alliance soon grew up between Allied authorities and the "most prominent" local citizens, many of whom had been fixtures in the *clientela* system for decades and had collaborated openly with the Fascists both prior to and during the war. On December 13, 1943, a front-line correspondent for the *Chicago Daily News* reported:

> 206. [Neapolitan] conservatives are wining and dining American and British officials, exactly as they formerly wined and dined Germans, absolutely convinced in their little minds that Britain and

CHAPTER 8. THE ERA OF CATASTROPHES, 1914–1943

America will really rule Italy, and that the way to save themselves is to curry favor with Englishmen and Americans. They love us. They do indeed. They love us exactly the way night club proprietors love millionaire playboys. [Quoted in Ellwood, *Italy*, p. 60.]

Thus, at the very moment when the destruction and hunger in the city were at their peak, local administration was left in the hands of some of the most corrupt and discredited elements of the population. During the winter of 1943–1944, Naples would suffer through one of the worst periods of deprivation in its history. But it had managed to survive the war.

■ ■ ■

MODERN NAPLES, 1799–1999

96. *May 1, 1920. Street fighting disrupts the Socialist May Day Celebration, Piazza Dante.*

THE TWENTIETH CENTURY brought economic and political upheaval to Naples, as to most of Italy. Here long-contending forces broke out into open conflict in the wake of World War I and the economic slump of the postwar era. Public confrontations and official inaction led to the eventual victory of the Fascists.

97. *October 24, 1922. Blackshirt squads take over Naples.*

98. *Benito Mussolini (second from left) reviews his troops in Naples before the March on Rome, October 1922.*

99. *Edmondo Rossoni, President of the Fascist National Labor Syndicates, addresses the crowds at Piazza del Plebiscito, 1927.*

POLITICAL CULTURE & EVENTS: 20TH CENTURY

THE COLLAPSE OF FASCISM. As the Germans prepared to withdraw before advancing Allied armies, Neapolitans civilians rose up against the occupiers in the revolt known as the Four Days of September 1943. Allied columns entered the city on October 1 amid the adulation of the people and the collapse of all aspects of Naples' urban life.

100. *The "Four Days," September 1943.*

101. *The Allied Fifth Army enters the city, October 1, 1943.*

102. *Neapolitans greet U.S. soldiers, October 1943.*

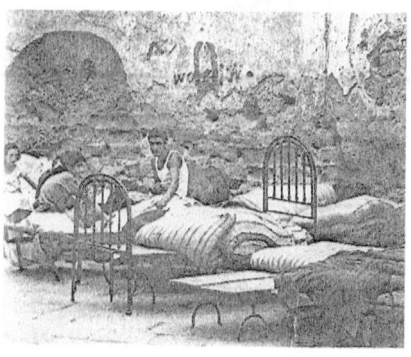

103. *Neapolitans sleeping in streets amid bombed-out buildings, 1944.*

MODERN NAPLES, 1799–1999

THE POSTWAR REALITY: physical and economic devastation, the indifference of the Allies, and the overwhelming problems of unemployment and lack of material resources forced many Neapolitans to extreme measures in the wake of the Italian defeat.

104. U.S. sailors and Neapolitan women, 1944.

105. Demonstration against bread shortages, 1947.

106. Unemployment after the war: the port area in 1946.

POLITICAL CULTURE & EVENTS: 20TH CENTURY

107. *Achille Lauro at a rally...*

POLITICS AS USUAL? The postwar economic "miracle," Cold War politics, the Christian Democratic ascendancy, and the system of "clientelism" made the cronyism of monarchist mayor Achille Lauro the standard mode of Neapolitan politics from the 1950s into the 1990s.

108. *in Piazza del Plebiscito, 1950s.*

The gradual emergence of grass-roots movements of women, environmentalists, the resurgent Left, the cultural revival of such groups as Napoli '99, and the collapse of the DC in the scandals of the 1990s combined with the excesses of the Camorra to produce the political and urban renewal of the late 1990s symbolized by the mayoralty of Antonio Bassolino.

109. *Women demonstrate for equal pay, 1970s.*

110. *Crackdown on the Camorra, 1990s.*

111. *Mayor Antonio Bassolino, 1998.*

112. Scugnizzi during the Four Days, 1943.

9
The Incomplete Recovery, 1943–1999

In early 1944, Alan Moorehead wrote:

> 207. For anyone who loved Italy it was a bitter experience to come to Naples. The traditional talents of the people, their charm and generosity, seemed for a time to have vanished in the savage and abject struggle for existence. I met quite a number of distinguished and honourable Italians in Naples, good haters of Fascism for many years, and the thing that they saw clearly at last was this: "We failed to revolt. Everything had derived from that. Nothing we could have suffered in revolt against Fascism would have been as bad as this."
> [Moorehead, *Eclipse*, p. 63.]

In Naples, as elsewhere in Italy, the results of that failure were there for all to see: tens of thousands of Neapolitans dead; many tens of thousands more injured or mutilated; men without work; women and children reduced to vagabondage and prostitution; the accumulated wealth of centuries — churches, factories, schools, hospitals, palaces, paintings, statues, archives in ruins. Naples, in short, had reached its nadir. Fascism, with its mindless violence and fanatical dream of a "Mediterranean Empire," had completed the process of decline that had begun more than a century before. Among the many writers who have attempted to capture the consequences of that decline, none stand out more than Norman Lewis. A British intelligence officer assigned to the American Fifth Army in Naples, he describes in his diary a physically and psychologically traumatized people, whose indomitable will to survive alone seems to have allowed them to endure:

> 208. *October 6*: The city of Naples smells of charred wood, with ruins everywhere, sometimes completely blocking the streets, bomb craters and abandoned trams. The main problem is water. Two tremendous air-raids on August 4 and September 6 smashed up all the services, and there has been no proper water supply since the

first of these. To complete the Allies work of destruction, German demolition squads have gone round blowing up anything of value in the city that still worked. Such has been the great public thirst of the past few days that we are told that people have experimented with sea water in their cooking and families have been seen squatting along the sea-shore round weird contraptions with which they hope to distill sea-water for drinking purposes....

October 8: Today [on my way back from] Afragola...I saw a remarkable spectacle. Hundreds, maybe even possibly thousands of Italians, most of them women and children, were in the fields all along the roadside driven by their hunger to search for edible plants. I stopped to speak to a group of them, and they told me that they had left their homes in Naples at daybreak, and had had to walk for between two and three hours to reach the spot where I found them — seven or eight miles out of town. Here a fair number of plants could be found, although nearer the city the fields had been stripped of everything that could be eaten. There were about fifteen different kinds of plants which were worth collecting, most of them bitter in flavour. All I recognized among their collections were dandelions....

October 20: ...This evening, after a day so full of alarms, the city was plunged into deep misery by the first German air-raid. Bombs fell in the port area, and the nearest explosion caused our *palazzo* to teeter hideously. As soon as the all-clear sounded I went out to inspect the damage.... Apocalyptic scenes as people crawled about in the ruins, some of them howling like dogs, in the hopeless attempt to rescue those trapped under the masonry. In Pizzofalcone a team of roadsweepers were working by lamplight clearing up what looked like a lake of spilled stew where a crowded shelter had received a direct hit.

October 23: A tremendous scare this morning following information given by a captured enemy agent that thousands of delayed-action mines would explode when the city's electricity supply went on. This was timed for 2 PM today. An order was given for the whole of Naples to be evacuated.... The scene as the great exodus started, and a million and a half people left their houses and crowded into the streets, was like some biblical calamity. Everyone had to be got away to the safety of the Vomero, Fontanelle, and the Observatory, overlooking the town. This meant that the bed-ridden and dying,

CHAPTER 9. THE INCOMPLETE RECOVERY, 1943–1999

and all the women in labor had to be coped with in some way or another, not to mention the physically and mentally sick persons in clinics all over the town.... I saw men carrying their old parents on their backs, and at one moment a single, small explosion set off a panic with women and children running screaming in all directions, leaving trails of urine.

At the Vomero we took up positions at a spot on the heights where the road had been intentionally widened to assist visitors to appreciate the view.... All Naples lay spread beneath us like an antique map.... For the first time I appreciated the magnificence of this city, seen at a distance which cleansed it of its wartime tegument of grime, and for the first time I realized how un-European, how oriental it was. Nothing moved but a distant floating confetti of doves. A great silence had fallen and we looked down and awaited the moment of devastation. At about four o'clock the order came for everyone to go home....

October 25: It is astonishing to witness the struggles of this city so shattered, so starved, so deprived of all those things that justify a city's existence, to adapt itself to a collapse into conditions which must resemble life in the Dark Ages. People camp out like Bedouins in deserts of brick. There is little food, little water, no salt, no soap. A lot of Neapolitans have lost their possessions, including most of their clothing, in the bombings, and I have seen some strange combinations of garments about the streets,... Everyone improvises and adapts.

November 1: ...Lattarullo [a local informer] looked even weaker with hunger today than usual, and swayed from the waist, eyes closed, even sitting down. After our chat I decided to take him for a meal to one of the side-street restaurants that have opened up in the past few days.... We found a restaurant and took our seats among the middle-class patrons, who kept their overcoats on against the cold.... Ragged, hawk-eyed boys — the celebrated *scugnizzi* of Naples — wandered among the tables ready to dive on any crust that appeared to be overlooked, or to snatch up leftovers before they could be thrown to the cats. Once again I couldn't help noticing the intelligence — almost the intellectuality — of their expressions. No attempt was made to chase them away. They were simply treated as non-existent. The customers had withdrawn from the world while they communed with their food. An extraordinary cripple was dragged in, balancing face downwards on a trolley, only a few inches from the ground, arms and legs thrust out in spider fashion. Nobody took his eyes off his food for one second to glance down at him. This youth could not use his hands. One of the *scugnizzi* hunted down a piece of bread for him, turned his head sideways to stuff it between his teeth, and he was dragged out.

Suddenly five or six little girls between the ages of nine and twelve appeared in the doorway. They wore hideous straight black uniforms buttoned under their chins, and black boots and stockings, and their hair had been shorn short, prison-style. They were all weeping, and as they clung to each other and groped their way towards us, bumping into chairs and tables, I realized that they were all blind. Tragedy and despair had been thrust upon us, and would not be shut out. I expected the indifferent diners to push back their plates, to get up and hold out their arms, but nobody moved. Forkfuls of food were thrust into open mouths, the rattle of conversation continued, nobody saw the tears.

Lattarullo explained that these little girls were from an orphanage on the Vomero, where he heard — and he made a face — conditions were very bad. They had been brought down here, he had found out, on a half-day's outing by an attendant who seemed unable or unwilling to stop them from being lured away by the smell of food.

The experience changed my outlook. Until now I had clung to the comforting belief that human beings eventually come to terms with pain and sorrow. Now I understand that I was wrong.... These little girls, any one of whom could have been my daughter, came into the restaurant weeping, and they were weeping when they were led away. I knew that, condemned to ever-lasting darkness, hunger and loss, they would weep on incessantly. They would never recover from their pain. And I would never recovery from the memory of it. [Norman Lewis, *Naples '44: An Intelligence Officer in the Italian Labyrinth*. New York: Henry Holt, 1976, pp. 26-53.]

Two of the most tragic side effects of the poverty and suffering in postwar Naples were a dramatic increase in prostitution and a revival of the Camorra. On October 22, 1943, Lewis, who was highly sensitive to the role that Allied soldiers and authorities played in the development of both problems, described an incident at his headquarters which demonstrated the harsh realities that many Neapolitan women had to face:

CHAPTER 9. THE INCOMPLETE RECOVERY, 1943–1999

> 209.1. There is no relief in sight to the near-famine conditions in the city and surrounding country.
>
> Friday, at least ten jobs came up, among which was the visit to a peasant house near Aversa where people had been assaulted by deserters. Having found nothing lootable, they had molested the women, subjecting them to every conceivable indignity, including attempted buggery. The women were evidently spared from outright rape by the fear many of our soldiers share of contracting syphilis. One of the girls involved in this nightmarish business was outstandingly pretty, although spoiled by a puffiness — a sogginess of flesh showing particularly about the eyes. This I've noticed so often in people close to starvation. I did my best to pacify the sufferers with vague promises of redress. There was nothing else to do. [Lewis, *Naples '44*, pp. 42-43.]

And, six months later, on March 26, he made a second entry in his diary that indicated that very little had changed:

> 209.2. The streets of Naples are full of people hawking personal possessions of all kinds: pieces of jewelry, old books, pictures, clothing, etc. Many of them are members of the middle class, and the approach is made in a shamefaced and surreptitious way. One and all, they are is a state of desperate need.
>
> Today at the top of the Via Roma near the Piazza Dante I was stopped by a pleasant-faced old lady, who had nothing for sale but who implored me to go with her to her house in a side street nearby. She had something to show me, and was so insistent that I followed her to a typical *basso* in a side street, where she lived. The single windowless room was lit by a minute electrical bulb over the usual shrine, and I saw a thin girl standing in the corner. The reason for the appeal now became clear. This, said the woman, was her child, aged thirteen, and she wished to prostitute her. Many soldiers, it seems, will pay for sexual activity less than full intercourse, and she had a revolting scale of fees for these services. For example, the girl would strip and display her pubescent organs for twenty lire.
>
> I told the woman that I would report her to the police, and she pretended to weep, but it was an empty threat, and she knew it. Nothing can be done....

> The Bureau of Psychological Warfare has just stated in its bulletin that there are 42,000 women in Naples engaged either on a regular or occasional basis in prostitution. This out of a nubile female population of perhaps 150,000. It seems incredible. Three out of four of these girls that I have interviewed will probably cease to be prostitutes as soon as they can hope to keep alive by any other means.... Nine out of ten [Neapolitan] girls have lost their menfolk, who have either disappeared in battles, into prisoner-of-war camps, or been cut off in the north. The whole population is out of work. Nobody produces anything. How are they to live? Some Neapolitans have not tasted meat for two years.... [Lewis, *Naples '44*, pp. 109-15.]

The implied criticism that Lewis aimed at British and American soldiers became explicit when dealing with the Camorra. Here the Americans, in particular, were willing to grant active or tacit support to known criminals in both Naples and Sicily in return for the maintenance of political and social order behind Allied lines. In two entries recorded in early 1944, he wrote:

> 210. I have been placed in charge of the security of a number of small towns to the north of Naples and within approximately 25 miles of the city; of these the largest are Casoria, Afragola, Accera, and Aversa. Although the Army certainly doesn't realize this, they are all located in the notorious *Zona di Camorra*....
>
> Seen from the outside, through the orchards that surround them, all these towns look attractive enough: tiny versions of Naples itself, clustered around their blue-doomed churches. On the inside [however] they are show cases of poverty and misery.... A handful of families own all of the land, and the peasants who work it have always done so in conditions that come very close to slavery.... The new *sindacos*, the mayors who have been appointed by the AMG, the Allied Military Government of the Occupied Territory, to replace the old Fascist *podestàs*, are stated in the main to be members of the *criminal Camorra*. It is common knowledge that these have been appointed with the knowledge of Vito Genovese, the American gangster who, having obtained employment as an interpreter, has now manoeuvered himself into a position of unassailable power in the military government.... As far as anyone rules here at all it is the *Camorra*....

CHAPTER 9. THE INCOMPLETE RECOVERY, 1943-1999

Genovese controlled most towns within fifty miles of Naples. He leased out rackets to his followers, took a toll of everything, threw crumbs of favour to those who kept in step with him, and found a way of punishing opposition.

What was to be done? Nothing, Edwards said. The CIC [American Counter-Intelligence Corps] had soon learned to steer clear of any racket in which Genovese had a finger — and his finger was in most.... An American CIC agent who cottoned on the fact that the notorious Genovese was in virtual control of Naples and set out to investigate his present activities, soon found himself isolated and powerless, and all the reward he had had for his pains was a loss of promotion.... [January 5 and May 9, 1944, in Lewis, *Naples '44*, pp. 74-76, 127-29, 134-40.]

For Allied leaders, the question of the Camorra, like that of the re-establishment of the old Neapolitan political elite, was simply a matter of military expediency. During the winter of 1943-1944, Churchill and Roosevelt were determined to leave the administration of the South in the hands of local (and, ostensibly, "pro-Western") political authorities, and to concentrate exclusively on the prosecution of the war. As for the South's dire economic condition, Churchill, in particular, tended to view it will callous indifference. On August 13, 1943, a note that appeared in the secret and high-level *Whaley-Eaton Newsletter* reported:

211. Churchill has made it abundantly clear that Britain is not fighting this war in order to engage freely hereafter in a vast humanitarian campaign to transfer into the farthermost places an Anglo-American standard of living. Neither is the United States, despite the slogans of wartime. It was the Hitler thesis that the time had come for the "have-not" nations to take away from the "have" nations a part, if not all, of their possessions. It may be assumed that the "have" nations will not voluntarily give away that which they are spending unlimited blood and treasure to prevent being taken from them by force. [Cited in Ellwood, *Italy*, p. 64.]

Thus, throughout most of 1944, Naples remained in the economic doldrums, with local industry at a virtual standstill and much of the population unemployed. The American army, on the other hand, possessed an enormous economic surplus, including everything from cigarettes and blankets to uniforms and food. Under such circumstances, it was estimated that 60 percent of American goods ended up on the Neapolitan black-market, producing a substantial profit for unscrupulous soldiers and local criminals alike. On May 9, Lewis wrote:

212. The impudence of the black market takes one's breath away. For months now official sources have assured us that the equivalent of the cargo of one Allied ship in three unloaded in the Port of Naples is stolen.... Stolen equipment sold on the Via Forcella and round the law courts...is now on blatant display, tastefully arranged with coloured ribbon, a vase of flowers, and neatly-written showcards advertising the quality of the looted goods....

The trouble now is that certain items which can be freely and easily bought on the black market are in short supply in the Army itself. This applies currently to photographic equipment and materials, practically all of which had been stolen to be sold under the counter in shops in the Via Roma, and to certain medical supplies, in particular penicillin.... At last the time has come when the effect of the black market on the war effort has become evident. It could have been wiped out, but because of the secret involvement in it through their Italian connections of some of our high authorities, it was not.
[Lewis, *Naples '44*, pp. 136-37.]

It was, in fact, only in the spring of 1945, after Mussolini's puppet regime in the north had collapsed and Germany had surrendered, that the Allies began to show a more active interest in Italy's economic revival; and, even then, it was more due to the fear of communism than to a desire for humanitarian reform.

■

During the first three decades that followed the Second World War, Naples experienced a long, slow, and, decidedly, uneven economic recovery. Although fighting in the city had effectively ended in October 1943, eighteen months later conditions for much of the population had undergone little appreciable change. As one American soldier, Robert B. Ellis, who was stationed in Naples at the end of the war, wrote:

213. While waiting a week in Naples for our troopship to arrive and be prepared for our transport, I wandered through many areas of the city, much of which was still in ruins, and I was greatly depressed by the hunger and poverty which caused extensive prostitution and countless young children to pimp for their sisters, mothers, or aunts. I was repeatedly approached by the inquiry, *"figi, figi, meester?,"* followed by assurances that the solicitor had a sister only 14 years old or some other inducement to follow him or her. One cute little girl explained that she had to sell trinkets because

CHAPTER 9. THE INCOMPLETE RECOVERY, 1943–1999

her father died in Germany and her mother was sick. Even Pompeii, we learned, was overrun with prostitutes.

We had been warned that anyone infected with venereal disease would not be allowed to board ship, and whether true or not, the warning gave some of my companions real concern....

One curious incident occurred while I was ambling about the city. I entered an alley with many badly damaged buildings and came upon a long line of GIs waiting their turn in a house whose women were offering sexual favors. As I walked along wondering how one could be enticed to wait in line for such an activity and then enjoy some women who had just had sex with numerous others, I heard piano music. Somewhere in the surrounding devastation, someone was playing a piece of haunting beauty by Rachmaninoff. The whole experience seemed like a dream, but I finally found the source in a partially ruined building nearby, where a young Italian man was playing an undamaged grand piano. I watched and listened spellbound for a while, but did not intrude on his playing. [Robert B. Ellis, *See Naples and Die: A World War II Memoir of a United States Ski Trooper in the Mountains of Italy*. London: McFarland, 1996, p. 230.]

The profound physical and psychological trauma suffered by the Neapolitan people during the war did not effect their attitude towards the monarchy. For most Italians, the Savoyard dynasty had been deeply compromised by Fascism. In October 1922, during the March on Rome, Victor Emmanuel had refused to sign a declaration of marshal law in the face of the advance of the Blackshirts and had tolerated Mussolini's excesses until defeat seemed certain in 1943. On June 2, 1946, therefore, a national referendum was held on whether to continue the monarchy. In the country as a whole, 54 percent of the population (or 12 out of 22 million people) voted to establish a republic. In Naples, however, where the monarchist tradition ran deep, 79 percent (903,651 to 241,973) cast their ballots in favor of the dynasty, the highest percentage of any city in the Italian South. The referendum highlighted the difference between Naples and its counterparts in northern Italy, where, in some places, as many as 8 out of 10 people had voted against the king.

Throughout the 1950s and much of the 1960s, in fact, Naples remained a bastion of political conservatism. During this time, it was run by a series of political "bosses," who, in the 19th-century tradition, exchanged votes for jobs and favors, and thus were able to establish unshakable political control. Between 1952 and 1958, the city was dominated by the wealthy ship owner Achille Lauro, who had been a member of the Fascist chamber of corporations and national councilor during the 1930s, and had reemerged as a leader of the Monarchist Party after the war. From 1958 to 1975, leadership passed to the Christian Democrats under Silvio and Antonio Gava — a father-and-son team who had made a fortune in banking and construction, and directed one of Italy's most powerful political machines.

In both cases — whether under Lauro or the Gavas — Naples remained a city ridden with fraud and corruption. "Friends" of the government were granted lucrative public-works contracts and high positions in office, and the time-tested "clientele" system was allowed to continue undisturbed. The key to that system, of course, remained the "grand elector," who maintained a network of clients, and thus was able to produce hundreds of votes on command. Usually a respected member of the community himself, the grand elector provided a crucial link between the party candidate and the individual voter. Hard working and unscrupulous, he was often willing to use *any* method – bribery, favoritism, ballot tampering, and even, in some cases, physical intimidation — in order to accomplish his ends.

Given the degree of corruption that pervaded the system, it is small wonder that so many Neapolitans developed a cynical attitude towards politics and political life. In 1958, a local treasury official told the Italian social scientist, J. LaPalombara:

> 214.1. I personally know a significant number of individuals who in recent years joined the DC for purely opportunistic reasons. Often these individuals thoroughly detest the party, but they nevertheless understand that possibly the only way to make a career in public administration today is to achieve this kind of rapport with the party in power. [Cited in Allum, *Politics and Society*, pp. 158-59.]

And, in 1963, another Christian Democratic member stated in even blunter terms:

> 214.2. A priest suggested to [me] that the only party was the DC.... I became a member because they said to me: "If you don't become a party member you can't find work." They made me understand [that] the party is good.... They convinced me, in short...because they got me a job.... I don't know, perhaps its my own conviction: I think that the party of which I am a member gives me security of employment, that this party gives me life. [Cited in Allum, *Politics and Society*, p. 161.]

As for those on the left — whether Communist or Socialist — they often paid for their convictions in lost promotions or jobs. In 1963, one PCI militant stated:

> 215. After 1950, party activity got less because some factories were opened and in hiring workers discrimination was practiced. At the Allocca and the Belli Companies, you had to pass through the Cardinal,

CHAPTER 9. THE INCOMPLETE RECOVERY, 1943–1999

the Captain of the Carabinieri, etc. Hence this limited participation in party life and we on the Executive were left all alone. We faced up to the blow well, by not accusing comrades who tried to slip in among the friends of the Cardinal: we told them that they did the right thing if they remained active. We leaders were much too well-known and we bear the consequences even today: if, for example, my son was to make a request to be employed, they would tell him: "Oh, you are Sempronio Navone, son of Tizio Navone." [Cited in Allum, *Politics and Society*, p. 162.]

Ultimately, such discriminatory practices had a profound effect in alienating many Neapolitan workers from their employers and the state alike. In 1963, "Vittorio I," an electrician living in Porto, told an interviewer:

216. The State is the Christian Democrats and the government. I think that the State does not take care of us because it gets hold of our votes by fraud. I too have to deal with the government offices where I am treated like a dog because I'm not too clever. I only went to elementary school. But when the Christian Democrats get all the votes under false pretenses, then they have no need to behave honestly or organize the offices or police properly. In the Questura, they are all thieves.... Then again, in the State there is nobody to give anybody any help. A poor man died of hunger without a pension, without medical care, without assistance of any kind. Another elder man gave him something to eat because he was forced to beg.... I believe that nobody matters to the State. [Cited in Allum, *Politics and Society*, p. 95.]

Since the state could not or would not help, and local industry remained insufficient to soak up the unemployed, emigration to the north or staying at home and engaging in *"arrangiarsi"* — or "the art of manipulating the system" — were, for many, the only viable alternatives. Between 1950 and 1975, over five million workers left southern Italy for northern Europe. The migration was totally unplanned, and most headed for the booming factories of Turin and Milan as well as those of Belgium, Holland, Germany, and France. As for those who stayed at home, the majority remained loyal to the Socialist and Communist Parties, despite the Christian Democrats' extensive system of political patronage. Indeed, as the chart below shows, in the 1968 election in Naples urban workers and agricultural laborers provided the bulk of support for the Socialist and Communist parties, while white-collar employees, business owners, managers, and many small farmers gave their votes to the CD and the parties of the extreme Right:

217. Voting Pattern in Naples Broken Down by Social Class (1968)				
	PCI (%)	Soc. (%)	DC (%)	Right (%)
Urban workers	45	42	25	8
Agricultural workers	15	7	5	6
Small farmers	13	12	25	16
Artisans	8	12	25	12
Shopkeepers	6	8	9	10
White-collar	11	17	21	26
Prof./Managers/Owners	2	3	5	12
	100	100	100	100

[Allum, *Politics and Society*, p. 142.]

Given the persistence such class loyalties, the Christian Democrats found it increasingly difficult to maintain themselves in power. Between 1953 and 1976 alone, in fact, the Communist-Socialist combination increased their share of the vote in the national elections in the city of Naples from 28 to 47.7 percent:

218. Percentage of Votes: City of Naples, 1953–1976				
	COMMUNIST	SOCIALIST	CATHOLIC	RIGHT
1953	21.3	6.7	30.3	36.5
1958	25.0	8.3	32.0	31.2
1963	25.0	15.5	30.2	19.4
1968	28.1	10.1	29.2	19.5
1972	27.8	9.3	28.4	26.3
1976	40.8	6.9	29.9	15.5

[Adapted from Judith Chubb, *Patronage, Power, and Poverty in Southern Italy*. Cambridge: Cambridge University Press, 1982, p. 261.]

It was this steady growth in Communist and Socialist power that would eventually topple the Christian Democrats in 1975.

■

One of the main reasons for the Christian Democratic Party's inability to maintain political control in Naples was the failure of its program for economic reform. In

CHAPTER 9. THE INCOMPLETE RECOVERY, 1943-1999

1950, Christian Democratic leaders in Rome had created a special government agency, the Cassa per il Mezzogiorno, for the express purpose of bridging the gap in economic development between the North and the South. Between 1950 and 1975, the Cassa had spent billions of lire in an effort to bring about southern Italy's economic modernization — promoting industry, improving agriculture, building new housing, and upgrading public health. Much of this money was spent in Naples. There the overwhelming emphasis was placed on the development of manufacturing and the creation of new jobs. By 1975, in fact, sixty-five percent of all southern industry was located in the Campania. Huge new industrial plants — such as the government-owned Italsider steelworks (with 8,000 workers) and the Alfa Sud automobile factory (with 15,000) — had arisen in and around the city, and hundreds of new apartment buildings dotted its hills.

In the end, however, the Cassa's main goal was never achieved. For during the years of Italy's so-called "economic miracle," the gap between North and South actually increased. In Naples, in particular, unemployment remained as high as ever. In 1981, official figures placed it at 126,000 (or 25 percent of the "active" population), and unofficial estimates ranged up to twice as high. In addition, estimates of the *sottoproletario* — or "underclass" of part-time wage earners, itinerant laborers, petty street venders, and small-scale dealers who lived from day to day — ran as high as one-third of the adult population. Even worse, child labor, one of key indices of economic underdevelopment, continued to flourish. In 1982, the American political scientist, Judith Chubb, after a careful study of the city's economy, wrote:

> 219. One of the most characteristic aspects of life in the slums of Naples...is the widespread dependence, of the individual family as well as of the local economy, on child labor. The city boasts a vast army of child workers, compelled by sheer necessity to begin working part-time at the age of 7 or 8, and then to leave school altogether at 11 or 12, upon completion of the 5th grade (the last year of elementary school in Italy).... Given the clandestine nature of such activity, there are no exact data on the numbers of children involved; unofficial surveys, however, have produced estimates of...an incredible figure of 100,000 in Naples.
>
> These children work 10-12 hours per day, earning an average of 3,500 lire (about 4 U.S. dollars) per week; they are totally deprived of social-security and health-insurance coverage, and are frequently exposed to serious health and safety hazards. Despite stringent laws prohibiting child labor, local officials of the State Labor Office are powerless to enforce compliance in the face of the complicity of the child and the family.... [Such child labor provides] a horrifying index

of the stark poverty that haunts the slums of Naples, where a child can find work more easily than an adult and where, as a result, whole families eke out a bare subsistence on the meager wages of several children. [Chubb, *Patronage, Power, and Poverty*, p. 52.]

As for those adults who could find work, the conditions of their employment were not much different than they had been in the past. Most were underpaid and labored in small-scale workshops in which job security was precarious at best. Indeed, despite the Cassa's creation of a few large factories, in 1971, over 90 percent of Neapolitan industrial firms employed less than 10 workers, and, among commercial firms, the number rose to an astounding 97 percent:

220. Distribution of Industrial and Commercial Firms by Size
Naples vs. Milan (1971)

Size of Firm: (in employees)	INDUSTRY: Naples	Milan
0-9	10,683	25,579
% of total	(90.5%)	(83.5%)
10-49	884	3,964
% of total	(7.5%)	(12.9%)
50+	235	1,076
% of total	(2.0%)	(3.5%)
	COMMERCE Naples	Milan
0-9	23,687	41,350
% of total	(97.5%)	(93.8%)
10-49	545	2,398
% of total	(2.2%)	(5.4%)
50+	54	340
% of total	(0.2%)	(0.8%)

[Chubb, *Patronage, Power and Poverty*, pp. 42-43.]

Thus, the Cassa, despite all of its vast expenditure, had failed to alter one of Neapolitan industry's basic weaknesses: in 1975, as in 1875, most Neapolitan factories remained small-scale and uneconomical, and thus were unable to compete with those of the North. As for the larger firms—far from their raw materials and markets and totally dependent on government capital—they too would soon prove to be unprofitable. By as early as 1970, many had already gone bankrupt, and, in 1990, even the showcase

CHAPTER 9. THE INCOMPLETE RECOVERY, 1943-1999

Bagnoli steelworks was forced to close its doors. As a result, large parts of the Neapolitan work force were once again jobless, and much of the Neapolitan landscape was scared by industrial ruins. Environmental degradation and urban sprawl — in short, the destruction of much of the city's legendary natural beauty — were also part of the Cassa's legacy. In 1964, Luigi Barzini, after viewing the early stages of what many Neapolitans would eventually come to call the "urban massacre," wrote:

> 221. Since 1950, the new democratic republic has spent in the South more than double what had been spent in the previous half century.... Progress has been immense. Nevertheless the old ills are still present.
>
> A short journey through any part of southern Italy by train or car will bear out the truth of this. Wherever he goes, the visitor will see a larger number of public structures and buildings erected with public money than in the North or in any other country in Europe. He will see first, chronologically speaking, the Cyclopean structures of his great-grandfather's time, erected by the first Bourbons, Joseph Bonaparte, and Joachim Murat, at the end of the eighteenth century and the beginning of the nineteenth. He will then see the incredible amount of construction done by Ferdinand II. All this still constitutes the majority of basic works: roads, harbours, government buildings, hospitals and schools. Then he will recognize the more familiar and modest buildings of the early Victor Emmanuel II era, the years before the First World War, followed by the more numerous, lavish and 'imperial' attempts of Mussolini to perpetuate his name and the fame of his regime in perennial marble and concrete. Lastly, he will see the glittering new buildings erected by his contemporaries, the Christian Democrat governments of this post-war period.
>
> Each epoch shows a state of disrepair naturally proportionate to its age. In the suburbs of Naples, for instance, some of the oldest factories built at the beginning of the century, are literally falling down. The plaster is peeling from the walls. It is sometimes impossible to read the name of the firm painted on the facade, obliterated by the sun and dust. Rotten roof-beams bend under the weight of moss-encrusted tiles. Doors hang from rusty hinges. The courtyards are littered with refuse, dilapidated machinery, weather-beaten packing cases, tin cans. The factories still run, of course. Somehow, on the verge of collapse, the wheels turn. The reason is that economic criteria are considered secondary. The factory is seldom

a strictly money-making enterprise. It is not meant to function efficiently. Its shoddy products are probably cheap enough to sell on the market, but cheap because the capital came largely from public funds and not loans; the company enjoys special tax facilities, interest is kept low, and little money is spent on modernization, upkeep or renovation. Wages are (or were until a short time ago) lower than elsewhere, miserably low in fact.... The recent post-war factories, dramatically ultra-modern, with plastic roofs and painted in the bright dazzling colours of sherbets, strawberry, peach, pistachio nut, are still in relatively good condition. Even here, however, flakes of plaster and large spots of moisture reveal their dubious future....

This disregard for upkeep is revealing. Even today the law enabling the Cassa del Mezzogiorno to spend billions of lire on the development and modernization of the country contains no provision whatever for maintenance. The older generation, watching the decay of expensive projects sadly called the region the 'Cemetery of public works'. The definition is still often used today. [Luigi Barzini, *The Italians*. New York: Bantam Books: 1964, pp. 253-55.]

And, nine years later, in 1973, after the full extent of the damage had become apparent, the noted Neapolitan historian and journalist, Antonio Ghirelli, wrote:

222. The current massacre of Naples is the result of a total lack of urban discipline. Government officials, city administrators, architects, engineers, judges, in other words, the finest professionals and university professors, have allowed themselves to be mobilized and corrupted in order to provide justification for the violation of laws and standards, and even some of the most elementary norms of civil life. Technicians and urban planners have assumed responsibility for a plundering that has inflicted infinitely more damage on the city than the Anglo-American bombings and the German demolitions combined. [As a result] the most enchanting bay in the world has been transformed into an immense, malodorous, pestiferous sewer...[and Naples] has become an inferno of squalid dormitories devoid of the most essential [public] services. The uncontrolled construction has destroyed the natural beauty of the hills,... obscured the sun, and converted the most incandescent panorama in Europe into a nightmare of cement. The economy of the *vicolo* having been destroyed, the most impoverished parts of the population have been squeezed into the city's periphery, where delinquency, prostitution, and

CHAPTER 9. THE INCOMPLETE RECOVERY, 1943–1999

> contraband are the only alternatives to unemployment, [and]...the last traces of traditional Neapolitan life are being erased. [Antonio Ghirelli, *Storia di Napoli*. 2d ed. Turin: Giulio Einaudi, 1992, p. 539.]

■

Throughout much of the 1970s and the 1980s, Naples seemed to be locked in a never-ending downward spiral. Noise, water, and air pollution reached dangerous levels; schools deteriorated; garbage went uncollected; and hospitals, sewers, and museums lapsed into various states of disrepair. Year after year, the city remained at-or-near the top of Italian municipalities in a number of negative categories: it had the highest rate of infant mortality; the greatest level of infectious disease; the most substandard housing; and even the greatest number of rats. A cholera outbreak in 1973 was followed by a major earthquake in 1980. Tourists fled, industries languished, and crime soared. In 1983, the moderate leftist government of Maurizio Valenzi — which had made a valiant, but, ultimately, futile effort since 1975 to arrest the deterioration — was driven from office. In its place, there reemerged the Christian Democrats under the Gavas, and the city lapsed into the same pattern of misgovernment and corruption that it had experienced since the end of the war. Worst still, the 1980s witnessed a drastic increase in the power of the Camorra. Up to then, Camorra leaders had largely contented themselves with bribing local politicians in return for government contracts and special favors. After 1980, however, they began to put forward their own candidates for office and launched a systematic campaign of violence and intimidation in order to guarantee that they would succeed. In testimony given to a special government investigating committee in 1993, Carmine Schiavone, a leader of the Camorra organization in Caserta, described his "family's" efforts to influence the 1982 elections in Casal di Principe at follows:

> 223. [Three of our men] went from house to house looking for votes. To those who proved hesitant or undecided, threats were directed against their personal safety or their business.... As a result, the Christian Democrats increased their percentage of the vote from thirty to fifty percent. I believed that "Ciccio" [the nickname for the Camorra candidate] should be nominated for mayor. He had sufficient experience in administration and, together with supporters in the council, would be able to guarantee the results that we wanted to achieve.... The town council was practically under the thumb of [the Camorra], which made its wishes known through Nicola Schiavone and Peppe Natale, both of whom were spokesmen for our point of view. The town council would never dare to oppose the directives of our

organization...because it knew that the consequences would have been fatal. [Cited in Francesco Barbagallo, *Il potere della Camorra*. Turin: Giulio Einaudi, 1999, pp. 104-5.]

By the end of the 1980s, dozens of camorristi or their supporters occupied positions of power in local or regional government, and crimes, such as drug trafficking, cigarette smuggling, extortion, and even murder, became endemic to Neapolitan life. In November 1990, Pope John Paul II, alarmed by reports of the city's further deterioration, made an extraordinary five-day visit to Naples. Traveling through some of the city's worst neighborhoods, he excoriated corrupt politicians, encouraged businessmen and ordinary citizens to stand up to criminal violence, and denounced the degradation of Neapolitan life. A short time later, local prosecutors announced that they had begun an investigation into reports that organized crime had skimmed off as much as seven million dollars from the monies that had been set aside by the government to provide security and organize gatherings during his stay.

If there was one bright spot in the history of Naples during the postwar period, it was in the area of thought and culture. Freed from dead hand of Fascism, Neapolitan artists and writers returned to their creative traditions — although they were never able to reestablish fully the reputation that the city had enjoyed prior to the First World War. In theater, Eduardo De Filippo proved to be a worthy successor to the great Eduardo Scarpetta. In literature, such writers as Carlo Bernari, Giuseppe Marotta, Domenico Rea, Anna Maria Ortese, Michele Prisco, Luigi Compagnone, and Raffaele La Capria created works of outstanding fiction. In cinema, Francesco Rosi, Salvatori Piscicelli, Massimo Troisi, Mario Martone, and Pappi Corsicato directed films in the neo-realist tradition; and Antonio de Curtis (the famous "Totò") gained international recognition for his comedic roles. Only in song writing and fine arts did Naples fail to live up to its 19th-century tradition; and, even here, a number of talented artists and singers continued to appear. In 1989, the city opened a newly-constructed group of skyscrapers known as the Nuovo Centro Direzionale. Located behind the central railway station and designed to house its administrative offices, the Centro contained an underground highway system that separated traffic from pedestrians, a necessity in a city which faced a daily influx of over 700,000 cars.

■

In spite of its formidable cultural creativity, by the early 1990's, most authorities on Naples continued to view the situation as hopeless. In 1992, it was estimated that 58 percent of all Neapolitan businesses paid protection money to the Camorra, and that one out of every six public officials was under investigation for crime. That year, only 200 foreign visitors per day came to the city, compared to 6000 in war-torn

CHAPTER 9. THE INCOMPLETE RECOVERY, 1943–1999

Belfast. *"Scippatori,"* or purse-snatchers, roamed the streets on motorbikes tearing away handbags, and an astounding 140,000 people made their living by selling contraband goods. In articles dealing with Naples in the northern Italian and foreign press, the overwhelming emphasis was placed on the lurid, the violent, and the exotic. Naples was depicted as a city without laws or morals, a land of ungovernable people totally devoid of civic sense. In a typical article that appeared in *The New York Times* on November 11, 1993 under ther title, "Naples Ready to Elect a Mayor, But Does It Matter?" Alan Cowell wrote:

> 224. It's voting season here, and everywhere the Neapolitans look they are being offered a choice for Mayor — a neo-Fascist or an ex-Communist or a candidate from one of the many hybrid tickets reflecting Italy's confusion-of-the-hour.
>
> Underlying the election on November 21, though, the question is not so much who will govern the city but whether it can be governed at all. Some might say the question applies to all of Italy as it struggles to right itself after 20 months of scandal that has tainted virtually all its institutions, discredited its political class and business elite and deepened divisions between north and south. This place, though, is in a league of its own....
>
> As things stand right now, Naples has no city council because too many councilors are under suspicion of corruption. The city is bankrupt, with $1.5 billion in unpayable debts. The buses, when they arrive, crawl at an average of 1.3 miles an hour in the city's snarled traffic.... The number of people formally registered as unemployed is 350,000, around half the work force in this city of 1.1 million people. Schools and hospitals don't work. The traffic lights usually don't work either.... The water is polluted, and, earlier this year, so was the milk....
>
> As if that were not enough to daunt any candidate, Naples is a fief of the Camorra...whose 42 clan bosses are not exactly interested in turning their haven of extortion, narcotics, and cigarette smuggling into the world's best-run city.
>
> "The drama of Naples is that to change the way it is run, you need to change the entire socio-economic structure," said Aldo Masullo, a well-known left-wing philosopher here. "But changing the socio-economic pattern is beyond the power of any administration."
>
> Amato Lamberti, a leader of the city's Greens environmental group, concurs, saying, "The forces against change outnumber the forces in favor of it...."

Here, though, the vote has a particular piquancy: one of the candidates for mayor, a neo-Fascist running on the Italian Social Movement ticket, is Alessandra Mussolini, granddaughter of the dictator. Recent opinion surveys show her running second to an ex-Communist, Antonio Bassolino, and slowly closing the gap....

"To understand this city, you always have to remember that there are two cities," Mr. Lamberti said, "there's a modern Naples, with schools, universities, research centers. Then there's a second Naples, which is two degrees hotter and two centuries behind."

The distinction in temperature refers to the fact that the wealthy Neapolitans live in the cooler heights, while the poor inhabit the tangles of the back streets below, where the Camorra holds sway. The distinction in centuries, Mr. Lamberti said, refers to the improvised lives of the poor in the Dickensian alleys of the Spanish Quarter, the oldest [sic] part of Naples.

"We have one-third of the population that has never had a regular job," Professor Masullo said, describing the city as a "society where people live off other people" and that functions — for rich and poor alike — through hidden networks of patronage and protection. Much of that protection comes from the Camorra.

"The Camorra fulfills two functions," Mr. Lamberti said, "It keeps the two cities apart, and insures the survival of the sub-proletariat through the creation of illegal jobs."

Thus, he said, up to 100,000 people live from illegal jobs guaranteed by the Camorra.... The gang's illegal income is drawn from vast cigarette and narcotics smuggling, up to 7,000 illicit parking lots, protection money, unlawful lotteries, and widespread loan-sharking. The funds are then invested in legal fronts — clothes shops and pizza parlors and dry-cleaning outlets that provide a front for drug-peddling.

All that made for an idiosyncratic city run by organized crime and political barons in cahoots with them. Indeed, Mr. Lamberti said, in the 19th century it was the tradition for newly-appointed police chiefs and newly-appointed Camorra bosses to exchange gifts denoting their mutual respect.

What turned Naples into a real mess was the booming corruption of the 1980s. Few things work here because so much money to improve city services was diverted to private pockets and political parties. On just about every project, from relief funds after the 1980 earthquake to the building of stadiums for the 1990 World

CHAPTER 9. THE INCOMPLETE RECOVERY, 1943–1999

Cup soccer tournament, most money from government coffers filtered into private pockets.

Under such circumstances, it might almost seem worth asking what difference a new mayor will make.

"All the candidates find it convenient to argue that it would be a success just to have basic administration — make the traffic work, make the schools work, create administrative order," Professor Masullo said. "This is a huge lie because in our city, if administrative order does not exist, it is because of the structural defects of the city."
[Alan Cowell, "Naples Ready to Elect a Mayor, But Does it Matter?" *The New York Times*, November 11, 1993, p. 3.]

Masullo's comment, despite all of its perspicacity, had one fatal flaw: it underestimated the forces of change. By 1993, those forces were sweeping not only Naples, but all of Italy. The postwar political system, which had been dominated by the Christian Democrats for four decades through patronage and foreign support, was collapsing. The end of the Cold War had deprived it of its rationale. In 1992, accusations of corruption, illicit party financing, politically-inspired appointments, and, most of all, deep and enduring links with organized crime brought the national political class down. During the following two years, over 3,000 people were indicted, including several ex-prime ministers, dozens of parliamentary deputies and high government officials, and virtually the entire Christian Democratic leadership in Naples.

In November 1993, Bassolino became mayor of the city; and he immediately set out on a program of political reform. At first, most domestic and foreign observers, as if incredulous to the possibility of a meaningful change in Naples, tended to ignore his initiatives and continued to depict the city almost exclusively in negative terms. In March 1994, in an article that appeared in *The New York Times*, John Tagliabue wrote:

225. Nobody is saying Naples is not a normal city, least of all Amato Lamberti. But he still fidgets when explaining why, for now, he is the only municipal official in Italy with the title of Commissioner for Normalcy.

"The idea was to return to normalcy the city and all its productive activities, like industry, the crafts, commerce," said Mr. Lamberti, a sociologist in his 40's from the Environmental League, part of the leftist coalition elected in December to run the city. "Unfortunately, in Naples there were rules that were never applied, and the model was one of controlled disorganization."

That fact was never clearer than in February when several hundred vendors of contraband cigarettes demonstrated for three consecutive days in downtown Naples,

265

shouting "Bread! Bread!" and "The Mafia is in Rome, not Naples!" They were protesting efforts to stamp out their business, which controls roughly three-fourths of cigarette trade in this city....

The last thing that Naples needed was for the cigarette smugglers to take to the streets. For everyone knows, though they may be controlled by the local organized-crime syndicate, the Camorra, they are a legendary force not only in the economy but also in the folklore hereabouts. After all, wasn't it Maurizio Valenzi, a much-loved mayor in the 1970s, who declared that "smuggling is to the people of the south what Fiat is to the North."...

Simply put, Naples is the kind of place that has a hard time being normal.... The problem is, as Mr. Lamberti explained, that the Camorra had always been part of the local economy. "In our system the Camorra had two functions," he said, explaining to the visitor the mob's various businesses, like cigarettes. "One was to assure control of the margins of society. The other was the economic survival of these marginal groups. Remember that one-third of the active population, that's 300,000 people, is officially unemployed, and yet the city does not explode."...

"For every 100 cigarettes sold in Naples, 72 are contraband," said Sergio Baronci, secretary of the Federation of Italian Tobacconists in Rome. Naples, the clearing house for most contraband tobacco, he said, "must stop being a Middle Eastern city." [John Tagliabue, "Naples Journal: Live by the Rules? A Smugglers' Haven Smolders." *The New York Times*, March 7, 1994, p. 4.]

Nevertheless, despite such overwhelmingly negative characterizations, as the decade wore on, the growing evidence that something important was happening in Naples could no longer be ignored. During the first six months of 1994, a massive effort was made to clean up the waterfront and the historic center of the city. New parks and squares were opened, the shoreline was closed to traffic on Sundays, and a wide variety of cultural activities were set in place. In July 1994, the leaders of the Group of Seven industrial democracies held their annual meeting in the city amid much fanfare. Four months later, in November, representatives from 138 countries gathered together in the Palazzo Reale to attend a three-day United Nations' conference on how best to combat the spread of international crime. In both cases, the choice of Naples as a meeting place seemed to indicate that perceptions of the city had begun to change. In March 1994, Bassolino announced during a speech in Strasbourg:

CHAPTER 9. THE INCOMPLETE RECOVERY, 1943–1999

226. Naples is experiencing a great renewal. There is a new city that is freeing itself from the legacy of years marked by the nefarious connection between politics and business. There is a new Naples, for which culture is the most precious resource. [*La Repubblica*, March 14, 1994, cited in David Forgacs and Robert Lumley, eds., *Italian Cultural Studies: An Introduction*. New York: Oxford University Press, 1966, p. 306.]

Meanwhile, as the efforts to draw on Naples' enormous cultural legacy proceeded, a sustained effort was begun to reduce the power of organized crime. Between 1993 and 1998, many of the Camorra's most prominent leaders were arrested. Others were forced to flee the country and brought back through extradition, and the army was called in to reestablish local control. On July 14, 1997, *The New York Times* reported:

227. The first Italian troops arrived in Naples today to try to halt a wave of mob violence that had spilled out onto the city streets. Some 300 troops arrived in buses, trucks and jeeps to prepare to take up surveillance and security duties in and around the city starting Monday. The Government's decision to send in troops was announced last Monday after a weekend of terror in which two suspected mobsters were killed in broad daylight, and a number of innocent bystanders, including an eight-year old girl, were wounded in shoot-outs.

Some 86 people have been killed and dozens injured since the start of the year as rival clans of the Camorra, the Naples Mafia, have fought each other for territorial control.

Italian newspapers today published maps highlighting where troops will be stationed, including the law courts, the jail, the synagogue, and a number of foreign consular offices. [*The New York Times*, July 14, 1997, p. 9.]

Given such determination on the part of the Bassolino government, the popular image of the city — although never completely sanitized — rapidly began to be transformed. On February 13, 1998, a reporter for the *San Francisco Chronicle*, Frank Viviano — while not ignoring the city's problems — summarized the events of the previous five years and the changed mood that they had produced as follows:

228. Nobody expected Antonio Bassolino to declare war on southern Italy. He was meant to be the passive sacrificial goat in the 1993 mayoral election in Naples — a party hack so orthodox and lackluster that his own Italian Communist colleagues had dubbed him "*l'apparatchik.*" But against the odds, Bassolino won that 1993 race,

edging out Alessandra Mussolini, neo-Fascist heir to her grandfather, Benito, and the photogenic niece of Sophia Loren.

Then he promptly declared war: Against the organized crime clans that ran his city for generations. Against the 50 year old legacy of corruption and grotesque mismanagement...that made Naples the byword for urban nightmare in Europe....

"When the 1990s opened," says Giovanni Maglio, president of *Progetta Europa*, a local citizen's group, "Napoli was *morta*." Dead.

The demise was not a sudden reversal of fortune, like the industrial failures that undid cities across the American Rust Belt. The death of Naples was a prolonged, six-decade free fall that shattered every aspect of urban life. As Mister Tony himself puts it, "We were the city of 'mosts.' The most corrupt. The most filthy. The most criminal. The most unemployed. The most hopeless."

The numbers measuring those dubious achievements were spectacular.

"In 1990, at least 300,000 people — 25 percent of the city's population — were living on the black economy," according to Carlo Tesauro, a researcher at the Institute for Planning and Regional Management in Naples. The black marketeers were the impoverished but visible tip of a criminal iceberg.... Their "stores" were often no more than a six-foot-square folding table, set up in ranks on every city block. The products were anything that was supposed to be controlled, taxed or banned, from smuggled cigarettes and liquor to fruits and vegetables, meat and fish, stolen radios and fake Rolex watches — and by the 1980s, heroin and cocaine.

An additional 7,000 families were supported by *"parcheggiatori,"* who sold "permission" to park cars on public streets. The fees were handed over to the Camorra...which also oversaw the contraband trade.

Between 1963 and 1980, the number of cases heard annually by criminal courts in metropolitan Naples rose from less than 72,000 to more than 317,000, just under 900 per day.

Tourists — in a city with 3,000 years of history, an architectural treasure trove, a sun-drenched subtropical climate and a setting framed by Mount Vesuvius and an azure sea — were terrified to set foot in the place.

During the 1990 soccer World Cup tournament, $60 million vanished into the construction sites of sports facilities that were never completed and in many cases never begun. In the decade after the

CHAPTER 9. THE INCOMPLETE RECOVERY, 1943-1999

1980 earthquake that killed 5,000 people [in the Campania, 120 in Naples], the Italian government and international agencies poured 50 trillion lire ($30.3 billion) in emergency funds into Naples and its surrounding region.

What ensued was arguably the biggest rip-off of all time. "Most of the 50 trillion lire disappeared without a trace into the pockets of camorristi, politicians and a swarm of building contractors from northern Italy," says Maglio. "The only evidence of their work is a vast network of unfinished bridges and roads that lead nowhere."

"Nowhere" is a perfect description of Afragola, an outlying district of relentlessly nondescript apartment buildings, weedy vacant lots and far more than its share of those unfinished roads. It was the sight of a ferocious intra-Camorra bloodletting in the early 1990s, fought over earthquake funds, that took 200 lives. Locals call Afragola and two neighboring towns the *"triangulo della morte."* The triangle of death. Mister Tony was born there 50 years ago.

Bassolino shies away from the subject of his youth, just as he declines to talk about the several rumored attempts on his life since 1994.... With no regard...for court maneuvering or empty rhetoric...he went after the bosses. "I took away their houses, their land, their businesses," he says, making it sound much simpler than it was. "I deprived them of their base and their income."

The police force was purged of *camorristi*, retrained and sent into the streets on its own fleet of motorcycles to break up smuggling rings and chase off *scippatori*. Six hundred officials were suspended on various malfeasance charges.... In the dead of night, municipal crews surrounded the Piazza del Plebiscito, an immense ornate square next to the former royal palace of Naples, and hammered in metal retainers that closed the area to traffic. "The Piazza was the historic heart of the city. But it became Europe's biggest parking lot, worth a fortune to the Camorra," says architect Antonio Bertini. Elsewhere, blue lines were painted along the curbs, identifying "official" parking spaces that could be occupied only by cars displaying prepaid city vouchers. Calling in the chits from his years of party loyalty in Rome, the mayor wheedled millions of dollars in special grants from the central government. By 1996, 750 new buses — many of them pollution-free electric vehicles — were crisscrossing the city, dramatically reducing the traffic and smog that had nearly strangled it....

When the Camorra struck back in a series of shootings, 8,000 soldiers were sent to Naples, where they still guard courts and City Hall with armored cars and machine guns. By the end of 1997, Bassolino was re-elected with the largest majority in the history of contemporary Italian politics. The air of menace has lifted from Europe's urban nightmare....

The [present] cleanup built on the work of *Napoli '99*, a foundation that began putting historic monuments "up for adoption" by municipal schools in 1992. The students are trained as guides, leading paid tours of Naples' glorious but crumbling heart, with the fees applied to an extensive restoration effort. The first year, 5,000 people signed up for the tour. By 1995, according to *Napoli '99* founder Mirella Barracco, half a million tickets were sold — most of them to residents of Naples. "It is as though Neapolitans had reclaimed their own city," says Bertini. "From the traffic, from the *parcheggiatori*, from their fears. Above all, from the Camorra. One of Bassolino's chief supporters in the sweep was a deceptively mild-mannered engineering professor, Giuseppi DiMaria, leader of an anti-Camorra organization called *"Napoli Libera"* — "Free Naples" — that had been waging a perilous fight against the mob since 1990. Like *Napoli '99*, it is one of the scores of grassroots associations that emerged from the desperation of the 1980s and paved the way for Bassolino. "It isn't my revolution you see here," the mayor says. "Its a revolution from the bottom up, a revolution of citizens' groups...."

Bassolino was the first mayor to be directly elected by the voters, he notes. "Before 1993, the post was appointed, and the choice was made by the same local party leaders who had been mired in corruption for decades. The direct vote was instituted during Italy's enormous wave of political scandals in the early 1990s. "It gave Bassolino a popular backing that no Neapolitan mayor before him had ever enjoyed," says Sergio Loj, a teacher and longtime political organizer in the Camorra-ridden city center.... "I understood what my predecessors somehow failed to recognize — that the Camorra had already lost its hold on *Napoli's* soul," Bassolino says. "They only controlled her assets, and I had the power to take them away."...

"Drugs were their greatest mistake," DiMaria says. "The camorristi were traditionally part of the community — they supported people in their peculiar way, and in the old days they enjoyed a trust that politicians never commanded.... The Government was "them"...[and] the home-grown Camorra was "us." [But] drugs began loosening [the Camorra's] hold on Naples' soul.

"People stopped protecting the bosses. The link between the gangs and the people was broken," says restaurateur Giovanni Serritelli, founder of another citizens' group, Let the City Live. "The theft of the earthquake money finished the process," says Carlo Tesauro, the institute researcher. "It was too much, twice-over, and it was Bassolino's genius to recognize it."...

"Listen," the mayor tells a reporter, "don't write that Bassolino changed Napoli. It was Napoli that changed Bassolino." [Frank Viviano, "Naples' Surprising Mayor Brings City Back to Life." *San Francisco Chronicle*, February 13, 1998, p. A1.]

Viviano's overwhelmingly positive assessment of the progress made in Naples during the 1990s may have been a bit too sanguine. Although the Camorra has been damaged, it is far from eliminated, and many of the structural weaknesses that have burdened Neapolitan history (such as the inadequacy of its economic base in relation to the size of its population) have not disappeared. In this regard, a much more measured — and, decidedly, more judicious — estimation of the city's prospects for the future was made by Antonio Ghirelli in 1996:

229. The successes initially achieved by the progressive government, in spite of the catastrophic financial and psychological legacy that it inherited from the past, have led many observers to adopt an attitude of hopeful expectation with regard to Bassolino, even though the fundamental problems of Naples — unemployment, the widespread disrespect for the law, the tragic situation faced by thousands of young people, the chaotic, ungovernable traffic, and, most of all, the continued underdevelopment of industry and public services — require both a strong municipal administration and the availability of resources which only the government and Parliament can provide.... Nevertheless, it is not an exaggeration to state that the experiment of this government probably represents the final opportunity, the last chance of preventing the city from sliding irreversibly into the inferno of the Third World. [Antonio Ghirelli, *Napoli*. Milan: La Fenice, 1996, p. 90.]

It was on this note of cautious optimism that Naples would enter the 21st century.

■ ■ ■

113. *At the Sailing Club of Naples, 1908.*

114. *The prince of Santobono and group at the Agnano racetrack, c. 1903.*

LIFE GOES ON. In the 20th century the rich and the upper-middle class continued much as they had in the 19th. Industrial society afforded them more and better opportunities for leisure and display.

But for the urban poor and the working class Neapolitan industry created conditions that only deteriorated from the craft and small-scale organization of the previous century.

115. *Industrial workers, Ilva plant, Bagnoli, 1905.*

116. *Work and life in the bassi, 1914.*

DAILY LIFE & MATERIAL CULTURE: 20TH CENTURY

A CITY OF CHILDREN? Into the mid-twentieth century the poverty and unemployment of large percentages of Naples' working classes forced many children into the black and grey economy. Child labor, and the continued poverty of their urban environment, made for what many observers called the "Third-World" condition of the city.

117. *Child Labor, 1968.*

118–19. *Children at play in the* bassi, *1968.*

120. *Families separated by emigration. Farewell at the port, 1958.*

MODERN NAPLES, 1799–1999

121. *Central Railroad Station, c. 1900.*

THE CITY THAT WORKS. The postcard image of Naples through most of the 20th century was one of orderly urban life, well regulated trade and commerce, of seaside leisure set against the natural beauty of sky and bay, an image unchanged from that of the early 19th century.

122. *Luigi Cosenza, Palazzo Forquet project for Riviera di Chiaia, 1933. Photo montage.*

123. *Pizzofalcone from the air, 1937.*

124. *Mergellina, c. 1960.*

125. *City and harbor, c. 1965.*

THE CITY THAT DOESN'T. THE "urban massacre" of the 1950s and 1960s, continued overbuilding and overcrowding, polluting industries and outdated facilities had left Naples a nightmare of bad air, undrinkable water, and crime-ridden streets: realities that brought the city to its knees in the 1980s.

126. The "urban massacre" on the slopes of the Vomero, c. 1960.

127. Spaccanapoli, c. 1960.

129. Bagnoli, Italsider plant, c. 1980.

128. The Spanish Quarter, c. 1975.

130. The Stazione Marittima, c. 1960. Castel Nuovo is in the background.

MODERN NAPLES, 1799–1999

131. *Enrico Alvino, Casa Armonica Kiosk, Villa Comunale, 1877.*

132. *Giorgio Botta, Villa Pappone, 1912.*

20TH-CENTURY ARCHITECTURE. Naples remained within the mainstream of European directions from the Beaux Arts and Arts Nouveau styles of the turn of the century, through the Art Deco and Fascist periods of the 20s and 30s.

133. *Gaetano Costa, Stazione di Mergellina, 1924–27. Detail.*

134. *Mostra d'Oltremare, 1937–40.*

135. *Giuseppe Vaccaro, Palazzo delle Poste, 1936.*

136. Luigi Cosenza, Olivetti Plant at Pozzuoli, 1951. Detail.

137. Angelo Mangiarotti, Prefabricated housing at Caserta, 1962.

THE POSTWAR PERIOD brought the new age of Italian architecture and design to Naples and its suburbs, encouraged by positive efforts to develop the economy of the South and by the continuing catastrophes of earthquake and urban congestion.

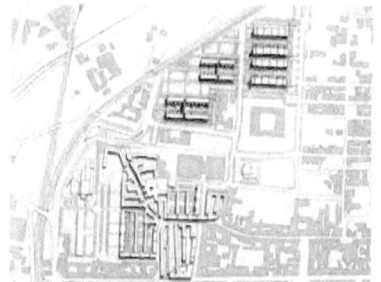

138. Housings plans for suburbs after 1980 earthquake.

139. Plans realized at Maiano, c. 1985.

140. Kenzo Tange, Centro Direzionale, begun 1982. View along central axis.

141. New Skyline. View across Borgo Marinari from Castel dell'Ovo toward Centro Direzionale, 2000.

CHRONOLOGY

1734   Charles III becomes king of Naples, establishing the Neapolitan branch of the house of Bourbon.

1759   Charles succeeds to the throne of Spain, Ferdinand IV becomes king of Naples.

1789   Outbreak of the French Revolution.

1793   Naples joins First Coalition against France.

1794   Conspiracy to overthrow Ferdinand IV fails.

1796   Napoleon begins invasion of Italy.

1798   Naples joins Second Coalition against France. Ferdinand and Maria Carolina abandon capital.

1799   January: Overthrow of Bourbon Dynasty by Neapolitan revolutionaries; Parthenopean Republic declared.

         June: Counter-revolutionary armies under Cardinal Fabrizio Ruffo recapture city, Bourbon dynasty restored.

         June–September: Over 100 revolutionaries executed; thousands imprisoned.

1801   Vincenzo Cuoco publishes *Saggio storico sulla rivoluzione di Napoli*.

1802   Ferdinand IV returns to Naples.

1805   Napoleon becomes king of Italy.

1806   January–March: Ferdinand IV forced to flee a second time; French armies overrun city; Napoleon's brother, Joseph Bonaparte proclaimed king of Naples.

         August: Abolition of feudalism in Kingdom of Naples.

1807   Carbonari emerges out of older secret societies; begins to organize active opposition to French occupation.

         French census places population of Naples at 341,047.

1808   Joseph becomes king of Spain; Joachim Murat, Napoleon's brother-in-law, replaces him as king of Naples.

1812   Napoleon's Grand Army defeated in Russia, start of general French retreat in Europe.

1814   April: Napoleon abdicates.

         September: Congress of Vienna meets; Great Powers allow Murat to remain king of Naples temporarily.

1815	March: Murat supports Napoleon during "Hundred Days," marches north and issues "Declaration of Rimini." May: Neapolitan Army defeated at battle of Tolentino, Murat forced to flee to France. June: Ferdinand IV returns to Naples for a second time. October: Murat defeated and executed in Calabria; Bourbons firmly reestablished, and period of general repression begins.
1816	Canosa becomes chief of police. Carbonari outlawed. Royal decree renames the Kingdom of Naples the "Kingdom of the Two Sicilies"; Ferdinand IV takes the title "Ferdinand I." Dutch painter Anton Pitloo arrives in Naples, begins "Posillipo School" of painting.
1817	Cholera epidemic strikes city.
1818	Concordat with Rome increases power of Church. First steamboat in Naples.
1820	July: Popular revolution in Naples forces Ferdinand to grant liberal constitution. October: Great Powers meet at Troppau, issue "Troppau Protocol."
1821	March: Austrian army crushes revolution in Naples; constitution abrogated, and policy of political repression deepens.
1825	Frances I becomes king.
1827	Austrian troops leave kingdom.
1830	Ferdinand II becomes king.
1834	Pietro Colletta's *Storia del Reame di Napoli* published.
1836/7	Cholera epidemic decimates city.
1839	Naples-Portici railway opened.
1840	Gas lights first introduced on city's streets.
1847	Settembrini's *Protest of the People of the Kingdom of the Two Sicilies* published.
1848	January: Outbreak of revolution in Palermo sparks mass demonstrations in Naples and granting of new constitution. April: Neapolitan parliament elected; government decides to send volunteers to join in war against Austria. May: Ferdinand II launches counter-revolution; royal troops retake control of city after heavy fighting; parliament dissolved; Neapolitan volunteers in North recalled.
1849	September–March: Sicilian revolution crushed; remaining constitutional concessions in both Naples and Sicily withdrawn.
1850s	Decade of intense political and social repression.

1851 Gladstone's *Two Letters to the Earl of Aberdeen* published.
1854/55 Cholera strikes city for the third time since 1800.
1858 July: Plombières meeting between Napoleon III and Cavour.
1859 April: Outbreak of Franco-Austrian War.
 May: Ferdinand II dies; Francis II becomes last Bourbon king of Naples.
 June: Francis II rejects Cavour's offer to join with France and Sardinia in war against Austria; battles of Magenta and Solferino; Austrians driven from Lombardy; uprisings in Central Italy.
 July: Peace of Villafranca ends fighting between France and Austria.
1860 March: Treaty of Turin. Piedmont-Sardinia annexes Lombardy and much of central Italy.
 May: Garibaldi sails for Sicily with one thousand "Redshirts"; Neapolitan Army defeated at Calatafimi; Palermo occupied.
 August: Garibaldi crosses Straits of Messina.
 September: Francis II abandons Naples for Gaeta; Redshirts enter city.
 October: Last Bourbon army defeated in battle of Volturno; Neapolitan plebiscite produces overwhelmingly majority for incorporation into Italy; Teano meeting between Garibaldi and Victor Emmanuel II; Cavour appoints Giuseppe La Farini temporary civilian governor of city; "Piedmontization" of Neapolitan legal and administrative institutions begins.
 November: Victor Emmanuel and Garibaldi make triumphal entry into city.
1861 March: Last Bourbon strongholds in former Kingdom of the Two Sicilies surrender; Francis II flees Gaeta for Rome; Naples officially incorporated into newly-proclaimed Kingdom of Italy.
1861–65 Piedmontese army undertakes massive military campaign to eliminate "brigandage" in countryside; virtual civil war rages in South.
1862 Office of temporary civilian governor for Naples abolished; first prefect for city appointed by central government.
1863 Pica Law passed in order to repress "brigandage."
1864 Fifteenth Congress of the Mazzinian "Workers' Society" held in city.
1866 Francesco De Sanctis publishes first of *Saggi critici*.
1867 Bakunin founds anarchist "Association for Liberty and Justice" in Naples.
1868 De Sanctis publishes his *Storia della letteratura italiana*.
1876 Victory of the Sinistra in local elections.
1877 Publication of Jessie White Mario's *Miseria di Napoli* and Renato Fucini's *Napoli a occhio nudo*.

1878	Anarchist attempt to kill King Umberto I on via Toledo during visit to city.
1880	Funicular railway begins service at Vesuvius.
1881	Lamont Young draws up first plan for Neapolitan subway system.
1884	Massive cholera epidemic decimates city for the fourth time in century; Umberto I and Prime Minister Agosto Depretis visit the city; Matilde Serao publishes *Il ventre di Napoli*.
1885	Italian Parliament passes law providing relief for the city; large sections of *quartieri bassi* (slum areas) demolished and program of urban renewal (*"Risanamento"*) begun.
1888	Eduardo Scarpetta's *Miseria e Nobilità* opens.
1890s	Naples becomes primary port of embarkation for southern Italians leaving Italy for foreign countries.
1890	First Socialist deputy elected from Naples to Chamber of Deputies in Rome.
1892	Galleria Umberto I opens. Eduardo Scarfoglio and Matilde Serao found *Il Mattino*.
1896	Alfredo Cottrau's *La crisi della città di Napoli* published.
1898	Strikes and social disorders throughout Italy spread to Naples; city placed under martial law.
1900	Umberto I assassinated; Neapolitan population reaches 564,000, still largest in Italy.
1901	Saredo study published highlighting backwardness of the Neapolitan economy; 70,000 southern emigrants leave Naples for foreign lands in a single year.
1902	Francesco Nitti calls for an "industrial risorgimento" for Naples.
1903	Nitti publishes *Napoli e la questione meridionale*.
1904	First "Special Law" enacted by Rome to stimulate Neapolitan economic development (others follow in 1908 and 1911).
1906	Murder of Genaro Cuoculo and his wife lead to arrest and eventual conviction of several Camorra leaders; record 90,000 emigrants depart from city for the Americas.
1909	Salvatore di Giacomo publishes *Assunta Spina*.
1912	Universal male suffrage enacted.
1913	National elections confirm drift towards political polarization; Socialists make important gains in Naples.
1914	Outbreak of "Red Week" in central Italy provokes widespread disorders in Naples; a coalition of progressives (*"Blocco popolare"*) assumes control of city.
1915	Italy enters World War I.

1917	Milan surpasses Naples as Italy's largest city.
1917	Benedetto Croce publishes *Teoria e storia della storiografia*. Battle of Caporetto.
1918	November armistice brings end to the war.
1919	Working-class strikes and demonstrations rock city; first Neapolitan Fascio di Combattimento founded in April.
1920–22	Fascist squads launch two-year reign of terror against rivals throughout the Campania.
1921	January: Italian Communist Party founded.
1922	August: Socialist "legal strike" (*"sciopio legalitario"*) suppressed by government. October: 40,000 Blackshirts march on city; Mussolini speaks at Teatro San Carlo; Fascists consolidate their hold over city; Mussolini launches "March on Rome."
1923	Aurelio Padovano purged as Neapolitan Fascist leader.
1924	Crucial national elections held; Liberals join Fascists in forming a national list.
1924	Matteotti Affair begins.
1926	Death of Padovani.
1925	L'Alto Commissariato instituted, urban administration under Fascist control.
1929	Great Depression begins. Lateran Pact signed.
1931	Mussolini gives major speech in Piazza del Plebiscito.
1933	Istituto per la Ricostruzione Industriale established.
1935	Invasion of Ethiopia.
1938	Hitler visits Naples.
1940	June: Italy enters World War II. November: British launch first of 105 air raids on city.
1941	December: Italy declares war on United States.
1943	July: German Army occupies Naples; city subjected to heavy bombardment by Allies for two months. September: Four Days, uprising against German forces by Neapolitans; German garrison decides to leave city; priceless Neapolitan archives destroyed. October: Americans and British enter city, completing its liberation.
1944	Eruption of Vesuvius.
1946	June: National referendum on Monarchy; seventy-nine percent of Neapolitans vote to preserve monarchy and reject Republic.

CHRONOLOGY

1947	Giuseppe Marotta's *L'oro di Napoli* and Domenico Rea's *Spaccanapoli* published.
1950s	Beginnings of Camorra revival.
1950	Neapolitan population surpasses 1 million.
1951	Cassa per il Mezzogiorno established.
1952–58	Achille Lauro dominates Naples.
1953	Anna Maria Ortese publishes *Il mare non bagna Napoli*.
1958–75	Christian Democrats under Gava family run city.
1970	First Regional Council for the Campania meets in Naples.
1973	New cholera epidemic strikes city.
1975–83	Moderate leftist administration under Valenti runs government.
1980	Earthquake results in heavy damage to metropolitan area.
1983	Gavas return to power; governmental corruption begins to peak.
1989	Centro Direzionale di Napoli established by Christian Democrats to act as new administrative headquarters for city.
1990	Local elections take place amid widespread violence by *camorristi*; visit of Pope John Paul II.
1992/93	Scandals drive Christian Democrats from power.
1993/94	Bassolino elected mayor; city initiates a program of gradual reform; clean-up of streets and parks begins; cultural revival gains strength.
1994	Huge crackdown on the Camorra launched. July: "G7" holds annual meeting in Naples. November: United Nations conference on crime.
1997	Bassolino reelected by huge majority.
1999	"Napoli '99" celebration.

■ ■ ■

In the 20th century the literary life of Naples often continued to center around the political and social issues of the city and the new nation.

142. With works like his 6-volume history of Italian literature and numerous works on poetry and history, Benedetto Croce (1866–1952) was perhaps the writer who most profoundly influenced Italian culture of the 20th century.

143. Salvatore Di Giacomo (1860–1934), author of Assunta Spina, wrote both lyrically and realistically of life in Naples.

144. Raffaele Viviani (1888–1950), dialect poet and playwright who brought scenes of daily life to the stage.

LITERATURE: 20TH CENTURY

145. *Colonnese Bookstore, via S. Pietro a Maiella.*

A THRIVING LITERARY CULTURE supports dozens of bookshops lining the streets of Port'Alba and the surrounding area, numerous presses and publishing companies, and an active interest in new writers either born or living in Naples.

146. *Book covers, from Electa and Alfredo Guida, Naples.*

THREE WRITERS OF NAPLES. Luciano De Crescenzo (b. 1928) is the author of *Thus Spake Bellavista: Naples, Love and Liberty.*

Anna Maria Ortese (1914–1998) made the city the subject of many stories and of her *Il mare non bagna Napoli.*

Fabrizia Ramondino (b. 1936) is the author of *Althénopis.* The city of Naples often serves as an integral part of her work.

147. *Luciano De Crescenzo.*

148. *Anna Maria Ortese*

149. *Fabrizia Ramondino*

MODERN NAPLES, 1799–1999

150. *A popular engraving shows a mother teaching her daughter the Tarantella, a ancient dance usually accompanied by guitars and tambourines.*

Music, including both song and dance, form an important part of the cultural heritage of the city of Naples.

151. *Gioacchino Rossini (1792–1868) was the music director of both the San Carlo and San Bartolomeo Opera Houses in Naples, where he composed* The Barber of Seville, *the most popular comic opera in the world. He composed a total of 39 operas in 19 years, retiring in 1829, at the age of thirty-seven.*

152. *Songsheets from some of Naples' more famous popular songs:* Funiculi-Funicula *by Luigi Denza (1846–1922);* Torna a Surriento *with words by Giambattista De Curtis (1860–1926) and music by Ernesto De Curtis (1875–1937); and* Marechiare, *words by Salvatore Di Giacomo (1860–1934) and music by Francesco Paolo Tosti (1846–1916).*

286

MUSIC

154. *The great Neapolitan tenor, Enrico Caruso (1873–1921) who with an extraordinarily beautiful and powerful voice sang in Moscow, Paris, Lisbon, London and at the Metropolitan Opera House in New York.*

153. *The songsheet of a famous Neapolitan song,* Io Te Voglio Bene Assaie, *composed before Unification. It is illustrated by Edoardo Dalbono (1841–1915), an artist more famous for his paintings.*

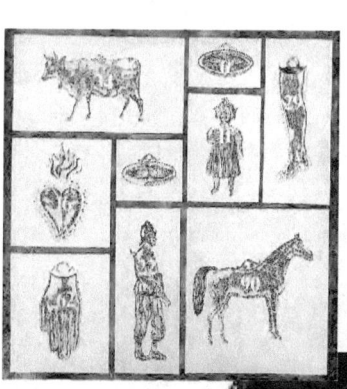

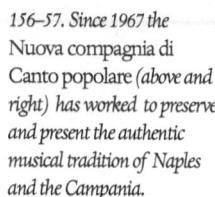

155. *Roberto Murolo (above), a present-day master of Neapolitan song.*

156–57. *Since 1967 the Nuova compagnia di Canto popolare (above and right) has worked to preserve and present the authentic musical tradition of Naples and the Campania.*

MODERN NAPLES, 1799–1999

SPECTACLE IN NAPLES found its outlet in the 19th century on the stage and also, in the 20th century, in film. Everyday life and local politics, both as comedy and tragedy, often dominated both forms.

158. *Eduardo Scarpetta (above left, 1853–1925), actor and comic playwright, created the famous Don Felice Sciosciammocca, who appeared in over 100 works.*

159. *Roberto Bracco (1862-1943), author and playwright of such works as* The Infidel *and* The Little Saint.

160. *Eduardo De Filippo (below right, 1900–1985), actor, poet and playwright, was a preeminent figure in Neapolitan theater and achieved his greatest success in creating and directing sensitive comedies about Naples and Neapolitans.*

161. *The wildly popular comedians Totò (Antonio De Curtis, 1898–1967) appeared in dozens of films over his 30-year career and put a comic face on the Italian of the pre-war era who could not quite get in step with the postwar "Miracle."*

THEATER & FILM

162. Gold of Naples.

162–63. Vittorio De Sica (1901–1974) presented two different views of postwar Naples: in The Gold of Naples (right, 1954, with Neapolitans Sophia Loren and Totò), he displayed the postwar get-by, or arrangiarsi, attitudes of the

163. On the set of Marriage Italian Style.

Neapolitans. Ten years later in Marriage Italian Style (above, Di Sica with Marcello Mastroianni and Loren) he skewered the upward mobility and hypocrisy of the economic "Miracle."

164. Rosi, Hands on the City.   166. Wertmüller, Camorra.

164-65. Francesco Rosi's Hands on the City (1963) and The Mattei Affair (1972) and Lina Wertmüller's Camorra (1985) condemned corruption and crime in Naples; while Pappi Corsicato's Libera (1991) added scorn and provocation to Neapolitan humor.

165. Rosi, Mattei Affair.

167. Corsicato, Libera.

168. *Toward Centro Direzionale. Open-air market on via Venezia, 2000.*

BIBLIOGRAPHY

GENERAL

Bouvier, René, and Lafforgue, André. *La vie napolitaine au XVIIIeme siècle.* Paris: Hachette, 1956.

Croce, Benedetto. *History of the Kingdom of Naples.* H. Stuart Hughes, ed., Frances Frenaye, trans. Chicago and London: University of Chicago Press, 1970.

—. *Storie e leggende napoletane.* Milan: Adelphi, 1991.

Collison-Morley, Lacy. *Naples Through the Centuries.* London: Methuen, 1925.

D'Agostino, Guido. *Per una storia di Napoli capitale.* Naples: Liguori, 1988.

Della Donne, Vincenzo, ed. *Naples.* Boston: Houghton Mifflin, 1995.

De Seta, Cesare. *Napoli.* Rome and Bari: Laterza, 1981.

Doria, Gino. *Storia di una capitale.* Naples: Guida, 1935.

Forgacs, David, and Robert Lumley, eds. *Italian Cultural Studies: An Introduction.* Oxford: Oxford University Press, 1996.

Galasso, Giuseppe. *Napoli.* Rome: Laterza, 1987.

—. *Mezzogiorno medievale e moderne.* Turin: Einaudi, 1965.

—. *Il mezzogiorno nella storia d'Italia.* Florence: Le Monnier, 1977.

—. *Italia democratica: Dai Giacobini al Partito d'Azione.* Florence: Le Monnier, 1986.

—. *Intervista sulla storia di Napoli.* Bari: Laterza, 1978.

Gambardella, Alfonso. *Naples: Portrait of a City.* Genoa: Sagep, 1993.

Ghirelli, Antonio. *Storia di Napoli.* Turin: Einaudi, 1992.

—. *Napoli: Gli intellectuali, la metropoli, la questione napoletana.* Milan: Fenice, 1996.

—. *Un' altra Napoli: Gli uomini di una città che è stata grande e voule esserlo ancora.* Venezia: Marsilio, 1993.

—. *Napoli italiana.* Turin: Einaudi, 1977.

Gleijeses, Vittorio. *La Storia de Napoli: Dalle origini ai nostri giorni*. Naples: Società Editrice Napoletana, 1977.

Gunn, Peter. *Naples: A Palimpsest*. London: Chapman and Hall, 1961.

Mack Smith, Denis. *Italy: A Modern History.* Ann Arbor: University of Michigan Press, 1959.

Romano, Salvatore Francesco. *Storia della questione meridionale*. Palermo: Pantea, 1945.

Russo, Giuseppe. *La città de Napoli dalle origini al 1860*. Naples: Risanamento di Napoli, 1960.

Sepe, Giovanni. *Napoli nella vita unitaria*. Naples: F. Fiorentino, 1964.

Seward, Desmond, ed. *Naples: A Travellers' Companion*. London: Constable, 1984.

Spagnoletti, Angelantonio. *Storia del Regno delle due Sicilie*. Bologna: Il Mulino, 1997.

Storia di Napoli. 10 vols. Naples: Società Editrice Storia di Napoli, 1975–1981.

Venturi, Franco. *Italy and the Enlightenment: Studies in a Cosmopolitan Century.* New York: New York University Press, 1972.

DIARIES AND MEMOIRS

Andersen, Hans Christian. *A Poet's Bazaar.* Boston: Houghton Mifflin, 1879.

Bixio, Nino. *Epistolario de Nino Bixio*. Emilia Morelli, ed. Rome: Vittoriano, 1942.

Blessington, Lady Marguerite Power Farmer. *Idler in Italy.* 2 vols. London: Hamish Hamilton, 1979.

Colet, Louise. *L'Italie des Italiens*. Paris: E. Dentu, 1863.

Craven, Richard Keppel. *A Tour Through the Southern Provinces of the Kingdom of Naples*. London: Rodwell and Martin, 1821.

De Damas, Comte. *Memoires du Baron di Damas*. Paris: Librairie Plon, 1922.

De Nicola, Carlo. *Diario Napoletano: Dal 1798 al 1825*. 3 vols. Naples: Società Napoletana di Storia Patria, 1906.

Dickens, Charles. *Pictures from Italy.* Paris: A. and W. Galignani, 1846.

Du Camp, Maxime. *Expedition des Deux-Siciles: Souvenirs personels*. Paris: 1861.

Ellis, Robert B. *See Naples and Die: A World War II Memoir of a United States Army Ski Trooper in the Mountains of Italy.* London: McFarland, 1996.

Goethe, J.W. *Italian Journey, 1786-1788*. W.H. Auden and Elizabeth Mayer, trans. Harmondsworth, England: Penguin Books, 1962.

BIBLIOGRAPHY

Lewis, Norman. *Naples '44: An Intelligence Officer in the Italian Labyrinth.* New York: Henry Holt, 1978.

Kelly, Michael. *Reminiscences.* London: Cassell, 1956.

Kubly, Herbert. *American in Italy.* New York: Simon and Schuster, 1955.

Massari, Giuseppe. *Diario dalle cento voci, 1858–1860.* Emilia Morelli, ed. Bologna: Cappelli, 1959.

Metternich, Prince Clemens von. *Memoirs of Prince Metternich, 1815–1829.* Prince Richard Metternich, ed. 3 vols. New York: Howard Fertig, 1970.

Minichini, Luigi. *Luglio 1820: Cronaca di una rivoluzione.* Rome: Bulzoni, 1979.

Moorehead, Alan. *Eclipse.* London: Hamish Hamilton, 1967.

Morgan, Lady. *Italy.* 3 vols. London: Henry Colburn, 1821.

Morton, C.V.A. *A Traveller in Southern Italy.* New York: Dodd, Mead, 1969.

Munthe, Alex. *The Story of San Michele.* New York: E.P. Dutton, 1957.

—. *Letters from a Mourning City.* London: John Murray, 1899.

Orlov, Grigorii Vladimirovich. *Memoires historiques, politiques, et litteraires sur le royaume de Naples.* Paris: Chasseriau et Hecart, 1819–1822.

Pepe, Gugliemo. *Memoirs.* 3 vols. London: Richard Bentley, 1846.

—. *Delle rivoluzione e delle guerre d'Italia nel 1847, 1848, 1849.* Turin: Einaudi, 1850.

Petrucelli della Gattina, Ferdinand. *Ricordi: La rivoluzione di Napoli nel 1848.* Genoa: Moretti, 1850.

Settembrini, Luigi. *Ricordanze della mia vita.* Bari: Laterza, 1934.

Stendhal, Henri di. *Rome, Naples, and Florence.* Richard N. Coe, trans. New York: George Braziller, 1959.

Swinburne, Henry. *Travels in the Two Sicilies.* Dublin: Price, 1783–1786.

—. *The Courts of Europe at the Close of the Last Century.* London: H. White, 1841.

Symons, Arthur. *Cities.* London: J. M. Dent, 1903.

Taine, H. *Italy: Rome and Naples.* J. Durand, trans. New York: Henry Holt, 1889.

PART I: NAPLES UNDER THE BOURBONS, 1799–1860

Acton, Harold. *The Bourbons of Naples, 1734–1825*. London: Methuen, 1956.

——. *The Last of the Bourbons, 1825–1861*. London: Methuen, 1961.

Atteridge, A.H. *Marshall Murat: King of Naples*. London: Worley, 1992.

Battaglini, Mario, ed. *Napoli 1799: I giornali giacobini*. Rome: Alfredo Borzi, 1988.

Beales, Derek, ed. *The Risorgimento and the Unification of Italy*. London: George Allen & Unwin, 1971.

Bianchi, Nicomede, ed. *Storia Documentata della Europa in Italia dell 1814 all'anno 1864*. Turin: Unione Tipografica Editrice, 1865.

Bingham, D.A., ed. *A Selection from the Letters and Dispatches of the First Napoleon*. London: Chapman and Hall, 1884.

Brethon, Paul le, ed. *Lettres et Documents pour servir a l'histoire de Joachim Murat*. 9 vols. Paris: Librairie Plon, 1913.

Cantimori, Delio. *Utopisti e riformatori italiani, 1794–1847*. Florence: Sansoni, 1943.

Capecelatro, Domenico Gaudioso. *1860: Crollo di Napoli capitale*. Rome: Ateneo, 1972.

——. *Ferdinando I di Borbone: Re illuminista*. Naples: Gallina, 1987.

Cimbalo, Antonio. *La lunga marcia del Cardinale Ruffo alla reconquista del Regno di Napoli*. Rome: A. Borzi, 1967.

Cingari, Gaetano. *Mezzogiorno e Risorgimento: La restaurazione a Napoli dal 1821 al 1830*. Bari: Laterza, 1970.

Colletta, Pietro. *History of the Kingdom of Naples, 1734–1825*. S. Horner, trans. 2 vols. Edinburgh: T. Constable, 1853.

Croce, Benedetto, ed. *La riconquista del Regno di Napoli nel 1799: Lettere del Cardinale Ruffo, del Re, della Regina, del ministro Acton*. Bari: Laterza, 1943.

——. *La rivoluzione napoletana del 1799*. Bari: Laterza, 1912.

Cuoco, Vincenzo. *Saggio storico sulla rivoluzione napoletana del 1799*. Bari: Laterza, 1929.

Coletti, Alessandra. *La regina di Napoli*. Novara: Istituto Geografico De Agostini, 1986.

Da Molin, Giovanna. *Popolazione e società: Sistemi demografici nel Regno di Napoli in età moderna*. Bari: Cacucci, 1995.

Demarco, D. *Il crollo del Regno delle Due Sicilie*. Naples: Instituto di storia Economica e Sociale, 1963.

BIBLIOGRAPHY

De Sivo, Giacinto. *Storia delle Due Sicilie dal 1847 al 1861.* 2 vols. Naples: Arturo Bersilio, 1964.

Doria, Gino. *Murat: Re di Napoli.* Naples: Di Mauro, 1966.

Espitalier, Albert. *Napoleon and Murat: A Biography Compiled from Unknown and Unpublished Documents.* London: John Lane, The Bodley Head, 1912.

Faraglia, N.F. *Storia dei prezzi in Napoli dal 1131 al 1860.* Naples: G. Nobile, 1878.

Fossati, A. *Lavoro e produzione in Italia dalla metà del secolo XVIII alla seconde guerra mondiale.* Turin: G. Giappichelli, 1951.

Gabrieli, Giuseppe. *Massoneria e carboneria nel Regno di Napoli.* Rome: Atanor, 1982.

Gladstone, William Ewart. *Two Letters to the Earl of Aberdeen on the State Prosecutions of the Neapolitan Government.* London: John Murray, 1851.

Giglioli, Constance. *Naples in 1799: An Account of the Revolution of 1799 and the Rise and Fall of the Parthenopean Republic.* London: J. Murray; New York: E.P. Dutton, 1903.

Grillo, Francesco. *La rivoluzione napoletana del 1799.* Cosenza: Pellegrini, 1972.

Haskell, Francis. *The Age of the Grand Tour (1720–1820).* New York: Crown, 1967.

Hearder, Harry. *Italy in the Age of the Risorgimento.* New York: Longman, 1983.

Lacour-Gayet, Michel. *Marie-Caroline: Reine de Naples.* Paris: Tallandier, 1990.

Mack Smith, Denis, ed. *The Making of Italy, 1796–1870.* London: Macmillan, 1968.

———. *Garibaldi.* Englewood Cliffs, NJ: Prentice-Hall, 1966.

———. *Cavour and Garibaldi: A Study in Political Conflict.* Cambridge: Cambridge University Press, 1954.

Marraro, Howard R., ed. *Diplomatic Relations between the United States and the Kingdom of the Two Sicilies: Instructions and Dispatches, 1816–1861.* 2 vols. New York: S.F. Vanni, 1951.

———. *American Opinion on the Unification of Italy, 1846–1861.* New York: Columbia University Press, 1930.

Martuscelli, Stefani, ed. *La popolazione del Mezzogiorno nella statistica di Murat.* Naples: Guida, 1979.

Moscati, Ruggero. *La Fine del Regno di Napoli: Documenti borbonici del 1859–1860.* Florence: Le Monnier, 1960.

———. *I Borboni in Italia.* Naples: Edizioni Scientifiche, 1970.

Napoleon Bonaparte. *The Confidential Correspondence of Napoleon Bonaparte with His Brother Joseph.* New York: D. Appleton, 1856.

Nitti, F.S. *Napoli e la questione meridionale.* Naples: Pierri, 1903.

Paladino, Giuseppe. *Governo napoletano et la guerra del 1848.* Milan: Segati, 1921.

———. *Il 15 Maggio 1848 in Napoli.* Rome: Segati, 1921.

Pedio, Tommaso. *La repubblica napoletana del 1799.* Bari: Levante, 1986.

———. *Giacobini e Sanfediste in Italia Meridionale.* Bari: Adriatica, 1974.

Petraccone, Claudia. *Napoli nel 1799: Rivoluzione e proprietà.* Naples: Morano, 1989.

Procacci, G. *Le elezione del 1874 e l'opposizione meridionale.* Milan: Feltrinelli, 1956.

Romani, M. *Storia economica d'Italia nel secolo XIX, 1815–1914.* Milan: A. Giuffre, 1968.

Romeo, Rosario. *Mezzogiorno e Sicilia nel Risorgimento.* Naples: Edizioni Scientifiche Italiane, 1963.

Schipa, Michelangelo. *Nel regno di Ferdinando IV Borbone.* Florence: Vallecchi, 1938.

Schroeder, Paul. *Metternich's Diplomacy at Its Zenith, 1820–1823.* Austin: University of Texas Press, 1962.

Settembrini, Luigi. *Opuscoli politici edite e inediti: 1847–1851.* Mario Themelly, ed. Rome: Areneo, 1969.

———. *Protestà del popolo delle Due Sicilie.* Naples: 1847.

Southey, Robert. *The Life of Lord Nelson.* London: J.M. Dent, 1906.

Talamo, Giuseppe. *Napoli: Da Murat alla morte di Ferdinando I di Borbone, 1808–1825.* Rome: Elia, 1972.

Valente, Angela. *Gioacchino Murat e l'Italia meridionale.* Turin: Einaudi, 1965.

———. *Il Sud nella storia d'Italia: Antologia della questione meridionale.* Bari: Laterza, 1972.

Walker, Mark, ed., *Plombières: Secret Diplomacy and the Rebirth of Italy.* New York: Oxford University Press, 1968.

Weil, M.-H., and C.D. Di Somma Circello, eds. *Correspondence inedité de Marie-Caroline, reine de Naples e de Sicilie, avec le Marquis de Gallo.* 2 vols. Paris: Emile-Paul, 1911.

Woolf, Steward. *A History of Italy, 1700–1860: The Social Constraints of Political Change.* New York: Methuen, 1979.

———., ed. *The Italian Risorgimento.* London: Longman, 1969.

PART II: NAPLES IN ITALY, 1860–1999

Allum, P.A. *Politics and Society in Postwar Naples*. Cambridge: Cambridge University Press, 1973.

Bairoch, Paul. *Revolution industrielle et sous-developement*. Paris: Mouton, 1974.

Barbiero, Maria Carmela, ed. *Gli eredi della povertà: Stabilità e mutamento nel sottoproletariato napoletano*. Naples: Guida, 1981.

Barbagallo, Francesco. *Il potere della Camorra, 1973–1998*. Turin: Einaudi, 1999.

Bassolino, Antonio. *Mezzogiorno alla prova: Napoli e il Sud alla svolta degli anni ottanta*. Bari: De Donato, 1980.

Bernabei, Marco. *Fascismo e nationalismo in Campania, 1919–1925*. Rome: Edizioni di Storia e Letteratura, 1975.

Capecelatro, Domenico Gaudioso. *Reazione a Napoli dopo L'Unità: Conguire e processi politici*. Naples: Delfino, 1976.

Carlucci, Giuseppi, ed. *Storia d'Italia nei discoursi di Mussolini, 1915–1945*. 2 vols. Rome: Centro Editore Nazionale, 1966.

Caizzi, B. *Storia dell'industria italiana dal XVIII secolo ai giorni nostri*. Turin: UTET, 1965.

—. *Nuovo antologia della questione meridionale*. Milan: Edizione di Comunità, 1970.

Colapietra, R. *Napoli tra dopoguerra e fascismo*. Milan: Feltrinelli, 1962.

Compagna, F. *Lauro e la Democrazia Cristiana*. Rome: Opere Nuovo, 1960.

Cottrau, Alfonso. "La crisi della città di Napoli." *Nuovo Antologia* 64.14 (July 16, 1896): 229-56.

Corsi, E. *Napoli contemporanea*. Naples: Edizioni Scientifiche Italiane, 1995.

Cutrufelli, Maria Rosa. *L'Unità d'Italia, guerra contadina, e nascità del sottosviluppo del Sud*. Verona: Bertani, 1974.

Chubb, Judith. *Patronage, Power, and Poverty in Southern Italy: A Tale of Two Cities*. Cambridge: Cambridge University Press, 1995.

D'Agostino, Guido. *Napoli alle urne, 1946–1979*. Naples: Guida, 1980.

De Antonellis, Giacomo. *Napoli sotto il regime: Storia di una città e delle sua regione durante il ventennio fascista*. Milan: Cooperativa Editrice Donati, 1972.

—. *Le Quattro Giornate di Napoli*. Milan: Bompiani, 1973.

De Fusco, Renato. *Napoli nel Novecento*. Naples: Electa, 1994.

De Jaco, A. *Il brigantaggio meridionale: Cronica inedita dell'unità d'Italia*. Rome: Riunti, 1969.

Ellwood, David W. *Italy, 1943–1945*. New York: Holmes & Meyer, 1985.

Erra, Enzo. *Napoli 1943: Le quattro giornate che non ci furono*. Naples: Longanese, 1993.

Fortunato, G. *Il Mezzogiorno e lo stato italiano*. Bari: Laterza, 1911.

——. *Appunti di storia napoletana dell'ottocento*. Bari: Laterza, 1931.

Figurato, Marisa. *Storia di contrabando: Napoli, 1945–1981*. Naples: T. Pironti, 1981.

Guglielmi, Tommaso. *Napoli: Cronache sempre vive*. Naples: Giannini, 1996.

Imbucci, Giuseppe. *Per una storia della povertà a Napoli in età contemporanea, 1880–1890*. Naples: Edizione Scientifiche Italiane, 1985.

Jeuland-Meynaud, Maryse. *La ville de Naples après l'annexation, 1860–1914: Essai d'interpretation historique et litteraire*. Aix-en-Provence: Éditions de l'Université de Provence, 1973.

King, Bolton, and Thomas Okey. *Italy Today*. London: James Nisbet, 1904.

Lambiase, Sergio, and G. Battista Nazzaro. *Napoli, 1940–1945*. Milan: Longanesi, 1978.

Loungo, E., and A. Oliva. *Napoli come é*. Milan: Feltrinelli, 1959.

Magni, Cesari. *Vita parlamentare del Duca di San Donato: Patriota e difensore di Napoli*. Padua: Antonio Milani, 1968.

Marno, Marcella. *Il proletariato industriale a Napoli in età liberale, 1880–1914*. Naples: Guida, 1978.

Mazzacane, Leilo. *I bassi a Napoli*. Naples: Guida, 1978.

Milanesi, Bruno. *Napoli, città difficile*. Naples: Guida, 1972.

Minozzi, Alfredo. *L'operaio muratore di Napoli*. Salerno: Pietro Laveglia, 1985.

Monnier, Marco. *La Camorra: Notizie storiche, raccolte e documentate*. Lecce: Argo, 1994.

Molfese, F. *Storia del brigantaggio dopo l'unità*. Milan: Feltrinelli, 1964.

Nitti, F.S. *La città di Napoli: Studi e ricerche su la situazione economica presente e la possibile trasformazione industriale*. Naples: L. Alvano, 1902.

Pallotta, G. *Il Qualunquisimo, e l'avventura di Guglielmo Giannini*. Milan: Bompiani, 1972.

Petrone, P. *Rapporto su Napoli, 1965: Indagine statistica sulla città de Napoli*. Naples: Roma, 1965.

Porcaro, Giuseppe. *Processo a un anarchico a Napoli nel 1878: Giovanni Passannatte*. Naples: Delfino, 1975.

Rocco, Marco. *Le condizioni del commune di Napoli*. Naples: Pierro & Veraldi, 1898.

BIBLIOGRAPHY

Russo, G. *Napoli come città*. Naples: Edizione Scientifiche Italiane, 1966.

Salerno, Nicola. *Dalle liberazione alla constituente: Cenni di vita politica napolitana*. Naples: Arturo Berisio, 1973.

Salvadori, M.S. *Il mito del buongoverno, la questione meridionale da Cavour a Gramsci*. Turin: Einaudi, 1960.

Salvemini, G. *Scritti sulla questione meridionale, 1896–1955*. Turin: Einaudi, 1955.

Spaventa, Silvio. *Discoursi parlamentari*. Rome: Tipografia della Camera dei Deputati, 1913.

Snowden, Frank. *Naples in the Time of the Cholera, 1884–1911*. Cambridge: Cambridge University Press, 1995.

Serao, Matilde. *Il ventre di Napoli*. Milan: Treves, 1884.

Stefanile, Aldo. *I cento bombardamenti di Napoli: I giorni delle Am-lire*. Milan: Alberto Marotta, 1968.

Susmel, Eduardo, and Duilio Susmel, eds. *Opera omnia di Benito Mussolini*. Florence: La Fenice, 1951–1962.

Varvaro, Paolo. *Una città fascista: Potere e società a Napoli*. Palermo: Sellerio, 1990.

Ulloa, Pietro Cala. *Lettres napolitaines*. Rome: Civiltà Cattolica, 1864.

Villari, R. *Mezzogiorno e contadini nell'età moderna*. Bari: Laterza, 1961.

■ ■ ■

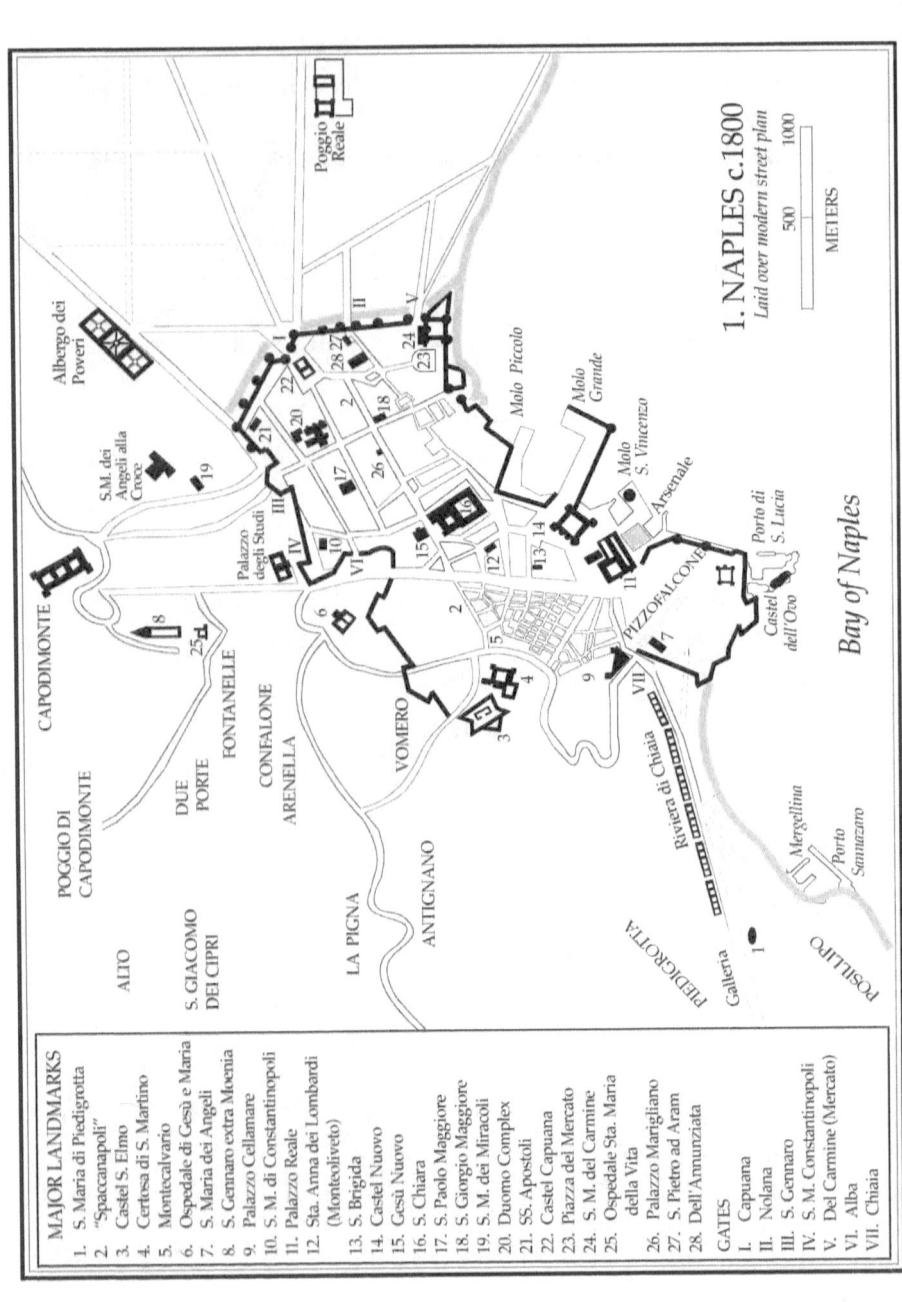

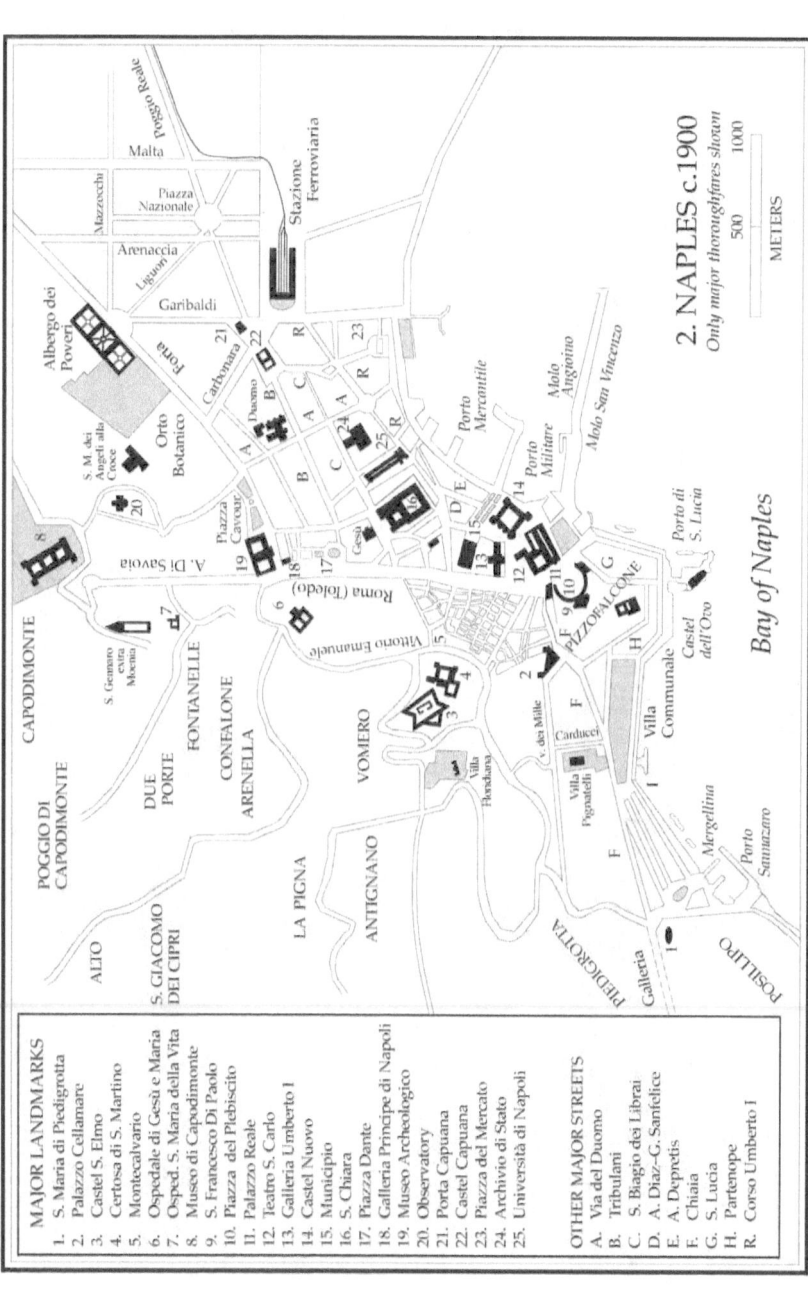

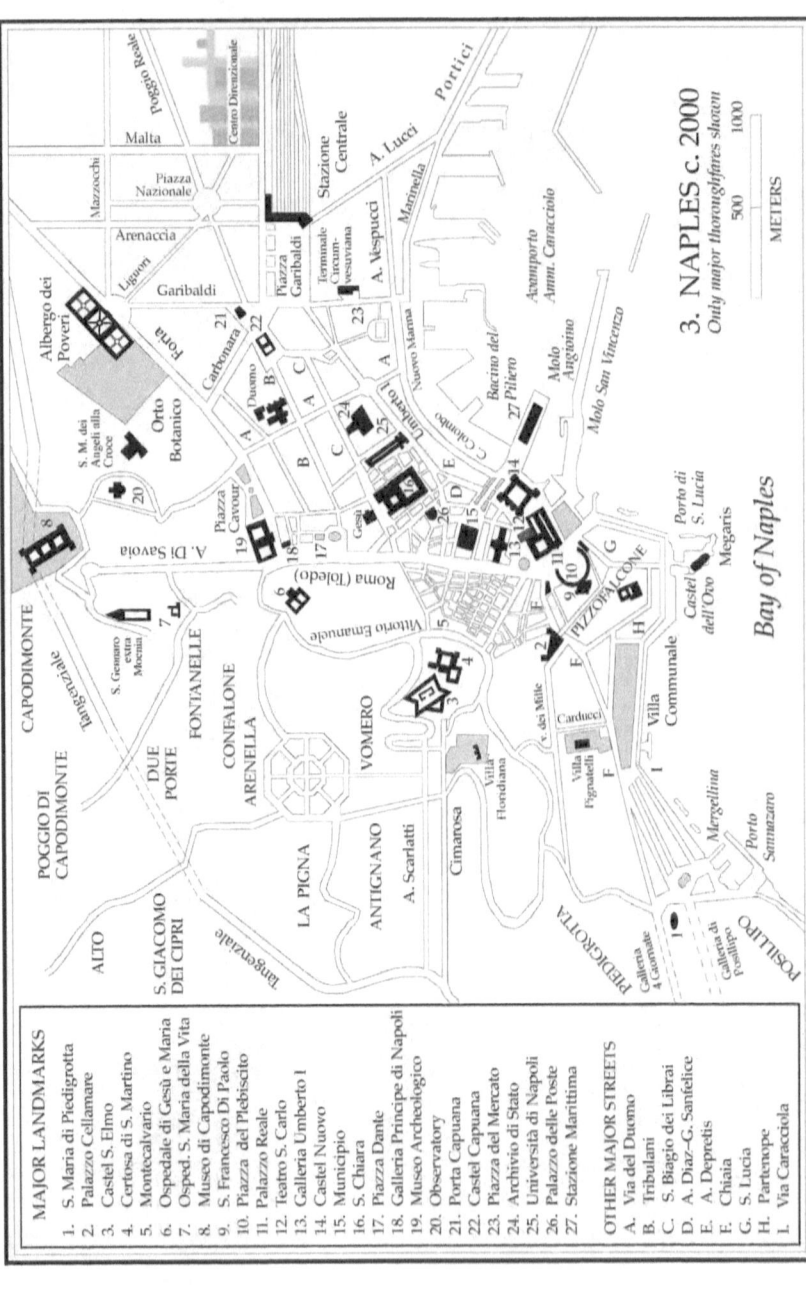

INDEX

A

Abba, G.C. 170
Abbamonte, Giuseppe 29
Aberdeen, earl of. *See* Gordon, George Hamilton, earl of Aberdeen.
Aboukir, battle of 42
Abruzzi 22, 47, 56, 205; agriculture 142
Accera 250
A'Court, William 112, 119
Acton, John 17, 20, 34, 38, 39, 42, 49; exile 60; fall 51; Napoleon's hostility to 50
Afragola 246, 250, 269
Africa 42
Agnelli, Comm. 238
agriculture: abundance XXXIV; decline under Ferdinand II 142; post-WWII 255; and Cassa per il Mezzogiorno 257. *See also* economy.
Albergo dei Poveri. *See* public structures.
Alexander, Czar of Russia 106
Alfredo Guida Editore 285
Aliberti, Gennaro 201
Alquier, Baron 48, 52
Alvino, Enrico 276
"amalgamation" 102

Ambrosio, General 109
Amendola, Giovanni 224, 225
Amiens, Peace of 48, 50
Amore, Nicola 203, 208
Anacapri 76
Ancona 56, 68; March of 138
Andersen, Hans Christian 3
anti-Fiumianism 225
Apennines 56
Apulia 51, 54, 66, 107, 165; agriculture 142
architecture. *See* cultural life.
archives: destruction of, 1943 XLV, 237
Argentina 211
Ariano 107
aristocracy XXXIV, XXXV, XXXIX, 10; effects of Napoleonic period 98; households 12; Risorgimento 190; social ethos 11
Arsenal. *See* public structures.
Ascoli, Troiano Marulli, duke of, 109
Augusta 19
Austerlitz, battle of 54, 71
Austria 18, 21, 48; war of 1848 153, 155; war with, 1858/59 165
Avellino: revolution of 1820 107–10, 111
Aversa 249, 250
Avvocata. *See* districts.

303

B

Baffi, Pasquale 29, 43
Bagnoli steel works XLVI. *See also* industry.
Banco di Napoli XLI; gold reserves, 1860 197
Bandiera, Attilio and Emilio 197
Bari 222
Baronci, Sergio 266
Barracco, Mirella 270
Barras, Paul François Jean Nicolas, de 52
Barzini, Luigi 259
bassi XXXIX, 204; and Risanamento 209; living conditions 211, 272; under Mussolini 231. *See also* housing.
Basso Porto. *See* districts.
Bassolino, Antonio 243, 264, 265, 266–268; reelection in 1997 270
Battistini, Elso 238
Bay of Naples 5, 182
Bayonne 68
Beauharnais, Eugene de 85
Belgium 255
Benevento 235
Bentinck, William 86, 100, 102
Bernari, Carlo 262
Berthier, Louis Alexandre 21
Bertini, Antonio 269
Bianchi Nuovi. *See* districts.
Biblioteca Nazionale. *See* public structures.
Bisceglia, Domenico 29
Bixio, Adelaide 194
Bixio, Nino 135, 170, 194
Blessington, Marguerite Power Farmer, countess of 2, 15, 126, 180
Bologna 104

Bombelles, Charles comte de 131
Bonaparte: Caroline 71, 77–78, 85, 87; Joseph 55, 58, 59, 60; as Joseph I 6, 8, 47, 60, 101, as king of Spain 68, friction with Napoleon 67, 68, public building 259, reforms 62, 63; Louis 81; Napoleon 20, 21, 47, 48, 50; 100 Days 86
Borghetto, battle of 20
Borjes, Don José 197
Borodino, battle of 85
Bosco. *See* Carbonari: revolt of 1828.
Botta, Giorgio 276
Bottai, Giuseppe 229
Boulware, William 138, 141, 146
Bourbonists 99, 101, 102; after Risorgimento 192, 194
Bourbons XXXIII, XXXVI; absolutism 10; and Camorra XL; Parma, duchess of 165; public building 259; restoration of 1815 87, 99; reactionism 105; restorations XXXVIII; royal court 6
Bourcard, Emmanuel, Lieut.-Gen. 77
bourgeoisie XXXVIII, XXXIX
Bozzelli, Francesco Paolo 149, 150, 155
Bracco, Roberto 288
Brancaccio, Carlo 184
bridges: first Italian suspension 139; Maddalena 38, 39, 110; Ponte Rotto 27
brigandage 103; Apulia 104; resistance to Napoleon 64; after Risorgimento 190–92, 212; support by local population 195; war of 1861–65 135, 192, 194
Broussier, Jean-Baptiste 27
Buono, Leon Giuseppe 183

INDEX

Buonocore, Vincenzo 185

C

Cadiz 80
Calabria 64-66, 77, 103, 107, 205; agriculture 142; Napoleonic 73; anti-Napoleonic resistance 67; and Murat 80; and Garibaldi 173; revolt of 1860 174
Calabrians 35, 37
Calatafimi, battle of 135, 170
Camorra XL, XLVI; organized vs. Garibaldi 173; and Risorgimento 188; political influence after 1860 202-3; political influence, 1900 203; post-WWII 248; Zona di, post-WWII 250; and Allies after WWII 238, 250, 251; 1980s 261; political takeover of 1980s 261, 264; and job creation 264, 266; in government, 1980s 262, 1990s 262, 263, 266; crackdown on, 1990s 243, 267; army brought in against, 1997 267, 270. See also crime.
Campagna Felice 6
Campana, Prince 108, 110
Campo Formio, Treaty of 21
Campo Santo 2
Campochiaro, Morile 79
Camposanto dei Colerosi. See districts.
Canosa, prince of 105, 125. See Minutolo, Antonio Capace.
Cante, Giuseppi 220
Cantu, Cesare 176
Capecelatro Gaudioso, Domenico 24
Capodimonte 27
Caprera 178, 191
Capri 2, 67, 76, 237; Murat's recapture 77

Capua 19
Caracciolo: Domenico XXXVI; Francesco XXXVII, 41, 43, 44
Carafa, Ettore 43
Caraffa, Luigi 165
Carascosa, General 109, 110-11
Carbonari 99, 102, 108, 109, 133; origins 105; outlawed 1816 107; revolution of 1820 111, 114, 118, 122; repression after 1820 128; revolt of 1828 131; revolt of 1847/48 149. See also political life: effects of Napoleonic period.
Carità. See districts.
Carlo Alberto 149
Carrara 164
Carrino, Giuseppe 184
Caruso, Enrico 287
Casa Lanza, Treaty of 87, 100
Casal di Principe 261
Casalduni, destruction of 196
Casale, Alberto 201
Casciaro, Guido 183
Caserta 277; and Camorra 261; massacre at 197
Casoria 250
Cassa per il Mezzogiorno XLV; failure 260. See also economy.
Cassola, Carlo 223
Castellammare 237; 1924 visit of Mussolini 227; massacre of 196
Castile, Supreme Council: Napoleonic 69
Castlereagh, Robert Stewart Viscount 100
Catanzaro 19, 36
Cavour, Camillo Benzo di XLI, XLII, 162, 163, 212; and Garibaldi

305

169; attitude to Naples after Risorgimento 189; favors inclusion of Naples 176; invasion of Papal States 176; monarchism vs. Garibaldi 171; plans pro-Piedmontese revolution in Naples 170; plans to exclude Naples from new Italy 169
Celentani, Colonel 110
ceramics. *See* cultural life: sculpture.
Champagny, Jean Baptiste Nompère 76, 79
Championnet, Jean Antione Étienne 21, 22, 25, 29, 31, 33
Charles Albert 148
Charles, archduke of Austria 77
Charles I XXXV
Charles III XXXIV, XXXVI, 173
Charles IV, of Spain 68
Charles X, of France 132
cholera. *See* public health.
Christian Democratic Party. *See* political life.
Chubb, Judith 257
Church, Richard, General 126
Church, Neapolitan 12; restoration of 1815 102; concordat of 1818 102; complicity in political corruption: post-WWII 254
churches: Annunziata 217; Duomo 59, 178; San Francesco di Paolo 91; San Martino 199; San Pietro ad Aram 217; Sant'Agostino alla Zecca 217; Spirito Santo 71; Sta. Chiara XLIV; Sta. Maria di Piedigrotta 92; Sta. Maria Egiziaca a Forcella 217; Sta. Maria Nova 216
Churchill, Winston 251
Cialdini, Enrico 196

Cilento 149
cinema. *See* cultural life.
Cirillo, Domenico XXXVII, 43, 111
Cisalpine Republic, of 1789 29
Clarke, Henri Jacques Guillaume 80, 81
Cleopatra 10
climate 13, 138; as a paradise 5
Colet, Louise 178
Colletta, Pietro 22, 97, 111, 117, 124; and revolt of Sicily, 1820 122
Colonna, Giuliano 44
Colonnese Bookstore 285
Compagna, F. XXXVI
Compagnone, Luigi 262
Comus 13
Conforti, Francesco XXXVII, 43, 45
Constitution: of 1820 112, 122; of 1848 150–51, 153, 154–56; annulled 159; Cavour's plan to revive 167; reestablished under Garibaldi 173; Piedmontese, of 1848 190
Continental System XXXVIII, 63, 68
Corfu 53, 80
corruption XXXII, XLIV; under Francis I 128, 129, 130; under Ferdinand II 140; after Risorgimento 189, 191; post-WWII 254; 1970s-80s 261, 264; 1990s 263, 269. *See also* political life.
Corsicato, Pappi 262, 289
Cosenza 19; rebellion of 1844 141
Cosenza, Luigi 274, 277
Costa, Gaetano 276
Costa, Mario 211
Cotrone 36
Cottrau, Alfonso XLIII, 210
Cowell, Alan 263
Cozzolino, Baron 147

INDEX

Craven, Keppel 114
crime XXXII, XL, XLIV; 1880s 204; money laundering 264; narcotics 263, 264, 270; *"parcheggiatori"* 268, 269, 270; protection 264; pushed to periphery 260; restoration of 1815 105; *"scippatori"* 263; smuggling 263, 264, 268, cigarettes 265, 266. *See also* Camorra; prostitution.
Crimea 42
Croce, Benedetto 211, 224, 284; on decline of Naples 211; South as "counterweight" 212
cultural life 211; architecture: 19th century 89, 20th century 276; arts XXXI, and 1990s reforms 267; cinema: post-WWII 262, 289; literary 211, 19th century 180, 20th century 284, fiction 211, poetry 211, post-WWII 262; *meridionisti* 211; museums: deterioration in 1970s–1980s 261; music 211, 286, popular song 211, 262, 286, 287, World War I 219; Napoli '99 243, 270; painting 211, 19th century 182, Neapolitan School 182, School of Posillipo 89; philosophy 211; post-WWII 262; sculpture 185, 211; theater 211, 288, post-WWII 262; visual arts 211
Cuoco, Vincenzo 30, 180
Cyndnus 10

D

Dabormida, Giuseppe, General 168
Dalbono, Edoardo 287
Damas, Roger, General, count of 53, 57, 60, 66, 77, 78
Daure, Jean 81, 86
Davanzati, Domenico Forges 29
d'Ayala, Mariano 147, 150
d'Azeglio, Massimo 191
De Crescenzo, Luciano 285
De Curtis: Antonio 262, 288; Ernesto 211, 286; Giambattista 211, 286
De Filippo, Eduardo 262, 288
De Gregorio, Salvatore 184
de Meo, Niccola 43
De Nicola, Carlo 26, 33, 59, 102; Enrico 221, 224, 226
De Nittis, Giuseppe 95, 211
De Santis, Francesco 181, 211
De Sica, Vittorio 289
Deconcili, Matteo 111
Dego, battle of 54
Del Carretto, Francesco 132, 139, 148, 149; revolt of 1847/48 150
Delfico, Melchiorre 29
della Torre, duke of 23
d'Enghien, Duc 52
Denza, Luigi 286
Depretis, Agostino 199, 208
Desaix, Louis-Charles-Antione 104
Di Capua, Edoardo 211
Di Giacomo, Salvatore 211, 284, 286
DiMaria, Giuseppi 270
districts: Avvocata 200; Bagnoli 275; Basso Porto 28, 206; Bianchi Nuovi 206; Borgo Marinari 277; Camposanto dei Colerosi 205, 207; Carità 231; Centro Direzionale 262, 277, 290; Fontanelle 246; Fuorigrotta 209; Granili 115; Largo 13; Marechiano 13; Mercato 198, 204, 207, and Risanamento 209, World War II 235; Mergellina 207, 274; Mola 13, 25; Molo and

Lighthouse 90; Monte Camaldoli 9; Monte Sant' Angelo 9; Mostra delle Terre d'Oltremare 231; Pendino 207, and Risanamento 209; Piedigrotta 92; Pizzofalcone 246; Porta Capuana 90; Port'Alba 285; Porto 204, 207, 255, and Risanamento 209; Posillipo 95, 145, 231; Pozzuoli 277; San Giuseppe 231; Santa Lucia 3, 25, 90, 205, 274, and Risanamento 209, 215; Scoglio 13; Spanish Quarter 199, 264, 275; suburbs 259; Vicaria 207, and Risanamento 209; Villa Comunale 276; Vomero 9, 231, 275, World War II 235, 236, 246-48

Du Camp, Maxime 177

Duce. See Mussolini, Benito.

Duhesme, Philbert-Guillaume 27

Dumas, Alexander 175

Duomo. See churches.

Durant, Baron de 80, 82

E

earthquake: of 1980 261, 269, 277; theft of emergency funds 271

economy XXXVIII; decline under Murat 84; 1840s 139; modernization 139; crisis of 1846/47 145; after 1848 163; in 1850s 163; crisis after Risorgimento 192; backwardness after Risorgimento 197, 210; marginalization with Risorgimento 187, 198; stagnation of 1870s 204; WWI: women in workforce 219; post-WWI: strikes 220; Great Depression 232; infrastructure:

WWII destruction by Germans 236; post-WWII 249, 256; post-WWII revival 252; "economic miracle" of 1950s/60s 257, 289; Cassa per il Mezzogiorno 257; artisans 12; black-market XLV, 1990s 263, 268, post-WWII 251, 252; capitalization 258; child labor 257, 273; clandestine 257; fishing 12; industrial decline: under Mussolini 231; industrial workers: after World War I 226; emigration to North 255; industry: destruction in World War II 232; job creation XLV; modernization XXXIX; per-capita income XLV; revivals XXXIII; small-scale workshops 258; unemployment XLIII; 1880s 204, post-WWI 220; post-WWII 242, 251, 1950s–60s 257, 1980s XLV, 1990s 263, 264. *See also* industry; trade.

education XLV; mandatory, in 1877 204; public building 259; schools: deterioration in 1970s–80s 261, in 1990s 263; and illiteracy: 1880s 204, 1900s 212

Elba 86

Electa Napoli 285

Ellis, Robert B. 252

emigration, to the U.S.A. 226, 273. *See also* population.

Emmanuel II, king of Italy XLII

Enlightenment XXXI, XXXVI, XXXVII

Ethiopian War 231

Etna, as symbol of South 193

Eustace, John Chetwode 1

Excelmans, Joseph-Isadore 81

F

Facta, Luigi 223
Fardella, General 109
Farini, Luigi XLI, 187, 188, 189
Fascist Party, Naples 227; Silone report 229; national congress in Naples, 1922 221. *See also* political life: Fascism.
Fascists. *See* political life: Fascism.
Faypoult, Guillaume 33
Ferdinand I, of Two Sicilies. *See* Ferdinand IV.
Ferdinand II 137, 213; as *"La Bomba"* 161, 192; character 139; early reign 137; reforms 139; absolutism 139, 140; corruption under 140; popular unrest under 141; and Sicily 141; economic decline under 142; revolt of 1847/48 149, 154, 156; post-1848 repression 159; human-rights violations 160; mysticism 140, after 1848 163; neutrality in Austrian war of 1858/59 165; death 166; public building 259
Ferdinand IV *(after 1815 Ferdinand I of Two Sicilies)* XXXVII, 6, 9, 10, 37, 39, 41, 42–44, 45, 133; and French Revolution 17; condition under Napoleon 52; and Murat 77; second flight 47; second return to Naples 48; restoration of 1815 100; as Ferdinand I 100; revolution of 1820 112; third flight 59; restoration of 1821 125; at Laibach 123; death and funeral 125, 127
Fergola, Salvatore 93
Filangieri, Carlo, count, prince of Satriano 109, 167, 213; Gaetano XXXI

Firrao, Archbishop 71
First Coalition 97
Florence 146, 165; Treaty of 47, 51
Foggia 235
fondaci. *See* housing.
Fontanelle. *See* districts.
fortresses: Carmine 28; Castel Nuovo 28, 38, 39–41, 101, 275; dell'Ovo 38, 39; St. Elmo 4, 9, 25–28, 29, 38, 39, 40–43, 101
Fortunato, Giustino 200, 211, 224
Four Days. *See* World War II: revolt of Naples.
France 255; Army of Italy 20, 47; Army of Naples 26; Directory 26, 33, 37, 47; domination of Naples XXXVII; invasion of Regno XXXVII; revolution of 1789 XXXVI, 17; Neapolitan support of 19; Paris 18
Francis I 59, 112, 130, 133; character 127; revolution of 1820 113; death 137
Francis I, of Austria 125
Francis II: early rule 166; relations with Piedmont-Sardinia 166; Austrian war of 1858/59 167; neutrality 167; and Garibaldi 173; pleas for French aid 173; farewell proclamation 174; flight to Gaeta 174; and Risorgimento 175; movement for his restoration 192; after Risorgimento 193; in exile 195
Frimont, Johann Maria Philipp von 125
Fucini, Renato, *Napoli a occhio nudo* 204
Fumel, General 196
funicular. *See* public transport.
Fuorigrotta. *See* districts.

G

Gaeta 19, 188, 189, 190
Gagliano in Basilicata 226
Galateri, General 193, 196
Galiani, Ferdinando, Abbé XXXVI
Galleria Umberto I. *See* public structures.
Gallo, Marzio Mastrilli, marchese di 17 20, 50, 51–54; deserts Bourbons 59; Napoleonic years 71, 82
Garibaldi, Giuseppe XLI, 189; in Sicily 135, 169; plans for Risorgimento 169; on Sicilian and Neapolitan campaigns 172; in Calabria 173; arrival in Naples 175; in Naples with Victor Emmanuel 177; effect on Neapolitans 178; after Risorgimento 191
Garibaldini: in Naples 178, 179
Gava: Antonio 201, 254; Silvio 254, 261
Gemito, Vincenzo 185, 211
Genoa XLIV, 68, 146, 172
Genovese, Vito 250
Genovesi, Antonio XXXVI
Gentz, Friedrich von 123
German Confederation: as model for Cavour's Italy 164
Germany 255
Ghirelli, Antonio 260, 271
Giambarba, Adolfo 209
Gigante, Giacinto 182
Giolitti, Giovanni 203
Giorgini, G.F. 156
Giovini, Raffaele 185
Giugliano 220
Giusso, Girolamo XLI, 203
Gladstone, William Ewart 134, 159, 161
Goethe, Johann Wolfgang von XXXIII, 1
Gorchakov, prince of Russia 165
Gordon, George Hamilton, earl of Aberdeen 159
Goretti, O. 185
government: bureaucracy XXXII, XXXVI, 12; civil service: after Risorgimento 202; Council of Ministers 71; Council of Regency 60; lawyers 12; and Risorgimento 188, 191; legal system: reforms under Risorgimento 189; martial law: after Risorgimento 196; Ufficio Tecnico 214. *See also* Constitution; corruption; Parliament.
Granili. *See* districts
Gravina, Cardinal 118
Gregory XVI, pope 146
Grenier, General 79, 81, 82
Griffoli, Giuseppe 156
Gropello, Giulio 162
Group of Seven 266
Guardascione, Ezechiele 182
gypsies: after Risorgimento 199

H

Hamilton: Emma Lady 41, 44; William Lord 17, 41, 42
Hanover 50
Herculaneum XXXVI, 29, 33; as image of corruption 161
Hesse, Prince of 66, 77
Hitler, Adolf XLV, 251
Holland 57, 255
hospitals. *See* public health.
housing: Cassa per il Mezzogiorno 257; deterioration in 1970s–1980s 261; *fondaci* XXXIX, 92; middle class 93. *See also bassi.*

INDEX

I

Imbriani, Vittorio 180
industry XXXII, XXXIX, XL, 12; 1970s–80s XLV; Alfa Sud auto factory 257; Allocca 254; and Cassa per il Mezzogiorno 257; Belli 254; decline 1950s–1980s 259; Fiat factory 266; Ilva plant 272; Italsider steelworks 257, 275; Olivetti Plant at Pozzuoli 277; postwar XLV; Royal Porcelain Factory 185. *See also* economy.
Intonti, Niccolo 128, 139
Ireland 42
Ischia 60, 77
"*Italia irridenta*" 219
Italian Customs League 147
Italian League 153
Italian Social Party. *See* political life.

J

Jacobinism 19, 24, 29, 30, 33, 34, 38, 39–41. *See also* political life.
John Paul II, pope: 1990 visit 262
Joseph I. *See* Bonaparte: Joseph: as Joseph I
Jourdan, Marshall 69

K

King, Bolton 201
Kingdom of Naples 6; Cavour's plans for 164 *et passim*.
Kingdom of the Two Sicilies XXXII, XXXV, 6 *et passim*.

L

La Capria, Raffaele 262
La Farina, Giuseppe 172
Labriola, Arturo 211, 220
Laibach, congress of 121, 122
Lamarque, Maximilien 76
Lamberti, Amato 263, 265
Lanusse, General 81
LaPalombara, J. 254
Largo. *See* districts.
Lauberg, Carlo 26, 29
Laura 110
Lauro, Achille 201, 243, 253
lawyers. *See* government.
lazzaroni XL, 12, 13, 14, 22–24, 27, 94; condition of 14; opposition to Napoleon 48; opposition to Parthenopean Republic 30, 38, 44; repression under Napoleon 64; resistance to French 25; revolution of 1848 155; under Joseph I 61
League of Nations: Ethiopian War XLIV; sanctions' effects on Naples 231
Leopold of Tuscany 148
Levi, Carlo 226
Lewis, Norman 245
Liberal Party; and Mussolini 223. *See also* political life.
Liberal-Fascist coalition 224
Liberals (-ism). *See also* political life.
literature. *See* cultural life: literary.
Livardi, massacre at 197
Lodi, battle of 20, 54
Lombardy 20; in Piedmontese kingdom 169
London 15
Loren, Sophia 268, 289
Lotto 45, 209; and Camorra 264
Louis Philippe, of France 138, 141; revolution of 1848 156
Louis XVI 17, 21
Lowe, Hudson 76
Lucania 226

311

Lucca 146
Luneville 54
Lyons 69

M

Macdonald, Jacques Étienne, Marechal 33, 36, 37
Mack, Karl 21, 27
Madrid 69
Maglio, Giovanni 268
Maiano 277
Maida, battle of 77
Malta 48
Mancini, Antonio 183
Mangiarotti, Angelo 277
Manthone, Gabriele 41
Marechiano. See districts.
Marengo, battle of 47, 54
Marghieri, Alberto 210
Maria Carolina, queen 6–7, 17, 19, 20, 36, 41, 47, 50, 78; and end of Parthenopean Republic 39, 42; during Napoleonic period 49, 53, 57, 65; and Murat 77; death 100
Maria Cristina, queen 140
Maria Sophia, of Bavaria, queen 167
Marie Antoinette, queen 6, 17, 19, 21
Marie-Louise, archduchess of Austria 78; ex-empress of France 9
Mario, Jesse White, *La miseria di Napoli* 204
Marotta, Giuseppi 262
Marseilles 41
Marsico, Baron 147
Martone, Mario 262
Masonic lodges 19
Massa 164
Massari, Giuseppi 169
Massena, Marshall 55

Mastai-Ferretti, Giovanni Maria. See Pius IX.
Mastroianni, Marcello 289
Masullo, Aldo 263, 265
Matania, Edoardo 215
material culture: 19th century 92; 20th century 272
Matteotti, Giacomo 227; assassination crisis 224
Matteucci, Carlo 191
Mauro, Domenico 147
Mazzacurati, Marino 185
Mazzini, Giuseppe XLII
Mazzinians 176, 189, 191. See also political life: after Risorgimento.
Medici, Luigi de' 101, 102, 107, 110, 130
Melito 173
Mercato. See districts.
Mercogliano 109
Mergellina. See districts.
Messina 19, 35, 192; revolt of 1847/48 147–49, 156; straits of 63
Metropolitana. See railroads.
Metternich, Klemens von 86, 100, 106; and Francis I 131; revolution of 1820 116, 117
Micheroux, Antonio 51
Milan XXXVIII, XLIV, XLV, 61; and Fascists 221; convention of 131; illiteracy 204; La Scala 10; population 1860 197; population 1940 232; post-WWII 255; revolt of 1847/48 156; society 11
Mileto, battle of 66
military 11; Army of Naples 28; Bourbon army: defects to Garibaldi 174; Christian and Royal Army 36
Minghetti, Marco 187
Minichini, Luigi 108, 109, 114

INDEX

Minutolo, Antonio Capace 101
Mirabeau, Honoré Gabriel Riquetti 104
Misiano, Francesco 225
Modena 169
Mola. *See* districts.
Molise 194
Moliterno, G. Pignatelli, prince of 27, 29
Mondovi, battle of 54
Mont Cenis 69
Monte Camaldoli. *See* districts.
Monte Sant' Angelo. *See* districts.
Monteforte 111
Moorehead, Alan 237, 245
Morelli, Domenico 183
Morelli, Michele 108, 109
Morgan, Lady Sydney 12
Mosbourg, Agar de 75, 81
Moscow 85
Mostra delle Terre d'Oltremare. *See* districts.
Mounier, General 27
Munthe, Alex 205; *Letters from a Mourning City* 205
Murat, Joachim XXXVII, 47, 60, 62; early life 71; named king of Naples 69, 70; as ruler of Naples 71; relations with Napoleon 71; Declaration to the Neapolitan People 71; relations with Napoleon 73; amnesty to resisters 74; and Code Napoleon 75; and Neapolitan finances 75; relations with Napoleon 76; plans invasion of Sicily 78; invasion of Sicily 79; relations with Napoleon 80; Decree on Naturalization 81; relations with Napoleon 81; Clarification of the Decree on Naturalization 84;
fall from power 82, 84, 97; with Grand Armée in Russia 84; relations with Napoleon: after Russia 85; return to Naples 1814 85; Italian independence 86; abandons Napoleon 86; Rimini declaration for Italian independence 87; last stand in Calabria 87; death 87; public building 259
Murat, Lucien 162–64, 166
Muratists 99, 101, 105; after Risorgimento 191; repression under Ferdinand IV 102
Murolo: Ernesto 211; Roberto 287
Museo Nazionale. *See* public structures.
music. *See* cultural life.
Mussolini: Alessandra 264, 268; Benito XLIV, 220, 240; as prime minister 223; fall and death of 252; Piazza del Plebiscito speech, 1931 230, 231; public building 259; San Carlo Theater speech 221

N

Naples, Treaty of 86
Napoleon. *See* Bonaparte: Napoleon.
Napoleon III of France 163, 173
Napoleonic Code 62, 97
Napoletano, General 110, 114
Naselli, General 118
Natale, Peppe 261
National Junta of 1820 115
Navarrini, Enea 232
Navone: Sempronio 255; Tizio 255
Negri, Gaetano 195
Nelson, Horatio, Admiral 21, 41, 42
Neri, General 196
Neuchatel, prince of. *See* Berthier, Louis Alexandre.

313

New York City: as Southern ideal 226
Nicotera, Giovanni 201
Nigra, Constantino 170, 190, 198
Nitti, Francesco Saverio 225
Nocera 139, 223
Nola 38, 108, 109; massacre at 197
Nugent, Laval, count von Westmeath 109
Nunziante, Vito, General 77, 172
Nunziata hospital. *See* public structures.
Nuova compagnia di Canto popolare 287
Nuovo Centro Direzionale. *See* districts: Centro Direzionale.

O

Observatory. *See* public structures.
Okey, Thomas 201
Olivieri, bishop of Arethusa 129, 130, 140
Orlando, Vittorio 224
Ortese, Anna Maria 262, 285
Otranto 47

P

P.S.I. *See* Italian Social Party.
Padovani, Aurelio 220, 228, 229–230; resignation and death 228
Pagano, Mario XXXVII, 29, 34, 43
painting. *See* cultural life.
palaces: Belvedere 52; Capodimonte XXXVI, 22, 126; Caserta XXXVI, 21, 145, 166, 177; Castellammare 137, 145; Portici XXXVI, 7, 48, 52, 115, 190; Reale 115, 145, 266
Palazzo degli Studii. *See* public structures.
Palazzo delle Poste. *See* public structures.

Palermo: after unification 192; and revolution of 1799 XLIII, 19, 21, 39, 41, 42–44; and revolution of 1820 117; and Risorgimento 171; Bourbon restoration 47, 48, 50; in Fascist schema 222; revolt of 1847/48 148, 149, 156
Pallavicino, Giorgio 178
Palmi 35
Palmieri, Giuseppi XXXVI
Papal States 21, 47, 103, 146; Cavour's plans on 164
Paris: Congress of 1856 164; Grand Opera 11
Parliament: revolution of 1820 121, 122–23, 124; of 1848 133, 155; Italian, after 1860 188; post-WWI 220
Parma 169
Parthenopean Republic. *See* periods.
Passanante, Giovanni 204
peasantry: 1840s 143; and Fascism 226
Pendino. *See* districts.
Pepe: Florestano 109, 118, 153; Guglielmo 19, 107, 108, 113, 114, 117; Austrian war of 1848 153; revolt of Sicily, 1820 119
periods: Anjevin XXXV; Aragonese XXXV; Spanish XXXV; 18th century 1–16; French & Napoleonic 97, impact of 97–100; Parthenopean Republic XXXVII, 29, 32, 36, 37, 47; *il decennio* 60; Risorgimento XLI, XLIII, 159, and Neapolitan loss of autonomy 187, impact XXXII, XXXIII; Plebiscite of 1860 135, 176, 186, 187; Piedmontese XLII, 190, "pacification"

INDEX

196; era of catastrophes 219-39; Fascism XLIV; Great Depression 230; incomplete recovery, 1943-99 245-71; post-WWII nadir XXXII, 245, 247; Cold War 265; 1990s reforms XLVI, 266; transformation of late 1990s 267
Persano, Carlo 171
Peruzzi, Ubaldino 212
Pescara 87
Phalaris: as image of corruption 161
Philip II of Spain 103
piazze 90; and Risanamento 209; Bovio 216; Carlo III 235; Carmine 44; Cavour 214, 235; Dante 220, 240, 249; Florentina 3; Largo delle Pigne 22; Mercato XLIV, 15, 25, 71; Nicola Amore 217; Plebiscito 91, 223, 230, 240, 269; annual art installation 185; Poerio (Carità) 90; public lighting in 1840s 139
Piedmont-Sardinia 147; as Kingdom of Upper Italy 169; negative attitude toward Naples 187; pressures Ferdinand II on reforms 162; relations with Naples: 1850s 163; after 1859 168; under Francis II 166
Pignatelli: di Strongoli, Ferdinando 43; Francesco 21; Mario 43; family land holdings XXXIV
Pimentel, Elenora Fonseca de XXXVII, 30, 43, 44
Pinelli, General 196
Pisa 146
Piscicelli, Salvatori 262
Pitloo, Anton Sminck 182
Pius VI, pope 35

Pius IX, pope 146, 148, 153; as reformer 147; revolt of 1847/48 149
Pizzofalcone. *See* districts.
Plebiscite of 1860. *See* periods.
Plombières agreement 163, 165, 169
PNF. *See* Fascist Party: Naples.
Poerio, Carlo 134, 147, 149, 150, 152, 154; after 1848 159
political life: 1880s: franchise 199, 201; 19th century 133; 20th century 240; after Risorgimento 188, 191, 192; *"arrangiarsi"* 255; "bosses" 201; post-WWII 243, 253; Camorra 200; Catholic Popular Party XLV, 221; Christian Democrats 254, 255, and Camorra in 1980s 261, fall from power, 1975 25, 1992 243, 265; City Council 200; "clientelism" 199, 202, 226, 238, 254; Communists: post-WWII 254, 255; conservatism: post-WWII 253; corruption 200, 212; cynicism: post-WWII 254; Democratic Union 224; effects of Napoleonic period 98; liberalism 104; electors 201; Environmental League 265; Fascism XXXII; 1920s 220, 240; and workers 226; post-WWI 220; Fascists: "national militia" 223; *"grandi elettori"* 199, 254; Greens 243, 263; intelligentsia 200; Italian Social Movement 264; Legitimists 102; Let the City Live 271; liberalism: under Ferdinand II 141; Liberals 99; 1848 146; mayoralty 200; Monarchist Party: post-WWII 253, 254; *Napoli Libera* 270; political prisoners: 1840s 142; after 1848 134, 159, international outcry 161, Popular Party:

315

and Mussolini 223; *Progetta Europa* 268; reforms of 1990s 265; restoration of 1815 102, 104; retreat of intellectuals 213; *sedili* 42; Socialists 240; post-WWII 254, 255; "transformism" 199; women and 243

Polk, William H. 146

Pompeii XXXVI, 8, 29, 33, 237; a s image of corruption 161; post-WWII 253

Pontelandolfo massacre 195, 196

population XXXI, XXXIX, XLIII; 1656 204; 18th century 6; 1791 1; census of Joseph I 63; decrease under Napoleon 84; 1860 163, 197; decline in 1860s 198; overcrowding, 1880s 204; 1940 232; 1990 268. *See also* urban growth.

port: post-WWII 252; Stazione Marittima 275; WWII destruction by Germans 236, 246

Porta Capuana. *See* districts.

Port'Alba. *See* districts.

Porto. *See* districts.

Portugal 69, 70

Posillipo *See* districts; *see also* cultural life: painting, School of 89.

poverty XXXIV, XXXV, XL, XLII; 1840s 144; 1880s 208; 18th century 5, 12, 13; 1900s 211; 1950s-1980s 258; after Risorgimento 194, 199; and political corruption 203; post-WWII 248, 252; restoration of 1815 105; rural XXXIV; under Mussolini 231. *See also* economy.

Pozzuoli 236

Pralormo, count of 128

press: after Risorgimento 191; censorship: after Risorgimento 192, 196; foreign: *Chicago Daily News* 238, criticisms 1980s–1990s 263, 265, criticisms of Bourbons after 1848 161, New York *Daily Times* 161, *San Francisco Chronicle* 267, *The New York Times* 263, 265, *Whaley-Eaton Newsletter* 251; freedom of: revolt of 1847/48 150; under Garibaldi 173; journalists 211; negative stereotypes in 213; newspapers: *Il Contemporaneo* 147; *Il Mattino* 224, 225; *Il Mezzogiorno* 228; *Il Monitore Napoletano* 30, 81; *La Patria* 147; *L'Alba* 147; *L'Italia* 147; revolution of 1820 118; political connections 201; ties with Camorra 203

Principati: agriculture 142

Prisco, Michele 262

prisons: conditions, 1840s 144; conditions, after 1848 159; Vicaria 45, 142. *See also* crime.

Procida, island 60, 77

prostitution XL, 203; post-WWII 242, 245, 248–50, 252; pushed to periphery 260

Provisional Government 26, 29, 30, 32, 34, 37, 38

public health: and Cassa per il Mezzogiorno 257; cholera epidemic XXXII; 1836 XXXIV, 140, 141, 205, 1854 205, 1884 XLII, 204, 215; 1884, description 205; 1910/11 211; 1973 261; comma bacillus 210; consumption 210; death rate XLII, 211; diet: under Mussolini 232; environmental degradation: 1950s–80s 259; gastroenteritis 210; homelessness 211;

INDEX

hospital conditions, 1840s 144; hospitals: public building 259, Santa Maddalenna 205; infant mortality XLV; deterioration in 1970s–80s 261; infectious disease: deterioration in 1970s–80s 261; life expectancy XLV; other diseases XLII; plague of 1656 204; plague of 1764 204; pollution 261; 1990s 263, 269; rat infestation: 1884 206; sewer system: and Risanamento 209; starvation: 1840s 146; syphilis 249; typhoid: in 1860s 190, after Risanamento 210; under Mussolini 231; venereal diseases: post-WWII 253. *See also* Risanamento.

public structures 91; Albergo dei Poveri 143, 235; Arsenal 190; Biblioteca Nazionale XXXVI; Casa Armonica 276; Galleria Principe di Napoli 91; Galleria Umberto I 91, 235; Mostra d'Oltremare 276; Municipio 91; Museo Nazionale: renovations under Mussolini 231; Nunziata hospital 144; Observatory 246; Palazzo degli Studii 23, 24; Palazzo della Borsa 216; Palazzo delle Poste 231, 276; University 216; Villa Floridiana: renovations under Mussolini 231; Villa Pappone 276; Villa Pignatelli 91. *See also* palaces.

public transport: airport: under Mussolini 231; funicular: Vesuvius 203, Vomero 231; roads: 1840s 145; development 259; tramways 204. *See also* railroads.

Punta del Pezzo 35

Q

Quarto 175
"Quattro giornate di Napoli." *See* World War II: revolt of Naples.
"queen of the Mediterranean": for Mussolini 223

R

railroads: Capua 145; destruction in World War II 232; expansion under Mussolini 231; *Metropolitana* 93, 204, 231; Portici 93, 139, 145; Stazione Centrale (Ferroviaria) 217, 262, 274; Stazione di Mergellina 276. *See also* public transport.
Ramondino, Fabrizia 285
Rea, Domenico 262
Reggio Calabria 19, 66, 79; revolt of 1847/48 147; taken by Garibaldi 173
religious life: after Risorgimento 191; Bianchi 44; charities, 1840s 143; effects of Napoleonic period 98; lower classes 12
Resina 236
Rettifilo. *See* streets: Corso Umberto I.
Revolution of 1799 17-45
Revolution of 1848 137-57; government of 152
Riario Sforza, Giuseppe 43
Ricciardi, Francesco 75, 119
Ricotti, Cesare, General 191
Rieti, battle of 124
Rimini 86
Risanamento XLIII, 209-11, 214-17. *See also* public health.
rivers: Adige 167; Garigliano 139; Po 153, 167; Tronto 191; Volturno 142, 172

317

roads. *See* public transport.
Rocco, Marco XLIII, 210
Rodrigueze, Giovanni 238
Roederer, Pierre-Louis 68
Romagna 138; in Piedmontese kingdom 169, 176
Romano, Liborio 171, 173, 175
Romantics 1
Rome XLIV, 1, 205; central government XLIII; French rule 21, 33; population 1860 197; population 1940 232; Republic of 1798 21
Roosevelt, Franklin Delano 251
Rosi, Francesco 262, 289
Rossini, Gioacchino 286
Rossoni, Edmondo 240
Rothschild Bank XLII
Rotondo, Prosdocimo 29
Ruffo: Fabrizio 34–35, 36, 38, 39–40, 41, 43–44; Vincenzo 43–44, 45, 133
Russia: alliance with Ferdinand II 164
Russo: Ferdinando 181, 211; Colonel 108; Vincenzo XXXVII–XXXVIII, 29

S

Saint-Cyr, Laurent de Gouvion 55
saints: Gennaro 24, 61, miracle of 26, 59; Madonna 24; Madonna della Colera 206
Salandra, Antonio 224
Salerno 19, 149, 175; Garibaldi in 174; WWII: Allied landings 236, 237
Saliceti, Cristoforo 68, 150, 152
Salmour, Ruggero di 166
San Donato, Gennaro Sambiase Sanseverino, duke of 203, 213
San Giuseppe. *See* districts.
San Martino. *See* churches.

San Severo 107
Santa Chiara. *See* churches.
Santa Lucia. *See* districts.
Santangelo, Felice marchese de 125, 142, 144, 147
Santangelo, Felice marquese di 143
Santo Stefano, island of 188
Savoy, house of. *See* Piedmont-Sardinia.
Scarfoglio: Carlo 225; Edoardo 211, 225; Paolo 224
Scarpetta, Eduardo 211, 262, 288
Schiavone: Carmine 261; Nicola 261
Scholl, Colonel 236
Schonbrunn, Declaration of 54
School of Posillipo. *See* cultural life: painting 89.
Scoglio. *See* districts.
Scovazzo, Gaetano 151
scugnizzi 94, 244, 247
sculpture. *See* cultural life.
Second Coalition 37, 47
Serado Commission: on Risanamento 209
Serado, Giuseppe 203
Serao, Matilde 181, 211, 224; *Il Ventre di Napoli* 181, 208
Serino aqueduct 204
Serra, Gennaro 43, 44
Serracapriola, Nicola Maresca, duke of 152, 153
Serritelli, Giovanni 271
Settembrini: Luigi XXXV, 134, 137, 142 145, 149; after 1848 159; Peppino 149
Sicily 5, 52, 58; Murat's plans for invasion 78; revolution of 1820 117; revolt of 1847/48 150
Siena 47
Silone, Ignazio 229

INDEX

Silvati, Giuseppe 108, 109
Socialists: and Mussolini 224; post-WWI 220. *See also* political life.
Società degli amici della Libertà et l'Eguaglia 20
Society of Guelph Knights 105
Solferino, battle of 166
Sorrento 9; peninsula 237
sottoterrani. See bassi.
Southern Question XLIV, 219
Southey, Robert 43
Soveria 174
Spanish Quarter. *See* districts.
Spaventa, Silvio 212
Spirito Santo. *See* churches.
St. Helena 76
St. Petersburg 53
Staiti, Nicholas 109
Starace, Achille 228
Stazione Centrale. *See* railroads.
Stendhal, Henri de 10, 102
Stocco, Baron 147
street life 2, 13
streets: boulevards: and Risanamento 209; infrastructure improvement: 1870s 204; Corso Umberto I (Rettifilo) 216, 217; Gradelle di San Giuseppe 217; Gradinata di Chiaia 90; riviera di Chiaia 77, 274; rua Catalana 217; Spaccanapoli 275; via Calderai 217; via del Duomo 217; via Forcella 252; via Foria 93, 235; via Mario Pagano 235; via Mezzocannone 216; via Nazionale 216; via Petrarca 231; via S. Pietro a Maiella 285; via San Ferdinando 136; via Sant' Antonio Abbate 235; via Sedil di Porto 216; via Sta. Brigida 134; via Tanucci 235; via Toledo (Roma) 59, 93, 114, 136, 148, 184, 192, 204, in World War II 236; via Venezia 290; vicolo della Duchessa 206; vicolo di Santa Lucia 215. *See also* public transport: roads.
Stuart, John 77
Stuttgart 56
suburbs. *See* districts.
Swinburne, Henry 11
Sybaris: as image of corruption 161
Syracuse 148

T

Tagliabue, John 265
Taine, Hippolyte 198
Tange, Kenzo 277
Tanucci, Bernardo XXXVI, 6, 17
Tapputi, Lieutenant-Colonel 110
Tarantella. *See* cultural life: music.
Taranto 53, 58
Tasso, Torquato 13, 14
Teano: meeting of Garibaldi and Victor Emmanuel 177
Teatro San Carlo. *See* theaters.
telecommunications 232
Temple, William 140
Teramo 193
Terra di Lavoro XXXIV, 6, 224
Tesauro, Carlo 268, 271
theater. *See* cultural life.
theaters: Palermo 148; San Bartolomeo Opera 286; San Carlo XXXVI, 10, 91, 95, 115, 119, 145, 221, 286; renovations under Mussolini 231
Thiébault, Paul-Charles-François 24, 27
Third Coalition 54
Thouvenel, Edouard 170

319

Thurn, Count 43
Tischbein, Wilhelm 22
Tofano, Giacomo 152
Tolentino, battle of 87
Toma, Gioacchino 95, 183
Tommasi, Donato de 150
Torre, marchese di San Saturnino della 125
Tosti, Francesco Paolo 211, 286
Totò. *See* de Curtis, Antonio.
Toulon 19, 20, 41
tourism: post-WWII decline 262, 268
trade: 1840s 143; 1860s 197; harbors: construction 259; merchants 12; *mestieri:* under Joseph I 64; weakness in 1850s 163. *See also* economy.
Trapenese, Gennaro 232
Trevigno massacre 196
Trichera, Francesco 147
Trieste 153
Troisi, Massimo 262
Troppeau, Protocol of 121, 122
Troya, Carlo 153, 154
Turatism 225
Turco, Giuseppe 211
Turin XLIV, XLV, 69, 172, 188, 190; illiteracy 204; population 1860 197; post-WWII 255; Treaty of 169. *See also* Piedmont-Sardinia.
Turks: in Bourbon service 40
Tuscany: Cavour's plans for 164; in Piedmontese kingdom 169, 176

U

Ulloa, Pietro Cala 195, 197
Umberto I, king 204, 215
United States: Fifth Army in Naples 245; image of Naples: 20th century 211; relations with Naples: Bourbons 138, 146
Upshur, A.P. 138, 141
urbanism: 19th century 90; 20th century 274; growth XXXV; topography XXXI, 214; under Fascists 231; sprawl of 1960s–80s 259; "urban massacre" 259, 260, 275; planning: after Risorgimento 203; urban renewal: in wake of cholera epidemic 1884 208; 1870s 204; under Fascists 231. *See also* population.

##

Vaccaro, Giuseppe 276
Valenzi, Maurizio 261, 266
Venice 153
Vesuvius 1, 2, 9, 204, 236; as symbol of Naples 182, 211, 268; as symbol of South 193; eruption of 1944 237
via Roma. *See* streets: via Toledo.
via Toledo. *See* streets.
Vicaria. *See* districts.
Victor Emmanuel II, king 162–64, 167, 171, 172, 189; and Fascists 223, 253; and Garibaldi 176–177; in Naples 177–78; public building 259
Vienna, Congress of 86
Viennet, Guillaume 132
Villa Comunale. *See* districts.
Villa Floridiana. *See* public structures.
Villafranca: Truce of 169
Villamarina, marquis of 168
Villari, Pasquale 203, 211
Vilna 86
Vittorio Veneto, battle of 230
Viviani, Angelo 89
Viviani, Raffaele 211, 284

Viviano, Frank 267, 271
Voltaire 34
Volturno, battle of 176
Vomero. *See* districts.

W

Wagram, battle of 77
Waterloo, battle of 87
Wertmüller, Lina 289
World Cup, 1990 264, 268
World War I XLIII, 219
World War II XXXII, XLIV, 232; Allied liberation 237, 241; August 4, 1943 XLIV; bombings of 1943 232–35; effects on city 237, 241, 242; German occupation XLIV, 236, 241, 246; post-liberation exodus 246; post-WWII collaboration with Allies 238; post-WWII indifference of Allies 238; revolt of Naples 236-38, 241; State of Alarm 232; State of Emergency 233

Y

Young, Lamont 93

Z

Zerbi, Rocco De 200
Zichy, Count 116

This Book Was Completed on January 15, 2001
at Italica Press, New York, New York
and Was Set in Monotype Dante and
Adobe Gill Sans. It Was Printed
on 60-lb. Natural Paper by
LightningSource,
U.S.A. /
E.U.
■ ■

www.ingramcontent.com/pod-product-compliance
Lightning Source LLC
Chambersburg PA
CBHW021829220426
43663CB00005B/185